Transport, Climate Change and the City

Sustainable mobility has long been sought after in cities around the world, particularly in industrialised countries, but also increasingly in the emerging cities in Asia. Progress, however, appears difficult to make as the private car, still largely fuelled by petrol or diesel, remains the mainstream mode of use. Transport is the key sector where carbon dioxide (CO_2) emissions seem difficult to reduce.

Transport, Climate Change and the City seeks to develop achievable and low transport CO_2 emission futures in a range of international case studies, including in London, Oxfordshire, Delhi, Jinan and Auckland. The aim is that the scenarios as developed, and the consideration of implementation and governance issues, can help us plan for and achieve attractive future travel behaviours at the city level. The alternative is to continue with only incremental progress against CO_2 reduction targets, to 'sleepwalk' into climate change difficulties, oil scarcity, a poor quality of life, and to continue with the high traffic casualty figures. The topic is thus critical, with transport viewed as central to the achievement of the sustainable city and reduced CO_2 emissions.

Robin Hickman is a Senior Lecturer at the Bartlett School of Planning, University College London, and Visiting Research Associate at the Transport Studies Unit, University of Oxford, UK.

David Banister is Professor of Transport Studies and Director of the Transport Studies Unit, University of Oxford, UK.

Routledge Advances in Climate Change Research

Transport, Climate Change and the City

Robin Hickman and
David Banister

Routledge
Taylor & Francis Group

LONDON AND NEW YORK

First published 2014
by Routledge
2 Park Square, Milton Park, Abingdon, Oxon, OX14 4RN

Simultaneously published in the USA and Canada
by Routledge
711 Third Avenue, New York, NY 10017

Routledge is an imprint of the Taylor & Francis Group, an informa business

British Library Cataloguing in Publication Data
A catalogue record for this book is available from the British Library

Library of Congress Cataloging-in-Publication Data
Hickman, Robin, 1971–
    Transport, climate change and the city/Robin Hickman and
    David Banister.
    pages cm. – (Routledge advances in climate change research; 7)
    1. Urban transportation – Environmental aspects. 2. Sustainable
    urban development. 3. Climate change mitigation. I. Banister,
    David. II. Title.
    HE305.H53 2014
    388.4028′6 – dc23
    2013021962

ISBN13: 978-0-415-66002-0 (hbk)
ISBN13: 978-0-415-66003-7 (pbk)
ISBN13: 978-0-203-07443-5 (ebk)

Typeset in Times New Roman by
Florence Production Ltd, Stoodleigh, Devon, UK

Contents

Illustrations

Tables

Figures

Plates

Figure 0.1 Bangkok, Thailand. The rise of motorisation, traffic growth and congestion is remarkably similar throughout the world – though of course in parts of Asia the scale of traffic growth is rapid. The motor car has only been with us for 125 years, but has had a dramatic impact on our lives and our urban fabric.

Source: Armin Wagner.

Preface

Cities have become the centres of humanity – in their planning, design, degradation and regeneration – and in the last 10 years, in particular, much discussion has focused on sustainability, reducing greenhouse gas (GHG) and carbon dioxide (CO_2) emissions. Within this, there are aspirations towards sustainable travel. Progress, however, appears intractably difficult in the transport sector as the private car, largely fuelled by petrol or diesel, remains the mainstream mode of use and choice. We seem very poor at planning for and delivering low carbon mobility. In almost all cities we are experiencing increasing emissions in transport, the city fabric is being damaged by planning for the private car, and many people complain of the daily grind of the commute as 'the worst part of their daily lives'. We don't seem to be planning for attractive future lifestyles, and the quality of life in cities is often getting worse. Our travel behaviours and our strategies in transport planning do not match up with the requirements and ambitions of people, business and politicians.

In parallel, a remarkable story seems to be emerging in transport planning, all as yet at the niche scale, and perhaps best viewed at three levels. One, a small group of pioneering city leaders and other decision-makers are signing up to ambitious strategic GHG and CO_2 reduction targets, in advance of any agreements that are forthcoming from the international negotiations. Two, and perhaps most importantly, no one appears to be sure how these good intentions can be achieved. There is little understanding of how approaches should differ by context, how good practice can be transferred from one context to another. The result is that only incremental and adhoc progress is being made in reducing CO_2 emissions in transport. But three – more positively – there appears to be some emerging practice that offers much promise: in rail, light rapid transit, walking and cycling, and urban planning, in European cities such as Amsterdam, Cambridge, Freiburg, Gröningen, London, Manchester, Montpellier, Oxford, Paris and Zurich; and in mass and bus rapid transit and cycling in South America and Asia, in cities such as Bangkok, Bogotá, Curitiba, Jinan, Shanghai and Singapore.

The clear drivers for these moves are finite energy resources and oil scarcity, climate change, traffic casualties, and also wider ambitions towards improving the quality of life in and the urban fabric of cities. Some of these – perhaps most likely climate change as we continue to use oil-based resources and emit CO_2 – may prove to be the 'game changers' in our transition to sustainable mobility. The major difficulty being faced is that there is little understanding as to how the transport sector may contribute in any significant way to cross-sectoral emission reduction targets at the aggregate scale (national, regional and global). We don't seem to be planning for and enabling the future travel patterns we would wish, and certainly the public are a long way from showing they can adapt to and adopt low carbon travel behaviours. There is a gap between the views of the car-owning public and the aims of policy-makers, which perhaps can be seen as a hyperreality in transport: with the advertising of the car as a sought-after-product, of the commonly held aspiration to own and use the car, in the increasing motorisation internationally; versus the reality of the impacts in environmental, safety, urban fabric and even economic terms (Baudrillard, 1981b).

Conventional policy-making is dominated by the economic paradigm. Policy measures are often analysed as to their assumed costs and benefits, but often the monetisation of impacts is weak and partial. Transport is viewed as the most complex sector within which to act in climate change – travel behaviours are perceived as too difficult and expensive to change and they also form an essential part of everyday life. But we have to change. Conventionally, the response is framed in technological or economic pricing terms. This clearly cannot continue if we are to take seriously environmental goals: inaction, or underperformance, in one sector (transport) leads to huge demands for emission reductions in other sectors, and hence it becomes an impossible position to maintain. Continued intransigence in the transport sector means cross-sectoral targets will be missed. Achieving sustainability in transport certainly requires more than marginal improvements, yet 'muddling through' (Lindblom, 1959; 1979) remains the dominant position in policy-making and strategy implementation.

This book takes this difficult context as its starting point, developing its approach from an exciting body of work in scenario analysis and futures thinking. It draws on the conceptual origins from Thomas More's (1516) *Utopia*, and others such as Herman Kahn and Pierre Wack. Futures analysis has developed into a wide literature field: scenarios have been well used in many domains, notably in business and corporate strategy, and also in energy futures and, to an extent, in transport and city planning. We view scenarios from the tradition of Herman Kahn, encompassing a wide range of external and internal factors, such as changed environmental, economic and cultural factors, into composite images of different potential future lifestyles – forming a structured view of the future and framework for analysis. This is different to much of the common parlance in transport planning, where scenarios are conflated with option analysis, considering marginal changes, such as route alignments or changes in frequency of service. We use scenario analysis to explore much more fundamental possibilities for changed travel behaviours.

Parallels can be found in the literature world, with authors such as H. G. Wells and J. G. Ballard illustrating future possibilities (often as dystopian futures); Albert Camus can offer important metaphorical lessons in that the human condition (including travel behaviour) is often difficult to improve. Though there is a tendency to enhance 'value' in life, often there is a human inability to achieve this. Perhaps others are also important, such as Jonathan Swift, Lewis Carroll and Jorge Luis Borges, in using the closely related allegorical approach: the story being told may have multiple meanings, or a different realisation to that commonly understood or imagined. Different genres such as print, photography and film, can also powerfully illustrate the possibilities and the limitations of the conventional understandings within city futures. We use a number of different means to illustrate the richness of the possible conversations and interpretations, from the British Film Institute, Bridgeman Art Library and The Advertising Archives in particular. Berger (1972, pp. 1, 26) explains:

> It is seeing which establishes our place in the surrounding world; we explain that world with words [. . .] if the new language of images were used differently, it would through its use, confer a new kind of power [. . .] that is to say the experience of seeking to give meaning to our lives, of trying to understand the history of which we can become the active agents.

The use of scenarios in transport can thus be imaginatively used, to help to demonstrate the very different possible futures open to society, and the likely trajectories of current policy.

They can perhaps help us to plan for attractive future lifestyles, where city life offers attractive living, for all in society. Significant progress against CO2 emissions reduction goals and wider sustainability goals will mean very different transport strategies and investment programmes than have conventionally been developed. Achieving reduced CO2 emissions in transport involves fundamental change: the new 'medium' of sustainable transport will involve a different framing of the problems and a different framing of the solutions; including different modes, technologies, ways of living and accessing opportunities and activities, and all of these relating to each other (McLuhan, 1964). Getting the public to participate in the development of, and to 'own', new types of travel futures will remain difficult, and it is here also that there is much scope for improvement in practice. This perhaps remains the most significant challenge – shaping and achieving different low carbon travel patterns in the mainstream.

We often lack the imagination to conceive radically different travel possibilities, and we struggle to think in the long term. But the demanding strategic policy agenda, including climate change and resource depletion, combined with the current global economic difficulties, and structural changes in the global population resulting from growth, ageing, and migration, all necessitate a renewed focus on our possible options, on our knowledge development and on our learning tools. This debate is critical, it is exciting and can be attractive for the public in getting involved in the debate, but the discussion needs be carried out in a transparent and inclusive manner. The first step is to understand what could be possible, in various contexts, and then to move on again – to think through what would we like to attain, and how – in terms of our travel lifestyles in 2030, 2050 and beyond.

Robin Hickman and David Banister
London and Oxford, 2013

Acknowledgements

This publication, as with most others, would not have been possible without important inputs from a wide range of people. Huge thanks to all, in particular the co-collaborators who have helped develop the various studies on transport and climate change and sustainable transport over the last 10 years, some of which we draw on here. These were carried out at the Halcrow Group; the Transport Studies Unit (TSU), University of Oxford; and the Bartlett School of Planning, University College London. Thanks to Olu Ashiru, who developed the modelling in many of the studies; others from Halcrow including Catherine Seaborn, Wambui Gachaco, Gareth Walters, Will Saltmarsh, Martyn Brooks, Annabel Bradbury; Alain Chiaradia, Jorge Gil, Jasia Ward and Gavin Baily from Space Syntax and Tracemedia, who helped develop the analysis and visualisations; also Jimin Zhao, Jian Liu, Sharad Saxena, and others, at the TSU, University of Oxford, for collaborations on some of the research and wider discussions on the general sustainable transport topic.

There have also been a number of project funders, contributors and discussants. Thanks to Ian Hawthorne and Nick Barter at the UK Department for Transport; Alan Penn, David Cobb, Chris Anderson, Tina Crombie, Daniel Gilbert and Juliana O'Rourke at University College London; Catherine Jones, Mark Evers and Richard McGreevy at Transport for London and the Greater London Authority; Jamie Leather, Ko Sakamoto and Lloyd Wright at the Asian Development Bank; Jo Fellows and Roger O'Neill at Oxfordshire County Council; Tricia Austin and Megan Howell at the University of Auckland; John Davies and Jojo Valero at Auckland Council; Steve Rayner and Idalina Baptista at the Future of Cities Programme, University of Oxford; Shi Cheng and Tang Yang from Tongji University; and also Peter Hall, Peter Headicar, Tim Pharoah, Mayer Hillman, Miles Tight, Jillian Anable, Abigail Bristow, Dinesh Mohan, Ajay Mathur, Dilip Chenoy, K. K. Gandhi, A. Ganguli, Anumita Roychowdhury, Zhou Yong and Liu Zhengling for various related contributions and discussions. Also to our B.Sc., M.Sc. and Ph.D. students at UCL and the University of Oxford who have helped discuss and develop some of the thinking on particular issues.

Thanks to Richard Sanderson at Halcrow and especially David Banister for agreeing to Robin spending 3 years at the TSU, on a part-time fellowship, developing research in this area and working on the early parts of the manuscript.

Thanks to Louisa Earls and Helen Bell at Routledge–Earthscan, for running with the idea for the book, and the smooth commissioning, publication, guidance and patience along the way.

And – most importantly – to Helen, Martha and Oscar, and Lizzie, Alex, Florence and Sally for letting us 'disappear' to write and edit, often when we should really have been doing other things. Our thoughts for all are, of course, for the future . . . and for their futures.

The views expressed, and any errors, are from the authors and do not necessarily reflect those of any of the organisations or individuals who kindly gave funding, data, inputs and comments.

Publisher acknowledgements

Some of the work and ideas in this publication has also been published elsewhere, as journal papers, and in a slightly different and earlier form. The following, in particular, are acknowledged, with thanks to the respective publishers for allowing the core ideas to be republished. Hickman, R., Saxena, S., Banister, D. and Ashiru, O. (2012) Examining transport futures with scenario analysis and MCA. *Transportation Research A*, 46(3), 560–575; Hickman, R., Ashiru, O. and Banister, D. (2011) Transitions to low carbon transport futures: strategic conversations from London and Delhi. *Journal of Transport Geography*, 19(6), 1553–1562; Hickman, R., Ashiru, O. and Banister, D. (2010) Transport and climate change: simulating the options for carbon reduction in London. *Transport Policy*, 17(2), 110–125.

Illustration credits

All photographs and images from Robin Hickman unless as otherwise credited. Thanks to Manfred Breithaupt at GIZ (Deutsche Gesellschaft für Internationale Zusammenarbeit) for use of photographs from the GIZ urban transport collection, and the individual photographers whose photographs we have used, including Manfred Breithaupt, Shreya Gadepalli, Abhijit Lokre, Santhosh Kodukula, Carlos Pardo, Pongnarin Petchu, Andreas Rau, Lloyd Wright and Armin Wagner. Thanks also for images and photographs from Harry Rutter; Alexandra Gomes; Chia-Lin Chen; Narinder Sagoo, Foster + Partners; Mecanoo (Delft station); Team CS (Rotterdam Centraal station); Eurostar; Transport for London; Low Carbon Vehicle Partnership; Chehsiang Chen; mozartitalia.com; thetransportpolitic.com; Abu Dhabi Urban Planning Council; Delhi Development Authority; and Sophie Punte, CAI-Asia. Thanks to Sandra Vinge for initial thoughts and mapping for the London and Oxfordshire case studies; and Bally Meeda, James Lewis and Mark Woolf (Urban Graphics) for developing the mapping in each of the case studies and for the global CO2 images. Thanks to the Bridgeman Art Library for use of fine art prints, the British Film Institute for film stills, the Advertising Archives for advertising poster prints, the London Transport Museum and British Library for prints.

We have made every attempt to agree publication permissions wherever possible, but would be glad to correct these if we have overlooked particular rights.

Figure 1.1 *Things to Come*, 1936, screenplay by H. G. Wells, directed by William Cameron Menzies. By 2036, mankind lives in pristine, modern underground cities, including the British city of Everytown (which was based on London). 'And if we're no more than animals, we must snatch each little scrap of happiness, and live, and suffer, and pass, mattering no more than all the other animals do or have done. It is this, or that. All the universe or nothing. Which shall it be, Passworthy? Which shall it be?'

Source: British Film Institute Stills Collection.

1 Transport, climate change and the city

> More than any other time in history, mankind faces a crossroads. One path leads to despair and utter hopelessness. The other, to total extinction. Let us pray we have the wisdom to choose correctly.
>
> (Woody Allen, 'My Speech to the Graduates', 1979, lines 1–6)

Introduction

Cities are undergoing a renaissance, with a huge growth in urban population, including the emergence of the 'megacity' (over 10 million population), the 'metacity' (over 20 million population) and the 'megacity region' (with an aggregate population over 80 million). Examples can be seen in Japan (Tokyo to Nagoya and Osaka), in China (the Pearl River Delta), and in Brazil (São Paulo to Rio de Janeiro). In 1900, about 13 per cent of the global population was urban, but by 2000 this proportion was 47 per cent, and the 50 per cent threshold was reached in 2007 when 3.3 billion people became 'urban'. By 2030, the 60 per cent (4 billion) threshold will be crossed, and by 2050 nearly 70 per cent (6 billion) of the global population (9 billion) will be living in urban areas. This enormous urban growth is fuelled by population growth, longer lives and migration into the city. And the dynamics of urbanisation will change as the population will be young and active. Cities will provide the main sources of employment in manufacturing and service provision, the centres of social interaction, and the new growth in the knowledge economy and the networked society.

The traditional notions of work, as being construed by a 35-hour week and by 40 years of commitment to one employer, have already effectively been replaced. The new forms of work are much more flexible, with people moving around between different jobs, with hours to suit their own needs, and with time taken out to learn new skills or to raise a family. Gender barriers are being broken down – now the dads are dropping the children off at school (to some extent) – and home working has and will increasingly become the norm for a growing proportion of the population. Both work and leisure are becoming organised around the web in its many manifestations. All of these emerging trends, and more, have an impact on travel behaviours, and the way that we plan for transport systems in cities.

The cities that adapt to this new knowledge and network-based environment are the ones that will prosper, with tradition counting for little as labour becomes ever more mobile. In addition to being the centres of work, cities will retain their positions as centres of government, finance, education and culture, as this is where decisions will be made that affect the next stages in the increasingly globalised markets. The larger and multinational companies may still influence many aspects of life, but it is likely that the process of governance will evolve, as decision-making revolves increasingly around the power of the Internet. Small scale coalitions may form to address particular strategic challenges affecting resource use in cities, such as

Figure 1.2
Elevated Railway, 1915
(Indian ink and chalk), George
Grosz. How will cities adapt
their transport infrastructure to
help reduce transport CO2
emissions?

Source: Grosz, George
(1893–1959)/Private collection/
The Bridgeman Art Library. Estate
of George Grosz, Princeton,
N.J./DACS, 2013.

climate change and 'peak oil', economic growth, social equity and wider quality of life issues. Because of the greater transparency brought about by Internet-based transactions, there is a much greater flexibility in decision-making and potentially a strong movement against large government. Normative frameworks within city planning are likely to become much more important: to avoid the prophecy of Woody Allen we can seek to develop futures that we think are 'right' and attractive to live within. Most conflicting values of course have validity, often related to the support they gain; universal positions may become more difficult to maintain. Though it is often difficult to see beyond the vested and vocal interests, it is critical that attractive and consensual futures are developed and worked towards in a consistent manner – with the emphasis on improving the social good. It is unclear how many of these potential conflicts of interest between different lobby positions, from government, multinational companies and society in general, will actually be resolved. An uneasy tension may continue.

This is an evolving landscape of change. As cities restructure themselves to the new set of challenges brought about by the latest technological revolution, it is clear that social and environmental issues will demand careful attention. Cities are dependent on all people engaging in the opportunities that are presented, but there will still be exclusion, homelessness, crime and poverty, so social priorities are important to success, as are the needs to address energy constraints, pollution, clean water, waste management and climate change.

Figure 1.3 Manila, Philippines. The city is now where most people live globally, and is the context where the climate change problem needs to be resolved. Yet often transport infrastructure dominates and acts against the quality of urban life. In some contexts, including in many Asian cities, highway infrastructure has become very intrusive.

Figure 1.4 The Westway, London. In some contexts, urban highway building has been discredited and is no longer the main transport investment option. But, in many cities, there is still a reliance on highway infrastructure provision, and much less is spent on public transport, walking and cycling. Civilisation has only recently – in relative historical terms – become highly mobile. The car has become a common feature of everyday life since the 1950s and 1960s, almost a background to the background (Thrift, 2004), with our urban areas designed around the use of the car. Although it might be difficult to envision, perhaps we are only at the start of the modern era of travel. We are very likely to see very different mobility patterns in future years.

Figure 1.5 Beijing, China. Congestion, mainly from the private motor car, is appearing in cities the world over. It wastes time for people and business and frustrates the driver. The marketing dream of the 'free road' is seldom achieved in the city, and the associated growth in traffic volumes adversely affects the city in terms of liveability, and of course GHG and CO_2 emissions proliferate.

Source: Manfred Breithaupt.

The infrastructure in many cities was designed and built over 100 years ago and needs reconstruction. It is here that transport has a key role to play in the city, both in terms of the need for people to interact for work, leisure, social, educational and cultural activities, but also to enable the city itself to work. This includes the movement of people, freight and information around the city, and the support necessary for the efficient operation of the energy and waste. Physical movement and distribution are still central to the operation of the city, as not every activity or transaction can be undertaken electronically; the electronic interaction often adding another layer of mobility to the individual and to society.

What then are the challenges and opportunities for cities? Urban areas have grown and are likely to continue to grow at a much faster rate than the provision of new infrastructure and housing, and this situation is having a deleterious impact on the quality of life through sprawl, congestion and pollution; through poor quality housing and poverty; and through the need for more reliable energy supply, clean water and sanitation. The potential global risk is of increasing energy scarcity, poverty and social inequity, which may in turn lead to social unrest and higher rates of crime and disease. Although the role of governance and urban planning is often questioned, it is important to see transport and development as an investment in the future of the city, and to maintain and enhance the quality of the built environment as a key to which cities emerge as the new centres of innovation and affluence.

Cities account for 75 per cent of global energy consumption, and nearly 80 per cent of Greenhouse Gas (GHG) emissions come from cities burning fossil fuels. Many of the world's great cities are located on the coast and on river estuaries, making them vulnerable to floods and sea level rises (UN Habitat, 2011). Of the nineteen megacities[1] (2005), fourteen are coastal and these cities are growing faster than other cities. In certain countries, a high proportion of the total population are at risk of flooding, including Bangladesh (46 per cent of the population), Egypt (38 per cent of the population) and Vietnam (55 per cent of the population). Cities are robust and durable – and in the past they have lasted longer than many countries – but this stability might change in the future.

This is the background against which this book is set, but its scope is more modest than that of providing the answer to the future of cities. Our emphasis is on the instrumental role that transport can and should play in the sustainable city. Sustainability is, of course, a nebulous term, with many interpretations and different meanings to different people: 'an astonishing collection of claims and concerns brought together by a variety of actors. Yet somehow we distil seemingly coherent problems out of this jamboree' (Hajer, 1995, pp. 1–2). We focus on the environmental dimension of sustainability, and in particular with regard to transport's future contribution to CO2 reduction targets. The perspective taken is that cities have great potential to provide a very attractive way of life in terms of opportunity and social interaction, including with relatively short travel distances. In some of the leading cities urban living is becoming very fashionable, with a strong renaissance in the built environment and public realm. But there is a common frustration in terms of the actualisation in many other cities, where attractive urban living is often beyond the reach of many; where the frequent desire is to suburbanise, and city centre living is not seen as being attractive; where there is a better quality of life to be had beyond the urban area. Certainly the current trends in transport are not sustainable in environmental, social (including health) and economic terms (Banister, 2005). The aggregate trends do not help: more than 1 billion vehicles populate the world today, and we are accelerating towards 2 billion cars by 2020 (Sperling and Gordon, 2009). A key question is whether the planet can continue to sustain them. The answer is: not as we know them. And, unfortunately, many of these issues are of the 'wicked problem' variety (Rittel and Webber, 1973), meaning that there are few definitive and clear solutions.

The desire to move towards sustainable travel is becoming increasingly ubiquitous, with almost all jurisdictions adopting this as a policy objective. Often the reality is very different, and policy actions remain little more than statements of intent. Achieving sustainable travel behaviours, across the majority of cities, is still a distant dream. The end goal is in the development of a high quality and inclusive urban life, and sustainable transport has to be an important part of the means to achieve this.

The classic starting point is from Colin Clark (1957): that transport can be the 'maker and breaker of cities'. This is taken as our starting point – that transport systems, if designed well, can support the sustainable city. As part of this, we hope to take an 'outsider's view' of the role of the car in contemporary society, taking a long, hard and – if this is possible – an objective look at its benefits and also its adverse impacts. Our inspiration is something akin to the road trip of Ilf and Petrov (Wolf, 2007), a travelogue across the United States in 1935, involving a classic and loving satirisation of (the then) evolving motorisation trend as a central part of American life. The motor car had come to be supported by extensive advertising, the developmental structure of cities, and was viewed as contributing in a significant way to the growth of the US economy. It reflected and was part of the simple ideology of 'the American dream'. But the ideology as represented in the advertising – and as often believed by the public – can be very different to the realisation: 'All these dizzying careers have been history for a long time; millionaires long ago became a closed caste that governs the country; people have been inheriting their millions for a long time' (Wolf, 2007, p. 27).

Why is this interesting for a discussion on transport and climate change? Well, similarly, the motorisation reality is often very different to the dream that is sold. Of course there are major benefits to car ownership and use, and they differ according to individual and requirements and context. We are only just beginning to understand these issues, but the implications for city planning are fundamental. We know that, at times, travel can be more than a derived demand (Mokhtarian and Salomon, 2001); that there are instrumental factors to travel (the convenience and flexibility of getting from A to B) and affective factors to travel (the relaxation possibilities, the thrill of driving, the sense of freedom, the 'rite of passage', the ability to listen to music, or chat on the phone, to be 'in your own space', and to avoid the 'stress' of travel and life) (Sheller, 2004; Steg, 2005; Anable and Gatersleben, 2005). The combinations of instrumental and affective factors are likely to differ by mode, individual, context and trip. Indeed there are likely to be strong interrelationships. Many of the positive elements are high-lighted and promoted in the advertising of the car. Yet sometimes – perhaps most often in cities – the reality is of poor driving experiences, sometimes in congested conditions; there is a huge cost from mass motorisation on the environment, in CO_2 emissions from passenger transport and freight; on the impact of the car and its associated paraphernalia on the urban fabric (think highways, surface car parks, street clutter and severance of communities). And, of course, a critical issue that we all seem to forget: that of safety – there are over 1.2 million deaths per year from road accidents (World Health Organization, 2009). We cannot afford to ignore all of the above; they represent major costs to our current travel behaviours that need rethinking.

A parallel can perhaps be taken from Orwell (1937). Again he attempts to take an 'external' view of the failings of contemporary life, this time manifest in his shock at visiting the working class and their lives in the northern towns of the UK in the 1920s and 1930s. Like Orwell's hope for 'a classless society', the transition to sustainable travel is unlikely to be as easy as we might like to think, or as it first appears: it might be a 'wild ride into the darkness', but also: 'probably when we get there it will not be so dreadful as we feared' (Orwell, 1937, p. 215).

Hence, we are hoping to explore the potential for different travel behaviours at the city level, and within this perhaps a very different role for the car and other modes. How might this radical change in travel behaviours occur? What might be the equivalent storyline to Gladwell's (2000) populist recount of the fall and rise in sales of Hush Puppies, the American brushed-suede shoes? Gladwell translates this same story of the 'tipping point' to the 'white flight' to the suburbs of the middle class in the older cities of the American northeast in the 1970s; the sale of fax machines in the 1980s; and the fall of crime rates in New York in the 1990s. The wider lessons are in the very real potential for social trends and social behaviours to change, with niche behaviours becoming mainstream, sometimes over very short timescales. Gladwell talks of the 'law of the few' (some people matter more than others in leading the trends), the 'stickiness factor' (making a potentially contagious message memorable), and the 'power of context' (the smallest details of the particular local context are also important). Perhaps our current travel behaviours, and our dependence on the (petrol and diesel) car, are not bound to continue. But, of course, this implies major lifestyle changes if radical changes to travel behaviour are to be achieved, in particular in a mass scale movement away from the use of the car. This means a major break in the trends, and this is where policy-making and implementation becomes much harder to tackle.

Figure 1.6 'Map of the island of Utopia', Thomas More, 1516. This is perhaps the earliest recorded attempt to write our future history from the viewpoint of developing an attractive future society. 'Utopia' has come to represent any seemingly idyllic, fictional society – but the original text can be interpreted in various ways, and can be read as political manifesto, moral allegory, or even an elaborate joke.

> 'Those struck with a desire to visit friends in another city or to see the country may easily get leave [. . .] wherever he goes, however, he is given no food until he completes a morning's worth of work [. . .] if he fulfils his responsibility he may go where he pleases' (p. 73).

Ambrosius Holbein's *Map of the Island of Utopia* appeared in the 1518 edition of Utopia; a less fully-developed version by an unknown artist was used in 1516. The genre has of course expanded hugely, in print and film.

Source: Private collection/The Bridgeman Art Library.

Climate change: the story so far

Concerns about the exploitation of the planet are not new, but the climate change debate[2] has only really taken off, in the media at least, since around 1990. Before then, environmental concerns were more limited, and were mainly concerned with the use of resources and local pollutants. Conservation and environmental groups, however, have been active for more than 100 years, including the setting up of the Sierra Club in the USA and the campaigning by John Muir and others for the National Parks. The early town planning luminaries, such as Ebenezer Howard, Patrick Geddes and Frederick Law Olmsted, commentated on the social ills of the early twentieth-century urban life, and sought to build 'garden cities', as self-sufficient new towns surrounded by the countryside. Later, other figures such as Jacobs (1961) reminded urban planners of the potential problems inherent with comprehensive redevelopment and urban renewal. The early environmentalists actively campaigned on single issues, including population growth and food supply (Malthus, 1798); the detrimental effects of pesticides, such as DDT,[3] on the environment (Carson, 1962); the energy crisis, social well-being and equity (Illich, 1974); and the exploitation of resources more generally (Meadows et al., 1972). Many were questioning the (overly) consumptive lifestyles of humans and the limits to the planet's carrying capacity. Hence, the perspective was quite different to the current mainstream understanding, provided largely by the dominant economic paradigm, which marginalises ecological and social objectives, and in the main doesn't question economic growth as the overriding political objective. An alternative view is that economic development (and traffic growth) relies upon the exploitation of natural resources, and is not focused on wealth distribution, hence by its nature doesn't foster the goals of sustainable development (Castro, 2004).

The first concerted international governmental action on climate change was the UN Conference on the Human Environment held in Stockholm in 1972, where it was agreed that extended international cooperation was required to reduce the impact of humans on the environment. As many of the challenges were global in nature, the UN Environment Programme (UNEP) was set up to help integrate environmental measures into the full range of UN programmes. The World Commission on Environment and Development (1987), chaired by Gro Brundtland, the former prime minister of Norway, gave the most well used definition for sustainable development: '. . . that meets the needs of the present without compromising the ability of future generations to meet theirs' (WCED, 1987, p. 8). Hence inter-generational equity became an important dimension.

In 1988, the UNEP and the World Meteorological Organisation (WMO) set up the Intergovernmental Panel on Climate Change (IPCC) to assess the levels of existing knowledge about the climate system and climate change, together with the environmental, economic and social impacts of climate change and the possible response alternatives. In its First Assessment Report (1990), the IPCC confirmed the scientific basis for climate change:

- Human emissions of GHG are likely to cause rapid climate change;
- Climate models predict that the global temperature will rise by between 1.0°C and 3.5°C by 2100;
- Climate change has powerful effects on the global environment;
- Human society will face new risks and pressures;
- People and ecosystems will need to adapt to the future climate regime;
- Stabilising atmospheric concentrations of GHG will require a major effort.

At the Rio Summit (1992) a new convention was set up where governments would report on national GHG emission and climate change strategies, so that accurate monitoring could take place. There were early commitments for stabilising GHG emissions at 1990 levels by 2000, and the developed countries would transfer funds and technology to allow developing countries to take action on climate change (and facilitate continued emissions over target levels by the rich countries). The developed countries are responsible for about 75 per cent of current emissions and for 65 per cent of all past emissions, with the developing countries having much low per capita emissions levels.

The Conference of Parties (COP) became the Convention's main authority from 1995, and the IPCC's Second Assessment Report (1995) concluded that: 'The balance of evidence suggests that there is a discernible human influence on climate change.' COP3 was held in Kyoto (1997), where for the first time reduction targets were agreed, namely to reduce $CO2$ emissions by 5.2 per cent (1990–2012) in the thirty-seven developed countries (Annex 1 countries). It took over 7 years for the Kyoto Protocol to be ratified (February 2005) and the United States, as the largest producer of $CO2$ (until 2010),[4] refused to sign; but 191 other countries have signed (August 2011). International aviation and maritime transport were both excluded from the Protocol. Several mechanisms were introduced, such as emissions trading, the clean development mechanism (CDM), and joint implementation to allow the thirty-seven countries to meet their obligations, and there were also requirements for reporting progress, both in terms of emissions and sinks. The first period emission reduction commitments were due to expire at the end of 2012, but the Kyoto Protocol was extended to 2017 at the COP17 Climate Summit in Durban (2011).

Since Kyoto, little progress been made in reducing GHGs, and by 2005 energy related emissions had grown by 24 per cent (World Bank, 2010c). Little had happened in terms of the transfer of financial support to the developing countries, even though it is agreed that they are more vulnerable to climate change (Liverman, 2008). Progress has been slow in meeting the targets set and in moving global agreements forward, despite the regular meetings of COP. The COP15 meeting in Copenhagen (2009) was an intense disappointment, as expectations had been high that real progress would be made towards a new global agreement. There was agreement that global temperature increases should be kept below 2°C, but there were no supporting measures. Some progress was made on forests and biodiversity, and on pledges for financial help (US\$100 billion by 2020) to help poorer countries adapt to climate change, but these were relatively minor issues. COP15 may have signified the end of trying to get binding agreement through global consensus on climate change. Cancun (2010) and subsequent meetings saw little significant further progress and many are now questioning the value of international negotiations in reducing GHG emissions. The targets set for emission reductions are very low, and the possibilities for international consensus are almost impossible. It is looking like this is the wrong forum for progress to be made (Prins and Rayner, 2008). Pictures of thousands of international delegates flying around the world (and emitting $CO2$) to discuss the issues only add to the disappointment and irony.

Over time the IPCC has steadily become stronger in its views on the scientific evidence. For example, the Third Assessment Report states that 'There is new and stronger evidence that most of the observed warming of the past 50 years is attributable to human activities' (Intergovernmental Panel on Climate Change, 2001, p. 5). And the Fourth Assessment Report confirms: 'Most of the observed increase in global average temperatures since the mid-20th century is very likely due to the observed increase in anthropogenic greenhouse gas concentrations' (Intergovermental Panel on Climate Change, 2007, p. 9).

The evidence and the certainty of the language hence have become confident over time. But perhaps the focus has now moved to the national and city arenas – here it seems possible to implement more radical strategies for emissions reduction. In parallel, the data trends are revealing: concentration of atmospheric CO2 has increased from a pre-industrial value of about 280 parts per million (ppm) to 379 ppm in 2005 (Intergovernmental Panel on Climate Change, 2007), and the most recent, preliminary estimates suggest the 400 ppm level has been reached in 2013. Projections of global concentrations rise to 550 ppm by 2050, under current trends, or to 550–700 ppm by 2050, and 650–1200 ppm by 2100, without substantial intervention. Atmospheric CO2 concentration increased by only 20 ppm over the 8,000 years prior to industrialisation; multi-decadal to centennial-scale variations were less than 10 ppm and most likely due to natural processes. However, since 1750, CO2 concentration has risen by nearly 100 ppm. The annual CO2 growth rate was larger during the last 10 years (the 1995–2005 average is 1.9 ppm) than it has been since continuous direct atmospheric measurements began (the 1960–2005 average is 1.4 ppm).

The rate of atmospheric CO2 concentration growth (now at 2–3 ppm p.a.) means that we are likely to reach the 450 ppm threshold within 30 years (at the latest by 2040). The IPCC suggests that, for the next two decades, warming of about 0.2°C per decade is projected under the most likely range of emission scenarios. Even if concentrations of all greenhouse gases and aerosols had been kept constant at year 2000 levels, a further warming of about 0.1°C per decade would be expected based on the current build up of CO2 in the atmosphere.

There is a need to consider at least three factors when formulating policies for decarbonisation, namely the policy framework, the underlying philosophy and the likely impacts. The current public policy framework for decarbonisation is highly reliant on rational decision theory (Friedman and Savage, 1948) and on expected utility theory (von Neumann and Morgenstern, 1944), and these inform the dominant discourse on environmental economics (Nordhaus, 2008). In the Friedman framework, consumers maximise expected utility from the policies that have emerged from government. Under Nordhaus, it is assumed policy-makers will weigh costs and damages to arrive at a rational decision on decarbonisation. In the Stern Review (2007), it was argued that early action in CO2 mitigation is the most cost-effective option, but this view relies less on the conventional wisdom, as a lower discount rate is used, meaning that future generations' welfare (in terms of CO2 mitigation) should be valued almost equally to those that are currently alive.

Stern (2009; 2007) reports that a doubling of pre-industrial levels of greenhouse gases is very likely to commit the Earth to a rise of 2–5°C in global mean temperatures, a level that will be reached between 2030 and 2060, and argues for early action for financial reasons. Much of the evidence is presented in terms of probabilities and risk.[5] Holding global concentrations of CO2 to around 500 ppm CO2e gives a 96 per cent probability of a temperature rise over 2°C, a 44 per cent probability of over 3°C, and 11 per cent of over 4°C (Table 1.1). There are advocates for different stabilisation levels, but Stern argues that these are problematic: lower targets being implausible in the short to long term; higher targets associated with unacceptable negative impacts. In relation, the business-as-usual concentration level is estimated at around 750 ppm CO2e.

The difficulty in presentation to the public is that a 5–6°C temperature change does not sound cataclysmic, certainly not for the Western countries. However, this is a global average figure with much differentiation spatially, and an average rise of 5°C would result in dramatic climatic change in terms of flooding, drought, storms and rising sea levels. Such a rise in temperature was only experienced 30–50 million years ago, in the Eocene[6] period, when much of the world was swampy forest. The last ice age (100,000 years ago) was only 5°C cooler

Table 1.1 CO2 concentration levels and temperature increases

Stabilisation level (ppm CO2e)	Likelihood of exceeding					
	2 °C	3 °C	4 °C	5 °C	6 °C	7 °C
450	78	18	3	1	0	0
500	96	44	11	3	1	0
550	99	69	24	7	2	1
650	100	94	58	24	9	4
750	100	99	82	47	22	9

Note: Given the uncertainties, climate sensitivity is described in terms of probabilities against a range of stabilisation levels and temperature increases at equilibrium relative to 1850 – representing average global temperatures across the surface of the planet – ocean and land. Within this there will be much variation by area (Stern, 2009).

than at present. Huge climatic changes are likely, with very large adverse impacts on populations, particularly for those located at sea level or close to the major rivers or estuaries. This includes the majority of the world's major cities.

Stern (2009) draws on 'contraction and convergence' principles (orginally developed by Meyer, 2000) and develops a 'blueprint' for change, and he argues for an upper limit of 500 ppm CO2e. This implies a peak in global emissions within 10 years and an approximate limit in volume at 20 GtCO2e (30–35 GtCO2e would be consistent with a 550 ppm CO2e target; 10–15 GtCO2e with a 450 ppm CO2e target). Given that global emissions are rising strongly and are now at above 50 GtCO2e, reaching 20 GtCO2e implies a reduction in emissions by more than 50 per cent relative to current levels, and around 50 per cent relative to 1990 and 2000 levels, which for global totals were similar. For developed countries this means: around an 80 per cent reduction in CO2 emissions on 1990 levels – to around 2 tonnes per capita per annum by 2050 (with the Climate Change Act 2008, this is now a legally binding target for the UK). Economic growth also has an impact. If global output increases by 2 per cent per annum until 2050 it would expand by a factor of 2.5. Halving emissions would mean reducing emissions, per unit of output, by 80 per cent. The slow progress being made in reducing emissions is problematic, meaning we will require much more dramatic action in later years. Unless concerted global mitigation efforts are initiated soon, the goal of remaining below 2°C will soon become unachievable (Peters et al., 2013), if it hasn't already.

As we can see, much of the debate around climate change has been confined to the natural sciences and economics, and this has 'bounded' the analysis and also many of the proposed solutions. The role of society has largely been absent in discussions, and this is a major weakness: many social processes are predicated on high carbon lifestyles and travel behaviours, and it is in understanding these that we might be able to find pathways to more carbon efficient behaviours (Urry, 2011). This social science analysis, however, remains curiously remote from the political decision-making process. Similarly, policy-makers have conventionally placed their faith in technological options and their own ability to develop solutions to environmental problems. Compared, for example, to alcohol or drug use, which are conceived mainly as 'social problems', the social dimensions of climate change are hugely underplayed (Murphy and Cohen, 2001). Low carbon technologies are seen as a 'new market' for business and consumption, even as a huge commercial opportunity. Whereas the social scientists would see the economic growth paradigm as a significant contributor to the environmental problem, and certainly not the mechanism for solving the problem (Jackson, 2009). So, we can see that there are huge difficulties in the framing of the climate change problem, our understandings

Figure 1.7 Alphaville, Jean-Luc Godard, 1965. Although set far in the future and on another planet, there are no special effects or elaborate film sets; the film was shot on the streets in Paris, the night time becoming the streets of Alphaville, and the glass and concrete buildings represent the city's interiors. Lemmy is a secret agent, with a code number 003. Coming from 'the Outlands', he enters Alphaville in his Ford Mustang. The city is run by a central computer system – Alpha 60 – created by Professor Von Braun: 'People should not ask why, but only say because.'
Source: British Film Institute Stills Collection.

of it, and the likely solutions that might be developed. All of these should not be underestimated, and indeed they are leading in part to our problems in seriously tackling climate change.

A global transport perspective

Modern travel behaviours, though it is often difficult to imagine, have really only developed over the last 50 years or so, certainly in terms of the growth of mass motorisation, and there have been large increases in the distances travelled over the last 10–20 years. The first modern motor car was designed and built in 1885, by Karl Benz in Germany. Just 125 years later and the car has become central to society and many of our cities. The Fordist vision[7] has had an incredible prescience over a relatively short timescale: there are now over 600 million motor cars worldwide, around one per eleven people.

As a result, the transport sector is using a large share of (finite) oil resources, accounting for over 61 per cent of total oil demand in 2008. This represents a huge increase, from 1,021 million tonnes of oil equivalent (Mtoe) in 1973 to 2,162 Mtoe in 2008, an increase of 111 per cent (Figure 1.8) (International Energy Agency, 2010). Clearly oil is a finite resource, and there is much debate in the literature about the future supply of oil. Estimates for the peaking of oil supply range from '2007–08' to 'after 2010' (World Energy Council) and '2025' (Shell) (Strahan, 2007). The International Energy Agency suggests that peak oil production, of conventional oil supplies, may have passed in 2006. Oil peaking is likely to result in dramatically higher oil prices as suppliers and consumers react to perceived supply shortages, and there is already some evidence of this type of price volatility. There are startling forecasts of conventional oil supplies lasting for only '46 more years', assuming proven reserves and current consumption rates (US Energy Information Administration, 2009). In parallel, though, the scope for usage of non-conventional oil[8] seems very large, despite serious environmental concerns in extracting these sources. There is even potential for North America to again be a net exporter of oil by 2035 (International Energy Agency, 2012).

The 'average world citizen' in 2050 may travel as many kilometres as the average European did in 2005 (Schäfer and Victor, 2000; Schäfer et al., 2009). In 2005, the average West European travelled 14,000 km, and the range of global estimates for 2050 are between 11,400 km and 16,400 km, and there will be an increase of 44 per cent in the global population to 9,109 million. This means that the overall levels of mobility will be over three times those in 2005 (from 38,000 billion passenger km to between 140,000 and 150,000 billion passenger km in 2050). Sperling and Gordon (2009) predict a doubling of the current car fleet by 2030, with many more vehicles and motorised two-wheelers, and Dimitriou (2006b) notes the difficulties with the growth of motorisation in Asia, with fast-rising numbers of middle-class inhabitants within cities, and rapidly changing lifestyles and consumption patterns of 'the fortunate'. The net result is a rapidly rising demand for travel, and this has major implications for energy usage and oil consumption.

Closely linked, CO_2 emissions by country and region vary markedly internationally, globally and within regions, with the only consistent pattern being the steady increase over time, with a near doubling of CO_2 emissions between 1973 and 2008 (International Energy Agency, 2010b). The OECD countries, China, the former Soviet Union and other Asian countries are the largest aggregate emitters, reflecting their large populations (Figure 1.9).

Global CO_2 emissions can be compared over time (Figure 1.11), illustrating how much has been released from 1850 to 2000 (530 GtCO2); from 2000 to 2010 (380 GtCO2); emphasising the recent huge growth in emissions; and the perceived 'safe' level of emissions relative to 2°C warming (500 GtCO2); and through the use of conventional reserves (750 GtCO2). The difficulty in using non-conventional reserves is in the likely emissions that will follow (2,050 GtCO2).

China is now the highest emitter in aggregate terms, with 2010 CO_2 emissions at 8,320 MtC02 relative to 5,610 MtCO2 in the US (Figure 1.12). Considering per capita emissions shows the inequitable nature of CO_2 emissions internationally. Per capita emissions are highest in the countries with high car ownership and car dependent lifestyles, such as the United States (18.1 tonnes CO_2 per person, tpp), Australia (18.8 tpp), Canada (16.3 tpp), Japan (9.2 tpp), Taiwan (13.3 tpp) and the UK (8.5 tpp). Asia, on the whole, has low per capita emissions, such as India (1.4 tpp). China is rising quickly (6.3 tpp), as are Thailand (4.2 tpp), and Malaysia (6.7 tpp). Some countries in the Middle East have very high per capita emissions, such as the United Arab Emirates (40.1 tpp). The world average is 4.6 tpp (all energy consumption, 2010) (Energy Information Administration, 2010). The country time-series (Figure 1.13) shows rapid increases in CO_2 emissions over time from 1965 to 2005, particularly in countries such as Malaysia, where CO_2 emissions have more than trebled since 1990 (World Bank, 2010b).

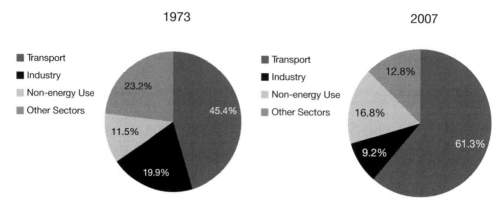

Figure 1.8 Global oil consumption

Note: * Other sectors include agriculture, commercial and public services, residential and other non-specified sectors.
Source: International Energy Agency, 2010b.

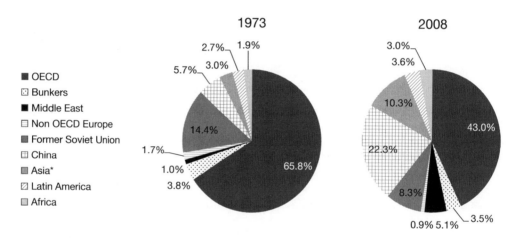

Figure 1.9 Regional share of CO2 emissions

Notes: *Asia excludes China. ** World includes international aviation and marine bunkers, which are shown together as Bunkers .
Source: Data from International Energy Agency, 2010b.

If the Stern (2009) '2 tonnes per capita per annum' equity argument is developed in the transport sector, and it is assumed that transport accounts for 25 per cent of CO2 emissions, this equates to around 0.5 tonnes per capita within transport. There are important issues to debate within this broad objective, whether an equitable target by city or wider jurisdictions is achievable, or indeed necessary, not to mention the costs and wider economic and social impacts. However, this approach does provide a benchmark for city comparison. A tradable element may provide some flexibility in emission allocation and 'spend', but the aggregate reductions would still need to be made somewhere in the transport sector or elsewhere, and at some spatial level.

The implications vary markedly internationally, and the response will need to be tailored according to city type, including a very wide range of measures which differ by context

Figure 1.10 Naples, Florida. Some societies such as the US are extremely energy and carbon intensive. Even many of the 'New Urbanist' developments, supposedly more attractive for walking and cycling and low in emissions, remain very car dependent, accounting for a disproportionate amount of finite resource 'spend'.

(Thomson, 1977; Gwilliam, 2002). A car-dependent US city would require an approximate 95 per cent CO2 emissions reduction within transport; similarly a Western city with extensive public transport networks (e.g. London) around a 60–80 per cent CO2 emissions reduction, and an Asian city with current low vehicle mobility (e.g. Delhi) may target an increase on current levels of around +200 per cent, all on 1990 levels. This increase in current CO2 emission levels for the emerging countries is consistent with the 'developmental imperative' – the poorer nations have contributed only marginally to historical CO2 emissions and must have the chance to develop even if this raises their emissions in the short term (Giddens, 2009). The key is to avoid, and achieve a reduction against, the business as usual (BAU) projection. These types of futures are all dramatic 'trend-breaks', but represent the scale of change implied by the strategic CO2 emission targets that are being adopted around the world. Targets set against historic emissions would be even more stringent for the industrialised West.

The difficulty is that this scale of change is not even being discussed by governments, industry or business, and the consequent implications for energy supplies, car production and distribution does not seem to be a key concern. Transport does not feature as a key sector in the IPCC debates, or at the COP meetings, and the growth in CO2 emissions from aviation and shipping have not yet been seriously discussed in any global forum. Yet it is in these sectors that much of the future growth in emissions will be concentrated.

Thomson's typology (1977) on city form and transport still serves as a benchmark on the ranges of choices available at the city level (Table 1.2 and Figure 1.14). But perhaps we now

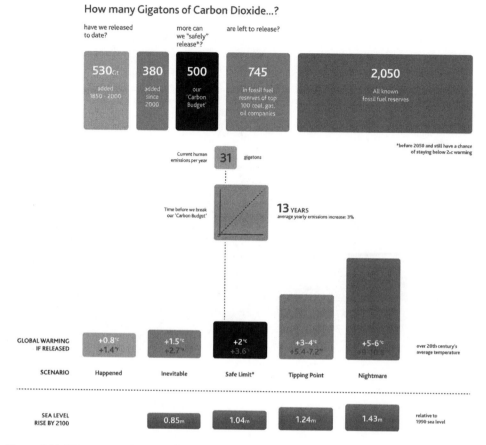

Figure 1.11 'How many gigatons of CO2?'

Source: *The Guardian* Datablog, 2012, redrawn by Bally Meeda and Urban Graphics.

need to look at this in the light of climate change and the most likely 'potential' futures available at the city level. Note there is some overlap between 'archetypes' (such as strong centre and traffic limitation), and indeed most major cities are hybrids of different types.

Increased motorisation

One of the main driving forces in the transport sector has been the growth in motorisation – largely that of the private motor car – and mainly powered by a common technology in the four stroke cycle, internal combustion engine (ICE) and using petrol or diesel as the fuel. The international story, however, is wider than cars, as there are large numbers of two (and three) wheeled motorised vehicles in developing countries, and these are augmented by vans, trucks and many other types of vehicle. Motorisation refers to the level of vehicle ownership within

Figure 1.12 (facing page) Global CO2 emissions (million metric tons)

Source: Energy Information Administration, 2010. Based on *The Guardian* Datablog, redrawn by Bally Meeda and Urban Graphics.

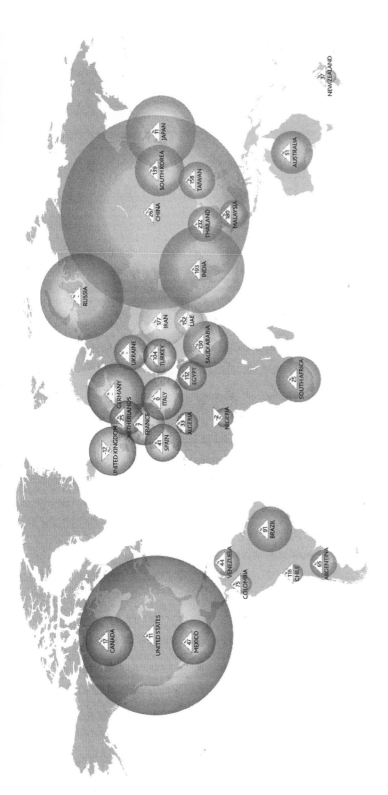

NORTH AMERICA

	TOTAL 2010	Per person emissions, 2010, tonnes	Rank 2010	% change 1990–2010
North America	6,605.67	14.5	–	14%
Canada	548.75	16.3	9	17%
Mexico	445.28	4.0	14	47%
United States	5,610.11	18.1	2	11%

CENTRAL & SOUTH AMERICA

	TOTAL 2010	Per person emissions, 2010, tonnes	Rank 2010	% change 1990–2010
Central & South America	1,257.74	2.6	–	76%
Argentina	169.83	4.1	31	65%
Brazil	453.87	2.3	13	91%
Chile	68.76	4.1	49	116%
Colombia	72.31	1.6	46	75%
Venezuela	158.44	5.8	32	44%

EUROPE

	TOTAL 2010	Per person emissions, 2010, tonnes	Rank 2010	% change 1990–2010
Europe	4,370.29	7.2	–	–4%
France	395.20	6.2	17	7%
Germany	793.66	9.6	6	–
Italy	416.37	7.2	15	0%
Netherlands	263.44	15.7	25	25%
Spain	316.43	6.8	19	41%
Turkey	263.54	3.4	24	104%
United Kingdom	532.44	8.5	10	–12%

EURASIA

	TOTAL 2010	Per person emissions, 2010, tonnes	Rank 2010	% change 1990–2010
Eurasia	2,454.13	8.7	–	–36%
Russia	1,633.80	11.7	4	–
Ukraine	275.51	6.1	23	–

AFRICA

	TOTAL 2010	Per person emissions, 2010, tonnes	Rank 2010	% change 1990–2010
Africa	1,145.16	1.1	–	58%
Algeria	110.90	3.2	38	33%
Egypt	196.55	2.4	27	112%
Nigeria	80.51	0.5	44	–2%
South Africa	465.10	9.5	12	56%

MIDDLE EAST

	TOTAL 2010	Per person emissions, 2010, tonnes	Rank 2010	% change 1990–2010
Middle East	1,785.93	8.4	–	145%
Iran	560.33	7.3	8	177%
Saudi Arabia	478.41	18.6	11	130%
United Arab Emirates	199.37	40.1	26	152%

WORLD

	TOTAL 2010	Per person emissions, 2010, tonnes	% change 1990–2010
World	31,780.36	4.6	47%

ASIA & OCEANIA

	TOTAL 2010	Per person emissions, 2010, tonnes	Rank 2010	% change 1990–2010
Asia & Oceania	14,161.44	3.7	–	169%
Australia	405.34	18.8	16	51%
China	8,320.96	6.3	1	267%
India	1,695.62	1.4	3	193%
Japan	1,164.47	9.2	5	11%
Korea, South	578.97	11.9	7	139%
Malaysia	181.93	6.4	29	180%
New Zealand	39.58	9.3	70	37%
Taiwan	305.38	13.3	20	158%
Thailand	278.49	4.2	22	232%

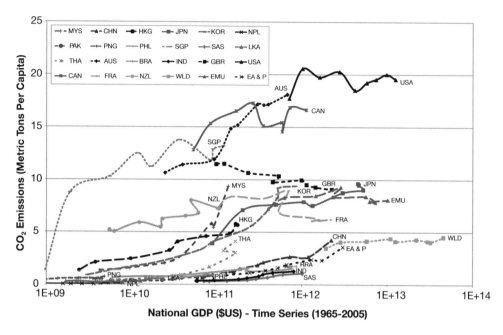

Figure 1.13 Global CO2 emissions over time (tons)

Note: * Total (all sector) CO2 emissions (tons per capita) are plotted against National GDP ($US, logged). ** Each country time series plots data for 1965/1970/1975/1980/1985/1990/ 1995/2000/2005

Source: Data from World Bank, 2010b.

the population and the ability to travel around in powered vehicles, either for passengers or goods or in combination. Williams (1991, pp. 7–9) describes the all-pervading influence of the car:

> In 1885 Karl Benz constructed the first automobile. It had three wheels, like an invalid car, and ran on alcohol, like many drivers. Since then more than seventeen million people [by 1991] have been killed in an undeclared war. And the rest of the world may be in danger of being run over in a terminal squabble over the oil. Were an alien visitor to hover a few hundred yards above the planet, it could be forgiven for thinking that cars were the dominant life-form, and that human beings were a kind of ambulatory fuel cell, injected when the car wished to move off, and ejected when they were spent.

Many vehicles are multi-purpose and this flexibility is part of the attraction; the growth in ownership and usage has been incredible (Table 1.3). Some of the car models produced have proved extremely popular: including the Toyota Corolla as the current best-selling vehicle of all time (32 million vehicles and counting, 1966–), and the VW Golf (25 million, 1974–), VW Beetle (22 million, 1938–), Ford Model T (16.5 million, 1908–1927) and Chrysler Voyager (11.7 million, 1984–) (Motortrend Forum, 2010).[9] Many models have an incredible longevity although of course change with different designs over time.

- In 1995, there were about 500 million cars, 77 per cent of which were in OECD countries, and some 750 million vehicles, 69 per cent of which were in the OECD countries;

Table 1.2 City typologies

Archetype	Description	Examples
1. Full Motorisation	Main aim is to allow people to drive freely and park easily, anywhere in the city area at any time; old radial roads are upgraded and inner and outer ring roads constructed; low density living and limited, if any, central business district (maximum ~120,000 workforce).	Los Angeles, Detroit, Denver, Salt Lake City
2. Weak Centre Strategy	A city with a radial road network serving a small city centre (~250,000 workforce) to which a relatively high proportion of city-centre workers travel by car. The large majority of jobs are located in suburban and peripheral places and are mainly served by car, with the benefit of high capacity ring roads. A few radial railway lines support commuting to the centre.	Melbourne, Copenhagen, San Francisco, Chicago, Boston
3. Strong Centre Strategy	A strong radial transport network, both road and rail, usually including mass rapid transit, with high speed orbital links except close to the city centre itself. The city centre is large (~500,000 workforce) and car ownership relatively low.	Paris, Tokyo, New York, Athens, Sydney, Toronto, Hamburg
4. Low Cost Strategy	A lower level of infrastructure investment, with a high density city and a major centre served by numerous bus or tram corridors in which employment and other non-residential activities are concentrated. A weak centre (~60,000 workforce) but with a large number of sub-centres of similar size (collectively ~250,000 workforce).	Bogotá, Lagos, Calcutta, Istanbul, Karachi, Manila, Tehran
5. Traffic Limitation Strategy	Deliberate limitation of the volume of traffic, including parking charges, prohibition of cars from certain streets or areas, extensive priority for buses, cyclists and pedestrians. A strong city centre (~500,000 workforce) supported by public transport, including mass rapid transit, but also strong regional, suburban and neighbourhood centres.	London, Singapore, Hong Kong, Stockholm, Vienna, Bremen, Göteborg

Source: Based on Thomson, 1977.

- By 2030, there will be over 1,000 million cars, 62 per cent of which will be in the OECD countries, and some 1,600 million vehicles of which 51 per cent will be in the OECD countries;
- This amounts to a doubling over the 35-year period or a 2 per cent annual growth rate overall, but in the non-OECD countries the growth rate for both cars and other vehicles is 3.5 per cent per annum;
- In China and India, growth rates in vehicle and two- and four-wheel vehicle ownership has now exceeded 10 per cent per annum;
- In 2005, the world's vehicle population reached 1,000 million.

The global picture is one of consistent growth in vehicle ownership and energy (carbon) use. The current and potential motorisation levels pose serious difficulties. China and India, for example, have a respective vehicle fleet of around 100 million and 50 million vehicles, but very low motorisation rates at less than 100 vehicles per 1,000 population (v/1,000). The projections are for motorisation rates to rise to somewhere between 200 and 300 v/1,000

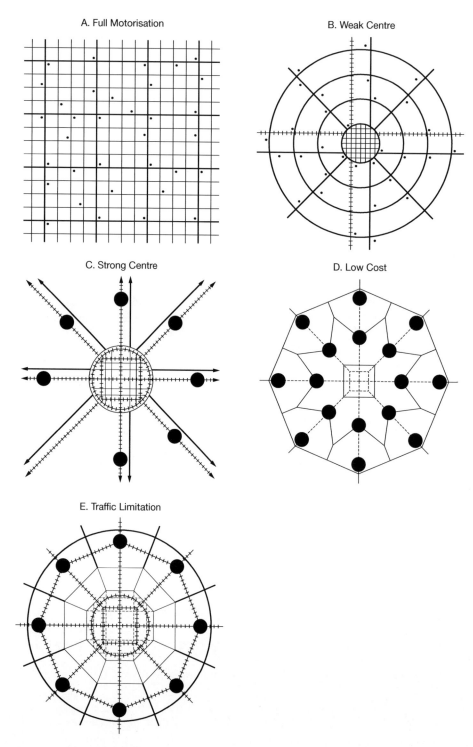

Figure 1.14 City typologies
Source: Based on Thomson, 1977.

Table 1.3 Growth in car and vehicle ownership

Area	1995 (1000s)		2020		2030	
	Cars	Vehicles	Cars	Vehicles	Cars	Vehicles
OECD	383,329	536,174	574,241	782,361	621,091	842,257
Rest of world	111,255	340,357	283,349	580,288	391,755	781,130
Total	494,584	776,531	857,590	1,362,649	1,012,846	1,623,387

Source: OECD, 1995.

by 2030, and hence vehicle populations become very large. If North American motorisation levels are reached then the vehicle populations become seriously unmanageable (Figure 1.15).

Mumford (1968, p. 93) points to the central problem here:

> As long as motorcars were few in number, he who had one was a king: he could go where he pleased and halt where he pleased; and this machine itself appeared as a compensatory device for enlarging an ego which had been shrunken by our very success in mechanisation. That sense of freedom and power remains a fact today in only low density areas, in the open country; the popularity of this method of escape has ruined the promise it once held forth. In using the car to flee from the metropolis the motorist finds that he has merely transferred congestion to the highway; and when he reaches his destination, in a distant suburb, he finds that the countryside he sought has disappeared: beyond him, thanks to the motorway, lies only another suburb, just as dull as his own. To have a minimum amount of communication and sociability in this spread-out life, his wife becomes a taxi driver by daily occupation, and the amount of money it costs to keep this whole system running leaves him with shamefully overcrowded, under-staffed schools, inadequate police, poorly serviced hospitals, underspaced recreation areas, ill-supported libraries. In short, the American has sacrificed his life as a whole to the motorcar, like someone who, demented with passion, wrecks his home in order to lavish his income on a capricious mistress who promises delights he can only occasionally enjoy.

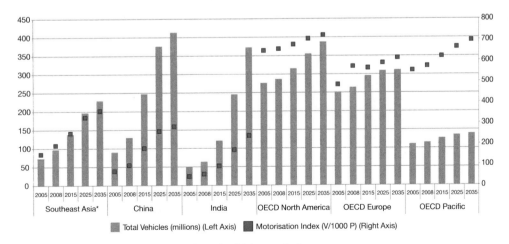

Figure 1.15 Regional motorisation trends and vehicle population

Note: * Indonesia, Philippines, Thailand, Vietnam

Source: CAI-Asia et al., 2009.

Table 1.4 Ground transport fuels, consumption and GHG emissions

City	Gasoline consumption, ML	Diesel consumption, ML	City transport tCO2e per capita	National transport CO2 emissions, tCO2e per capita
Bangkok	2,741	2,094	2.27	0.76
Barcelona	209	266	0.77	2.39
Cape Town	1,249	724	1.44	0.94
Denver	1,234	197	6.31	5.56
Geneva	260	51	1.85	2.21
London	1,797	1,238	1.22	2.04
Los Angeles	14,751	3,212	4.92	5.56
New York City	4,179	657	1.53	5.56
Prague	357	281	1.44	1.71
Toronto	6,691	2,011	4.05	4.86

Source: Based on Kennedy et al. (2009) and IEA (2010a).

Figure 1.16 Harlow, UK. Often it is the small-scale road building, undertaken time and time again, surrounded by a low quality urban fabric, which can only be reached by the car, that makes our cities and urban areas unattractive – and the resulting transport CO2 emissions very problematic. This type of development cannot be continued if climate change is to be taken seriously.

These motorisation trends are also reflected at the city level, as the following examples demonstrate (Tables 1.3, 1.4 and 1.5) (Kennedy et al., 2009; Kenworthy, 2011). The use of energy in transport in cities is very variable, dependent not only on levels of development, but on the cultural context, and the needs for energy in transport and other sectors (e.g. housing and industry). For example, urban transport accounts for about 50 per cent of energy use in the Bangkok Metropolitan Area, and the city level of CO_2 emissions is three times the national rate (Table 1.4). This is an exception as most cities have much lower levels of CO_2 emissions than the national average, the other two exceptions here being Cape Town and Denver.

Although growth in levels of motorisation is dependent on the context, income levels, availability of cars and motorcycles, and regulations on the necessary standards for driving and insurance, the actual ownership decision also depends on the availability of infrastructure and parking. The trends in road construction are variable and different strategies have been adopted in the cities towards infrastructure (Kenworthy, 2011), including road space per inhabitant and the overall amount of ground level space available (Table 1.5).

The problem here is that the space available in many cities is limited, as they were not designed for the car, and the space is often used for many different purposes, not just traffic. While 20–30 per cent of all land is taken by roads in US cities, the corresponding share for

Figure 1.17 Middlesbrough, UK. These types of sprawling suburban areas are perhaps the most common suburban housing style in the Western industrialised world, and are almost completely dependent on car usage for travel. Residents emit a large amount of transport CO_2 emissions per capita. If (or when) the price of oil rises, these types of developments will become very vulnerable; travel by the petrol car will become too expensive and there will be large drops in house values; some areas will perhaps become redundant.

Source: Jonathan Spruce/Tees Valley Unit.

Figure 1.18 Manila, Philippines. The story is often the same in the developing world, especially in the areas
built for the emerging middle classes; the affluent residential enclaves are very car dependent.

> *Linda*:   We should've bought the land next door.
> *Willy*:   The street is lined with cars. There's not a breath of fresh air in the neighbour-
> hood. The grass don't grow anymore, you can't raise a carrot in the backyard. They
> should've had a law against apartment houses. Remember those two beautiful elm
> trees out there? When I and Biff hung the swing between them?
> *Linda*:   Yeah, like being a million miles from the city.

(Miller, 1949, p. 12)

Source: Chia-Lin Chen.

major cities in Asia is 10–12 per cent. Cities cannot accommodate high levels of motorisation
without sprawling over large areas; and centres of activity can only be effectively served
by mass transit and other forms of public transport – the car cannot deliver the appropriate
numbers to the centre without excessive levels of congestion.

In addition, an older vehicle fleet, poor maintenance practices and limited vehicle testing
mean that the environmental impacts of motorization are many times worse than those in the
West. The reliance in many cities on poor quality fuel results in high levels of pollution from
particulates, lead and other local pollutants. Transport is responsible for 80–90 per cent of the
atmospheric lead in cities where leaded gasoline is still used (World Health Organization,
2009). Even with relatively high levels of public transport and walking and cycling, these
cities face serious air pollution impacts from transport (Wright and Fulton, 2005). In Shanghai,
for instance, vehicle use contributed 87 per cent, 97 per cent and 74 per cent of CO, HC and

Table 1.5 Private transport infrastructure

City	Passenger cars per 1,000 persons, units/1,000 persons	Motorcycles per 1,000 persons, units/1,000 persons	Taxis per 1,000 persons, units/1,000 persons	Length of road per person, m/person	Length of freeway per person, m/ person	Parking spaces per 1,000 CBD jobs, spaces/ 1,000 jobs
Chennai	22.9	100.0	9.9	0.3	0.011	5
Harare	115.3	7.4	0.7	1.8	0.000	370
Mumbai	21.2	32.2	10.0	0.3	0.000	77
Ho Chi Minh City	7.9	291.0	0.4	0.3	0.000	105
Dakar	12.6	0.5	1.9	0.5	0.003	120
Beijing	42.9	27.7	6.9	0.3	0.005	24
Jakarta	90.9	168.2	3.6	0.7	0.007	175
Cairo	52.1	10.9	4.2	0.1	0.001	115
Tunis	63.0	14.7	3.6	2.0	0.018	170
Manila	82.4	7.7	2.3	0.5	0.004	29
Shanghai	15.2	44.0	3.9	0.3	0.003	2
Tehran	95.1	51.5	0.1	0.4	0.031	22
Guangzhou	20.2	93.7	4.7	0.5	0.000	24
Bogotá	89.4	5.8	7.2	1.8	0.000	3
Cracow	255.3	8.0	4.7	1.5	0.023	31
Cape Town	143.4	8.0	0.2	2.3	0.051	298
Johannesburg	269.0	6.3	0.8	3.4	0.018	221
São Paulo	301.2	21.5	1.9	1.0	0.009	183
Budapest	298.7	6.7	3.8	2.2	0.013	147
Riyadh	221.4	0.2	3.8	2.1	0.142	1,883
Bangkok	249.1	205.4	10.0	0.6	0.013	304
Curitiba	216.5	15.7	1.2	3.2	0.000	84
Kuala Lumpur	208.7	174.5	6.3	1.5	0.068	298
Prague	441.8	47.8	3.4	2.3	0.059	48
Seoul	160.1	39.1	5.2	0.9	0.017	25
Athens	303.0	57.7	4.3	4.5	0.039	225
Eastern Europe	331.9	20.8	4.0	2.0	0.031	75
Middle East	134.2	19.1	2.8	1.4	0.053	532
Latin America	202.3	14.3	3.4	2.0	0.003	90
Africa	135.1	5.5	0.9	2.0	0.018	252
Low income Asia	105.4	127.3	6.0	0.6	0.015	127
China	26.1	55.1	5.2	0.4	0.003	17
USA	587.1	13.1	1.0	6.5	0.156	555
Australia/NZ	575.4	13.4	1.4	8.1	0.129	505
Canada	529.6	9.5	1.3	5.3	0.122	390
Western Europe	413.7	32.0	2.2	3.0	0.082	261
High income Asia	210.3	87.7	4.5	2.2	0.020	105

Source: Kenworthy, 2011.

NOx emissions in 2002, respectively (Zhao, 2011). Though the built environment, pollution and associated health problems are large, they are perhaps superseded by (road) safety as transport's key negative externality. About 85 per cent of the 1.2 million people killed annually in road accidents across the globe lived in developing and emerging economies, and this is now the major source of child mortality (5–14-year-olds) in low- and middle-income countries (World Health Organization, 2009). Williams (1991, pp. 32–35) describes: 'The new theatre of war [. . .] seventeen million dead, and counting [. . .] a humdrum holocaust: the Third World War nobody bothered to declare'.

Despite the physical limitations and the social costs of the car, the aspiration to own a motor vehicle seems to be embedded within all societies, as owning and driving a car is seen as a right or as a sign of prosperity, and many lifestyles are now impossible without the car. It is the major item of consumer expenditure (possibly after housing) in terms of the costs of ownership, and it is seen as a status symbol in many, if not most, societies. Variability in levels of car ownership is not just based on income, but on a range of other factors (Table 1.4; Mitric, 2008). For example, many emerging cities have higher levels of car ownership at equivalent income levels to those in the developed countries, and motorcycle ownership in some cities far outnumbers cars. An example is Bangkok, with 30 per cent more cars than Japan had at the equivalent income level (Barter, 2000).

The price of fuel is also a significant variable, again with a very large variability by country due to level of subsidy and taxation (Figure 1.20). The price of crude oil was US$110 a barrel

Figure 1.19 Abu Dhabi, United Arab Emirates. The oil-rich societies often show incredible desires towards – and realisations of – the consumer society. These types of societies have extremely high levels of CO2 emissions per capita, in travel and wider lifestyles.

Source: Abu Dhabi Urban Planning Council.

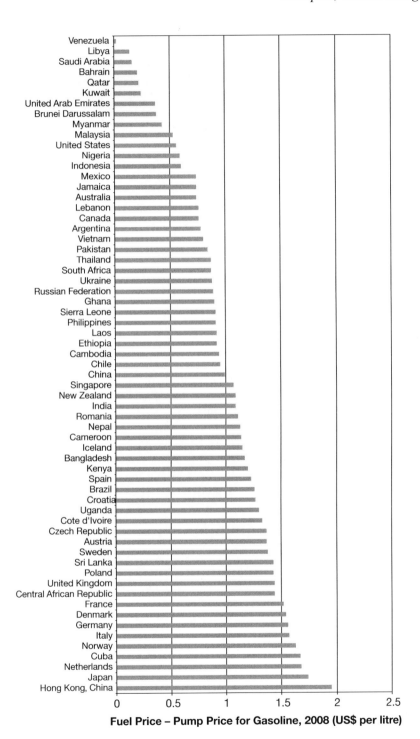

Figure 1.20 Fuel price differential by country

Source: Data from GIZ, 2008.

(US$0.68/litre) in early 2013. The retail price of gasoline is much below this level in countries where there are very high gasoline subsidies (Libya, Saudi Arabia, Kuwait – usually where plentiful domestic oil supplies are available); other countries have high subsidies (Malaysia, USA, Mexico, Vietnam, Philippines); some have limited taxation (Singapore, India, Sweden, UK); and some have higher taxation (Denmark, Germany, Japan, Hong Kong).

In Asia there is an additional dimension to mobility as the ownership levels for motorcycles (two- and three-wheelers) are substantial. In Delhi, for example, over 80 per cent of households have motor vehicles, but these are mainly motorcycles which cost 10–15 per cent of a small car. The new challenge in India is the introduction of the cheap, mass produced car, such as the Tata Nano, and the impact this will have on both motorcycle and car ownership. The importance of motorised two-wheelers may reflect situations where previously there was high cycle use. As usual, there is more to ownership of different types of vehicles than narrow economic criteria. For example, the implementation of management schemes and the allocation of dedicated space is also important, and there are also strong cultural issues. Overall, a 'ladder of mobility' has evolved with implications for the distance travelled, the transport energy (carbon) used, and for sustainable transport.

For society, the car industry provides employment through manufacture, servicing, repairs and recycling, potentially employing about 10 per cent of the total workforce directly and many more indirectly through suppliers of components and other support services. Many national governments encourage and support the car industry, both in terms of generating demand in their own country, but also in the export potential. The encouragement of a domestic motor industry is often a key economic goal, providing a successful sector for employment, with examples from the early Fordism in the West to the current encouragement of automobile manufacturing in India and China. The car industry is also global in its reach, and uses a huge range of raw materials and other sourcing through complex and extensive supply chains.

Within the context of sustainable transport, there are many challenges for city transport. The huge growth in private motorised transport and the demand for fuel form the central debating issues for transport, as the sector is virtually dependent on carbon-based energy sources. This may be reduced over time with the use of alternative fuels and more efficient vehicles, but any reductions in the carbon emissions per vehicle are likely to be more than outweighed by the growth in demand. In cities there are many opportunities for using the land-use planning system, together with physical restraints and pricing to slow down the growth in travel and to explore the means by which travel distances can be reduced. These are key issues taken up in the case studies explored later in this book. In addition to the carbon challenge, there are several other key elements to be addressed, and these include the externalities: congestion, noise, safety and accidents (Table 1.6 and Figure 1.21), community severance, local air pollution, space requirements (for parking), etc. There are also huge variations by context in the levels of emissions allowed and the enforcement of regulations is variable, as are vehicle emission standards.

Comparative analysis of global trends in private motorised transport in urban areas provides one means to understand the scale of the problems being faced and the range of differences that exist between cities (Table 1.7 and Kenworthy, 2011). New technology has an important role to play in improving the efficiency of all transport, but there has been little significant improvement in vehicle efficiency as measured by fuel consumption until recently. Until 1973, there was no pressure on the price of fuel and it was considered to be abundant, with few problems relating to the environment. It is only in the last 30 years that both the local and more recently the global environmental issues have become dominant, together with the increasing levels of accidents and most recently the health implications.

Table 1.6 Environmental impacts of motorised transport

Natural environment		Built environment
Biodiversity		Liveability
Water – runoff and biosystems	Air quality	Health, noise
Vehicles – reprocessing and disposal	Land take for roads and urban sprawl	Safety
Fuels – energy		Urban fabric, community severance
Materials – steel, rubber and technology		Open space and green space

Source: Based on Ernst, 2011.

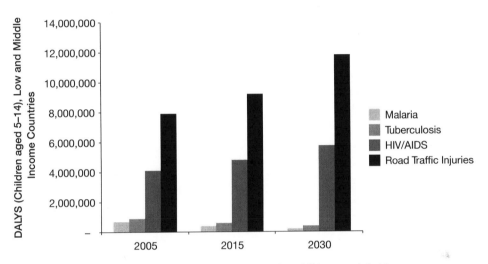

Figure 1.21 DALYS in low- and middle-income countries, children aged 5–14

Note: DALYS are the disability adjusted life years lost – the number of years lost due to ill-health, disability or early death – and are a common measure used in the health literature.

Source: WHO, 2009.

The trend has been for vehicles to use more energy, as smaller two-wheelers and cars are replaced by larger vehicles, and these tend to have an increasing number of 'add-ons' that all consume energy (e.g. air conditioning). Speed, comfort and image have all become important determinants of choice. The increasing price of fuel and environmental concerns have led to more efficient Internal Combustion Engines (ICEs), the increased use of diesel engines (which are more efficient in CO_2 emission terms, but are associated with greater mileage and greater local pollutants), and the development of hybrid cars. Technology is also being used extensively in cars to make them run efficiently, to have greater diagnostic capabilities, to help in route guidance and to assist the driver. Hybrid electric cars (HEVs) provide the most notable example of a new technology, and the future seems to be with ultra lean ICEs and HEVs, together with a new generation of electric cars and Plug in Hybrid Electric Vehicles (PHEVs). The much vaunted hydrogen car appears only possible in the long term, post-2050, if at all.

As with all fuels, the electricity needs to be generated cleanly from renewable sources, as there is likely to be carbon embedded in all sources of energy. For example, there are large variations in emissions from electric vehicles in France and the UK due to the difference in

Table1.7 Trip making, modal split, together with car, motorcycle and taxi use

City	Total daily trips per capita, trips/ person	Proportion of total daily trips by non-motorised modes, %	Proportion of total daily trips by motorised public modes, %	Proportion of total daily trips by motorised private modes, %	Passenger car passenger kilometres per capita, p.km/ person	Motorcycle passenger kilometres per capita, p.km/ person	Taxi passenger kilometres per capita, p.km/ person
Chennai	1.25	43.9	42.3	13.8	129	375	53
Harare	2.03	43.0	30.9	26.2	2,244	81	52
Mumbai	1.30	49.8	40.9	9.3	212	214	200
Ho Chi Minh City	1.70	44.2	1.7	54.2	81	1,253	15
Dakar	1.58	34.5	47.1	18.3	301	3	141
Beijing	2.44	47.9	27.8	24.3	1,492	373	548
Jakarta	1.83	46.4	25.5	28.1	1,040	554	118
Cairo	1.41	36.2	23.1	40.6	507	10	102
Tunis	2.00	51.6	28.4	19.9	1,493	99	248
Manila	2.04	21.4	59.0	19.6	2,372	60	151
Shanghai	3.16	77.9	15.1	7.0	378	132	307
Tehran	2.98	29.6	19.7	50.6	1,385	331	4
Guangzhou	2.30	69.3	14.2	16.5	572	364	581
Bogotá	1.56	23.0	47.2	29.8	1,102	18	421
Cracow	1.75	30.3	48.6	21.1	1,255	15	70
Cape Town	1.37	35.4	14.7	49.9	3,136	94	10
Johannesburg	2.08	52.5	12.5	35.0	4,927	49	42
São Paulo	1.86	35.1	32.9	32.0	3,650	130	48
Budapest	2.47	23.3	46.6	30.1	3,122	19	79
Riyadh	2.23	2.2	1.3	96.5	7,807	2	479
Bangkok	2.61	11.5	42.7	45.8	2,991	1,411	751
Curitiba	2.05	34.0	21.6	44.4	3,833	165	57
Kuala Lumpur	2.72	24.0	7.2	68.8	4,345	1,365	288
Prague	4.56	24.9	45.8	29.3	4,346	22	98
Seoul	2.41	17.9	34.8	47.3	3,667	239	240
Athens	1.93	11.8	22.3	65.9	4,528	582	520
Eastern Europe	2.93	26.2	47.0	26.8	2,907	19	83
Middle East	2.09	26.6	17.6	55.9	3,262	129	185
Latin America	1.82	30.7	33.9	35.4	2,862	104	175
Africa	1.76	41.4	26.3	32.3	2,652	57	61
Low income Asia	1.98	32.4	31.8	35.9	1,855	684	288
China	2.63	65.0	19.0	15.9	814	289	478
USA	3.81	8.1	3.4	88.5	18,155	45	67
Australia/NZ	3.86	15.8	5.1	79.1	11,387	81	127
Canada	2.88	10.4	9.1	80.5	8,465	21	71
Western Europe	2.88	31.3	19.0	49.7	6,202	119	114
High income Asia	2.67	28.5	29.9	41.6	3,614	357	348

Source: Kenworthy, 2011.

Figure 1.22 The Truman Show, 1998, written by Andrew Niccol, directed by Peter Weir. Truman Burbank has lived his entire life unaware that he is living in a constructed reality television show, broadcast 24 hours a day to millions of people across the globe. Truman lives in Seahaven, a complete filmset (and home) built under a giant dome, including all of the show's actors and crew. The executive film producer, Christof, can control every aspect of Truman's life, even the weather: 'We accept the reality of the world with which we are presented.'

Source: British Film Institute Stills Collection.

fuel sources. France is 80 per cent nuclear and 12 per cent renewable or hydro, but the UK has 40 per cent gas, 33 per cent coal, 19 per cent nuclear and only 5 per cent renewable or hydro. There are additional environmental benefits in the city as there is less pollution of all types of emissions at the point of use, so city air becomes cleaner (King, 2007; 2008). Electric motorcycles are also becoming more popular, with over 50 million now in operation in China (2012). But technology on its own will not resolve many of the environmental challenges posed by transport in cities – and this is a point that does not seem to be understood by governments and decision-makers – as there is also the problem of growth in demand that overwhelms much of the technological innovation. This is evident in the Western industrialised countries, but a much larger problem – and intractable as yet – in Asia and South America. All countries and cities are becoming more dependent on motorised transport in all its forms, but the car has become dominant, and this is not likely to change as rapid growth is taking place as economies and prosperity are raised. Indeed, the level of motorisation is often synonymous with development, and it appears difficult to develop pathways that would substantially move away from this. However, transport must decarbonise and become more sustainable, and breaking the projected growth in motorisation and distances travelled are a critical element here.

Reperceiving: after car dependence

Transport and mobility in the twentieth century hence has been centred on the automobile.[10] The motor car has had a primary role in the location of homes and workplaces, and in access to activities and social interactions, and has helped shape our cities. The manufacture and consumption of the car has been at the heart of the Western and increasingly global developmental model, and it has had major impacts on society, social interactions and cultural patterns; on resource consumption, GHG and CO_2 emissions, and environmental quality; on economic growth and decline; and options for the spatial mobility and inclusivity of different sections of society. To a degree, consumption has come to define 'happiness' and 'success' in life, and we find ourselves inhabiting the city as part of the commercial imperative (Debord, 1967). The response to the economic crisis is to encourage further materialism, as 'a matter of duty' to 'kickstart' the economy.

As we have seen, the car is associated with both instrumental and affective emotions. For many, ownership and use of a car is thus inherently desirable. Mobility is important to social relations and activities, and very often this is delivered by the car (Freund and Martin, 1993; Urry, 2007; Dennis and Urry, 2009). The complexities of modern day life are often only achievable by use of the car (Sheller and Urry, 2004), but of course the resulting lifestyle can be less than originally envisaged:

> Automobility is a Frankenstein-created monster, extending the individual into realms of freedom and flexibility whereby one's time in the car can be positively viewed but also structuring and constraining the users of cars to live their lives in particular spatially stretched and compressed ways.
>
> (Sheller and Urry, 2004, p. 744)

All of this is at least partly a social construction.[11] There are other possible attractive societal arrangements, including a changed organisation of home, work and lifestyles, and means of travel. Beyond the individual benefits, which are often perceived rather than real, there are significant collective adverse impacts. The wider impacts of natural and built environmental degradation, the health effects of inactive lifestyles, and the enormous casualty toll (World Health Organization, 2009)[12] receive surprisingly little attention. They seem to be a substantial cost – in a form of false consciousness – that society is prepared to pay for high (and fast) levels of mobility. The dream sold is of freedom in terms of the 'zero friction society' (Flyvbjerg et al., 2003) and of being able to visit the 'open road', but in reality, for the journey at least, the individual is confined in a small box of steel. Individuals spend an increasing amount of time on the road, alone in their cars; this doesn't appear to be a 'positive' spend of time in social interaction terms. The finite resource consumption and CO_2 emissions, of course, are not viable in the longer term. The explicit policy of planning for the private car, and of not planning for other means of travel, is almost an experiment of 'Non-Plan' (Banham et al., 1969), but applied to the transport domain. There is a rejection of the public modes, and instead a focus on personal liberty as delivered through the private car.

Baudrillard's (1981b; 1988; 1998) concept of 'hyperreality' refers to the virtual or 'unreal' nature of contemporary culture and perhaps can be important here. It can be viewed in terms of mass communication, consumption and materialisation, and perhaps also mass motorisation – a heavily-mediated 'real'. For Debord (1967) this is seen as a 'spectacle' of the social relation between the advertising and communicated image and the 'genuinely lived life'. The mutation is into 'commodity fetishism'. We seem to have lost the capacity to comprehend reality as it actually might exist, or to comprehend what our lifestyles – and travel behaviours – currently offer, relative to the advertising and marketing dream, or what they might be in a more sustainable world. We experience only prepared realities – the latest car advert, the need for volume and throughput, speed and high specification, the joy of the open road, the necessity in modern life. But often the motorised realisation is one of queuing in congested traffic, the horrific safety record, the destruction of the urban fabric, the consumption of finite resources, and high social inequality. The adverse costs are very high to support the motorisation model, but are given little weight in discussion:

> The very definition of the real has become that of which it is possible to give an equivalent reproduction [. . .] the real is not only what can be reproduced, but that which is always already reproduced: that is the hyperreal . . . which is entirely in simulation.
>
> (Baudrillard, 1983, p. 146)

And perhaps in a similar manner:

> We have annexed the future into the present, as merely one of those manifold alternatives open to us [. . .] the balance between fiction and reality has changed significantly in the past decades [. . .] we live in a world ruled by fictions of every kind – mass merchandising, advertising, politics conducted as a branch of advertising, the pre-empting of any original response to experience by the television screen. We live inside an enormous novel. It is now less and less necessary for the writer to invent the fictional content of [the] novel. The fiction is already there. The writer's task is to invent the reality.
>
> (Ballard, 1973, p. 1)

The motorisation culture, as it is presently framed, produced and used is therefore problematic on many levels. There are important issues in the practice of using the car, and its central role in everyday life and society (Bourdieu, 1972; Urry, 2007). There are Habermasian (1981) dimensions in the legitimacy of the political debate, in the extent of participation, and in the selling of and use of the motor car and societal organisation. Many of the practices are continuing only under inertia, an example of adverse path dependency (Arthur, 1994; Mahoney, 2000) in terms of the environmental and health impacts. The response is often very conventional, in arguing for a greater use of low-emission vehicles, but essentially within the same system of mobility (King, 2008; Stern, 2007). The roadmap to survival for many is largely technologically-based (Sperling and Gordon, 2009), comprising:

* Electric drive technology (electric hybrids and emerging forms);
* Low carbon fuel standards, high prices for petrol and diesel at the pump;
* And, almost as an afterthought, new forms of mobility: smart paratransit (neighbourhood electric vehicles), car sharing, dynamic ride sharing, telecommuting (facilitated by ICT) and bus rapid transit.

Hence the assumption is that society still values continued mobility as now, but the technology should become much cleaner. It is difficult to persist with this view in many contexts, perhaps particularly in Europe and Asia, but also elsewhere. The basic paradox is that the car is likely to remain in the short and even medium term, providing the major form of (primarily) individual transport. In the longer term, however, travel behaviours are likely to change markedly, with a different use of technologies, and a different balance in terms of

Figure 1.23 Film set from Georges Méliès's *A Trip to the Moon*, 1902, a French black and white silent film. In our collective trip to the world of motorisation, what will be our Méliès rescue ship?[13]

Source: British Film Institute Stills Collection.

access, ownership, urban structure, and relation to walking, cycling, and mass public transport systems. The very evident problem is in thinking of ways in which a radically different set of relationships between the different modes of transport can be designed, with a transition occurring more quickly than the slow rate of current progress. The consumption-led business model seems to be the only pathway within the current economic and political system. But this is inherently unsustainable, and it is likely to become very inequitable, as the price of travel increases under constrained energy supplies and as the impacts of climate change become clear. Levels of consumption in the wealthy countries must be substantially reduced if more sustainable futures are to be achieved, where social and environmental priorities are given greater weight relative to the growth in wealth.[14] Such a change must involve a wider range of interested parties if progress is to be made; hence inclusivity is an important principle. Otherwise, the default option is that the vested and powerful interests continue to dominate, perhaps increasingly so, as seen in the North American model, and manifest partly through the auto-industrial complex.[15] This future is very likely, as the powerful interests continue to dominate the political and public interest groups that contest it (Freund and Martin, 1993), whilst in the main the public remain unaware and disinterested in the forces that shape their lives and lifestyles.

Why should the public be concerned with climate change as long as they can consume their next vehicle, hopefully slightly larger and quicker than their previous model? Dunn and Perl (2010) discuss these issues in terms of 'policy monopolies', with the successful debate driven by interests and alliances. The difficulty, of course, in calling for widened participation to overcome the organised lobbies, is that the local vested interests may also come to the fore, the vocal and active participants shaping decision-making, but simply changing the debate to represent their own self interests.[16] The experience of neighbourhood planning in the UK is perhaps a good example here.

In terms of the trends, distance travelled has increased dramatically over time as faster transport has replaced slower forms of transport, but it has only been in the last 50 years that real growth in both speeds and distances have taken place. Until about 150 years ago (1860), daily travel distance was limited to travel by foot and on horseback, but the railway changed this with speeds increasing from 5 km/hr (walk) and 10 km/hr (horse) to over 40 km/hr (rail). By 1900, daily travel distances had increased to about 1 km per person per day, and to 10 km by 1960, and 50 km by 2000, with a large increase in use of the car (Grübler, 1990; 2004) (Figure 1.24). The question here is where does this exponential increase end – is there a plateau – or are there no limits to the distance that can be travelled? Of course, it is all down to the availability of different means of travel: the growth in usage of the car, and more recently short-haul air and high-speed rail, often facilitates yet further the average distances travelled. What travel patterns are around the corner? Will speed be so important in the future? Perhaps the quality of the journey, and the possibility for 'productive' travel (reading, working, listening to music, chatting to friends, surfing the web) might become a much greater inspiration for the public and also an objective for transport investment.

The expected levels of mobility and distance travelled are forecast to increase by over three times (2005–2050), with much of this growth taking place in countries and cities that currently have low levels of mobility (Schäfer, 2009). The use of ICT and electronic interaction, including email, but also wider electronic social interaction, offers an additional 'mode' of interaction to the Grübler analysis, and potentially one that can substitute for physical travel. Though the evidence suggests that complex adaptations occur rather than substitution (Mokhtarian, 1988), which at times lead to additional travel, there is much larger potential in the longer term to develop very different travel behaviours where substitution becomes a greater reality (Castells, 2000). There are signs, in the Western context at least, that we may have hit the peak of car ownership and use (Millard-Ball and Schipper, 2010) – if this has happened, and lasts beyond the current economic downturn, then perhaps a tipping point has been reached.

The current pathway of increased mobility is unsustainable, unless the expected growth in transport mobility is more than matched by a decarbonisation of the transport sector – this is the key nexus faced. The choice seems to be clear: either transport is decarbonised so that travel can take place without the carbon costs, or the growth in transport needs to be moderated and reduced substantially, or more likely, a combination of both. To a certain extent, it is the wealthy countries that have the knowledge and resources to facilitate such a revolution in transport, and some global leadership must come from these countries. However, recent progress in the BRIC countries (Brazil, Russia, India and China) may mean that the real innovations come from here or other emerging economies. Recent events illustrate the problems of finding a global consensus for change at the international level (cf. Copenhagen, 2009; and Cancun, 2010, etc.), and this means that the onus for action has also moved to national, regional, subregional and city governments to develop local strategies for carbon-efficient lifestyles, including transport. The major problems at these more local levels are, however, in implementing strategies of sufficient scale and innovation to contribute significantly to (inter)nationally

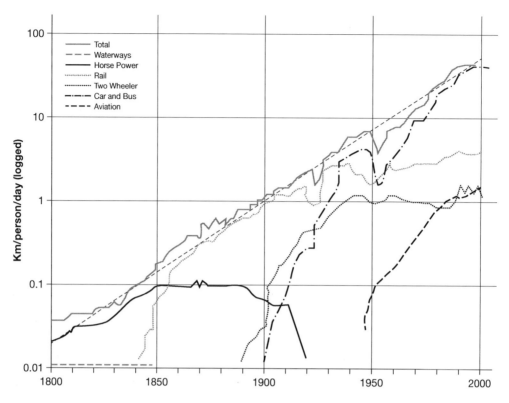

Figure 1.24 Distance travelled in France since 1800 (km/person/day)
Source: From Grübler, 1990, 2004.

agreed cross-sectoral CO2 reduction targets, and in understanding the wider sustainability impacts of low carbon mobility strategies.

Car dependence (Goodwin, 1995)[17] is still likely to be the reality, both now and in the short term future. Low carbon and sustainable travel, in the form of walking, cycling, public transport and low emission vehicle use, is at present only a niche activity relative to the volume of travel by car. Many people have built their daily life around the use of the car, including the location of home, workplace and access to family, friends and activities. The early car dependence analysis (using UK evidence) suggests there are 5–10 per cent of car owners whose commitment to cars is marginal, perhaps a third would like to travel less by car if circumstances allowed, and 50–80 per cent of car owners perceive themselves to be generally dependent on car use for their lifestyles (Anable, 2005). A smaller proportion of specific car trips, around 10–30 per cent, can be identified as 'strictly necessary and with no alternative'. The concept of car dependence can be viewed as a temporal process, with potential for change over time, as 'constraints intensify or relax' (Goodwin, 1995, pp. 151–152), but of course there is much inertia in the system and in behaviours.

Framing the debate

Much has been made in this extensive introductory chapter of the great challenges that need to be addressed if transport is to decarbonise, and many of solutions must be found in the cities, and the links between cities, where more than half the population are now living.

Any significant progress towards sustainable lifestyles and travel behaviour is proving difficult to achieve, and many of the options discussed may seem undesirable in the sense that they require substantial change. Even where efforts are being made, significant reductions in GHG and CO_2 emissions have not been delivered. Actions can usually only be described as ineffective at best, but perhaps also in terms of 'greenwash'[18] and even strategic misrepresentation in the case of decision-making and investment in particular large infrastructure projects (Flyvbjerg et al., 2002; Flyvbjerg et al., 2003). The lack of progress in delivering implementation programmes, transport systems and travel behaviours that match the rhetoric is startling, but seems to be overlooked. Most urban areas, beyond a few central parts of selected cities and towns, remain wedded to very high car mode shares. Transport CO_2 emissions remain high and are projected to grow across almost all cities. Actions need to be much more progressive in policy development terms and much more successful in terms of implementation. Funding, of course, plays a major role here; investment and application in walking, cycling and public transport, and restructuring of urban form, all very rarely matching the conjecture of the politics. The time between the leaders and the laggards in particular policy areas appears lengthy, and there are many 'false starts' along the way. Again this is an area that is overlooked – even if we have the ideas, and even if the good practice is beginning to emerge in terms of low carbon transport, transferring this to the mainstream involves significant lead times and considerable obstacles.

Articulating an appropriate level of response to the transport and climate change problem hence appears hugely problematic, in the sense that the solutions are perceived to be politically unpopular, and consequently either no action or weak action is taken. This is the major theme within implementation, that of 'muddling through' (Lindblom, 1979). The political window is often very short (4–5 years), and issues concerning the global environment appear a long way down the list of priorities at the local level, so delay and inaction proves inevitable. Decisions made now will have significant effects (both positive and negative in terms of CO_2 reductions) for many years to come, so there need to be approaches that can encompass the longer term perspective. Perhaps global practice is, however, converging post-2010 in the development of sustainable transport options; at least there appears to be some emerging consensus in the policy approach. But the problem remains that the issues of the environment and climate change need to go beyond politics and the conventional policy-making perspective. These do not seem to be amenable to making substantial commitments to addressing longer term global issues. This book considers these difficult issues and explores our potential pathways towards achieving sustainable transport at the city level. Although the policy-making has developed, it is still the conventional transport paradigm that is dominant, with the primary focus on increasing traffic volume, in throughput and speed, and investment largely justified in terms of saving travel time. In parallel, the business model is to sell more vehicle units at the highest possible margin, hence the aggressive marketing of the higher end, larger vehicles with many add-ons in terms of comfort, equipment and style. The consumption of resources follows, and this results in more and more energy being used for transport.

Increasing mobility has, however, become a very dated objective – for societal needs at least – with the quality of the social interaction (the destination) and the journey (the potential for 'productive' travel) now becoming much more important together with the environmental and social impacts. Some authors describe the potential large difficulties in reducing road traffic volumes and congestion. Stopher (2004), for example, suggests there is a need for 'a reality check'. He argues that even massive increases in public transport are unlikely to lead to much reduction in traffic volumes and congestion because of the large market share of the car. And, further, that:

> Unparalleled mobility . . . is generally a good thing, and has probably helped to bring us to the level of economic development that we currently enjoy . . . perhaps those in less developed countries that aspire to similar levels of mobility are not deluded, but have put their collective fingers on the main root of economic well-being.
>
> (Stopher, 2004, p. 129)

Taylor (2004) similarly argues against investing in public transport as a response to congestion difficulties, arguing that moving public transport 'back' to the mass market scale in many cities is likely to be impossible, and that congestion or road pricing options are more beneficial. Hence there is much debate as to future possibilities and pathways, and even as to the necessity for any change at all.

A similar debate and scepticism occurs over links between urban form and travel. The mainstream view is that urban form, covering various facets of development (homes, workplaces, leisure, retail and other facilities), location, design and layout, makes a large difference to the resulting travel behaviour. The early research developed from an international city comparative analysis on density and energy consumption in transport (Newman and Kenworthy, 1989; 1999); the general thesis being that higher densities were associated with reduced travel distances and transport energy consumption, and this could support greater use of public transport, walking and cycling. It was recognised that land use and travel decisions co-determine each other, i.e. there are close linkages between the location of development, urban structure and travel (and the reverse – that transport investment is associated with a resulting urban form) (Wegener and Fürst, 1999; Albers, 1974). A typology of approaches (Figure 1.25) was put forward, including:

- Point structures: cities are orientated towards the central point of the urban system, usually the core urban area, e.g. the compact city or polycentric city model;
- Linear structures: cities built along a corridor, usually along major transport infrastructure, e.g. Soria y Mata's linear city.
- Area structures: low density development, lacking a clear spatial hierarchy and central structure, e.g. Wright's Broadacre City.

A rich literature has developed, eventually covering a wide range of built environment factors, including density, settlement size, jobs–housing balance, mix of use, the location of development, extending into local neighbourhood and street design. All these factors are associated with travel at various levels of significance. Different metrics of travel (by mode, distance, energy consumption, CO_2 emissions), scales of analysis, and socio-economic and attitudinal variables have also been incorporated over time, and there is now a quite sophisticated understanding of urban structure and travel relationships (including Cervero, 1989; 1996; Banister et al., 1997; Headicar and Curtis, 1998; Ewing and Cervero, 2001; Stead, 2001; Schwanen and Mokhtarian, 2005; Hickman et al., 2009c; Aditjandra et al., 2012). The built environment variables have been translated into the three Ds (density, diversity and design) (Cervero and Kockelman, 1997), five Ds (with the addition of destination accessibility and destination to transit) (Ewing and Cervero, 2001) and even seven Ds (demand management and demographics) (Ewing and Cervero, 2010; Hickman et al., 2010c). The 'meta analysis' view is that destination accessibility, distance to urban centre and neighbourhood design (intersection density and street connectivity) are the most significant built environment variables.

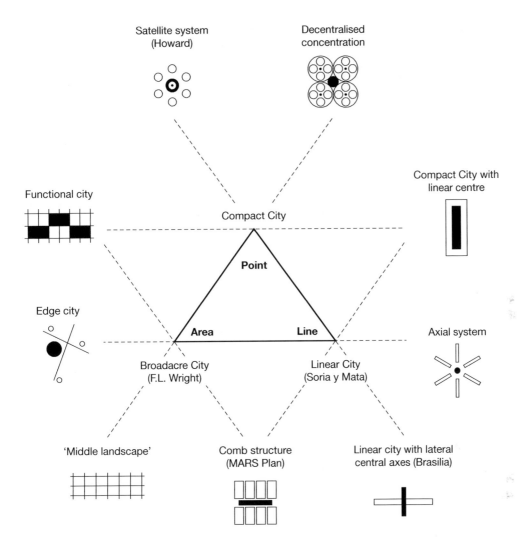

Figure 1.25 A typology of land use organisation plans
Source: Wegener and Fürst, 1999; Albers, 1974.

Of course, this is tempered by the complexity of decision-making in travel, as people don't always select their nearest destinations, and there may be issues of 'self selection' (whether particular locations may be associated with certain travel behaviours, or whether people with particular types of attitude are attracted to certain urban forms) (Bohte et al., 2009; Cao et al., 2009; Naess, 2009). There is certainly an uncertain level of 'discernment' in activity choice, including issues beyond the travel implication; and there are also acceptability and affordability concerns around urban living for a large cohort of the population (Breheny, 1992; 1997; Hickman and Banister, 2012).

There is a more controversial position, largely from the neo-liberal or free market perspective, of not supporting public intervention in planning, or in deeming that policies to combat urban sprawl are ineffective, or that the public, in the main, wish to live in areas at low density levels, with large houses and gardens, and access to the motor car (Gordon and Richardson, 1995; Bruegmann, 2006; Echenique and SOLUTIONS Consortium, 2009). For example:

> The idea of planners turning our lives upside down in pursuit of a single-minded goal is as horrible as it is alien. Newman and Kenworthy's world is the Kafkaesque nightmare that Hayek always dreaded, a world where consumers have no choice, relative prices have no role and planners are tyrants . . . Newman and Kenworthy have written a very troubling paper. Their distortions are not innocent, because the uninformed may use them as ammunition to support expensive plans for central city revitalisation and rail transit projects or stringent land use controls in a futile attempt to enforce urban compactness . . . perhaps Newman and Kenworthy would be well advised to seek out another planet, preferably unpopulated, where they can build their compact cities from scratch with solar powered transit.
>
> (Gordon and Richardson, 1989, p. 342)

Hence the debate remains very much alive, and some important points are being made that need to be addressed. The focus on the importance of individual preference is a useful critique of the built environment determinism, but in the end offers no solution to societal problems such as climate change and resource usage. There remains a huge gap in implementing the policy relative to intentions, in terms of developing mass market rapid transit, walking and cycling, integrating urban planning and transport planning, achieving polycentric urban form, and in changing the vehicle fleet to more efficient vehicles. Much of this is due to the business model we operate within (profit maximisation very often works against wider societal goals) and also public aspirations (the sign value of products is developed by the marketing effort, and consumption is shaped in a manner that makes profit). But the intractable problem remains: that the climate change imperative demands a different pathway in terms of lifestyles, and some progress soon.

Many alternative approaches are being developed to counter the entrenched level of motorisation in most contexts. There are some very good emerging examples of sustainable transport initiatives, but again progress is slow and the inertia is substantial. The good practice is usually concentrated in a few urban centres, rather than being introduced across the city as a whole. Such novel approaches can perhaps be encapsulated in the sustainable mobility paradigm (Banister, 2008) with some emerging thinking in terms of addressing the convention of increasing speed, distances and the need to prioritise slow transport and local activity (Banister, 2011). In the richer countries, a major part of decarbonising the transport sector is to reduce the need to travel (and actual travel), and in developing countries this translates to reducing the projected (business as usual) growth in motorisation and distances travelled.

In addition to the strength of the case to decarbonise transport, there are substantial co-benefits from reducing car use, particularly in cities. These include the health gains from active lifestyles (Woodcock et al., 2007; Woodcock et al., 2009), urban design quality and liveability in urban areas, costs of congestion, frustration in journey quality, independence gains for children and others, and reductions in the numbers and severity of road accidents. The key problem is in understanding how and to what extent the trend-break in car dependence can be achieved. In many developing countries, this story is of prospective nature, in terms of the incredible growth projected in car ownership and use. Many are on the growth path in motorisation that the Western industrialised countries followed 50 years ago, although their rate of increase is much faster. In these countries and cities, it is difficult to suggest that no

Figure 1.26 Amsterdam, Netherlands. There are alternative models for travel in cities – and it is time to replicate these internationally. People in the Netherlands don't cycle because they are poor and can't afford a car, but because it is an attractive and healthy way to get to work and access other facilities.

increase in travel take place (i.e. the ladder is drawn up). But the consequences of following the same pathway need to be very carefully considered, not just in transport, but in terms of how cities should develop in the future. There are considerable opportunities to 'leapfrog' from low mobility and low carbon use, to high accessibility and low carbon use, without passing through the very wasteful 'ICE motor car phase'.

The transport sector is hence at a major crossroads in terms of the direction it takes. Achieving sustainable mobility around the world is proving to be extremely problematic. At the moment there are very selective efforts to develop strategies to reduce GHG and CO_2 emissions, with some limited consideration of potential policy pathways. The ambitions of the policy are not being met in practice. Meanwhile transport CO_2 emissions continue to rise. Even in the cities that are taking the lead in moving towards transport emissions reductions, progress is very slow. There are few examples of sustainable transport behaviours in suburban areas. There are no examples in the industrialised countries where area-wide transport CO_2 emissions have been reduced by 80 per cent or even 60 per cent on 1990 levels, despite the targets and the postulation; and in the emerging countries there are few significant reductions against BAU projections. International targets,if they are set, are often unambitious, and the pathways followed do not reveal significant progress and substantial savings in the short term.

Only slow and ad hoc implementation has taken place,and incremental progress is actually made against objectives, with levels of transport CO2 emissions stabilising at best. Relative to the other emitting sectors (industry and domestic), the transport sector is performing very poorly in terms of decarbonising. By default, the politicians are waiting for the 'silver bullet' technological solution, to enable a dramatic reduction in transport emissions – but this will not happen – and in the meantime CO2 is still being produced and it will remain active in the atmosphere for up to 100 years.

The aim of this book is to arrive at a better understanding of how transport can contribute to sustainability in cities. It uses case study analysis – from London, Oxfordshire, Delhi, Jinan and Auckland – to explore the richness and heterogeneity in approach for different contexts. It seeks to understand the different baselines, the potential policy interventions on offer, the approaches for strategy and policy-making, and the most effective means of reaching strategic targets. This is tackled through using scenario analysis methodologies, not conventionally used in the transport sector, and combining these with a quantification of likely policy measure and scenario impacts, and more conventional multi-criteria analysis against scenarios. The different contexts are considered in the following five case study chapters, exploring the possible mitigation pathways that also give benefits against wider sustainability aspirations. The approach might be viewed as Panglossian[19] insofar as we seek to demonstrate that alternative and attractive futures are possible. We hope this improved understanding, and discussion around the key strategic decisions that need to be made – the 'strategic conversations' (Van der Heijden, 1996) – will help us move beyond our current unsustainable transport behaviours. However, alongside, the current transport trends and dependence on the car in almost all cities is also very evident, and we are realistic about the trends and also the attractiveness of the car for many people, if not most. This can be viewed as representing a form of false consciousness (and certainly complacency), perhaps of hyperreality in transport.

Lewis Carroll (1893) and Jorge Luis Borges (1960) famously describe the process of map making, where the map first represents the territory, but then replaces it and ultimately precedes it – as an illustration of the process of simulacra. This concept might be used to help us understand the representation of motorisation and travel – the difference between the advertising dream and the reality of the impact of mass motorisation on the environment, social inclusion, the economy and the city – and perhaps encourage us to frame and shape the debate around sustainable travel in a different and more realistic manner:

> In that Empire, the craft of Cartography attained such Perfection that the Map of a Single province covered the space of an entire City, and the Map of the Empire itself an entire Province. In the course of Time, these Extensive maps were found somehow wanting, and so the College of Cartographers evolved a Map of the Empire that was of the same Scale as the Empire and that coincided with it point for point. Less attentive to the Study of Cartography, succeeding Generations came to judge a map of such Magnitude cumbersome, and, not without Irreverence, they abandoned it to the Rigours of sun and Rain. In the western Deserts, tattered Fragments of the Map are still to be found, Sheltering an occasional Beast or beggar; in the whole Nation, no other relic is left of the Discipline of Geography.
>
> (Borges, 1960, p. 181)[20]

These are, of course, huge ambitions. Achieving sustainability in transport will involve a major break from current mainstream trends and aspirations, even beliefs, with many of us needing to think and act in very different ways. The tools of government are often very limited, particularly in the industrialised countries, where the tendency has been to follow neo-liberal thought and not to try to influence (or 'socially engineer') individual behaviours, or to implement 'politically controversial' projects, or to spend large amounts of money on public transport schemes (relative to spending on the private car). Thinking around this transition represents a major intellectual challenge, and also a major implementation challenge for practitioners and the public. Our final chapter discusses some of the (as yet) unsolved difficulties that arise as we seek to move to more sustainable travel behaviours; how we might move beyond our 'conspicuous consumption'and 'technological unconscious' (Veblen, 1899; Thrift, 2004), but also more fully understand and respond to the car as a central part of society (Baudrillard, 1981a; Urry, 2007). We need to more fully understand the intractability of the current situation, in that:

> Cars will not easily be given up just (!) because they are dangerous to health and life, environmentally destructive, based on unsustainable energy consumption, and damaging to public life and civic space. Too many people find them too comfortable, enjoyable, exciting, even enthralling. They are deeply embedded in ways of life, networks of friendship and sociality, and moral commitments to family and care for others.
>
> (Sheller, 2004)

The narrative of the motor car has lasted for only 125 years – but this seems much longer – as if the car has been around forever. The impact on the fabric of the city, on individuals' lives and society has been incredible, and it is easy to overlook the relatively short term nature of the trends. In 50 years time we hope to be looking at very different means of movement and interaction within our everyday lives, but changing the trajectory in the trends is and will be difficult. However, the stakes are high – potentially the ultimate for humanity – in terms of the use of oil, the increasing scarcity, the political skirmishes over the supply of oil, and the changing climate. Perhaps resulting in the rise or the fall of civilisation as we know it (Diamond, 2005). We really should be discussing our future options, and the major political directions that we need to take, in earnest.

The dream and the reality: the picture of unsustainable mobility

The following images illustrate the development of car-based travel, as sold in the marketing and advertising and then – in juxtaposition – as realised in travel in the city. The car has been very successfully marketed and sold in different ways, in terms of style, features and aspiration, including the early emphasis on affordability, reliability and suitability for the mass market; moving onto a more seductive pitch in terms of 'aspirational' lifestyles and fashion. In parallel, there has been some marketing for public transport and cycling, but this has been very limited in relation and much less sophisticated in approach. The common theme in car advertising has been to encourage private car ownership, to illustrate the (real and unreal) benefits to the individual, and to downplay the reality of the environmental and social dimensions of mass motorisation, including the impact on the city.

Plate 1.1
Poster advertising Ford, the 'general utility car',
c.1912 (colour litho)
Source: Cuningham, Oswald Hamilton (b. 1883)/Victoria and
Albert Museum, London, UK/The Bridgeman Art Library.

Plate 1.2
Bangkok, Thailand. Cities the world over are suffering from traffic growth, aspirations for increased motorisation, and the projections are that this will only get worse. Congestion and lengthy journey times are most evident in Asian and South American cities, some cities have horrific average journey times.
Source: Carlos Pardo.

Facing page:

Plate 1.3 Advertisement for the Oldsmobile Olds Sixty, 1939 (litho), American School (20th century). Motor car ownership becomes affordable for the masses, or at least a wider selection of 'the privileged'. And, of course, low density suburbia is an integral part of the motorisation dream.
Source: Private collection/Peter Newark American Pictures/The Bridgeman Art Library.

Plate 1.4 The Studebaker Land Cruiser, 1948 (colour litho), American School (20th century). Even the high-end styling is offered to the masses.
Source: Private collection/Peter Newark American Pictures/The Bridgeman Art Library.

Plate 1.5 Tokyo, Japan. Many cities have been expanded in the 1970s to 1990s, when the emphasis was on increasing highway capacity, including with urban motorways. This has been less effective at relieving congestion than envisaged, with traffic filling the space provided. There are severe problems in environmental terms, including severance, poor air quality, CO_2 emissions, and adverse impacts on urban quality.
Source: Manfred Breithaupt.

Plate 1.6 Magazine illustration, 1950s (colour litho). The car offers opportunities that seem attractive – how can we refuse the car purchase?

Source: Sarnoff, Arthur (1912–2000)/Private collection/© The Advertising Archives/The Bridgeman Art Library.

Plate 1.7 'Driving a Peugeot car is fashionable', 1934 (colour litho), French School.

Source: Private collection/Archives Charmet/The Bridgeman Art Library.

Plate 1.8 Advertisement for Morris Motors, 1935 (illustration). The car offers the open road, freedom and opportunity; there is no other way that you can see these beautiful sights. And, of course, your view is not spoiled by others being there.

Source: The Illustrated London News Picture Library, London, UK/The Bridgeman Art Library.

Plate 1.9
UK (M62). The tangential and inter-urban trips are also rising rapidly in volume, with few attempts to curb the growth. Most efforts at traffic demand management focus on the conventional radial trip into the urban area – and this has long since been superseded by the 'many to many' origins and destinations.
Source: Highways Agency.

Plate 1.10
Manila, Philippines. Where there is provision for public transport, services are often uncoordinated, with little priority given for buses on the roads, hence the service is poor.

Plate 1.11
Brochure advertising the Renault Primaquatre
Automobile, c.1930 (colour litho), French School.
The higher the unattainability of the good, the
higher its value (Simmel, 1978).

Source: Private collection/Archives Charmet/The Bridgeman
Art Library.

Plate 1.12
German advertisement for the Volkswagen,
produced by the Nazi organisation KdF, 1938
(colour litho)

Source: Axster-Heudtlass, Werner von (fl.
1938)/Deutsches Historisches Museum, Berlin,
Germany/© DHM/The Bridgeman Art Library.

Plate 1.13 Hanoi, Vietnam. There are often
competing demands for road space in cities, and
usually public transport, walking and cycling lose
out. There is a reticence to reduce the space given
to the private car; usually capacity for vehicles is
increased over time.

Source: Manfred Breithaupt.

Plate 1.14 Bangkok, Thailand. Two- and three-
wheelers are very popular in some cities; there is a
great opportunity to make these clean in fuel terms,
with very low CO_2 emissions.

Source: Carlos Pardo.

Plate 1.15 'New housing'. The new transportation possibilities allow a new style of housing and the growth of the suburbs.

Source: The Advertising Archives.

Plate 1.16
'Moving furniture'. Car ownership facilitates the development of the ubiquitous suburban plot.

Source: The Advertising Archives.

Plate 1.17
Poster advertising the 1955 Chevrolet car (colour litho), American School. The styling gets more complex.

Source: Private collection/The Stapleton Collection/The Bridgeman Art Library.

Plate 1.18
'Lion hearted' Chrysler, 1959

Source: Flickr Creative Commons, Paul Malon.

Plate 1.19
Hanoi, Vietnam. Local air quality, including high levels of particulates, nitrogen oxide and sulphur dioxide, remains a problem in many cities.

Source: Manfred Breithaupt.

Plate 1.20
Manila, Philippines. Many Asian cities have different types of paratransit, including jeepneys, and this offers an important form of public transport. They however need to utilise clean vehicles in terms of CO2 emissions.

Facing page (bottom):

Plate 1.23 *LMS for Speed and Comfort*, poster advertising the London, Midland and Scottish Railway (colour litho). The railway advertising is similarly constrained and doesn't approach the aspirational and consumerisation dimensions.

Source: Secretan, Murray (fl. 1935)/Private collection/Photo © Christie's Images/The Bridgeman Art Library.

Plate 1.24 The London Underground. Some of the messages are powerful, but get lost amongst the car advertising.

Source: London Transport Museum collection.

Plate 1.22
Raleigh bikes, 1970s
Source: The Advertising Archives.

Plate 1.21
Poster advertising 'The Perfect' bicycle, 1895 (colour litho), Belgian School. There have been some efforts to advertise alternative modes such as the bicycle – but these have been extremely limited in comparison to the car. There is not the same potential in the profit margin, hence the effort seems to be much reduced.

Source: Private collection/© Ackermann Kunstverlag/ The Bridgeman Art Library.

Plate 1.25
Toyota Corolla, 1974. A change in styling with 'must have' gadgets
Source: The Advertising Archives.

Plate 1.26
Ford Cortina, 1970s
Source: The Advertising Archives.

Plate 1.27
Mini, 1978
Source: The Advertising Archives.

Facing page:

Plate 1.28 Surrey, UK. Many of the developments located on the edge of, or beyond, the central urban areas are often very car dependent. They are sometimes built with very good accessibility to the strategic road network – these developments have virtually 100 per cent car mode share.

Plate 1.29 Harlow, UK. In addition, retail and employment centres are often built in out-of-town locations, and with a design, that can only be accessed by the car. These types of developments are virtually impossible to serve by public transport and are difficult to cycle or walk to. They are very difficult to retrofit for sustainable mobility options – the only realistic option is via low-emission vehicles.

Plate 1.30
Toyota Starlet
Source: The Advertising Archives.

Plate 1.31
BMW, 1970s: 'The ultimate driving machine'
Source: The Advertising Archives.

Plate 1.32 Volvo, 1987. Vehicle safety is introduced as an angle for selling vehicles.
Source: The Advertising Archives.

Plate 1.33 Washington DC, USA. Some cities were designed around the use of the car, and remain very dependent on the car. Where the built fabric is interesting to the pedestrian, it can still be very difficult to negotiate the space reserved for car usage.

Plate 1.34 East London, UK. Even in the cities lauded as 'good practice' examples in sustainable transport planning, the suburbs and dispersed outer areas tend to be very car dependent, and there are often very limited facilities for public transport, walking and cycling.

Plate 1.35
Volvo 740 Turbo
Source: Flickr Creative Commons.

Plate 1.36 Manila, Philippines. It is usually the pedestrian and cycling environment that loses out to the private car – these are the modes that are given least consideration in transport planning and funding – but, of course, in environmental terms should be given the greatest priority.

Plate 1.37 Seattle, USA. Internationally the result is the same: the infrastructure involved in catering for the car has subsumed the city fabric – we have spent the last 50 years planning our urban areas for the car, rather than for the people who live there. The motorisation dream has spread from the USA and the industrialised West to much of the globe. Echoing Vonnegut (1963, p. 116): 'Son, my father said to me, someday this will all be yours.'

Source: Chehsiang Chen.

Plate 1.38
Toyota Prius, 2010. Climate change becomes the focal selling point.

Source: The Advertising Archives.

Plate 1.39
Lexus RX 400h, 2007. Even for SUVs.

Source: The Advertising Archives.

Plate 1.40
Porsche 911, 2007

Source: The Advertising Archives.

Plate 1.41 Land Rover, 2010. The emerging markets become critical.
Source: The Advertising Archives.

Plate 1.42
'Home sweet home'
Source: mozartitalia.com.

Plate 1.43
For All That We See or
Seem a Dream Within a
Dream, 1967 (oil on
canvas), Jacques Emile
Louis Monory

Source: Monory, Jacques
Emile Louis (b. 1934)/
Musée Cantini, Marseilles,
France/Giraudon/
The Bridgeman Art Library.
Copyright ADAGP, Paris, and
DACs, London 2013.

Bill took off his jacket and chucked it on the back seat of the car. Then he swung himself into the front. He rammed the key into the ignition, turned it, and the car thrummed and pulsed into life. The CD chirruped – then some John Cage came on. Bill scraped the big saloon around a hundred and eighty degrees, and shot back up on to the A9, this time heading south.

For the next hour he drove hard [. . .]. It was exhilarating – this headlong plunge down the exposed cranium of Britain. After twenty miles or so Bill had a spectacular view clear of the Moray Firth to the Grampians. The mountains pushed apart land, sea and sky with nonchalant grandeur; their peaks stark white, their flanks hazed white and blue and azure. Not that he looked at them, he looked at the driving, snatching shards of scenery in the jagged saccades his eyes made from speedometer to road, to rearview mirror, to wing mirrors, and back, over and over.

[. . .] In a way Bill was praying. In the concentration on braking and accelerating, and at these speeds essentially toying with life and death – others' as well as his own – he finally achieved the dharmic state he had been seeking all morning: an absorption of his own being into the very act of driving.

(Will Self, *Tough, Tough Toys for Tough, Tough Boys*, 1999, pp. 120–121)

Plate 1.44 In the Car, 1963 (magna on canvas), Roy Lichtenstein. The painting is based on the comic book
series *Girls' Romances*, number 78, published by Signal Publishing Corporation in 1961. It is part
of a series of 'fantasy drama' paintings of women in love affairs with domineering men causing
the women to be miserable. The original comic book text reads: 'I vowed to myself I would not
miss my appointment – that I would not go riding with him – yet before I knew it . . . '

Notes

1 Megacities (over 10 million population) in rank order (2005): Tokyo, Mexico City, New York–Newark, São Paulo, Mumbai, Delhi, Shanghai, Kolkata, Buenos Aires, Dhaka, Los Angeles–Long Beach, Karachi, Rio de Janeiro, Osaka–Kobe, Cairo, Beijing, Manila, Moscow, Istanbul. By 2020 it is expected that there will be 9 metacities (over 20 million population): Tokyo, Mumbai, Delhi, Mexico City, New York–Newark, Dhaka, Jakarta and Lagos.

2 In 1898 the Swedish scientist Svante Arrhenius warned that CO_2 emissions could lead to global warming.

3 DDT (dichlorodiphenyltrichloroethane) is one of the most well-known synthetic pesticides. DDT was used with 'great success' in the second half of World War II to control malaria and typhus, and after the war as a widespread agricultural insecticide. Rachel Carson described the environmental impacts of indiscriminate DDT use in the United States and questioned the release of large amounts of chemicals without understanding their effects on the environment or human health. Use of DDT was subsequently banned in the US (1972), and internationally, but with some limited continued use.

4 In 1990, the US was responsible for 36 per cent of CO_2 emitted by the thirty-seven Annex 1 countries.

5 Stern also uses the CO2e metric (equivalent CO_2), which is an estimate of the concentration of CO_2 using the six greenhouse gases considered under the Kyoto Protocol, hence involves higher numbers than CO_2. As a guide, 379 ppm CO_2 approximates to 455 ppm CO2e (Kyoto).

6 Eocene: derived from Greek ἠώς (eos, dawn) and καινός (kainos, new) and refers to the 'dawn' or appearance of new mammals. The end of the Eocene is associated with a major extinction event called the *Grande Coupure* (the 'Great Break' in continuity), which may be related to the impact of one or more large bodies in Siberia, in what is now Chesapeake Bay. Hence the temperature changes being contemplated, and in effect risked, are extremely concerning.

7 'I will build a car for the great multitude. It will be large enough for the family, but small enough for the individual to run and care for. It will be constructed of the best materials, by the best men to be hired, after the simplest designs that modern engineering can devise. But it will be so low in price that no man making a good salary will be unable to own one – and enjoy with his family the blessing of hours of pleasure in God's great open spaces' (Henry Ford, founder of the Ford Motor Company, 1922).

8 Unconventional oil is petroleum produced or extracted using techniques other than the conventional oil well method. The main sources are in oil sands and shale. The two most important deposits are the Athabasca oil sands in Alberta, Canada and the Orinoco deposit in Venezuela. Unconventional oil production has greater environmental impacts than that of conventional oil production – extraction involves much landtake, requires large volumes of water and energy, and the mining process releases additional CO_2.

9 Further details are found in the Annex.

10 The derivation of 'auto' is in itself instructive – taken from the Greek 'αὐτο' (auto-), and meaning 'self, one's own'. It is used with reference to the private car, one's own mobility.

11 Social construct: the concept or practice (artefact) of a particular group. The practice is dependent on the contingent variables of the social self (the individuals) rather than the particular inherent quality that it possesses in itself (the car) (Berger and Luckman, 1966).

12 The numbers are uncertain, but the estimates are that traffic accidents result, worldwide, in up to 1.2 million deaths each year, and 50 million injuries each year. The majority of victims are poor, and pedestrians or cyclists (Mohan, 2002).

13 A Trip to the Moon was also used as the inspiration for the well-known music video to 'Tonight, Tonight', a single by the Smashing Pumpkins, released in 1996. The storyline in the video shows a trip to the moon by Zeppelin: the central characters are attacked by aliens, but manage to escape, vaporising the aliens with their umbrellas. They are then rescued by a ship – the S.S. Méliès.

14 The argument here is for a form of social capitalism that moderates the primary concern over profits and returns to shareholders, with objectives to also enhance social and environmental capital, through giving much greater value to the protection of resources and environmental assets, as well as promoting social well being – this is at the heart of sustainable mobility.

15 The auto–industrial complex is seen as comprising the private sector highway lobby (oil companies, the auto industry, road freight and road construction companies), the development industry, many private sector consultancies, and the public sector professionals and bureaucrats. Taken together these interests have conventionally dominated the formulation of transport policies at the governmental level.

16 Meaningful participation is not easy to achieve. The desirable goal of 'diverse voices contributing to decision-making' may be very difficult to attain. Participation may in effect not be an attractive device

to achieve some form of optimised consensus, rather a mechanism for vocal minorities to act in their own self interest. The participation process hence needs very careful definition (Abram, 2000; Bruton, 1980).

17 The nature of 'car dependence' is broad – covering reliance in trips (there is no other form of transport available), car reliant activities (carrying heavy goods or undertaking multi-destination trips), car reliant locations (remote), car reliant persons (limited mobility), car convenient journeys (alternatives modes are available, but perceived as less attractive), car dependent persons (a statement of status or self esteem), car addiction (those who talk 'incessantly' about cars and whose life revolves around the need to drive), a car reliant society (high observed levels of car use, where people without cars are excluded from essential activities) (Lucas and Jones, 2009).

18 Greenwashing (green whitewash) is a term for the disingenuous 'spinning' of policies and products as environmentally friendly. Reputedly coined by environmentalist Jay Westerveld in 1986, greenwash was used to describe the hotel industry's practice of promoting the reuse of guest towels, ostensibly to 'save the environment'. In most cases, little or no effort was being made towards energy efficiency, waste recycling or other environmental practices, and the distances travelled to the hotel were often extensive, and perhaps by air. Westerveld viewed these 'green' efforts as being motivated by profit rather than for the environment. Examples can be seen in many other fields.

19 Voltaire's *Candide* (1759) begins with a young man, Candide, living a sheltered life, indoctrinated with optimism by his mentor, Pangloss. Over time Candide becomes disillusioned at the pain experienced in the world. He maintains that 'We must cultivate our garden', moving beyond the naivety of Pangloss that 'all is for the best in the best of all possible worlds' (Voltaire, 1759).

20 Lewis Carroll provides us with a very similar story (in *Sylvie and Bruno Concluded*): a map so detailed that it covers the very things it was designed to represent – the hyperreal: 'a map of the country, on the scale of a mile to the mile'. Baudrillard, Urry and others develop these themes to describe the concept of hyperreality: a hypothetical inability of consciousness to distinguish 'reality' from 'fantasy'. The logical extension into the transport world is perhaps in the use of the car and car dependency: the hyperreality of motorisation – in the utility, convenience and freedom it supposedly offers – but often fails to deliver, and certainly only with significant external costs to the environment and society.

Figure 2.1 *Blade Runner*, 1982, written by Philip K. Dick, directed by Ridley Scott. Genetically engineered organic robots, called replicants, visually indistinguishable from adult humans – 'more human than human' – are manufactured by the Tyrell Corporation. Their use on Earth is banned, and replicants are exclusively used for dangerous or menial work on Earth's off-world colonies. Replicants who defy the ban and return to Earth are hunted down and 'retired' by police special operatives known as 'blade runners'. The blade runners drive 'spinners', or flying cars, which can be driven as ground-based vehicles, or in vertical take-off mode, hover, and cruise using jet propulsion. Despite restrictions, wealthy people can also acquire spinner licenses.

> *Deckard*: She's a replicant, isn't she?
> *Tyrell*: I'm impressed. How many questions does it usually take to spot them?
> *Deckard*: I don't get it, Tyrell.
> *Tyrell*: How many questions?
> *Deckard*: Twenty, thirty, cross-referenced.
> *Tyrell*: It took more than a hundred for Rachael, didn't it?

Source: British Film Institute Stills Collection.

2 Futures, scenarios and strategic conversations

Goldberg:	Is the number 846 possible or necessary?
Stanley:	Neither.
Goldberg:	Wrong! Is the number 846 possible or necessary?
Stanley:	Both.
Goldberg:	Wrong! It's necessary but not possible.
Stanley:	Both.
Goldberg:	Wrong! Why do you think the number 846 is necessarily possible?
Stanley:	Must be.
Goldberg:	Wrong! It's only necessarily necessary! We admit possibility only after we grant necessity. It is possible because necessary but by no means necessary through possibility. The possibility can only be assumed after the proof of necessity.
McCann:	Right!

(Harold Pinter, *The Birthday Party*, 1960, p. 50)

Futures thinking

We are all naturally interested in our futures, including how our own lifestyles may pan out, and how the world might develop over time. The examination of possible futures, and eventually leading to the development of a literature field in futures studies, has a lengthy and fascinating history. Perhaps the earliest and well-known accounts are from the Oracle at Delphi,[1] from 580–570 BC onwards (Chappell, 2006). For example, in 547 BC, King Croesus of Lydia famously consulted the Oracle, anxious to know the likely outcome of his war with Cyrus the Great. He was told that if he crossed the river between his army and his enemy a great empire would fall. Overjoyed, he attacked the Persians, only to discover that his was the empire to fall (Robinson, 1990; West, 2003). This is a problem for all futures studies: the difficulty in understanding what might happen.

From the social science domain, Popper (1957, Preface, xii–xiii) helps us understand the central problematic in futures analysis; he critiques historicism in that interpreting the past cannot always help predict the future:

> If there is such a thing as growing human knowledge, then we cannot anticipate today what we shall know only tomorrow [. . .] no scientific predictor – whether a human scientist or a calculating machine – can possibly predict, by scientific methods, its own future results.

Hence there are fundamental difficulties in projecting the future course of history. Over the years various related perspectives on societal change have evolved to tackle these issues;

a number of ideas have gained much coverage in the literature. Kuhn's (1962, p. 10) celebrated concept of paradigm shift, for example, attempts to explain scientific revolution. He suggests that there is a 'normal science', which scientists and practitioners accept for a time as a basis for everything they do. This is the accepted 'paradigm' or: 'some accepted examples of actual scientific practice – including law, theory, application and instrumentation – which together provide models from which spring particular coherent traditions of scientific research'.

At particular points in time, scientists, however, become aware of anomalies in their worldview; they find things that the prevailing paradigm does not explain well. Science then enters a new phase, in which the old paradigm is scrapped and a new one developed in its place – translated in the current economic jargon as the 'new normal'. Kondratieff (1935) similarly developed the notion of 'waves of development' in terms of profit crisis in the capitalist system, due to the possibilities of a given generation of technologies being exhausted. Only by the diversion of new capital into a new a new set of technologies, can this be overcome. Schumpeter (1939) translates these principles into business cycles, with new industries and technologies arising over time. Foucault (1966, p. 235), this time in terms of knowledge, asks:

> How is it that thought detaches itself from the squares it inhabited before – general grammar, natural history, wealth – and allows what less than twenty years before had been posited in the luminous space of understanding to topple down into error, into the realm of fantasy, into non-knowledge?

Hence we have a wealth of perspectives, from different domains, from key thinkers, and from different times, all considering issues relating to change, and whether the future is merely a continuation of the past or something much more imaginative. There is also the supplementary question of how change over time can be better understood, or as Foucault labels this: 'the order of things'.

Dealing with uncertainty

Future studies attempt to think through possible (and desirable) ways forward, but also to investigate alternative more radical possibilities through deliberative processes. This is very often a normative process: expressing value judgments as to where we might like to be, or go, from the societal perspective; as contrasted with stating facts, or analysing and/or extrapolating trends. Part of this process is a focus on assessing the potential for enhancing positive trends, or achieving breaks against more negative trends (this is often the policy-maker's goal), or how to make more effective strategic choices in view of uncertain trends (the corporate planning goal). All of these perspectives can be of relevance to transport, city planning and wider sustainability objectives. But it is perhaps surprising that normative analysis in transport planning is very seldom used, as there is a tradition of positivism and more quantitative modelling. For example, the analysis is made of the impact of city development on the transport network, or the traffic flow through a junction, rather than a more fundamental understanding of the potential role of transport in achieving societal goals.

The position taken by Popper was that the level of future uncertainty was only partly determined by the present conditions and societal trends as we know them. Dreborg (1996) terms this problem as 'indeterminacy', explaining that a change in public policy may not only affect an exogenous policy variable, but may change 'the rules of the whole game'. An actor's decisions are largely determined by the ideas and knowledge available; new knowledge may

Figure 2.2 Early twentieth-century trade card imagining fashionable travel in 2012. Woman travelling in a submarine 'car' using the intercom to ask the captain to stop at the station for Chocolat Lombard.

Source: Universal History Archive/UIG/The Bridgeman Art Library.

Figure 2.3
In the Year 2000: Balloon on a Long Course, 1912 (colour litho), French School

Source: Collection Kharbine-Tapabor, Paris, France/The Bridgeman Art Library.

Figure 2.4
In the Year 2000: A Whale Bus, 1912 (colour litho), French School

Source: Collection Kharbine-Tapabor, Paris, France/The Bridgeman Art Library.

Figure 2.5
(Above) Leaving the Opera in the Year 2000, Albert Robida (colour litho), French School. It is often difficult to anticipate the changes around the corner.

Source: Robida, Albert (1848–1926)/Collection Kharbine-Tapabor, Paris, France/The Bridgeman Art Library.

Figure 2.6
(Left) The Modern Style Road, Albert Robida, French School

Source: From *The Twentieth Century*, 1884 (litho), Robida, Albert (1848–1926), Collection Kharbine-Tapabor, Paris, France/The Bridgeman Art Library.

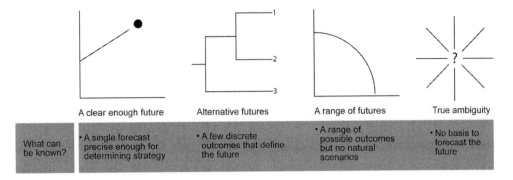

Figure 2.7 Levels of residual uncertainty
Source: Courtney et al., 1997; 2001; Frommelt, 2008.

tip the balance in favour of another known alternative, and may even open up entirely new options. A key concept within futures analysis is therefore that of uncertainty. Courtney (1997), Courtney et al. (2001) and Frommelt (2008) describe different levels of 'residual uncertainty', depending on the range of possible outcomes (Figure 2.7). These outcomes range from a clarity of the future direction as moving in one direction, or the choices made between clearly defined alternatives, or a range of possibilities placed within a solution space, or a more truly unknown and random set of futures.

If these alternatives are augmented by a timeline, then a different sort of uncertainty occurs. Van der Heijden (1996) (Figure 2.8) illustrates how the degree of predictability falls with reduced knowledge of predetermined trends, and the uncertainty rises, the further we look in time. In the very long term everything is uncertain and strategy is based, at best, on 'hope',

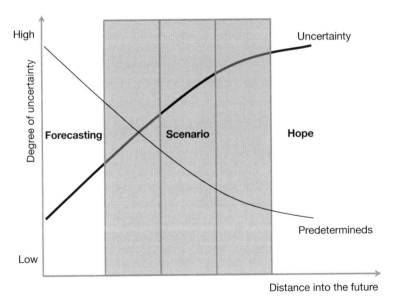

Figure 2.8 Predictability and uncertainty
Source: Van der Heijden, 1996.

but scenarios can play an important role in this intermediate space between short forecasting and long term hope.

Sources of uncertainty have been defined as a combination of demand side factors (e.g. interpreted within transport as traffic volumes and rates of growth and decline, etc.), supply side (perhaps including vehicular technology and the wider range of policy interventions) and external factors (e.g. governmental policy and social pressures) (Karnani and Wernerfelt, 1987). Perhaps the Van der Heijden view is also optimistic in today's world, as major uncertainties (and shocks) can appear in even the short term, for example through climate or financial related events, and these events are often from outside the transport system and not contained within it.

Figure 2.9 Metropolis, 1927, directed by Fritz Lang. In the sprawling futuristic mega-city Metropolis, society is divided into two classes: one of planners and management, who live high up in luxurious skyscrapers; and one of workers, who live and work underground.

> *Freder*:   It was their hands that built this city of ours, Father. But where do the hands belong in your scheme?
>
> *Joh Frederson*: In their proper place, the depths.

Source: British Film Institute Stills Collection.

Uncertainty can be viewed through different lenses, possibly as the 'Achilles' heel' of strategic planning (Allaire and Firsirotu, 1989), or as the means not to prevent action (Levine, 1997), or as a way of even inspiring action (Peterson et al., 2003).Van der Heijden (1996) perceives success and failure as inevitable and dynamic notions, as there are winners because there is uncertainty, and without uncertainty, there can be no winners. In a related manner, a common phenomenon in business strategy is 'satisficing' – where decision-makers do not seek maximally beneficial outcomes, but instead accept the outcome that meets a minimum set of criteria (March and Herbert, 1958), or as Simon (1991) suggests, within their 'bounded rationality'. This means that there will always be uncertainty in the future and it is important to be able to cope so that the competitive environment can be shaped (Allaire and Firsirotu, 1989). This view is supported by Wack (1985a), who suggests that the only solution is to accept uncertainty, to try to understand it and make it part of our reasoning. Porter (1980; 1990) has famously translated this type of thinking into theories of competitive advantage at the business and even national level, but even here the notions of uncertainty are embedded as part of those processes.

A lack of awareness in our environment may also have a large impact on future events, particularly when changes over time are involved, as large changes to objects and scenes are not detected (change blindness), and those objects themselves might not be even perceived (inattentional blindness). There is a tendency to only perceive those objects and details that receive focused attention (Simons, 1999; Frommelt, 2008). Such myopia can be due to inertia, over-confidence (too sure of a central view of the future), a failure of imagination; and, at times, a greater sensitivity to losses than to gains, resulting in risk aversion (Schoemaker, 1998; Schoemaker and Gunther, 2002). Simons and Chabris' (1999) 'gorillas in the midst'[2] explores these issues, and how the really important strategic issues are sometimes missed, or at least only slowly recognised. Such thinking has much resonance in transport planning, as there is often a very limited perspective taken in analysis, as solutions are seen to be technical. This means that some of the large strategic challenges (such as climate change) are ignored.

The forecasting problem

Forecasting has conventionally been the dominant methodology used in transport planning. Historical trends are typically extrapolated in the future, for example assuming stable relationships between incomes and car ownership. The relationships are derived from historical data, and are often non-context-specific (e.g. they may use national data in the absence of local data). There may be some sensitivity around variables, such as the growth rates used. Thus increases in household incomes will lead to rises in car ownership and use. We can see how, under conditions of uncertainty, forecasting approaches can be very unreliable, particularly over the longer term. They are of course not suited to situations where trend-breaks are required, such as in sustainable transport. Forecasting is rarely normative in nature, hence tends to lead to, or be associated with, policy-making that accentuates or reinforces existing trends. This means it is very path dependent, with a clear lock in to a particular way of thinking, and it is limiting in terms of incorporating policy alternatives.

Within the transport sector, forecasting has led to the 'predict and provide' approach, with schemes being built as a solution to the projected trend, often with self-fulfilling results. For example, traffic growth was forecast, roads built and the growth in traffic followed. The general convention in transport was to achieve 'the greatest mobility for the greatest number' (Adams, 1981), and this has dominated transport-planning thinking over the years, in terms of motorway and highway development, the design of links and junctions to increase volume and throughput, and indeed the planning of wider modes such as air and rail. For example: 'Car ownership [. . .] should increase, for personal mobility is what people want, and those who already have it should not try to pull the ladder up behind them' (Department of the Environment, 1976, cited in Adams, 1981, p. 3).

In the UK, this approach was best represented in the 'Roads for Prosperity' White Paper (Department of Transport, 1989), where over 500 new road schemes were proposed in 'support' of the economy and to cater for predicted traffic growth (Headicar, 2009). Though the policy discourse has changed markedly since, with almost all transport strategies internationally now being centred on sustainability aspirations, the implementation and investment programmes are still very much roads-focused. Many of the road schemes mentioned in 'Roads for Prosperity' were constructed in the following years in the UK, with 'sustainable transport' being interpreted as the maintenance of existing levels of mobility, with lower levels of delay and congestion. With almost every change of Secretary of State for Transport there is a renewed call for a road-building programme, and often investment follows.

Policy has thus been self-fulfilling. Transport analysis needs to be understood within the framework of promoting car-based transport (at least in recent history), with the 'socio-technical systems' reinforcing themselves through positive feedback loops and increasing returns (Figure 2.10). The socio-technical regime 'organises' the practices, the routines, the competences and materialities of travel behaviours, all of which create the varied patterns of movements. This system is being continuously reproduced. Individual interventions, for example through network investments or urban development, only usually lead to small changes and modifications in aggregate travel. The 'socio-technical transition' (the system of change) hence includes a number of dimensions, including user practices, institutions, financial rules and regulations, infrastructures, vehicle and artefact, industry structure, and cultural and symbolic meanings (Geels, 2002; Geels and Schot, 2007).

This systemic 'lock-in' poses very significant problems for transport planning. Changing external events (e.g. an economic downturn) or revised policy objectives are often overlooked, or at best only seen as a short delay to the general trend of traffic growth, rarely changing the projection to any significant degree. Planning for uncertainty and assessing the potential for achievement of trend-breaks is very limited, and traffic growth is seen as an inevitable outcome of economic growth

Adams (1981, pp. 205–206) explores the illogicality of this situation with his 'absurd scenario':

> The year 2205 is a milestone insofar as it is the year in which Britain becomes a millionaire society. It is the year in which, assuming that the government's growth target is achieved, average incomes will reach one million pounds [. . .] the volume of freight moving about on the roads will have increased one-hundredfold. To accommodate this our descendants would need 60 million lorries [. . .] people will spend most of the their time driving around in the family juggernaut picking up piles of machine-made stuff from automatic warehouses [. . .] such is the volume of stuff that will require shifting that it is doubtful whether they will have the time to do all the holiday to-ing and fro-ing expected of them by the road and airport planners.

Hence there are two epistemological problems to be faced: the greater uncertainty affecting transport and travel behaviours, as well as the need to more effectively address the underlying sustainability agenda, mean that a new set of methods need to be developed and tested. The limits of forecasting have been reached and their use should be restricted to short-term and

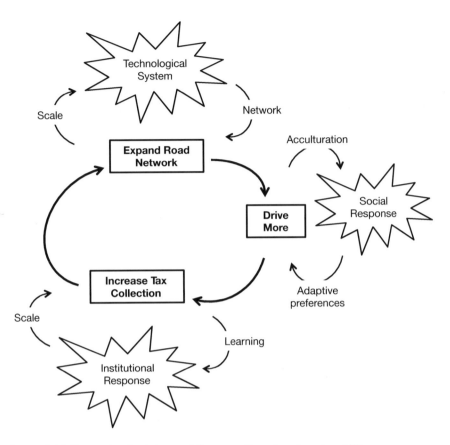

Figure 2.10 Conventional wisdom and the promotion of car-based mobility
Source: Unruh, 2000.

more technical, local-scale, traffic problems. The larger scale, longer term and more open-ended strategic decisions – which address technologies, climate change, energy use and emissions, demographic change (including ageing), societal priorities (including equity), and the types of cities that people and businesses would like to live in – all require innovative thinking. This has large implications in research and practice as conventional study approaches often have considerable inertia. However, where they are not suited to the problems being faced, alternative methods are required.

Utilising scenario analysis

A number of approaches have been developed to help overcome these difficulties. Scenario analysis is one of these, and has been used since the 1950s, in fields such as military and energy planning and corporate strategy. Scenarios are defined here as views of the (long) term future, structured around alternative societal trends or policy priorities. Scenarios encompass a wide range of external and internal factors into composite images of different potential future lifestyles, providing a structured view of the future and framework for analysis. This is different to the common usage in transport planning, where scenarios are conflated with option analysis, considering marginal changes, such as in a route alignment or change in frequency of service.

Scenarios are intended to describe alternative futures that are different to each other, so that pathways can be developed from the present towards that future direction. Ideally, future images can be developed and discussed that tend to be 'invisible' under more conventional forecasting approaches. This type of approach can help us think more deeply and imaginatively about the future, limiting to an extent the risk of being surprised and unprepared; and also, if the future is likely to be uncertain, scenario analysis can help us to prepare for multiple plausible futures, not just the one we expect to happen (Bishop et al., 2007).

The depiction of different images of the future hence offers a glimpse of alternative possibilities. Working definitions for scenario analyses date back to Kahn and Wiener in the mid-1960s and earlier, when scenarios were defined as 'hypothetical sequences of events for the purpose of focusing attention on causal processes and decision points' (Kahn and Wiener, 1967). A well-used definition also emanates from work in the Netherlands: 'a description of society's current situation (or a part of it), of possible and desirable future societal situations, and the series of events between current and future situations' (Becker and Van Houten, 1982).

Thus scenarios are aimed at understanding Lindblom's (1979) 'range of impossibilities' – the indeterminate factors – that we find difficult to understand to the left of the continuum (Figure 2.11). The complete synoptic analysis, however, is difficult against complex problems, as there always remain a number of issues we cannot foresee.

Figure 2.11 The analysis continuum
Source: Lindblom, 1979.

The early work by Herman Kahn was developed at the RAND Corporation, and it addressed military scenarios. Later, at the Hudson Institute, Kahn developed scenarios for the Air Defence System Missile Command and a radical critique of US military strategy in the thermonuclear age (Kahn, 1960; 1962; 1965; Kahn and Wiener, 1967; Kahn, 1984). He believed that military planning tended to be based on 'wishful thinking' rather than sensible expectations. One of his most well-known scenario-based studies was originally developed for the US federal government in the 1950s to study how nuclear wars might start and develop (Van der Heijden, 1996). He became known for 'thinking the unthinkable', including creative but dire scenarios of the 'winnable' nuclear war and life with fallout.[3] Kahn's view of the business as usual baseline was that it was very unlikely to happen, due to the frequency of 'uncertain' events occurring; he purportedly coined this as: 'The most likely future isn't' (Bishop et al., 2007). Kahn was extremely innovative in his approach, including in the use of phraseology and language to enrich his view of possible futures. But (with hindsight) he didn't consider one of the major societal problems of today, namely that of climate change.

Scenario analysis again proved popular in the 1970s, utilised to consider the 'possible, probable and preferable' futures in times of energy shortages and high prices (Toffler, 1972). Organisations such as General Electric, Shell Oil (Pierre Wack) and the Stanford Research Institute (Peter Schwartz) developed scenario analysis in terms of business planning. Shell's management team used scenarios to assess how consumers and countries might react to oil shortages, and to determine how they should respond relative to their competitors in dealing with the shock of the oil crisis in 1973 and its aftermath. Wack (1985b) utilised and developed the approaches, emphasising that scenarios were not predictions, simply a perception of likely futures, articulating this as 'the gentle art of reperceiving'. Porter (1985) also used scenarios to examine external uncertainties and forces on markets as a backdrop to planning. Scenario analysis has since become extremely popular, with much use in government in policy-making and also in business management for forward planning and strategy development (Schwartz, 1996; Frommelt, 2008), and many countries have carried out 'foresight programmes' that use scenarios.

Van Notten et al. (2003) develop a typology of the varied approaches used in scenario analysis, covering the following variables:

- Norms and values: descriptive (explore possible futures) or normative scenarios (probable or preferable futures);
- Vantage point: forecasting, anticipatory (exploratory) and backcasting (steps from a desirable future);
- Subject: issue, area or institution-based;
- Timescale: short (3–10 years) and long-term perspective (25+ years);
- Spatial scale: global, supranational, national, city, local;
- Nature of data: qualitative (often narrative) or quantitative, or hybrid;
- Temporal nature: developmental trajectory or end-state 'snapshot';
- Nature of variables: heterogeneous (wide variety) or homogeneous (limited);
- Nature of dynamics: trend scenarios (extrapolating existing trends) or peripheral scenarios (include unlikely and extreme events);
- Levels of deviation: business as usual (BAU) scenarios represent the status quo and alternative scenarios differ significantly from one another – to challenge assumptions and raise discussion about potential and emerging issues.

The classic starting point for many scenario studies is to identify 'predetermined' and 'undetermined' elements. The predetermined elements are the same in each scenario (sometimes called the external elements), and the undetermined elements are elaborated in several ways (sometimes called the internal elements), dependent on possible future developments, and thus result in different future images (Van der Heijden, 1996). Frommelt (2008) outlines the different potential elements of the scenario generation process, including the different starting points, methods, approaches and modes of development (Figure 2.12).

There are, therefore, a number of potential distinctions in the approaches that can be used. The explorative scenarios start from the present and move towards an end state, whilst the anticipative scenarios (sometimes also known as normative scenarios) start with a set of characteristics or images in the future and work backwards to see what it would take to get there. These are then assessed as to whether they are plausible. There is a similarity between this approach and the backcasting approaches (see later discussion).

Inductive methods derive scenarios based on experience or experiential building blocks, moving from the particular to the more general. Hence observations are used to develop general principles. The deductive method operates in reverse, reasoning from the general to the specific. A framework or general image may be added to with specific data. The incremental method uses an 'official future' as the starting point, and uncertainties or flaws within this can be identified and critiqued. Schwartz and Ogilvy (1998) see the official future as 'the scenario that the decision-makers really believe will occur' and 'usually an unsurprising and relatively non-threatening scenario, featuring no discontinuities, changes to current trends, no crises and continued stable growth'. The degree to which these approaches produce similar or different

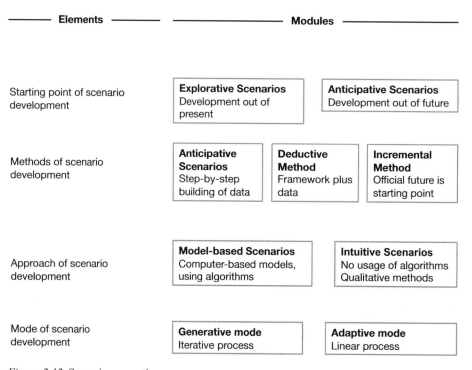

Figure 2.12 Scenario generation
Source: From Frommelt, 2008; drawing on Van der Heijden, 1996.

results depends largely on the level of uncertainty, range of factors (internal and external) being considered and the quality of the scenario-building exercises.

Model-based scenarios involve a quantification of prominent uncertainties, often using probabilistic tools. Intuitive approaches depend more on qualitative knowledge and insights from which scenarios are developed. The development of storylines is a typical approach. In some studies a combination of model-based and intuitive approaches is used, and increasingly scenarios are being quantified so as to illustrate their likely impacts, their 'realism' and the contributions of important policy measures within the scenarios. This is an important progression from the earlier narrative-based approaches, though of course a quantitative basis can often give a spurious level of certainty to future scenario impacts, when the assumptions taken in the modelling are driving the impacts as much as other issues (Hickman et al., 2010a; Hickman and Banister, 2007a).

There are two views concerning the means of scenario development. The generative mode is to 'raise important questions for the future and advance understanding until a new and unique insight has been gained' (Van der Heijden, 1996), whilst the adaptive mode considers a range of scenarios to see whether they can respond to the uncertainty, but still remain flexible. Coherence, plausibility, internal consistency and logical underpinning are obvious tests for the resulting scenarios (Bradfield et al., 2005), but are often not achieved in scenario-based studies.

One method has been to develop a scenario matrix, usually with two key parameters being used to define the scenario dimensions. Key factors and uncertainties can be used. These are clustered or ranked, with the scenarios typically using the key perceived uncertainties (ideally with high impact and high uncertainty) and high importance as axes, and a two-by-two scenario matrix is created, such that two driving forces produce four scenarios. The scenarios can be named at this stage, ideally with key words or a 'strapline' expressing the basic nature of the storyline.

The main benefits of scenario building within decision-making (May, 1982) are outlined as below:

- Providing useful frameworks to decisions: allowing a range of alternatives and different assumptions to be explored;
- Identifying dangers and opportunities: considering a range of alternative futures increases the likelihood of identifying possible problems and opportunities;
- Suggesting a variety of possible approaches: the use of scenarios may generate a range of approaches to tackle issues or problems whereas the use of forecasts, based on single theories or simple extrapolations, often leads to the pursuit of singular solutions;
- Helping to assess alternative policies and actions – scenarios may be used to identify the usefulness of different policies under alternative future conditions;
- Increased creativity and choice in decision-making: identifying possible future developments and avoiding the acceptance of current trends as inevitable opens up new possibilities for policy development.

Similarly Stauffer (2002) suggests there at least five reasons why scenario planning may be useful:

- To ensure that you are not focusing on catastrophe to the exclusion of opportunity;
- To help you allocate resources more prudently;
- To preserve your options;
- To ensure that you are not still fighting the last war;
- To give your company (or transport sector or city) the opportunity to rehearse for future challenges.

Few scenario studies are used as a blueprint of the desirable future or an action plan. Instead Steen (1997) and Van den Belt (1988) pursue the idea of a continual revision of targets as new knowledge is gained, labelled as constructive technology assessment (CTA). In addition, Van der Heijden (1996) raises an important dimension concerning the participatory elements, and the need for raising the level of debate and transparency around certain policy questions. He proposes the 'strategic conversation', a discussion around the scenarios and likely implications, leading to continuous organisational (or city) learning about key decisions and priorities.

Scenario analysis is still well-used in industry, including Shell's recent study that considers the likely impacts of the recession in the Western industrialised nations (Shell International, 2011). There are further applications throughout the energy industry, and also in wider corporate strategy. The UK government has used scenario approaches to help develop policy, particularly through the Foresight Programme, for example in Intelligent Infrastructure Systems (Department for Trade and Industry and Office of Science and Technology, 2006), and Land Use Futures (Department for Trade and Industry and Office of Science and Technology, 2010). There are many further examples internationally. These types of analyses help to define a broader conceptual framework for discussing the future and contribute to policy formulation. The Swedish have traditionally been very strong in developing futures studies, and their tradition (e.g. in backcasting) allows different actors a strong foundation for discussing goals and developing strategies that may help achieve societal goals. France has similarly followed a strong research tradition called *La Prospective* (translated as developing scenarios of future states), and Germany one of *Leitbilder* (inspiring visions or guiding images) (Dreborg, 1996; Banister et al., 2000).

Backcasting and the VIBAT approach

Backcasting approaches are often conflated with more general scenario analysis, and there are many overlapping elements, but backcasting also has a distinct element in being removed from historical and current trends and considering the pathway back from a future state. Hence, backcasting has developed as a particular form of scenario building. Many approaches to scenario analysis think of the future as extending from the present, an extrapolation of the timeline from the past. This perspective has the problem of carrying the 'baggage' of the past and present into the future. This can limit creativity, creating only conventional future images. The alternative is to ignore the previous and current trends, to envision a future state, and then 'cast backward' to establish the means by which we might get there. This future image can be 'plausible or fantastical, preferred or catastrophic' (Bishop et al., 2007).

The approach has its origins in the work of Lovins (1977), who developed the concept of the 'soft path', referring to the development of efficient, diverse and renewable energy usage. This was developed by Robinson (1982; 1990) and others from the late 1970s onwards. Robinson describes backcasting as:

> a concern, not with what futures are likely to happen, but with how desirable futures can be attained. It is thus explicitly normative, involving working backwards from a particular desirable endpoint to the present in order to determine the physical suitability of that future and what policy measures would be required to reach that point.
>
> (Robinson, 1990, p. 822)

Backcasting can thus be viewed as a normative scenario, but with an additional and explicit step in the development of the pathway back from an image or scenario of the future to the present. Dreborg (1996) sees backcasting as important where there are highly complex problems evident, where dominant trends are part of the problem, and where the scope of the problem and time horizon allow the development of very different futures. He also comments on the important role of backcasting in its role of 'discovery' rather than merely justification of different futures.

There was a particularly strong backcasting debate in Sweden over energy futures in the 1970s and 1980s. Many of the initial approaches were developed in this period, including by Steen et al., 1978, 1980 and 1983 (described in Johansson and Steen, 1978; Johansson et al., 1983; Lönnroth et al., 1983). More recently, futures studies have been carried out on broader sustainability issues and climate change, such as in household consumption, recycling and waste management, and passenger and freight transport (Dreborg and Steen, 1994; Jungmar, 1995; Peters et al., 1998; Steen, 1997). The well-known OECD project on Environmentally Sustainable Transport (EST!) (Organisation for Economic Cooperation and Development, 2000; Geurs and van Wee, 2000; 2004) and the EU POSSUM project (EU POSSUM, 1998; Banister et al., 2000) introduced the backcasting methodology to the transport planning field in Europe.

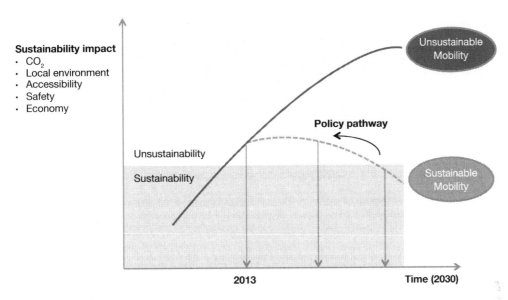

Figure 2.13 Scenario analysis and backcasting

Source: Hickman et al., 2009a; based on Organisation for Economic Co-operation and Development, 2000.

A common approach has been used in these studies to examine the possibilities of moving towards a sustainable transport system. The Business as Usual (BAU) projection forms the starting point as it reflects the trends, and this is taken as the upper limit for CO2 emissions (and other indicators of sustainable transport) in the future (Figure 2.13). A new image of the future is described, and often targets are used to quantify the level of reduction required in CO2 emissions or changes in other indicators. A combination of policy measures can be used and implemented over the intervening time period to help reach the new image. The present trends are perceived as important only in view of providing a comparator for an agreed future. The future change trend is a 'choice' for decision-makers rather than something to react to. Hence this is a fundamentally different approach to forecasting.

Participatory backcasting approaches have recently become been more frequently used, as involvement with key stakeholders – perhaps (ideally) even the public – mean that the acceptability of policy proposals is likely to be enhanced (Robinson et al., 2011; Quist et al., 2011). There are some concerns that participants can be overwhelmed by the complexity of the choices they are being asked to make, and of course there is a persistent problem in that only certain sectors of the community tend to get involved in the policy-making process. Often city authorities like to closely 'manage' their strategy development processes, and equally the participation process is carefully handled. This can be viewed as a little untransparent or undemocratic, but generally is done for resource reasons or in an attempt to reduce the risk of some projects being hijacked or disrupted by particular interest groups – which in themselves have little electoral validity. However, in the main, the participative approach is perceived as an extremely positive feature, allowing stakeholders to express their views as to what futures might be plausible and desirable, and to get their engagement. This should mean that implementation is more likely and that there will be support for the measures being introduced, meaning that outcomes match more closely with intentions.

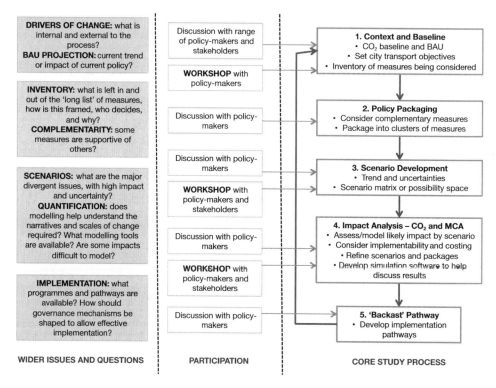

Figure 2.14 VIBAT scenario building and backcasting study process

A series of Visioning and Backcasting for Transport (VIBAT) studies have been carried out, over the period 2004–2013 (and ongoing), utilising and developing the backcasting approach. Much of the commentary in this book draws on this work, considering the different contexts and the likely different BAU projections and sustainable transport futures. Some of the VIBAT studies also include a simulation capability, either through a transport and carbon simulation (TC-SIM) or through an integrated multi-criteria appraisal simulation (INTRA-SIM), which helps to discuss the potential packaging of policies against end goals and also explore the trade-offs involved in decision-making. Both these simulation models have been designed to help in the participatory elements of the approach so that decision-makers and others can explore the implications of the different choices that are open to them.

The general approach in the VIBAT studies is shown in Figure 2.14, with a series of stages and different inputs in terms of participation. There are a number of critical issues and questions that need to be considered throughout the study process, many of which are seen as 'technical' issues, but of course reflect normative decisions in their own right. The definition of the BAU projection, type of measures considered, development of scenarios, choice of modelling tools, the decision to model itself, and the framing of possible governance mechanisms, all have important impacts. Much of this is often determined with regards to the context, but is also heavily dependent on the approach chosen by the researchers carrying out the work. These issues often remain hidden in studies, but are critical to the end results.

Table 2.1 outlines the list of VIBAT studies that have been carried out, some of which are explored in the later case study chapters. More details of the individual studies, including the simulation tools developed, are also available on the project website: www.vibat.org.

Table 2.1 The VIBAT studies

Study (coverage in this book)	Sponsor and date
VIBAT Auckland, New Zealand (Chapter 7)	University of Auckland and Auckland Council, 2010–12
Low carbon transport pathways in Jinan, China (Chapter 6)	University of Oxford, Future of Cities Programme, 2010
INTRA-SIM Swindon	Swindon Borough Council, UK Department for Transport; 2010
INTRA-SIM Oxfordshire (Chapter 4)	Oxfordshire County Council, UK Department for Transport; 2009–10
VIBAT Victoria, Canada, scoping study	Transport Canada, 2008
VIBAT Delhi, India, scoping study (Chapter 5)	Asian Development Bank, 2008
VIBAT London (Chapter 3)	UCL UrbanBuzz Programme, HEFCE; 2007–09
VIBAT UK	UK Department for Transport, 2004–06

A key motivation for, and emphasis, in the work has been to apply the thinking of Van der Heijden (1996) to transport; this means that the discussion of strategic policy choices – the 'strategic conversation' – is seen as being critically important. An additional part of this has been the development of the TC-SIM and INTRA-SIM simulation tools to help with the discussion process and to understand the key trade-offs in decision-making. There are related tools developed elsewhere, such as QUEST (Robinson et al., 2011), which is used to explore sustainability futures in British Columbia, Canada. TC-SIM and INTRA-SIM are both used as learning tools, but they are also meant to lead to social change in terms of city development and travel behaviour. The key elements are to: (1) simplify the likely multiple policy choices into key strategic decision points, (2) allow for multiple policy packaging and scenario analysis, and (3) develop a comparison of likely impacts by scenarios in real time, either against a single criterion (e.g. CO_2) or multiple impact criteria (e.g. CO_2, accessibility, accidents, employment, etc.). Hence elements are added to the conventional scenario analysis and backcasting methodologies to allow for a better strategic decision-making process against single- or multi-criteria impacts. The participatory element is carried out with the involvement of stakeholders using the simulation front end, but also in defining the scope of the policy options available, the images of the future and likely implementation pathways or mechanisms.

The scenario building and backcasting approach hence allows the development of policy pathways to agreed trend-break futures. These can represent desirable solutions to societal problems, and a pathway back from the image of the future to the present. A policy pathway or implementation programme can be developed to achieve the desirable future, and evaluated in terms of physical, technological, socio-economic feasibility, and indeed multi-criteria policy implications. Unlike the predictive forecast or scenario, backcasting is not intended to reveal what the future is likely to be, or to simply put together a feasible image(s) of the future, but instead indicate the relative feasibility of different potential policy futures. Similar to scenario analysis, there is no particular onus on developing a view of the 'optimum' strategy, rather an understanding of the possibilities under different futures. A participatory element of course strengthens the emphasis on achievability of different futures. Perhaps a key strength is in taking a 'fresh look' at difficult or intransigent issues – backcasting can operate as a 'protected experimental space' in which ideas can be articulated and discussed, while ignoring the 'vested interests and inherent rules of the outside world' (Quist et al., 2011).

Figure 2.15 Futuristic monorail and helicopter, 1971 (gouache on paper), English School (20th century). Our transport futures may involve new emerging vehicle technologies and ICT developments, but perhaps also the more 'mundane' in the sense of much more use of the 'old' transport technologies of walking and cycling.

Source: Private collection/© Look and Learn/The Bridgeman Art Library.

There is some discussion as to the possibilities for mapping out the path from future image to the current situation (Åkerman and Höjer, 2006), given that there is inherent uncertainty surrounding the future. However, most analyses will be able to develop a 'backcast' based on current knowledge. The difficulty that scenario analyses (and indeed forecasting) face are that without the backcasting stage and the development of an implementation pathway, scenario building remains focused on only a theoretical future and can be difficult to justify in terms of realism and acceptability (i.e. which scenario we believe is possible to implement, if any).

Policy development is, of course, much easier if it works in the same direction as the trends, perhaps anticipating emerging trends and working with them, perhaps shaping them to a limited degree. But, in terms of climate change and oil scarcity, and the quality of the urban fabric, there is a set of policy challenges that appear to be much more difficult to tackle. The dominant trends, such as the rise in CO_2 emissions, need to be broken, indeed reversed.

The scenario analysis and backcasting methodologies provide very useful approaches here, helping decision-makers discuss and respond to these strategic policy concerns. A more open discussion of the strategic policy choices can also lead to changed public awareness of the issues, and perhaps public demand for significant action on policy.

Developing scenarios

The scenario development stage is worth examining in more detail as it usually proves to be the most creative and interesting of all, and a method still needs to be followed to ensure a systematic development of future images. This is an approach that has not really penetrated the world of more conventional transport strategy development, but it could make a major contribution to strategies that look over the longer term, are more robust to external factors, and can help address societal problems. The following process utilises the matrix approach to scenario development (Wack, 1985b; Schwartz, 1996; Van der Heijden, 1996; Frommelt, 2008), and works best if largely carried out in a workshop setting in a participatory manner. This provides another essential involvement of the stakeholders, so that they can get an appreciation of the different opportunities available as well as the difficulty of achieving the targets set. The value of the participatory element is to add some level of acceptability, in the sense that the scenario has been tested with technical specialists, political leaders or local people, the very people who will be expected to change their travel behaviours. Their involvement increases the likelihood of successful implementation as they have some appreciation of the objectives and the means to achieve the desired outcomes.

Pre-workshop

1 *Study focus*: defining the key issue, perhaps formulated as a research question(s), upon which to build the scenarios. The objective, for example, may be to explore how transport may reduce CO_2 emissions for a particular city.
2 *Pre-workshop interviewing*: this may be used to understand people's viewpoints and current strategic thinking concerning the future. The results can be shared at the workshop to rapidly build a knowledge base of understanding concerning the external environment.

Scenario workshop

3 *The context*

(a) *Driving forces*: these will include variables that have large impacts on the main issue and potential scenarios in question. They are usually out of our control and consist usually of macro political and economic trends, or even strategic technological developments or environmental degradation. Some of these will involve predetermined elements (the numbers of people reaching retirement age) whilst others are more uncertain (migration flows and directions, economic growth, traffic growth, vehicle technology penetration rates). Some of these are critical uncertainties, and consequentially they will have large impacts.

(b) *Uncertainty review*: predetermined elements and critical uncertainties are closely related; perceived predetermined elements should be questioned and it may be possible to move some into the uncertainty category.

(c) *Ranking*: issues can be ranked by degree of importance and uncertainty, and the key factors (say the top two or three) identified as likely to have most impact yet be the most uncertain.

4   *Scenario creation*

(a) *Plot line*: the scenario is built around a logic and plot, describing how the driving forces might develop in the future. Several plot lines may intersect. A classic example is the 'winner' and 'loser' (Schwartz, 1996).

(b) *Scenario matrix*: two of the most important uncertainties are used to develop a set of four initial scenario themes, and this can be presented in a matrix. Determining the axes is one of the most important steps in the scenario generation process (Schwartz, 1996; Schoemaker and Gunther, 2002). Ideally the issues chosen are as 'mutually exclusive' as possible, i.e. cover very different issues, allowing a divergence in scenarios. The scenario is then extended to include fuller detail consistent with the key theme. All the uncertainties, or at least those deemed as the most important, can be used to create the detail of the scenario. If predetermined factors are used in developing the axes, then the process becomes more akin to forecasting; this is a common confusion within scenario development.

(c) *Wild cards*: these can be considered to cover possible 'discontinuities' (Drucker, 1968) that may have high impact and high uncertainty – these are also known as the 'black swans' (Taleb, 2007). Examples might be technological (such as development of the Internet, or a radical new vehicle technology), political (the change of government or regime), physical (an earthquake, volcanic eruption or climatic event), economic (financial meltdown), individual (changes in public attitude) or other factors. Very different worlds may emerge if a number of wild cards emerge together (Drucker, 1968). The scenarios are revisited for robustness in the light of the wild cards.

Scenarios perform different roles according to the requirements for their use. In the business field, they may be used to develop long-term strategy against uncertain trends, allowing organisations to more aware of potential likely market changes or to develop new market directions. In transport planning their use is more likely to be in developing and anticipating likely future policy trajectories, the potential for changes in policy direction, in understanding the risk behind certain policy positions, but also in developing an awareness and discussion of the different available policy trajectories. This latter point is especially important in view of the current climate change difficulties being faced. 'Windtunnelling' (Van der Heijden, 1996; Ringland, 1998) can be used to test the efficacy of the current policy approach or strategy against each of the developed scenarios. Again, this is rarely used in transport planning. The effectiveness of our policy-making is very rarely assessed over the previous years, if at all, and the progress towards goals at the required rate is rarely considered. This, however, would seem critical to effective policy-making. 'Path dependency' can also be a useful concept here – scenarios can be examined for adverse path dependent effects and flexibility. The classic form of the two-by-two scenario matrix is given in Figure 2.16, and two examples of future images are given in Figures 2.17 and 2.18, drawn from the DTI Foresight project on Intelligent Infrastructure Systems (Department for Trade and Industry and Office of Science and Technology, 2006).

Scenarios, when well developed, describe different worlds (Wack, 1985a), not just different outcomes in the 'same world'. Ideally, they shouldn't be based on simplistic differences, such as pessimistic and optimistic views. In terms of the number of scenarios, Wack (1985a) suggests that the ideal number is three, the first giving the 'surprise-free' view (but showing

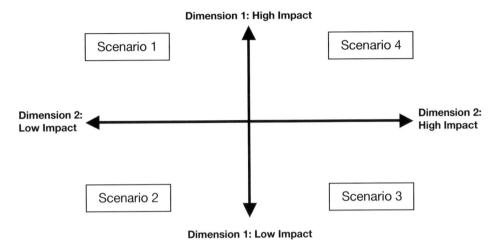

Figure 2.16 The classic scenario matrix

why this is fragile), and then two other worlds or ways of seeing the world. Schwartz (1996) advises that three scenarios are better than two to allow a greater range of thinking, but also because two scenarios tend to represent two extremes of the same thinking: the worst case scenario and 'utopia', which doesn't really offer any innovative insight into policy choice. There is a potential problem with three scenarios – the third tends to become the average between two extremes. Hence, the third scenario, and potentially a fourth, should follow a different logic and perspective to be of most use. Any more than four scenarios and the strategic issues tend to become muddied, and the exercise becomes unmanageable or less clear.

The classic view in scenario analysis is that the scenarios as developed are uncertain in themselves and none are preferred. When a preferred future scenario is chosen this can illustrate

Figure 2.17 Intelligent infrastructure systems, 'Good intentions'

Source: Narinder Sagoo, Foster + Partners. Department for Trade and Industry and Office of Science and Technology, 2006.

Figure 2.18 Intelligent infrastructure systems, 'Perpetual motion'
Source: Narinder Sagoo, Foster + Partners. Department for Trade and Industry and Office of Science and Technology, 2006.

the error of falling back into the 'old pattern' of fixing one view of the future, or of forecasting (Schoemaker, 1998; Schoemaker and Gunther, 2002). The point of scenario analysis is to explore and understand the implications of different futures, not to forecast what is most likely to happen. Within transport planning this can be viewed as problematic. Practitioners involved in preparing, for example, a local transport strategy, have to model and understand the future over the next 20 years, but the immediate intention is in developing a bid for transport funding over 3–5 years. The solution perhaps is to assess which future is most likely to have the most 'beneficial' impacts, or to be most likely to achieve against set objectives and targets, and the short-term investment programme can then be developed to be consistent with, and flexible and resilient to, the range of possible long-term futures, progressing towards the longer term goals.

Scenario analysis and MCA

A potential limitation with scenario analysis is that the scenarios as developed are often viewed only as a means of discussion, rather than one of the images signifying a preferable future or a 'blueprint' for future strategy. For policy-makers this can be difficult, as they may have an interest in application, and are attempting to map out a preferred route for policy and investment choices. In recent years the quantification of the likely impacts of scenarios has become more popular, usually against key metrics such as CO2, but sometimes using a broader range. The latter approach can be carried out by using multi-criteria analysis (MCA) in combination with scenario analysis (Saxena, 2012; Hickman et al., 2012b). We develop this approach to an extent, against CO2 and wider MCA impacts, in some of the case studies that follow. Figure 2.19 illustrates the methodology used, where policy measures are clustered into policy packages and scenarios, then the scenarios are examined against MCA impacts. The optimal scenario is chosen with the best results against the MCA criteria.

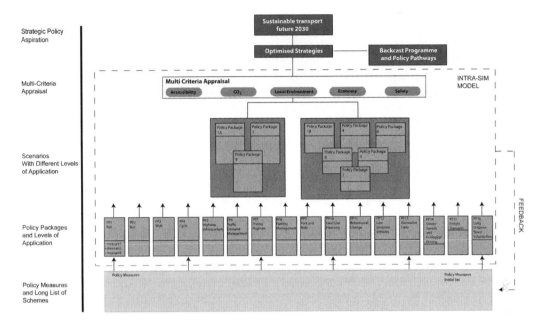

Figure 2.19 Scenario analysis and MCA
Source: Saxena, 2012; Hickman et al., 2012b.

An important issue is that there is an increasing contribution of the transport sector to CO2 emissions, and little sign that transport is managing to reduce its emissions to any significant degree. Measuring this, and discussing it, against MCA criteria, using a BAU scenario and different future scenarios, can help make this more explicit to decision-makers and stakeholders. For example, low CO2 strategies, whilst being effective in reducing CO2, may however have adverse impacts against other policy goals. This is an important area that is poorly understood, and there can be some progress made using MCA. Hence it is useful to move the debate within scenario analysis beyond the generation of 'possible pathways' to consider what the optimum pathways might be.

MCA is particularly useful where there is a wide range of potential impacts of projects or initiatives. These can be examined, either in terms of efficacy, or for prioritisation, and typically involve the assessment against a wide-ranging list of objectives or criteria. This can be a combination of quantitative and qualitative assessment, and is seen as a major step forward from using a cost–benefit analysis (CBA), where the impacts considered are often narrowly defined. In practice the cost–benefit ratio is often used as one of the criteria within the MCA. Transport investment planning is often described as a 'multi-criteria decision problem' because projects typically have conflicting objectives. There is often no single optimal solution to problems because objectives conflict and compensatory trade-offs cannot be established (Guiliano, 1985). In the UK, the Department for Transport's (2012) web-based Transport Analysis Guidance (WebTAG) represents the main MCA methodology used in transport planning in the UK, and is increasingly used internationally as the basis of appraisals.

Although the use of MCA could offer an important step forward in assessing the benefits of various scenarios, there are some inherent problems. A key difficulty, also found in the use of CBA, occurs when impacts are difficult to quantify, or where there is disagreement in the ascribed values. Many socio-economic impacts (land use, economic development, social cohesion) and environmental impacts (CO2 and resource consumption, local air pollution, accidents) are very difficult to quantify or monetise (Nijkamp et al., 2003; Bristow and Nellthorp, 2000). Also, the dominance of particular criteria in the final decision is often heavily criticised, either due to queries over the importance given or the validity of the metric. The dominance of time savings in many CBA and MCA calculations is a good example, where the time savings are often not realised or valued as expected at the individual level (Metz, 2008). In terms of considering the likely target achievement of packages and scenarios, there are additional issues. Although some policies can be modelled through elasticities, in other cases there is a need for careful empirical analysis over the scale and immediacy of policy impacts. There is good empirical information available in some cities on the effectiveness of policies individually and in combination, but much less in others. Care must be exercised over their transferability between cities, and indeed for some policy areas the evidence base is very weak.

Hence, many of the requirements of transport policy, particularly when developing scenarios over the long term, cannot be effectively measured in a quantitative manner. The 'value' of an attractive landscape, even life and death, or other such issues, should clearly be beyond quantification and monetisation, yet this is still the conventional approach used in appraisal, using techniques such as 'willingness to pay'. But often these simply discredit the process – famously becoming 'nonsense on stilts' (Self, 1970; Adams, 1981).[4] Where these types of impacts are important, the MCA and CBA give only a partial view of the costs and benefits of a scheme or strategy, and consequentially become less useful. There some possibilities to reduce these problems, for example by developing approaches to the weighting of impacts by different criteria, hence allowing composite scoring (Dodgson et al., 2009; Sayers et al., 2003). There is also an emerging preference for approaches that make greater use of 'multi-actor' participation in the design of appraisal frameworks, reflecting concerns over the lack of participatory input prior to decisions been made (Macharis et al., 2010).

A further difficulty in MCA is the lack of clarity concerning what to do with the large amount of data produced during the process. The choice of preferred option is still difficult despite the extensive background evidence gathering – with a difficult and often unsystematic analysis of results still remaining (Figure 2.20). In France, a move away from MCA has recently occurred, largely due to the lack of procedures for aggregating the evaluations of multiple criteria. It was concluded that the process became unworkable with a lack of credibility, and certainly transparency, in results. Evaluations and non-transparent weightings have been

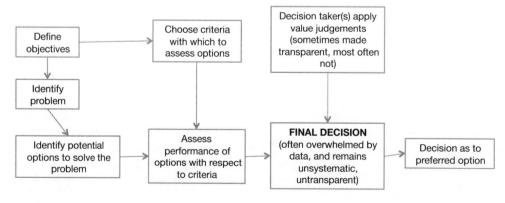

Figure 2.20 Decision-making with MCA
Source: Developing Sayers et al., 2003.

Figure 2.21 2001: A Space Odyssey, 1968, written by Arthur C. Clarke, directed by Stanley Kubrick. Elena and her colleague Dr Smyslov ask Floyd about 'odd things' occurring at Clavius Base (a US outpost on the moon), and the rumour of a mysterious epidemic at the base. The American declines to answer any questions about the epidemic.

> *Hal*: I've just picked up a fault in the AE35 unit. It's going to go 100 per cent failure in 72 hours.

Source: British Film Institute Stills Collection.

left to decision-makers, and this is seen as having limited legitimacy (Sayers et al., 2003); 'a waste of public funds and clearly irrational decisions' have occurred, and it becomes difficult to determine why options are taken forward (Quinet, 2000). The methods for appraisal, across different transport modes and timescales, clearly need a major rethink, but careful application of MCA provides one very useful approach.

Many countries are now using a mix of CBA and MCA in project appraisal, but the practice differs markedly. The UK and USA, for example, have a heavy reliance on 'economic' approaches (CBA, with importance given to time savings), whilst Germany is more concerned with 'technical' solutions (how systems are designed and engineered, and well integrated), and in France 'image' becomes much more important (such as found in 'Les Grand Projets', including high-speed rail and a series of tram schemes in cities, which seek to compete against each other in terms of quality of the city fabric and urban life) (Hall and Falk, 2013).

Conclusions

Ideally, when planning city and transport futures it would be desirable to be blessed with the foresight of Borges' Yahoos;[5] this would certainly simplify the difficult process of transport and city planning! In the absence of this, scenario analysis provides a very useful framework for considering transport futures within the context of uncertainty. It allows us to consider possibilities beyond the BAU trajectory, and it is exactly this that is required in the current transport planning domain, where many important issues, including climate change, demand a different type of response to that which comes from more conventional transport planning analysis.

In the urban planning world, Hall (1980) takes us through some *Great Planning Disasters*, where many high profile and 'problematic' major projects appear to have been initiated on the basis of planning that was later found inadequate and perhaps even misleading. These include: the London Ringways (proposed urban motorways in London, abandoned in the 1970s), which were planned on the basis of estimates of population, economic activity and car ownership which were later seen as over-estimates; the Bay Area Rapid Transit (BART) system in San Francisco, based on travel forecasts that were hugely over optimistic; Concorde (a supersonic aircraft), developed on the basis of inflated estimates of the demand for supersonic travel; and the Sydney Opera House, with multiple design and cost overrun problems. Many of these projects, and many others since, were started on the basis of cost estimates that were soon exceeded, some by a very large amount. There are various factors behind these difficult development stories (Friend and Jessop, 1969; Hall, 1980), including:

- Uncertainty about the planning environment (i.e. everything outside the immediate decision-making system). Planners in practice cannot easily predict the mass behaviour of people in society, such as propensity to have children, move about, or demand different goods and services.
- Uncertainty about decisions in related decision areas, such as those related to areas beyond the immediate problem, involving wider decision-makers in groups or organisations with their own discretion.
- Uncertainty about value judgments, including decisions where the final judgment involves questions of value, with different weightings according to group, all of which may change over time.

These issues have more recently been taken up in considering the planning and delivery of major infrastructure projects (Flyvbjerg et al., 2003; Priemus et al., 2008; Dimitriou et al., 2012), with concerns over the effectiveness of decision-making, the methodology applied in forecasting (often complexity and uncertainty is difficult or impossible to model); poor data availability; discontinuous behaviour (either inelastic; or very elastic, with sudden changes due to external factors which often are not modelled); political activities and even appraisal bias.

All of these issues have an important bearing on transport and city planning over the long term, and scenario analysis can assist in dealing with problems of uncertainty or difficulties in the accuracy of modelling. The current level of global motorisation, its impact on the city, life and the associated problems of climate change and oil scarcity, together with the intractability of changing travel behaviours, are similar examples of 'wicked problems' (Rittel and Webber, 1973) – and manifest themselves at the grand scale. There is certainly no well-prescribed solution to these issues, and to a large extent the current policy framework can only deal with 'tame problems'. It can work with emerging trends, changing their direction to only a minor degree. This is a major problem: we have very few examples of policy that changes trends to a radical degree, yet the strategic climate change agenda demands some major bending of the current trends.

The following concluding thoughts can be given:

1   The challenge of climate change is complex, and international efforts to gain political momentum are not affecting the trends to any significant level. The irony of thousands of delegates flying thousands of kilometres to talk about reducing CO_2 emissions is becoming all too clear.
2   National and city-based targets, on the other hand, have become very progressive at times, but there is much inconsistency in approach and difficulty in the targets set. The use and prioritisation of resources have changed in many contexts, yet the emphasis and levels of investment required for a more sustainable transport future are still not being reached.
3   Many of the transport policy measures that are required are well-known, and have been well-researched and developed over more than 30 years. Yet their potential levels of application, likely contributions, and most effective packaging with wider measures are poorly understood.
4   Other policy objectives beyond CO_2 reduction are also critical in the development of sustainable transport and urban planning, and MCA is a useful approach to use in combination with scenario analysis. There is potential for positive co-benefits (such as reduced CO_2 and improved health impacts), but there are also negative impacts, perhaps in terms of some low carbon pathways and economic or social equity dimensions. The scale and diversity of these impacts and interrelationships are very poorly understood.
5   Finally, it is likely that governmental 'direction' can only take us so far, certainly in view of tackling underlying trends. Hence participatory elements within the scenario process will be critical. These governance issues are explored in the case study chapters, and they form an essential element in successfully tackling climate change.

The approach developed in this chapter offers a very different approach to that used conventionally in transport planning, with its basis in scenario building, and a strong emphasis on working towards long-term futures, the quantification of scenarios, the usefulness of the backcasting stage and also the need to include participatory methods. The transition to more sustainable travel behaviours and wider sustainability in city lifestyles will require policy-making beyond the 'muddling through' (Lindblom, 1979). Scenario analysis can help us here: Porter (1985) suggests that we should use scenarios to help 'bet on the most probable one', 'bet on the best one', 'hedge so as to get satisfactory results under all scenarios', and to try to 'raise odds' that the preferred scenario will occur. Some of these options are explored in the ensuing chapters, applying the scenario building approaches in different ways to a set of international case studies.

Notes

1   Delphi, an archaeological site and modern town in Greece, was the site of the Delphic Oracle, the most important oracle in the classical Greek world. The Oracle was a site of worship of the god Apollo, associated with medicine and healing. The Oracle gave prophecies during the warmest months of each year (in the winter months Apollo deserted his temple). The Pythia, the priestess at the temple of Apollo, was widely known for her prophecies inspired by Apollo. The Oracle is one of the most documented religious institutions of the classical Greek world, mentioned by Herodotus, Plato and Aristotle.
2   Simons and Chabris (1999) show a number of individuals standing in a sports hall with a basketball. The exercise is to count how many times the individuals pass a basketball to each other. At the end the viewer is asked to share how many passes they counted. The viewer is then asked: 'Did you see the gorilla? If not, watch again, this time looking out for and spotting the individual dressed in a gorilla costume

who walks into the centre of the screen amongst the people passing the ball.' In a controlled experiment around 42 per cent saw the gorilla. This was later developed into a SAP business marketing video clip.

3   Herman Kahn's work was useful in searching for serious and workable alternatives to military difficulties, including the problems of annihilation and surrender. Kahn was reportedly one of the models for Stanley Kubrick's *Dr Strangelove* (1964). His ideas provided the genesis for the concept of Mutual Assured Destruction (MAD), the central tenet of US foreign policy with Russia in the Cold War era and still important today. Kahn's work developed over the years to cover the rise of Japan as a major power, the growth of the economy and capitalism, and into corporate fields. Kahn saw scenarios as fictional and playful, and certainly not rigorous forecasts.He developed the technique of 'future now' thinking – writing a report in the present tense, but representing some time in the future (Frommelt, 2008).

4   The 'nonsense on stilts' phrase was borrowed from Jeremy Bentham, originally used concerning the concept of 'natural law' and 'natural rights'.

5   'What baffles me is that men, while they can look indefinitely backward, are not allowed to look one whit forward [. . .] tomorrow morning is much closer to us than the crossing of the Red Sea by the Hebrews, which, nevertheless we remember. The witch-doctors of the Yahoos however are [. . .] endowed with the facility of foresight and can state with quiet confidence what will happen ten or fifteen minutes hence [. . .] that "a fly will graze the nape of my neck" or "in a moment we shall hear the song of a bird"' (Borges, 1976).

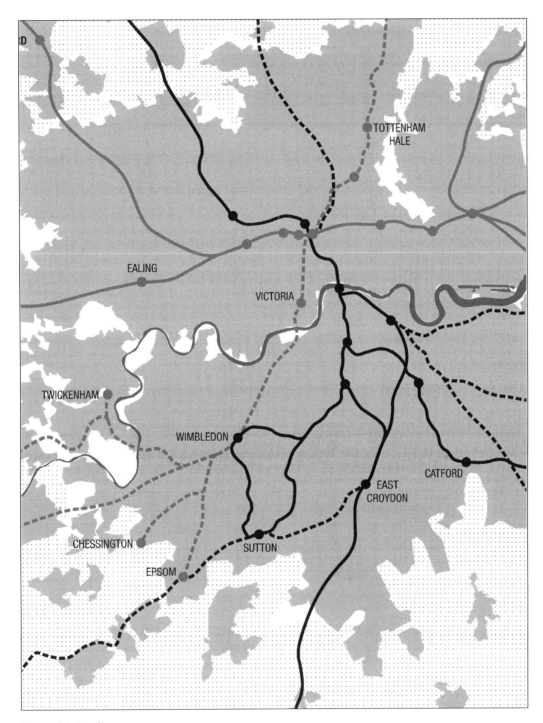

Figure 3.1 London

Source: Mapping by Bally Meeda and Urban Graphics.

3 Ambitions towards sustainable mobility (London)

'That is the Law. How could there be a mistake in that?' 'I don't know this Law,' said K. 'All the worse for you,' replied the warder. 'And it probably exists nowhere but in your own head,' said K.; he wanted, in some way, to enter into the thoughts of the warders and twist them to his own advantage or else try to acclimatise himself to them. But the warder merely said in a discouraging voice: 'You'll come up against it yet.' Franz interrupted: 'See, Willem, he admits that he doesn't know the Law and yet he claims he's innocent.' 'You're quite right, but you'll never make a man like that see reason,' replied the other.

(Franz Kafka, *The Trial*, 1925, pp. 12–13)

Introduction

London is used as our first case study and provides a good example of a progressive policy approach to reducing transport CO_2 emissions, building on an extensive experience of developing the city based around a multimodal public transport system. Over the years some very effective transport projects and initiatives have been developed. Yet, at the same time, relatively high private car usage, mainly in Outer London, highlights the significant challenges faced in responding in a meaningful manner to climate change. The UK itself is a modern industrialised country, with a fairly stable population at just over 60 million, a high GDP per capita at US$35,000, with some recent decline due to the economic meltdown. The level of motorisation is relatively high at 517 vehicles per 1,000 population, but less than that of the United States at 675 vehicles/1,000. Energy use and CO_2 emissions per capita are also relatively high, depending on the comparator used (9 tons per capita in the UK, relative to 20 tons per capita in the US, and 5 tons per capita globally) (Table 3.1).

Within London, the city authorities – Transport for London (TfL) and the Greater London Authority (GLA) – are developing broad-ranging strategies for sustainable transport, urban planning and climate change. The city can build on an already extensive public transport network and compact, polycentric urban form. The London Underground is the oldest in the world, celebrating 150 years in existence in 2013, hence there is a long history of investment in sustainable transport. The GLA has developed cross-sectoral CO_2 emission reduction strategies, with significant investment and implementation in the transport sector. The strategic aim is to develop a 'model' sustainable city that can combine population growth (largely high levels of in-migration) with economic prosperity, social equity, and at the same time reduce adverse environmental impacts.

This chapter draws on work carried out in the Visioning and Backcasting for Transport in London study (VIBAT-London) (Hickman et al., 2009a).[1] It assesses the likelihood of deep transport CO_2 emission reductions in London, developing a baseline and projections for

Table 3.1 UK – World Development Indicators

Indicator	1990	2000	2005	2008	2009
Population, total	57,247,586	58,892,514	60,226,500	61,406,928	61,838,154
Population growth (annual %)	0.3	0.4	0.6	0.7	0.7
GDP per capita (current US$)	17,688	25,089	37,859	43,361	35,165
GDP growth (annual %)	0.8	3.9	2.2	0.5	4.9
Life expectancy at birth, total (years)	75.9	77.9	79.1	79.9	–
Fertility rate, total (births per woman)	1.8	1.6	1.8	1.9	–
Energy use (kg of oil equivalent per capita)	3,619	3,803	3,699	–	–
CO_2 emissions (metric tons per capita)	10.0	9.2	9.0	–	–
Motor vehicles (per 1,000 people)	–	–	517	–	–
Mobile cellular subscriptions (per 100 people)	1.9	73.8	108.7	126.0	–
Internet users (per 100 people)	0.1	26.8	66.4	76.0	–

Source: World Bank, 2010a.

transport CO_2 emissions, followed by different images of the future to 2025 and 2050. The impacts of different policy packages and strategies are modelled, using a simulation model of the city that was developed during the VIBAT-London work. The analysis highlights the extreme difficulties – even in a city such as London – in meeting strategic transport CO_2 reduction targets using the current policy tools. This is an issue much underestimated by policy-makers and politicians. Reducing surface transport emissions is the main focus of the analysis, but when international air travel is also considered it provides an almost insoluble problem in a city with relatively high incomes. Focusing on seemingly low per capita transport emissions in surface transport often ignores a large problem in international air emissions (Holden and Linnerud, 2011).

The 'world city' context

London has globalised networks, an international 'world city' reputation (Sassen, 2000), as well as acting as the capital city in the United Kingdom (UK); many businesses and residents have strong ties with overseas. London has a strong tradition of utilising strategic urban planning to address the concerns of the day. Examples range from the Royal Commission on the Housing of the Working Classes (1885), which was concerned with the problems of the Victorian slum, to the development of the Garden Suburbs (including, for example, Bedford Park, built in 1876; Brentham, 1901; and Hampstead Garden Suburb, 1907), which were early attempts to design sustainable suburbs; and the post-war rebuilding of London under the Abercrombie Plan (1944),[2] as realised in the 1950s and 1960s at Alton West, Roehampton, and elsewhere. The Garden Cities and New Towns beyond the London urban boundary were also very significant attempts to improve the quality of urban life for London residents (Hall, 1988; URBED, TCPA, 2002). Though some of these city planning efforts are 'expressions of their age' and have faded in quality, they do highlight the intention and capacity to tackle strategic planning issues. Much of the development of London was, of course, incremental and not the result of large-scale planning; and many of the plans of the day have not been

Figure 3.2
Piccadilly Circus. The London Underground celebrates 150 years in existence in 2013, and provides the structural basis for urban development in the city.

Source: Alexandra Gomes.

realised, famously including Sir Christopher Wren's plans for reconstruction of the city of London in 1666 (Hebbert, 1998). But there is still a tradition in city planning, which remains strong and progressive today. Societal challenges have moved on, but perhaps the tradition and experience in city planning can assist in making progress against difficult issues.

The population of the London urban area has risen from just 850,000 (1801) to the current 8.17 million in Greater London (Office for National Statistics, 2012), and 12–14 million in the extended metropolitan regional area (Greater London Authority, 2009).[3] The urban fabric comprises relatively compact densities, with a dense central area and in polycentric centres in the outer areas. London is known as 'the city of villages' – there are two defined international centres (the West End and Knightsbridge), ten metropolitan centres (e.g. Ealing, Kingston, Croydon and Bromley), together with a series of major centres (e.g. Richmond, Chiswick, Wimbledon, Edgware, Dalston, Stratford and Eltham) and numerous district centres (Greater London Authority, 2004). Most of these centres have arisen from the original 'villages'. Average dwellings per hectare in the Victorian suburbs are around 30–60 dwellings per hectare (dph), so levels of density are relatively high (URBED, TCPA, 2002).

Central to much of the urban expansion debate has been the transport network, with transport often providing the framework for development. London provides a classic example of integrated urban and transport planning, so often called for – and seldom achieved – in the present day policy rhetoric. The Metropolitan Railway was developed as the first underground railway in the world from 1867, and later as part of a more extensive underground network.

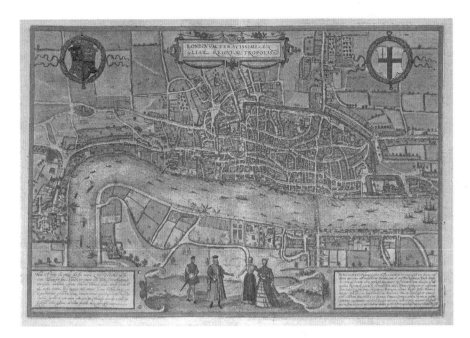

Figure 3.3 Sixteenth-century map of London, *Civitates Orbis Terrarum*, by George Braun (1541–1622) and Franz Hogenberg (1540–1590), engraving. London has been mapped extensively, highlighting its growth over recent times.

Source: The British Library.

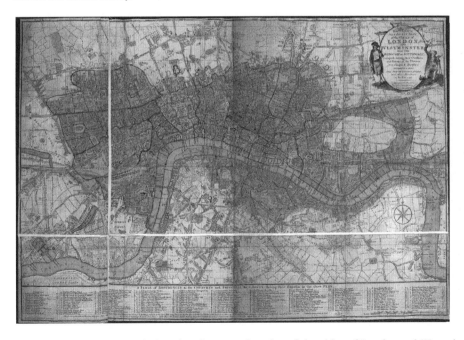

Figure 3.4 Carington Bowles's reduced new pocket plan of the cities of London and Westminster, with the borough of Southwark exhibiting the new buildings to the year 1780

Source: The British Library.

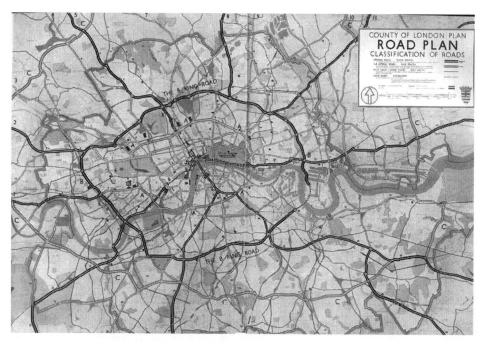

Figure 3.5 The Abercrombie Road Plan, 1943

Source: Macmillan & Co., 1943.

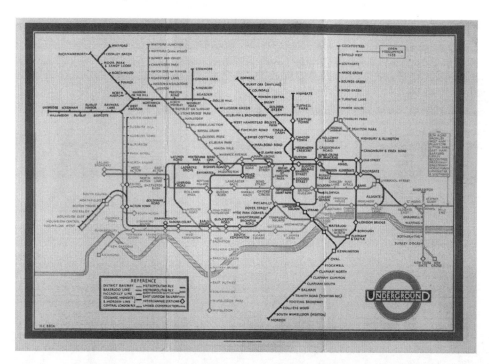

Figure 3.6 Harry Beck's iconic diagrammatic map of the London Underground system. Beck developed the design in 1931, whilst working as a draughtsman for the Underground. Following the formation of London Transport in 1933, Frank Pick gave the design a trial printing; it proved popular and easy to use for passengers, and has been used ever since.

Source: TfL from the London Transport Museum collection

Figure 3.7 1930s *Metro-Land* magazine
Source: The Advertising Archives.

This led to major urban redevelopment and the expansion of London from a pre-1850s urban area of around 20 km² (the 'walking city' of London, stretching west–east from Green Park to Bethnal Green, and north–south from Holloway to Elephant and Castle) (Ackroyd, 2003), to the present day Greater London area of 1,700 km² (effectively the 'railway city' and 'motor car city') (Newman and Kenworthy, 1999).The urban area that was built initially around the Metropolitan Railway famously became known as 'Metro-land'.[4] The London Transport marketing of the day was often based around the attractions of 'escaping' from the city by means of the Underground.

London has since developed an extensive public transport network, including national rail, the Underground, Docklands Light Railway, Overground (an orbital service) and bus network. The focus for much of the network is for radial trips into the central area; however, there are some orbital, tangential and cross-city routes.The number of trips in London is 24.8 million

Table 3.2 London – some statistics

Issue	Comment
Demonym	Londoner
Population	
Greater London (2011)	8.17 million
Metropolitan area (2007)	12–14 million
London urban area (1801)	850,000
Executive head	Mayor of London, created in 2000, currently held by Boris Johnson
Area	1,600 km²
Population density	5,100/km²
Commuters	1.06 million people enter central London during the morning peak (7–10 a.m.)
Mode share (by journey stage) (2010)	28.7 million daily journey stages,[a] per day 36% car, 21% walk, 20% bus, 10% Underground, 9% rail, 2% bicycle
Smartcard ticketing (2012)	The Oyster card accounts for 80% of journey stages on public transport
Travel cost, single, zones 1–4 morning peak, Underground ticket (2013)	£5.50 cash; £2.70 Oyster card
Congestion charge (into central London cordon – 2012)	£10.00
CO_2 reduction target	60% reduction in CO_2 emissions by 2025, applied across all sectors, on a 1990 base
Total transport CO_2 emissions (2010)	9.39 $MtCO_2$
Per capita transport CO_2 emissions (2010)	1.15 tCO_2 per person
Transport % of total	20%

Note:

[a] Journey stages and trips represent different travel metrics. A trip is a complete one-way movement from origin to destination by one person for a single purpose. A stage is a part of a trip using a single mode of travel (TfL, 2006).

Source: Transport for London, 2007; Hickman et al., 2009a; Transport for London, 2010; Transport for London, 2011; Office for National Statistics, 2012.

per day in 2010, increasing from under 21 million per day in 1994. In 2010, the car accounted for 40 per cent of trips, with most usage in outer London. Walking accounted for 24 per cent, bus 15 per cent, rail 9.3 per cent and Underground at 8.5 per cent (Transport for London, 2011). Public transport is of course very well utilised for commuting trips into central London.

In governance terms, London has also developed strong mechanisms to enable strategic planning. The Greater London Council (GLC) ran from 1965 to 1986, replacing the earlier London County Council (LCC) which had covered a smaller built-up area. The current GLA was established in 2000, with a directly elected mayor and London Assembly. The current mayor (Boris Johnson) is able to make and influence city-wide policies and strategies, including in urban planning, transport and climate change; set budgets and appoint the board of TfL and related organisations; hence has a wide-ranging remit. This scope of influence is often admired in other cities internationally.

Figure 3.8 Oxford Circus, 1842 (litho), Thomas Shotter
Source: Boys, Thomas Shotter (1803–74)/Private collection/The Bridgeman Art Library.

Figure 3.9 Buses at Victoria Station, London (oil on canvas), Martin Bloch
Source: Bloch, Martin (1883–1954)/Private collection/The Bridgeman Art Library, reproduced with permission of the Martin Bloch Trust.

Figure 3.10 Oxford Circus, 1905 (oil on board), Maxwell Ashby

Source: Armfield, Maxwell Ashby (1882–1972)/Private collection/Photo © The Fine Art Society, London, UK/The Bridgeman Art Library.

Figure 3.11 Paddington Station, 1949 (oil on board), Terry Frost

Source: Frost, Terry (1915–2003)/Private collection/The Bridgeman Art Library. Copyright Estate of Terry Frost. All rights reserved, DACS 2013.

The GLA and TfL have produced a series of strategic policy documents over recent years, including Transport 2025 (T2025) (Transport for London, 2006), a 20-year strategy for investment; and also a succession of transport strategies, with the current version being the Mayor's Transport Strategy (Transport for London, 2010). The transport strategy sits alongside the spatial development plan, published as the London Plan (Greater London Authority, 2011) and there is also a Climate Change Action Plan (CCAP) (Greater London Authority, 2007). So perhaps there is a proliferation of policy documents, often overlapping in coverage of issues, but this means that the strategic direction for policy is well established, well debated and can be updated over time.

Figure 3.12 A Carnaby Scene, from *Carnaby Street* by Tom Salter, 1970 (colour litho)
Source: English, Malcolm (b. 1946)/Private collection/The Bridgeman Art Library

Figure 3.13 The classic London Underground posters. New transport investment as providing employment possibilities, the quickest mode, the route to entertainment and shopping, and a means to escape to new housing in the new suburbs.

Source: London Transport Museum collection.

Baseline and projections

The CO_2 reduction target adopted for London (CCAP) is a 60 per cent reduction in CO_2 emissions by 2025, applied across all sectors, on a 1990 base (Table 3.3). The major current policy weakness is the lack of a specific transport sector target; however, the strategic target is very ambitious, certainly relative to other international, national and city-based aspirations.The target builds on a previous, less ambitious target, a 30 per cent reduction in CO_2 emissions by 2025 (T2025). London is, therefore, in policy terms, amongst the most ambitious cities internationally, certainly of those covered in this book.

Figure 3.14 Central London. Part of a high density and vibrant urban core, served well by public transport in the Underground, National Rail, Docklands Light Rail and an extensive bus network.

Figure 3.15 Canary Wharf. The extension of London's financial centre into the abandoned Docklands started in the 1980s, with over 100,000 jobs in 2010 and plans for over 200,000 in the future, supported by the Docklands Light Railway and Jubilee Line extension.

In relative terms, the policy response at the UK level has been extremely slow in development. Top-down target setting has gradually produced more stringent policy targets, but in all cases international aviation is excluded. In the UK, the Kyoto Protocol (1997) seeks to achieve a 12.5 per cent reduction in six GHG below 1990 levels over the period 2008–2012.[5] The Protocol has recently been extended to 2017, but negotiations are still ongoing for a replacement agreement and this has been very difficult to achieve (Copenhagen 2009 and Cancun 2010). A more ambitious domestic target has been adopted, an 80 per cent CO_2 emissions reduction target on a 1990 base, by the Department of Energy and Climate Change (2010). The new Climate Change Act (2008) means this has become legally binding. However, there are concerns that the commitment to action on climate change at the national level is weakening, and the targets – conveniently set a long time in the future with few interim milestones – can quite easily be delayed or broken at a later stage.

The current levels of CO_2 emissions (2010) for London are around 48 MtCO2 (million tonnes of CO2) (Transport for London, 2011). Achieving large reductions in CO_2 emissions, whilst retaining economic and quality of life goals, is likely to be difficult, even with a static population and employment base. Add in large population and economic growth and the task to reduce aggregate emissions becomes considerable. London's population is expected to grow from 7.5 million in 2006 to 9 million in 2050 (an increase of 23 per cent), and the economy by between 100 per cent and 150 per cent over the same period, notwithstanding some recent 'fluctuations' (Greater London Authority, 2009; Greater London Authority, 2003). Within London (2008), the transport sector accounts for 22 per cent of ground-based transport CO_2

Figure 3.16 Congestion charging. Private cars are charged at £10 per day to enter the central area, reducing the number of cars in the centre of London, improving conditions for pedestrian and cyclists, and also giving more space to buses.

Figure 3.17 Just Imagine, 1930, directed by David Butler. In 1880, the people believed themselves to be the 'last word in speed'; but by 1930, the streets are crowded with cars and lined with lights and telephone wires; and in 1980, the tenement houses have become 250-story buildings, connected by suspension bridges and multi-lane elevated roads.

> *Single O*:   Boys, I vouldn't know de old town! Vere is all de automobiles?
> *RT-42*:   [pointing skyward] Oh, they're in the upper level.
> *J-21*:   Hardly anyone drives a car now. They all use planes.
> *Single O*:   It looks like someone got even with Henry Ford!

Source: British Film Institute Stills Collection.

emissions (9.6 MtCO2) (Figure 3.18). Of these transport emissions, the vast majority are from car and motorcycle emissions (46 per cent), road freight (HGVs and LGVs) (17 per cent) and ground-based aviation[6] (12 per cent) (Figure 3.19). These proportions change dramatically if aviation is included. The allocation for London, as used in the Climate Change Action Plan (Greater London Authority, 2007), is that half of emissions from all flights landing at London airports are allocated to London residents' emissions. This results in the aggregate transport emissions rising to 48 per cent. Since 2008, transport-related CO2 emissions have fallen to 9.36 MtCO2, but these figures may not be entirely compatible with the earlier ones (Transport for London, 2011).

Per capita transport emissions are relatively low at 1.3 tonnes CO2 per person for Greater London (2008), though there are large differences between inner London, where use of public

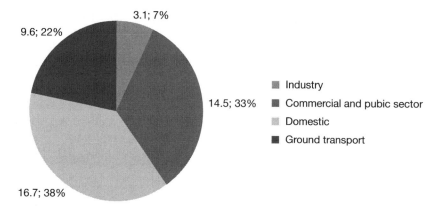

Figure 3.18 Cross-sectoral CO2 emissions
Source: Based on TfL, 2009.

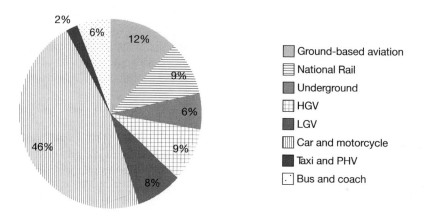

Figure 3.19 Transport CO2 emissions disaggregated
Source: Transport for London, 2011.

transport is higher, and outer London where there is greater car dependency. Even in the progressive cities such as London, areas around the key radial routes, such as along the Westway or parts of the suburbs, are designed around the car: 'whole parts of the built environment are now a mute but still eloquent testimony to the automobile' (Thrift, 2004, p. 46). This figure has now been reduced to 1.15 tCO2 per person (2010).

The analysis in this chapter develops and explores likely pathways towards the adopted strategic target – a 60 per cent reduction in transport CO2 emissions by 2025 on a 1990 baseline. This is a radical drop to 4 MtCO2 in aggregate, representing 0.5 tonnes CO2 per person. An 80 per cent reduction by 2050 is even more demanding (Table 3.3).

As well as 'end state' targets, carbon budgets are also important, as this is the 'area under the curve' and represents the amount of CO2 emitted over time (Anderson et al., 2008). A focus on budgets can, in theory, help improve implementation timescales, with a greater focus on speed of implementation; a different speed of CO2 reduction achieves a very different 'carbon spend'. The UK Committee on Climate Change has usefully developed 5-year budgets at the UK level (Committee on Climate Change, 2008) in an attempt to force the speed of action. In London similar budgets have not been developed, but assuming a linear reduction (1990–2025), the total budget available over the 35 years is around 247 MtCO2 for transport in London (Figure 3.21). The actual amount used already (1990–2006) is 166 MtCO2. Hence the problem is quite evident: the amount available for the next 20 years is 81 MtCO2 – meaning that the current budget per year is actually 4.3 MtCO2 (around 45 per cent of the current levels). Many of these core problems are not really discussed; and each year, this level is reduced if it is not met, making it harder to achieve. At the current levels of CO2 emissions in transport for London, the total allocation (247 MtCO2) will be used in 2014, some 11 years before the target date. The most likely pathway (the slow track –2.5 +7.5 +30.0 +60.0 per cent reductions over each of the budget allocation periods), means there will be a deficit relative to the linear projection of 70 MtCO2 by 2025. Even with an extreme fast-track approach (+35.0 +58.5 +59.8 +60.0 per cent reductions) there is a deficit relative to the linear projection of 14 MtCO2 by 2025. To follow the linear budget requires immediate fundamental action, and this seems very difficult to implement, as the actual pathway has always been substantially above this level. The slow-track route is the most attractive, as it leaves any real reductions to very late in the period to 2025, but it is the high-risk strategy as the 'magic solution' may not happen. There is already the additional problem that CO2 is continuously being released into the atmosphere, so any delay means that future reductions are less effective than those taken today (Anderson et al., 2008). It is already virtually impossible to meet the 60 per cent reduction target set for transport in London on a budgetary basis. It is essential to make immediate and substantial cuts.

Figure 3.20 Ealing, 'Queen of the Suburbs'. Many of London's Victorian suburbs were built from the late 1800s around the new Underground lines, including the Metropolitan and District Lines.

Table 3.3 CO2 projections and targets for London, excluding aviation (MtCO2)

Scenario	1990	2006 (per capita)	2025 (per capita)	2050 (per capita)
BAU projection (cross sectoral)	45.1	44.3 (5.9)	51.0 (6.2)	–
BAU projection (ground transport)	9.9	9.6 (1.3)	11.7 (1.4)	–
CCAP target (cross sectoral) *60% reduction by 2025 on a 1990 baseline*	–	–	18.0 (2.2)	–
VIBAT London target (ground transport) *60% reduction by 2025 on a 1990 baseline*	–	–	4.0 (0.5)	–
80% reduction by 2050 on a 1990 baseline	–	–	–	2.0 (0.2)

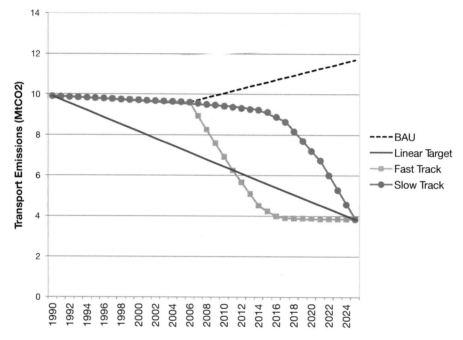

Figure 3.21 Transport CO2 emission budgets (London)

Though London is progressive in relative terms to other cities, any serious consideration of the targets and likely achievement provides serious concerns. The striking feature of the target and budgetary analysis is the huge gap between BAU projections and the emissions' reduction aspirations. Achieving this scale of change will prove to be very difficult. It will involve a fundamental and new rethinking, including the range and scale of available policy interventions, the levels of application and funding, and a much deeper understanding of travel requirements and possibilities for low carbon travel at both the individual and societal levels.

Available policy interventions and packages

An advantage is that we have been thinking about the possible components of sustainable transport for many years. A wide range of policy measures are available to help reduce transport CO2 emissions and to transition towards a low carbon mobility future. Moving from carbon inefficient travel to carbon efficient travel means a composite strategy of realising fewer trips, reduced trip lengths, mode shift and increased vehicle efficiency. Relying on one set of these mechanisms (e.g. increased vehicle efficiency) is likely to be offset by 'adverse' trends elsewhere (e.g. more trips and increased trip lengths). Hence any aggregate gains will be small, if any at all. Again, this seems to be a difficult point to appreciate in national governmental circles, certainly at the political level.

Over 150 individual policy interventions were reviewed in the VIBAT-London study that may help reduce transport CO2 emissions. Individual measures work best within packages, allowing complementary measures to work together and mitigation impacts to be quantified. Hence measures are grouped into complementary policy packages as components within scenarios. Apart from the measures, information was gathered on their effectiveness in reducing emissions, and the time scale necessary for their implementation. The difficulty here was in the packaging, and the potential number of packages. Originally the measures were grouped into fifteen packages, but these were reduced to twelve (including two that were seen as being more like supporting mechanisms – oil prices – or enabling mechanisms – carbon rationing). Most of the packages had variants that were more suited to one image of the future than the other.

These packages were then clustered together as scenarios to see whether the targets set in each of the images could be reached. In this study an additivity assumption was used, namely that the savings from each package were supportive of others. This assumption gives an optimistic view of target achievement, and it would be useful to explore non-additive effects, synergies and rebound effects in implementation (see concluding comments). The final stage was then to establish the sequencing of implementation, so that the targets set for 2025 in each image would be achieved – these are the policy pathways.

The packaging process was very fruitful as measures could be combined and efforts made to ensure their impact was made more effective. To achieve substantial reduction in emissions requires combinations of mutually supporting policies, often involving a variety of stakeholders. Individual policies will certainly not take us far down the lower carbon route. Combinations (together with the supporting soft measures such as awareness raising) can help control for rebound effects, where individual reductions in emissions are in turn increased as people travel further, thus negating some of the benefits. Many of the packages are extremely interrelated, and this includes the technological options, such as low-emission vehicles, as they require supporting behavioural change such as adapted consumer buying preferences towards low carbon vehicles.

The potential carbon savings were calculated through the estimation of the reductions in travel and/or change in mode share, and these figures were obtained from a wide range of empirical studies and commissioned model runs. The modelling is developed to allow quantification (in CO2 reduction terms) of the potential impacts of different scenarios. A range of data sources are used, including commissioned runs from the strategic highway model for London.[7] Other datasets utilised include the latest UK vehicle/speed CO2 emission factors (Department for Transport, 2008b), modal CO2 emission factors (Department for Food and Rural Affairs, 2009) and London Plan (Greater London Authority, 2009) spatial planning assumptions. The analysis proved to be enormously useful in working out how the targets set could be achieved, in illustrating likely levels of change, and they also give an indication of the importance of each package and their variants. The modelling hence proved critical in providing some quantitative input to an essentially qualitative process.

A transport and carbon simulator (TC-SIM[8]) was also developed to help visualise the likely impacts of packaging of policy options and the strategic policy choices that need to be made. TC-SIM was hence developed as a visualisation and participation tool, including elements of policy packaging, scenario building and a policy discussion platform, with a spatial base for London, around which decisions concerning possible future policy packages and scenarios can be made. The twelve policy packages (PP) considered for London cover:

- PP1: Low-emission vehicles
- PP2: Alternative fuels
- PP3: Pricing regimes
- PP4: Public transport
- PP5: Walking and cycling
- PP6: Urban planning
- PP7: Information and communication technologies (ICT)
- PP8: Smarter choice behavioural measures
- PP9: Ecological driving and slower speeds
- PP10: Long distance travel substitution
- PP11: Freight transport
- PP12: International air travel.

The application of a range of policy packages, clustered as a scenario, can then seek to meet the gap between BAU projections and strategic target (Figure 3.22). This is similar in approach to the 'stabilisation wedges' methodology (Pacala and Socolow, 2004), considering how individual measures or groups of policy measures contribute to an end target, but rather than similar-sized wedges, calculates what the different contribution might be according to

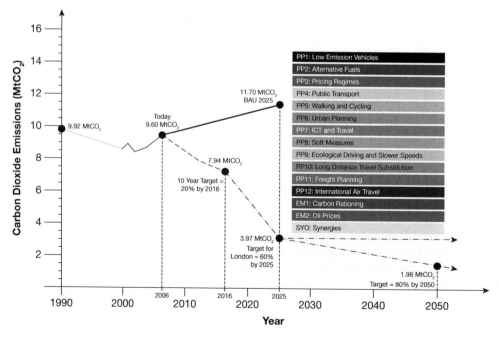

Figure 3.22 Policy packages to bridge the gap

policy area. Each policy package can be selected at a variety of levels of intensity of 'application' – typically at a 'low', 'medium' or 'high' level.

Relative to the rest of the UK and elsewhere internationally, London is unusual in that traffic growth has been limited in recent years, and it appears to have reached the top of the 'S' curve of traffic growth. This may be related to various factors, including changes in the macro economy, greater international travel and even a reduction in young people acquiring a driving licence, but also the availability of high-quality public transport alternatives and increasingly more comprehensive walking and cycling networks. Consequently, there are also substantially lower levels of CO_2 emissions in transport in London than for equivalent populations elsewhere in the UK, as car ownership levels are lower and the use of public transport is much higher.

Developing scenarios

Multiple scenarios can be developed within TC-SIM, allowing the comparison of potential future policy trajectories, including possible 'trend-breaks' towards sustainable transport. All can be examined relative to the BAU projection and each other. Each scenario includes a variety of 'clustered' policy packages, representing a level of 'application' and a strategy for implementation and investment.

For all policy packages and enabling mechanisms, the CO_2 reductions are computed relative to the BAU reference case. The BAU application is assumed to be the reference case (Scenario 1) in T2025 (Transport for London, 2006). This broadly represents the current fully funded investment strategy for TfL. It includes a significant amount of funding – approximately £2–7 billion per annum to 2025 (Transport for London, 2006). If no policy package is selected this is the equivalent of selecting the BAU option. Tailpipe emissions only are considered, and travel only within the Greater London boundary. Obviously the definition of the reference case is critical; a 'challenging' trajectory, with a large increase in emissions, means that the impacts from policy interventions need to be significant if targets are to be reached.

Drivers of change

Following the conventional matrix approach to deriving scenarios, a number of drivers of change, which at times compete in differing directions, are taken into account. These can be existing trends or uncertainties which may impact on travel in London (Table 3.4).

Overview of scenarios

Multiple combinations of policy measures can be explored within TC-SIM, but the following broad scenarios are examined within this chapter:

- *Baseline (1990–2006)*: historic trend in transport CO_2 emissions.
- *Scenario 1 BAU Scenario 2030*: this future is an extension of existing trends over the next 20 years – some investment in public transport, limited change in the efficiency of the car stock and in the use of alternative fuels, but there is no coherent strategy for accelerated change.
- *Scenario 2 – Lower carbon driving 2030*: achieves an approximate 25 per cent reduction in transport CO_2 emissions, on 1990 levels. However, this is reliant on an ambitious implementation of technological measures (low emission motor vehicles and alternative fuels) with a fleet wide average of 95 gCO_2/km.

Table 3.4 Drivers of change

Emerging socio-demographic trends	Potential travel implications
• Changing demographic and household structures • Ageing, yet more active population • Increasing world trade and globalisation • Economic volatility; including periods of financial collapse and recovery • Emergence of networked organisations, clusters and supply chains • Rising importance of local provision (complex flows) • Rapid technological developments and the emergence of 'digital natives' (the new generation growing up accustomed to technology) • Greater discernment in choice of activities and consumer purchases • Taxation increasingly based on resource consumption rather than income • Decline in the power of national governments and distrust in institutions (reduced ability to influence change) • Increasing awareness of sustainability issues and demand for change • Gradual emergence of radical solutions to climate change	• Steady increase in demand for mobility – passengers and goods; with periods of reduced growth related to economic volatility • Increased trip distances in goods movement; though partial reduction through localised sourcing • Gradual increase in share of low-emission vehicles and use of alternative fuels • Huge growth in demand for public transport, walking and cycling as environmental and health benefits become much more widely known • Much greater realisation of the 'Network Society' – electronic flows replace part of physical travel as well as opening up a new range of social interactions

Source: Drawn from the Department for Trade and Industry and Office of Science and Technology, 2006, with application to London.

• *Scenario 3 – More active travel 2030*: achieves an approximate 32 per cent reduction in transport CO2 emissions, on 1990 levels. It is less optimistic about the potential implementation of low carbon vehicles and relies more on public transport, walking and cycling and smarter choice investment.

• *Scenario 3 – Sustainable travel 2030*: this scenario combines the best technological and behavioural application of Scenarios 1 and 2 to deliver an approximate 60 per cent reduction in transport CO2 emissions, on 1990 levels. It is very optimistic about levels of application of policy levers.

Figure 3.24 illustrates the scenario matrix under a classic scenario 'dilemma'. Two of the major themes from the drivers of change – in this case the extent of technological change and behavioural change – are used to generate the axis of change. These were chosen, in discussion with transport planners at Transport for London and also the expert panel in the VIBAT-London study, to highlight the major problematic currently facing decision-makers in London (and indeed the UK and industrialised West): whether the gains in vehicle efficiency can allow us to remain as mobile as we are, and by use of a similar mode share, or whether travel behaviours also need to change as well to reduce transport CO2 emissions.

SCENARIO 2: LOW CARBON DRIVING

Under this scenario, London is developed with a strong emphasis on technological change (Table 3.5). The demand for transport remains strong and mobility continues to grow. There is a ready acceptance of new technology, both in the home and the workplace, but particularly

Figure 3.23 The City. The approach to development, and the type of activity encouraged,
generates particular travel behaviours – for example, financial employment
and long-distance rail commutes into central London. There is also a reverse
relationship evident – the type of transport investment affects the form of
city that can be developed.

Source: Alexandra Gomes.

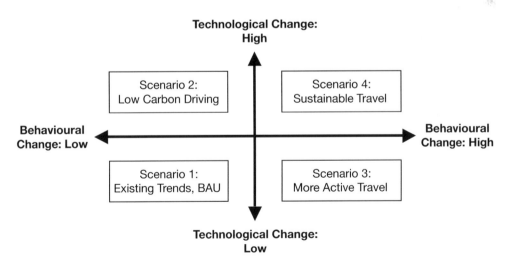

Figure 3.24 Scenario matrix

in transport, with a keen desire to overcome the consequences of CO_2 emission increases through clean technology. However, this concern is not backed up by major lifestyle changes; only marginal changes occur using ICT to reduce the need to travel for certain activities (e.g. some use of teleconferencing and home shopping). Mobility levels remain unaffected; particularly travel by private car in the suburbs.

The main aim of transport policy is to achieve the required CO_2 emissions target with a minimum of change in terms of behaviour. Car traffic still grows and dominates in terms of modal share, with trip lengths increasing and occupancy levels remaining about the same as in 2000. The key changes are in pushing hard on hybrid technologies and alternative fuels so that the overall average emissions profile of the total car stock reduces to below 100 gCO_2/km in 2025. There is also considerable investment in alternative fuels to reduce the carbon content of existing internal combustion engines (ICEs) and the non-electric parts of hybrids. Niche electric vehicles also have a limited role for low-speed vehicles in central London, provided that their source of energy is renewable. The cost of fuels rises overall, but this increase falls increasingly on those car users that continue to consume fossil fuels. New materials are used to make vehicles lighter.

A successful application of this technological ambition delivers a CO_2 efficient vehicle fleet (100 gCO_2/km car fleet, 800 gCO_2/km heavy goods vehicles) and a medium-level usage of alternative fuels (car – 60 per cent petrol, 25 per cent diesel, 5 per cent LPG, 5 per cent electric, 5 per cent biofuel; freight – 75 per cent diesel, 5 per cent LPG, 10 per cent electric, 10 per cent biofuel; bus – 60 per cent diesel, 5 per cent LPG, 5 per cent electric, 30 per cent biofuel). Hydrogen would only appear in a higher level application of alternative fuels, and beyond 2025. A level of application such as this achieves an approximate 25 per cent reduction in transport CO_2 emissions by 2025. This, however, may be very unlikely based on current vehicle penetration rates and difficulties with supplying alternative fuels to the mass market – the assumptions made within the scenario are not likely to be delivered.

Although the scenario acknowledges behavioural change as being important, the general view is that little lifestyle change is required, apart from clear pricing signals to encourage less fuel consumption and a switch to cleaner technologies. This position is illustrative of the conventional policy view at the UK level from the Treasury (HM Treasury, 2006; HM Treasury, 2007), and similarly at the Department for Transport and other related departments (Committee on Climate Change, 2008; Department for Transport, 2008a; Department for Transport, 2009; Department for Transport, 2011). Certainly not enough consideration is given to the massive investment required in policy areas such as public transport, walking and cycling, urban planning, smarter choice behavioural measures, slower speeds and ecological driving, freight planning, etc. These appear fundamental to reducing CO_2 emissions in transport. The wider behavioural and mobilities literature appears not to have penetrated the debate here. Much of the discussion is still framed in neo-liberal terms, i.e. of promoting 'travel choice', not being 'anti-car', of 'low carbon, not low mobility'. This clearly is a very weak position in terms of the potential to reduce transport CO_2 emissions, but of course the results are in the future, beyond the current terms of office. Only a narrow range of policy measures are being employed, including largely voluntary car emission agreements, limited fiscal tinkering, a renewable fuels target and other 'low intensity' application of the wider measures discussed above. The current financial cuts at the UK level only exacerbate this problem. Transport for London and the Greater London Authority lobby hard (to the Department for Transport) for large investments in public transport and the wider behavioural aspects of transport planning – hence investment patterns in the city are very different to elsewhere in the UK, but this scenario illustrates what

Figure 3.25 Robinson in Space, 1996, directed by Patrick Keiller. Robinson is commissioned by 'a well-
known international advertising agency' to undertake a study of the 'problem' of England, which
is never sufficiently defined, but seems all too clear.

John Robinson: There's a lot of space out there to get lost in.

Source: British Film Institute Stills Collection.

might happen if the national approach to transport was pursued in London – a fairly limited
reduction in emissions, if anything at all.

As well as concerns regarding the narrow aspect of policy under this potential scenario,
there are major risks in the assumed level of 'success' in policy implementation for the key
measures employed. The central assumption of a 100 gCO2/km average total car fleet by 2025
is very ambitious based on the current trajectory. Most of the gains in fuel efficiency are likely
to be offset by consumer preference for larger and heavier cars, and perhaps longer travel
distances over time. A more realistic assumption would be a lower level application of technological change (assuming a 125 gCO2/km average total car fleet and 4 per cent alternative
fuels, mainly in the freight and bus fleets, by 2025). The difficulty here is that this leads only
to a contribution reduction in transport CO2 emissions of around 6 per cent. Clearly the
assumptions embedded within scenarios, and more importantly achieved, are critical to the
end level of transport CO2 emissions.

The scenario analysis illustrates the different potential for vehicle technology to achieve
CO2 reduction targets in London if pushed hard (through regulation) or left to the voluntary
actions of motor manufacturers and individual choice. Importantly, there is still a substantial
shortfall against the headline target if the higher levels of application are achieved.

Table 3.5 Low-carbon driving

Policy package	Comment	% of VIBAT London target by 2025
PP1 Low-emission vehicles	High: 100 g/km car fleet; 800 g/km heavy goods vehicles	18.3%
PP2 Alternative fuels	Medium	5.2%
PP3 Pricing regimes	BAU	0%
PP4 Public transport	BAU	0%
PP5 Walking and cycling	BAU	0%
PP6 Urban planning	BAU	0%
PP7 ICT	Medium	1%
PP8 Smarter choice soft measures	BAU	0%
PP9 Slower speeds and ecological driving	BAU	0%
PP10 Long-distance travel substitution	BAU	0%
PP11 Freight transport	BAU	0%
Progress against VIBAT London target (60% reduction in CO2 emissions)		24.5%

Notes: Modelling using TC-SIM London v.3. Within the BAU for London, the T2025 Reference Case (Scenario 1) is normally used.

SCENARIO 3: MORE ACTIVE TRAVEL

Under this scenario, London develops with a stronger emphasis on environmental objectives (Table 3.6). Economic and social considerations are still important, but they are not pursued at the cost of environmental goals. The scenario is less optimistic about the potential implementation of low carbon vehicles and alternative fuels, though delivers some gains here. The majority of environmental gain is delivered through investment in public transport, walking and cycling and smarter choice behavioural measures. The scenario achieves an approximate 29 per cent reduction in transport CO_2 emissions by 2025.

The scale of technological implementation arguably assumes greater realism than in Scenario 2, reflecting more unimpressive penetration trajectories (achieving 140 gCO_2/km car fleet, 900 gCO_2/km heavy goods vehicles (fully loaded) and 4 per cent alternative fuels, mainly in the freight and bus fleets, by 2025). Some gains are made in terms of implementing the behavioural measures. Road pricing assumes the same scheme as currently operating – a limited congestion charging scheme in central London only. Public transport investment is at a 'medium' level of application, representing the T2025 Scenario 4, Full Programme, and includes major schemes such as Crossrail, and capacity and frequency upgrades on the Underground, National Rail and Docklands Light Railway. Similarly, investment in walking and cycling facilities and in the streetscape and public realm, together with effective urban planning, makes active travel options much more attractive. Supportive investments are made in smarter choice behavioural measures, slower speeds and ecological driving are encouraged and freight transport is made more efficient in CO_2 emission terms.

SCENARIO 4: SUSTAINABLE TRAVEL

Clearly the concern is in relying on a narrow range of options to deliver strategic goals. Some may not deliver the expected gains, and there may be unintended or rebound effects.

Table 3.6 More active travel

Policy package	Comment	% of VIBAT London target by 2025
PP1 Low-emission vehicles	BAU	–
PP2 Alternative fuels	BAU	–
PP3 Pricing regimes	High	11.0%
PP4 Public transport	Medium	5.1%
PP5 Walking and cycling	Medium	1.1%
PP6 Urban planning	Medium	1.8%
PP7 ICT	Medium	1.0%
PP8 Smarter choice soft measures	High	2.6%
PP9 Slower speeds and ecological driving	High	4.9%
PP10 Long-distance travel substitution	Medium	0.6%
PP11 Freight transport	Medium	0.8%
Progress against VIBAT London target (60% reduction in CO2 emissions)		28.9%

Note: Modelling using TC-SIM London v.3. Within the BAU for London, the T2025 Reference Case (Scenario 1) is normally used.

Scenario 4 attempts to balance the risk, combining the best technological and behavioural application of Scenarios 2 and 3 to deliver an approximate 60 per cent reduction in transport CO2 emissions, on 1990 levels (Table 3.7). It is, however, very optimistic about levels of application and delivery of policy levers, and the attractiveness of the measures to, and implied different travel behaviours from, the public. Serious attention is required in assessing the obstacles to delivering changing behaviours and in improving the incentives for change.

London again develops with a strong emphasis on wide-ranging sustainability objectives, including environmental, social and economic dimensions. Slowly, the importance of designing the urban environment for less travel and efficient use of resources becomes more obvious. There is a much greater focus on slower means of travel and less distances travelled (Banister, 2011). Over time, technology systems become essential to deliver carbon efficiency. Hence multi-disciplinarity becomes very important – the wider impacts of acting in particular fields are considered and synergies sought. For example, urban design also takes account of the travel impacts of different design options and is articulated to achieve aesthetic objectives and sustainable travel outcomes. Similarly ICT interventions are targeted towards achieving greater sustainability in travel (rather than improved throughflow).

Within London, the central activity zone is an important centre for growth, but growth is also concentrated in the suburbs, with local, polycentric growth, strengthening the former city of villages. Societal benefits accrue from a society integrated more at the local level. People are environmentally aware and more careful in their use of resources. This image is also market driven, but has a much stronger social and environmental emphasis, and is focused on improving the quality, rather than quantity, of life. The transition to the technological society is moderated by greater social intervention. The economy is a knowledge-based economy, producing specialist products for hi-tech businesses. It is accepted that behavioural change is the essential basis needed to address the adopted CO2 emissions targets; however, technology is also important – it is only the package that can deliver deep CO2 reduction cuts.

In the transport sector, the expectation is that there will be a slight reduction in the total amount of travel distance by each person in 2025 and again to 2050, on baseline 2006 levels,

Table 3.7 Sustainable travel 'optimised balance'

Policy package	Comment	% of VIBAT London target by 2025
PP1 Low-emission vehicles	High: 100 gCO2/km car fleet; 800 gCO2/km heavy goods vehicles	18.3%
PP2 Alternative fuels	Car low: (80% petrol, 20% diesel); Freight medium: (75% diesel, 5% LPG, 10% electric, 10% biofuel); Bus medium: (60% diesel, 5% LPG, 5% electric, 30% biofuel)	2.0%
PP3 Pricing regimes	High: a London-wide emissions-based pricing scheme; medium parking charging	9.9%
PP4 Public transport	High: investment strategy beyond even T2025 Scenario 4; medium: fare reduction	11.3%
PP5 Walking and cycling	High: investment strategy beyond T2025 Scenario 4, with an intensive network and facilities for active travel	2.1%
PP6 Urban planning	High: London Plan ++, assuming higher densities around key interchanges and local public realm improvements	3.9%
PP7 ICT	Medium: much greater application of the 'network society' with the substitution effect and reduced travel distances achieved	1.0%
PP8 Smarter choice behavioural measures	Medium: T2025 Scenario 4 investment strategy, reduction in car distance and mode shift to public transport, walking and cycling	1.6%
PP9 Slower speeds and ecological driving	Medium: application of slower speed limits and behaviours on strategic routes and in residential areas, changed driving styles	3.1%
PP10 Long-distance travel substitution	Medium: reduction in short haul air and substituted by rail (though only within London travel considered, hence minimal impact recorded here)	0.6%
PP11 Freight transport	High: reduction in freight travel distance and more CO2 efficient behaviours	1.3%
Oil price	High: $140 a barrel	5.1%
Progress against VIBAT London target (60% reduction in CO2 emissions)		60.3%

Notes: Modelling using TC-SIM London v.3.

1 Within the BAU for London, the T2025 Reference Case (Scenario 1) is normally used.

2 An 'additive' principle is mainly used in the modelling – assuming additive impacts between packages. A limited number of synergetic packages were considered where modelling outputs were available – the interventions covered under T2025 analysis. The additive assumption potentially double counts (sub-additivity) in some areas and misses synergies (super-additivity) in others. There are also issues concerning rebound effects. Much further consideration is required in terms of understanding these types of interactions between package implementation.

3 This scenario assumes oil prices are at $140 a barrel by 2025, but sensitivity tests can be made with different prices assumed.

but the aggregate effect of this will be offset as population will have increased in London. The main reduction has not taken place in the number of trips made, but in the length of trips. The distribution has hence changed, with some growth in long-distance trips, but these are more than compensated for by the increase in shorter more local trips. The desire for less travel (and distance for freight distribution) links in with the greater social awareness and conscience of the population, and the importance of community and welfare objectives. The 'lock-in' to car dependency (as found in image 1) is broken with social priorities pushing for greater use of public transport and other clean modes of transport. Walking and cycling levels are similar to those found in the Netherlands, in Gröningen, Delft and Amsterdam – so 30 per cent of trips are made by bicycle. The vehicle fleet becomes much cleaner to 2025, through new taxation and pricing incentives to use more efficient and cleaner technologies, with tax reductions for not owning a car or for participating in car sharing or different ownership schemes. Car clubs and new forms of ownership are encouraged because of the wider societal benefits. Real fuel prices increase over the period; increases in oil prices are an effective enabler to achieving carbon efficient transport.

This level of policy implementation is the scale of change required to achieve the overall target of 0.5 tCO2 emissions from transport per capita per annum. The very positive news is that the transport sector can de-carbonise in a city such as London to these levels, at least in theory. The scenario pushes extremely hard on all of the available policy levers and implements all technological and behavioural options to a relatively high intensity level. It envisages very high levels of walking and cycling. An important feature is that car distance reduces in Scenario 4 (and 3) – overall distance is broadly held constant, with the difference taken up by a very large increase in walking and cycling. The large difficulty is in achieving the assumptions within the modelled scenarios. This relates to technological and behavioural options. The rationales for achieving greater efficiencies in vehicle emissions and individual mobilities and behaviours hence need a very serious examination – from this knowledge we can perhaps improve our levels of policy implementation and effectiveness. A number of points are made against the assumed levels of policy package application under each package in Scenario 4.

PP1 low-emission vehicles: The take up of low-emission vehicles, based largely on hybrid technology, is likely to be very important to reducing emissions. Because most transport CO2 emissions derive from the car fleet, the achievement of targets is greatly reliant on the penetration rates of low-emission vehicles into the fleet, supported by efforts to induce mode share and changed trip distribution (shorter travel distances). Full introduction of an average car fleet of <100 gCO2/km by 2025 and/or 2050 requires substantial investment by car manufacturers and changes to consumer purchasing patterns; hence the technological and behavioural aspects are very closely interrelated.

The current best generations of new vehicles have emissions levels of around 100 gCO2/km (the Toyota Prius hybrid emits 89 gCO2/km; the Volkswagen Polo Blue Motion diesel emits 91 gCO2/km). Relying on the low-emission vehicle option may be high risk as there is no guarantee that the vehicles will penetrate the market to any great degree. The current consumer preference (in the mass market) is for higher specification and heavier vehicles, which emit more CO2. Recent reductions in average fleet CO2 emissions have largely been due to dieselisation rather than the introduction of hybrids. There are major issues concerning the costs and feasibility of converting the whole of the London car fleet to hybrids, and a poor understanding of incentives required to allow mass-market take up. Influencing the motor manufacturers as to which vehicles and technologies they develop is difficult; with the current business model very much focused on selling the ICE petrol car, with some limited effort in

Figure 3.26 Toyota Prius. Delivering low-emission vehicles to the mass market is of critical importance to the attainment of CO2 emission reduction targets.

Source: Low CVP.

emerging technologies. There are, however, major roles here for the UK and EU governments in terms of legislating for mandatory emission targets, the motor industry in delivering them and for changes in consumer-purchasing patterns. For London, the major legislative changes required concerning this policy package fall beyond the mayoral remit, and rely on the EU or UK governments to act. London has to concentrate on applying complementary measures – low-emission zones, preferential parking areas for low-emission vehicles, or perhaps altering the specification of the congestion charge to focus on emissions, and applying this over a wider area (see discussion under Policy Package 3).

PP2 alternative fuels: Additional benefits can be obtained if alternative fuels are used in conjunction with petrol and diesel hybrids. There are many possible alternative fuels on the market – including compressed natural gas (CNG), liquid petroleum gas, methanol, ethanol, biodiesel, hydrogen and electricity (Khare and Sharma, 2003). Many alternative fuels can be used on their own; others can be blended with existing fuels and used in vehicles without any major modifications to the engines. The International Energy Agency (2004; 2009) suggests that, by 2030, some 20–50 per cent of all fuels in transport could come from alternative sources, though this is now assumed to be very optimistic. Major issues here are the land take and water consumption, and the infrastructure required to support mass-market use of alternative fuels. More recent estimates assume 5–10 per cent of fuel sold as alternatively fuelled would be more realistic. The electric car has much potential, for city driving in particular. In London the G-Wiz is available, and theoretically could emit (virtually) zero emissions if the source electricity was clean. This is a major issue – electric vehicles in France are associated with very different emissions to the UK. There are also important issues to be overcome in developing electric vehicles that are attractive and deliverable to the mass market, in terms of body shape, battery life and distance between charges. A low-intensity application of this policy package is assumed for the car fleet, with higher levels of application for the freight and bus fleets.

PP3 pricing regimes: Congestion charging or area-wide road pricing could potentially make a substantial difference to CO_2 emissions on a London-wide scale. Road pricing is conventionally conceived as one or more of the following: link-based (tolling for a route or lane, sometimes including occupancy considerations); network-based (a congestion or distance-based charge for strategic routes or wider); and area-based (a cordon or area charge for an urban area or wider). There are large problems with all of these in terms of effectiveness, acceptability and ultimately implementability – hence the huge difficulties experienced in delivery (Levinson, 2010; Santos, 2005).

The history of road pricing illustrates nicely that theoretically 'efficient' interventions are not always politically achievable, and in the end it is often the politics that are more important than the technical options. Effectiveness issues are often related to equity and there are concerns that impacts on low-income drivers are regressive. Acceptability depends very much on the perceived distribution of winners and losers to the proposed charge. The current London scheme is a simple cordon-based congestion charge, covering a limited part of the central area. This scenario assumes a high-level application of the congestion charge (emission-based charging London-wide) and a medium application of parking charging (higher charges and a tighter supply). This gives clear signals to consumers to switch to more efficient cars or to other modes of transport. An improved focus on CO_2 reduction means re-specifying the charge as an emissions-based charge. The cost of travel is related to distance travelled and the emissions of the vehicle. In-vehicle GPS works out the charge – smaller, more fuel-efficient vehicles pay less per km than the large and heavier cars. This type of re-specification may also assist in implementation, articulating the scheme as a response to wider societal problems (CO_2 emissions) and even include hypothecation, where the funds being raised are then used for investment in other parts of the transport system. The problem here might be in scheme complexity. One of the advantages of the current congestion charge scheme is its simplicity in operation.

PP4 public transport: Public transport investment is critical in allowing consumers to choose carbon efficient means of travel. This scenario assumes a high-intensity investment in public transport (beyond even the T2025 Scenario 4 Full Programme) and a medium level of fare reduction. The scenario therefore includes all of the major Underground, National Rail, Docklands Light Railway and bus and transit network developments and frequency upgrades currently being developed, plus some potential additional proposals as discussed below. Crossrail, the east–west rail link across London, will add 10 per cent to the overall capacity of the public transport network and an additional 5.8 million passenger kilometres to peak capacity. The full Rail 2025 proposals will increase capacity on the rail network by 35–40 per cent. The public–private partnership (PPP) package on the Underground network (LU) will deliver an average capacity enhancement of 25 per cent across the LU (Transport for London, 2006). The additional schemes to T2025 Scenario 4 include light rapid and bus transit schemes in the suburbs, complemented by a revised urban planning approach (PP6). Transport planning in London has conventionally been focused on improving the radial links into the centre; there is still some way to go in improving options in outer London, which remains relatively car dependent.

Figure 3.27 King's Cross St. Pancras. Some of the recent investment in public transport in London has been of a very high specification and helps to improve the interchange experience.

There is more that could be developed in terms of public transport investment; for example Crossrail could be developed into a more extensive regional service – following the example of the Parisian RER (Réseau Express Régional) – with much more extensive through services than planned across the Southeast region. The central London tunnel could offer connecting services to Oxford, Milton Keynes, Guildford, Chelmsford, Southend, Dartford and Gravesend, along the lines of the 'Superlink' proposal of Michael Schabas and John Prideaux. Crossrail 2 (under consideration, but with no detailed design or funding approval) similarly could offer extended regional linkages into London, with the potential to link Guildford, Weybridge, Surbiton, across central London, to Alexandra Palace, Cheshunt and Hertford East (Hickman et al., 2013) (Figure 3.30), hence adding to an already extensive public transport network.

Figure 3.28 King's Cross St. Pancras, new western concourse

Figure 3.29 Oyster card. Useable across Greater London for all public transport journey payment, including travel on the London Underground, National Rail, Docklands Light Railway, Emirates Airline (the North Greenwich–Royal Docks Cable Car) and bus journeys.

Source: Transport for London image collection.

In support, there could also be new light rapid transit (tram) and/or bus rapid transit (BRT) schemes, many focused in outer London; possibilities include East London Transit, Cross River Transit, West London Tram, and a North- and South-Circular BRT. Some of these schemes have been well studied and partially designed in past years, but have failed to get to the implementation stage for various reasons. They, or variants, remain important to making Outer London much less reliant on private car usage. There could also be a series of new interchange improvements. High Speed 2 (a proposed new high-speed rail service, London Euston–Birmingham and Manchester), for example, offers the potential for a new 'western gateway' station akin to Stratford and Ebbsfleet on HS1. This would be located adjacent to North Acton, North Pole Depot and Willesden Junction, and could potentially help regenerate Park Royal and surrounds in Northwest London. There are further possibilities where

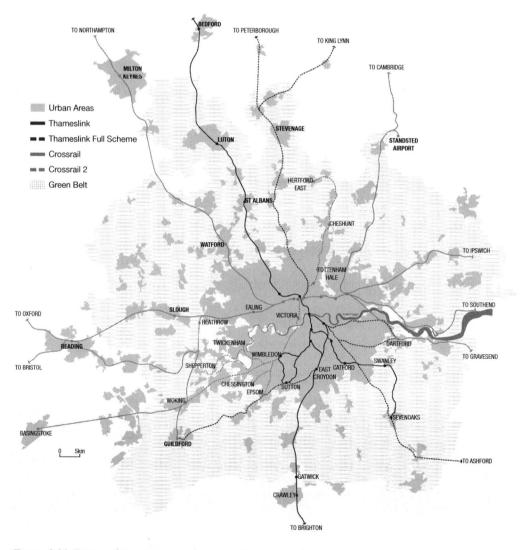

Figure 3.30 Future urban structure and transport investment for the London City-Region
Source: Mapping by Bally Meeda and Urban Graphics.

Underground lines cross but there is as yet no effective interchange, e.g. the Overground crossing the Piccadilly Line and Central Line in West London. These types of major public transport investments would see London develop as the central part of a wider London city-region, with the compact city urban form developing into a polycentric regional form, linked by the regional rail connections (Hickman et al., 2013). This will, of course, require some coordination in development and transport strategy at the regional level, and this is difficult under the current governmental context in the UK, which is unsupportive of regional planning efforts.

PP5 walking and cycling: Investment in walking and cycling facilities and in the streetscape and public realm makes carbon efficient means of travel more attractive, particularly for short journeys. London-wide, people make 7 million journeys on foot every day. Walking is hence an important means of travel, and accounts for about 20 per cent of all London's journeys (Transport for London, 2011). Despite this, investment in the pedestrian environment is traditionally low relative to other modes. London's streets need to be made more amenable and attractive in design terms to encourage pedestrian use, and there are many initiatives underway. The continued growth of cycling in London is critical for attracting trips from the private car and, perhaps to a lesser extent, the public transport network. Less than 2 per cent of trips in London are made by bicycle. Mumford (1968) highlights the relative efficiency of modes:

> We have forgotten how much more efficient and how much more flexible the footgoer [and cyclist] is. Before there was any public transportation in London, something like fifty thousand people an hour used to pass over London Bridge on their way to work: a single artery. Mass public transportation can bring from forty to sixty thousand people per hour, along a single route, whereas our best expressways, using far more space, cannot move more than four to six thousand cars [. . .] this is obviously the most costly and inefficient means of handling the peak hours of traffic.
>
> (p. 103)

This scenario assumes a very high-intensity investment in walking and cycling (much beyond the current level of planned investment in even T2025 Scenario 4, Full Programme). Walking kilometres increase by 160 per cent (on a high base) and cycling by a factor of nearly 10 (on a low base), both relative to 2006. The aim here is to achieve much higher levels of walking and cycling in London than previously envisaged, towards the levels found in many urban areas in the Netherlands and Germany, i.e. eventually 30–40 per cent of trips by cycling (Pucher and Buehler, 2008). Efforts here can be much more progressive than envisaged in the Mayor's Transport Strategy (Transport for London, 2009). The wider health gains from such a focus on active lifestyles are expected to be very important (Woodcock et al., 2009). There are a number of 'Greenways' (long-distance cycle and walkways) that could be developed, as along canal towpaths, such as the Grand Union Canal through North London. There is much greater potential to develop radial and tangential cycle and walkways in London, beyond the so-called 'cycle superhighways' of Boris Johnson. On most routes there are capacity difficulties (in terms of needing to take out car lanes if space is reallocated), but cycle routes still need to be provided along all strategic routes, and ideally these would be mostly made up of segregated cycling lanes, along the Dutch or Danish models.

PP6 urban planning: This package focuses on using urban structure to support and enable sustainable transport. There is a substantial literature on this topic (including Ewing and

Figure 3.31 Hungerford Bridge. Some of the new pedestrian crossings over the Thames are of excellent
quality, almost becoming tourist attractions in their own right.

Cervero, 2001; Handy et al., 2002; Newman and Kenworthy, 1989; Newman and Kenworthy,
1999; Banister, 2008).

Urban structure provides the underlying 'physical rationale' for travel, alongside wider
influences such as socio-economic and attitudinal/cultural characteristics, affecting the main
characteristics of travel – the numbers of trips made, trip distribution, journey lengths and
mode share, and consequently a major part of transport CO_2 emissions. Efforts can be directed
at both strategic as well as local scales (Hickman et al., 2009c). Despite this, urban planning
is often underplayed as a tool in traffic demand management strategies (Banister and Hickman,
2006; Hickman and Banister, 2005; Hickman and Banister, 2007b). Dispersed urban areas
and low densities, which are evident in suburban areas in London and elsewhere, certainly
preclude the use of public transport, walking and cycling, and tend to facilitate private car
dependency. Hence spatial structure sets the physical 'envelope' for travel.

This package assumes a high-intensity application of urban planning to reduce travel CO_2
emissions (London Plan++) – so a much greater effort than even the current policy approach
in using higher densities and the location of development to support sustainable transport.
Higher density development is clustered around an upgraded public transport system – with

Figure 3.32 High Street Kensington. Designing a streetscape environment to cater for multiple users, including for vehicles, pedestrians and cyclists, is often difficult given space constraints. The design for High Street Kensington showed what could be done to improve pedestrian space with even quite limited changes.

Figure 3.33 Exhibition Road. A shared-space approach was used in Exhibition Road, largely with success, though there are still too many vehicles using this important museum and university quarter.

Figure 3.34
(Left) Euston Road cycling. The cycling environment in London is very poor, with very few routes segregated from traffic – there is much scope for improvement here, with Dutch or Danish-style provision required.

Figure 3.35
(Below) East London. There is huge redevelopment potential, and the opportunity to build in low CO2 travel behaviours to new development.

polycentricity developed at the city-regional level – and, more locally, urban areas master-planned to vastly improve their urban design quality and attractiveness for living and working, and use of walking and cycling. This includes major public transport corridors and interchanges in the suburbs, and could also be carried out at the city regional level, hence London is planned as the centre of a much larger urban region (see earlier Figure 3.28) (Hickman et al., 2013). There is, of course linkage to the transport system, with complementary heavy investment in public transport and walking and cycling facilities. Extensive application of this package would potentially have a major impact, but largely over the medium term, as decisions on the location of new housing and other development takes place gradually over time. More immediate impacts are seen in major development areas – known as the 'Opportunity Areas' and 'Intensification Areas' in London (Greater London Authority, 2009).

PP7 ICT: This package explores the potential for CO2 reduction through the application of ICT, either in or on travel. The former includes measures to increase operating efficiency and vehicle occupancies, and the latter measures that reduce travel by providing an electronic alternative to physical travel. The current application of these types of measures are at very low/formative levels of 'intensity' and the levels of transport CO2 reduction are limited under current applicative patterns. Travel tends to adapt, with different types of activity taking place, including more travel in many places, rather than a simple substitution of physical travel for electronic interaction (Mokhtarian, 1988). Hence the rebound effects tend to be large here. There is much more potential in future years as the 'network society' is developed and becomes established (Castells, 2000; Hall and Pain, 2006); substitution in travel may even be realised. The current levels of CO2 reduction from this package are, however, limited. This scenario assumes a medium intensity application of ICT and the impacts remain minimal in terms of transport CO2 reduction.

PP8 smarter choice behavioural measures: This option includes a variety of measures targeted at achieving behavioural change. In the UK they have become known as 'smarter choices', after an influential early study on the topic (Cairns et al., 2004). Elsewhere, in areas such as North America, similar initiatives are known as traffic demand management or mobility management measures (Litman, 2010). Included here are workplace, residential and school travel plans, car sharing and leasing, car clubs, travel awareness and personalised travel planning programmes, information and marketing. There is some overlap in definition with previous packages, such as ICT, and even urban planning is mentioned in some of the work.

These types of measures provide an important support to other packages, and they also have an important impact on reducing CO2 emissions in their own right. In implementation terms there is a developing programme – the DfT Sustainable Travel Demonstration Towns programme has implemented smarter choice measures in Darlington, Peterborough and Worcester. The evidence has suggested that public transport trips have increased by 13–22 per cent, walking trips by 17–29 per cent and cycling trips by 25–79 per cent. Car trips have reduced by 11–13 per cent (Department for Transport, 2007). More recent evidence suggests similar levels of change – bus trips have increased by 10–22 per cent, walking trips by 10–13 per cent and cycling trips by 26–30 per cent. Car driver trips have reduced by 9 per cent and distance by 5–7 per cent (Sloman et al., 2010). TfL is similarly implementing smarter choice measures, funding a programme since 2002. £5 million is being spent in Sutton as part of the Smarter Travel Sutton programme. The objective here is to reduce car mode share by 5 per cent (Transport for London, 2009).

Despite the often impressive results, smarter choice investment remains low, certainly relative to infrastructure investment. The DfT and others appear sceptical about the effectiveness of spend. There are certainly concerns over the reporting and evaluation of results (Bonsall, 2009), the longevity of behavioural change, and the ability to spread take up over a wide population – there are likely to be diminished returns when spread beyond the initial enthusiastic take up. Certain cohorts of the population have little interest in reducing their levels of car use (inter alia). However, the effectiveness and cost effectiveness of investment appears to compare well against other interventions, and despite some concerns, investment should be increased (Sloman et al., 2010).

Although we will discuss later the sociological and psychological dimensions to travel behaviour, and the need to further understand these, the smarter choice measures are trying to understand and influence behaviour, and they provide an important initial step. The scale of impact is closely linked to the level of associated hard infrastructure investment and the location of development; and this is perhaps the point that is important, namely that any efforts that are likely to reduce travel to any degree are likely to include 'hard', 'soft' and planning interventions, and they cover the full range of interventions within the sustainable mobility paradigm. Working within these fields, with little wider action, is not likely to have large impacts on travel behaviour. Hence multi-disciplinary working within and beyond transport planning is important. This scenario assumes a medium intensity application of smarter choice behavioural measures to reduce travel CO2 emissions.

PP9 slower speeds and ecological driving: Much of the conventional thinking in transport planning is designed to speed traffic up, as congestion and delay are seen as 'wasted' time, resulting in loss of time that could be productively used on other activities. This raises important issues that need resolution. It has been demonstrated that lower speed limits, including less lane switching, may allow traffic to flow more smoothly, thereby increasing capacity. There are also major environmental and safety benefits, and potentially economic advantages from slower speeds and reduced traffic volumes. There has been a clear move towards lowering speed limits in residential areas (home zones) and in other locations (e.g. around schools or on routes with important design quality), where priority has been reallocated to people. Potter et al. (2001) advise on the safety benefits of slower speeds, namely that drivers of both cars and goods vehicles could typically save between 5 and 10 per cent on their fuel bills by adopting more fuel-efficient driving behaviour, and in some cases, a 20 per cent improvement in fuel economy could be achieved. There are therefore strong arguments to reduce the speed and volume of vehicles in some locations.

Lower speeds need to be combined with awareness programmes and better driving techniques to reduce fuel use. Ecological driving skills have been developed in the Netherlands and Germany and include simple measures such as driving at moderate speeds, avoiding excessive acceleration and harsh braking, changing gears at low engine revolutions, driving in the highest comfortable gear at any given speed, avoiding unnecessary use of in-car equipment (especially air conditioning), keeping tyres inflated and reducing unnecessary loads (Anable and Bristow, 2007).

This package has the potential for substantial immediate and long-term benefits if take up is high in terms of reduced speeds and changed driving styles. The major problem is likely to be in achieving and enforcing changed driving styles in the mass market. Slower speeds provide extensive savings, for example, with potential for some 15–20 per cent reduction in carbon emissions if a maximum speed limit of 80 km/hr is introduced on motorways and trunk roads, with lower speeds on other roads, both with effective compliance. Although the fuel use and speed value curves for new cars are flatter than those for older cars, there are considerable fuel savings from lower speeds. This scenario assumes a medium-intensity application of this package – a 30 km/hr (20 mph) speed limit on all residential roads and 80 km/hr (50 mph) on the strategic road network in London. Effective speed limit and driving style enforcement is also assumed; potentially this is assisted by ICT means, such as speed delimiters.

PP10 long-distance travel substitution: This package deals with long-distance travel substitution, say from short-haul air to rail, but considers the Greater London part of the journey only (the part of the trip within the urban area boundary). The increase in long-distance travel within the UK, particularly by short-haul air travel and air freight transport, causes particular concern for CO2 emissions. The modal share of air transport is still very low, but growth rates are much above those of all other modes. Also, air transport is operating with a type of 'extraterritorial' status, being exempted from taxes that in national contexts are charged to all other modes. Long-range leisure travel and airborne freight transport are growing on the basis of the present cost situation. As increasingly important economic structures are relying on cheap air transport, attempts to internalise at least a part of the considerable externalities will become increasingly difficult in future years. Some travellers are also becoming used to the availability of inexpensive, short-haul flights. This growth is being driven by growth in real income levels and in the globalisation of economies, at least until recently. Rail has the potential to offer a serious alternative to air travel over distances of around 300–500 km, particularly for High-Speed Rail (HSR). The considerable improvements brought by HSR on a limited number of national and international routes, together with faster services on existing infrastructure (e.g. with tilting technology and new signalling), technical harmonisation, organisational cooperation and strongly improved conditions for competition. These changes would mean that there is considerable potential for long-distance rail–air substitution (beyond the current Eurostar service) and even co-operation with HSR serving air travel for longer distance travel. This scenario assumes a medium intensity application of this package and the CO2 reduction impacts remain small.

PP11 freight transport: The freight sector has a major role to play in helping to reduce transport sector CO2 emissions. McKinnon (2007) gives a good overview of the possibilities. Load factors are particularly important in the freight sector – the use of average emission factors in analysis can over-simplify the analysis. In terms of the prevailing trends at the UK level, CO2 emissions from heavy goods vehicles (HGVs) account for the highest proportion of freight emissions (79 per cent). They appear to have risen by over 5 per cent (1990–2005), even though the data are a little uncertain. There is also rapid growth in distance travelled by light goods vehicles (LGVs). Because of the difficulties in finding good quality data in this sector, uncertainties remain as to the real nature of the trends. The current declining CO2 intensity per tonne-km for HGVs can be attributed to a combination of reduction in empty running, net consolidation of loads and improved fuel efficiency. Aggregate emissions continue, however, to rise over time.

McKinnon discusses a number of areas that may help reduce emissions in the freight sector, including improving handling factors (number of links in the supply chain), reducing length of haul, improving mode share, proportion of empty running, fuel efficiency and choice of fuel/power source.These can be considered in terms of subsidiarity (local production and knowledge transfer) and dematerialisation (miniaturisation, advanced logistics and distribution networks, load matching and material consumption). All can lead to savings, some substantial. This scenario assumes a high-intensity application of the package. CO2 reduction impacts remain small, due in part to only considering the part of the trip within the urban area boundary – many deliveries, for example, to London residents or businesses originate beyond London.

Synergies between policy packages

An important dimension here is how policy packages should be best grouped together to form a mutually supporting, synergetic strategy. Urban planning, for example, might be used well to support a higher public transport, walking and cycle mode share. Some policy packages may not work well together. The potential relationships evident include:

• Positive and negative interactions and synergies between policy packages/enabling mechanisms;
• Double counting of policy benefits (sub-additivity);
• Positive (super-additivity) and negative multiplier effects – greater or less than the sum of the parts;
• Positive or negative snowball effects over time, and the trigger points where these effects can be identified.

Synergies and additionality effects are poorly understood in the literature. There is little available evidence on these issues and an additive principle is adopted in the current TC-SIM modelling. This means that the relationships between packages are not modelled. Some of the research behind the VIBAT studies has attempted to assess likely effects (Hickman et al., 2009b) and there is potential for further development of these ideas. Conceptually, it is not difficult to identify where the most promising positive benefits of policy packaging may take place, but the real difficulty is in obtaining empirical evidence that can be used in modelling approaches where synergies are included.

'Known unknowns': international air travel, carbon rationing and oil prices

There are at least three difficult (and critical) policy areas that are currently far from being resolved. The first is international air travel, which has until recently been growing at a rate of 6 per cent per annum (doubling every 12 years). There is little acceptance of the need for reducing the growth in demand for aviation, yet emissions from air travel are soon to become a major problem to the achievement of CO2 reduction targets (Bows and Anderson, 2007). Even more concerning is the 'troublesome' leisure travel, as it is the high-income cohorts, who, despite living in (high-quality) urban areas and being environmentally aware, still travel most for leisure purposes, including by air (Brand and Preston, 2010; Holden and Linnerud, 2011).

Two further problems are evident. One relates to how international aviation should be accounted for in emission reduction targets. At present they are either excluded (as in most transport planning analysis concerning this topic) or they are considered as contributing a major part of city-based emissions. In London, the calculations used in this analysis are that half the full international aviation CO2 emissions are allocated to residents (Climate Change Action Plan: GLA, 2007). This is a high proportion as not all air trips end in London, as many travellers interline between flights (the London hub) and others travel on to destinations in the UK that are outside London. At present there are very few technological opportunities available to reduce emissions for the air sector. Many of the planes flying today will still be in use in 2025 and even 2050 (for example, the A380).

The only way to reduce emissions is therefore to reduce demand – through pricing, regulation and even rationing – and there is little political (or public) appetite for these policy levers. Even with the wide range of measures to tackle emissions in ground-based transport as suggested in Scenario 4, and including a 'medium' reduction in the projected growth in air travel (a 10 per cent reduction against BAU), the calculations are that the reductions in CO2 emissions fall to just 23 per cent (relative to the previous 60 per cent reduction in Scenario 4). The scale of emissions involved in air travel thus becomes very important.

There are further areas that are important to carbon efficiency in transport, but remain very poorly understood and developed. These might be termed 'enabling mechanisms'. The first is carbon rationing (Hillman and Fawcett, 2004) – there are a number of possible ways of implementing a rationing scheme in the transport sector. The most likely are through car manufacturers, fuel suppliers or as personal carbon allocations (PCAs). Each would involve a cap and trade system with an overall maximum total level of emissions, probably reducing in volume over time. This cap and trade mechanism might help achieve high-intensity application in the preceding packages. But there are very large implementation difficulties, particularly with PCAs (Department for Food and Rural Affairs, 2008; Environmental Audit Committee, 2008; Fawcett and Parag, 2010). There is, however, one related example of implementation. The EU Emissions Trading Scheme (EU ETS) is already running, where some major polluting industries are allocated tradable emission permits, and they can use or trade them according to the levels of CO2 produced. The transport sector is likely to be included in this scheme in future years, with international air emissions also being included. The idea is to set a cap on the aggregate level of emissions and trade within this level. Trading is likely to be at the business and/or national level. Much uncertainty, however, remains as to how to implement a trading mechanism for carbon.

One argument for including aviation in the scheme is that, as flying is a premium producer of CO2, the aviation industry would buy all available permits and then pass on the costs to the users. The additional costs would reduce the demand for air travel and would allow other industries to decarbonise at a faster rate. At present (2013), there is a delay in including aviation into the ETS as the airlines have undertaken to come up with their own scheme. The EU has given them a year to do this, as a result of intense pressure from international airlines and national governments against any form of charge on aviation CO2 emissions.

Second is oil price (and linked with the 'peak oil' debate). Over the past 30 years there has been some stability in oil prices – at relatively low levels – but recently this has changed, with high volatility and some concern we are reaching, or have already reached, a period of peak oil (Strahan, 2007; Heinberg, 2003). This is likely to result in dramatically higher oil prices as suppliers and consumers react to perceived supply shortages. The consumer is shielded to a certain extent by the high tax component in the price of petrol and diesel. Nevertheless, a large increase in the cost of oil impacts markedly on the price of petrol and diesel. Large price increases are likely to dampen the demand for travel using oil and provide clear signals to industry and consumers to increase efficiencies.

Recent price volatility may have an important impact on travel demand (in early 2013 Brent crude oil prices were at around $110 per barrel, and hit $140 per barrel in July 2008). The typical elasticity used for vehicle travel with respect to fuel price is assumed to be in the order of –0.15 in the short run and –0.3 over the long run (Graham and Glaister, 2002). Recent price rises, we would expect, should be feeding through to reduced demand for travel, and this may be acting as an effective enabler of reduced carbon dependency in travel. There is

Figure 3.36 South Bank. London is currently a very attractive and liveable city, with much vitality and life. Transport is a major part of this offer and further spending should be viewed as an investment in the city, for residents, businesses and visitors. Upgrading the transport systems is, however, expensive, particularly in view of challenging CO_2 reduction targets, and there needs to be some rethinking of funding mechanisms, including using the developmental value uplift following transport investment to fund transport and public realm initiatives.

some limited evidence of this. Large price increases may, perversely, 'help' achieve high-intensity application in the preceding packages. There are, however, very large difficulties in terms of acceptability of large price increases (with the public and business). With the recent discovery of oil shales and gas fracking, there may be downward pressures on oil prices that might in turn reduce the incentives to switch to low carbon mobility.

Conclusions: achieving deep reductions

This chapter outlines some of the difficulties being experienced in achieving ambitious CO_2 emission reduction targets, in even a progressive city such as London that aims to become 'sustainable'. London can perhaps be considered as one of the 'bellwethers' for experience elsewhere, developing an early, innovative strategy for low carbon transport. Though, of course, we should appreciate that transport CO_2 emissions remain high in Outer London relative to Inner London, with higher levels of car dependency. Per capita emissions levels in London are also much higher than those found in cities in countries such as India and China.

Multiple pathways are possible in moving towards low CO_2 emissions in transport in London, each with different levels of CO_2 reduction. All of the scenarios that reduce CO_2 emissions to a significant degree represent significant breaks against current trends and are likely to be very difficult to implement. There should also be some consideration of political realism, in terms of what can be implemented in the political and public arenas. These difficulties are soon apparent and it is clear that very considerable efforts are required across the whole range of policy packages, if the strategic targets are to be met. A number of conclusions can be drawn:

1   The current trends mean that the transport sector continues to perform poorly; it is the one sector that is not contributing to cross-sectoral CO_2 reduction targets. The clear message here is that actions must work much more effectively across the broader range of policy packages available, and at a much higher level of intensity relative to current trends.

2   An optimised package of measures, targeted at achieving sustainable travel, may take us a long way towards the 60 per cent CO_2 reduction target for London. A caveat here is that this assumes a successful level of application across a wide range of policy levers. Large investment is required to move beyond a 10–20 per cent reduction in CO_2 emissions, and further thought is also required concerning deliverability and public acceptability issues. Changed travel behaviours are notoriously difficult to encourage.

3   Low-emission vehicles and alternative fuel penetration are likely to remain very important policy innovations, as they tackle carbon efficiency in the dominant mode of travel (the private car). The main difficulty here is in achieving a significant level of penetration into the mass market. The motor industry and government need to develop mechanisms to achieve this, including mandatory targets for manufacturers. The 80 gCO_2/km average total car fleet could be developed as a mandatory target for an agreed future year such as 2025. A correspondingly hard target can also be developed for light and heavy goods vehicles. More thought is required as to what this means for particular manufacturers, but business models should be capable of being maintained at greater carbon efficiency. Indeed, the innovators here can gain competitive advantage in view of likely legislation.

4   The behavioural measures also offer great opportunities, including novel pricing regimes, the increased use of public transport, walking and cycling, ecological driving and slower speeds, and more efficient freight transport. Urban planning and smarter choice soft measures, as well as acting in their own right, potentially perform very important roles as supporting measures to other policy packages, enabling higher levels of success in implementation. The analysis also shows the high interrelationships between supposedly distinct technological and behavioural measures. Many options, for example the penetration of low-emission vehicles into the vehicle fleet, involve technological dimensions (the development of new car technologies) and behavioural change (changed consumer purchase patterns). The technological–behavioural dichotomy is thus a little misleading and distracting, as most actions require combinations of both.

5   Positive actions need to be more innovative as the headline targets are not being achieved over time. For example, we may need to consider much more imaginative ideas, perhaps including greater use of zero and low-emission vehicle zones, automatic low-speed city driving systems, new forms of car use and ownership (building on the recent growth of city car clubs and rental schemes), new forms of public transport to serve suburban areas, substantial increases in walking and cycling (including Vélib'-style city schemes across all urban areas), virtual mobility massively scaled up to reduce 'unnecessary' physical travel, and a whole host of ideas we have yet to think through.

6   A major problem is the inconsistency in political support over time. As political administrations change there is a tendency to revert back to support for road building and

highway capacity upgrades. The temporary lack of knowledge and familiarity with the issues at the centre is often exploited by the road lobby. This needs to be avoided with cross-party support developed for a long term vision and the broad strategy to achieve this. Hence, over time, more consistent progress can be made towards strategic goals.

The strategy discussed for London is to take a very ambitious approach and use as many of the potential policy levers as possible that have a high potential to contribute to carbon reduction targets. The assumption within the modelling is that a very high degree of successful implementation is possible, and that the benefits can be captured with limited rebound effects. This enhances the CO_2 reduction potential of the optimised strategy, and a positive conclusion can be reached, namely that the target of a 60 per cent reduction in CO_2 emissions in transport can be achieved. But this may be overly optimistic, as such a successful outcome would require major effort, including investment beyond that considered even in the T2025 Scenario 4 (which was itself a very ambitious strategy).

Continuing to 'exhort at the margins' will not lead to the required level of change in travel behaviour and transport CO_2 reduction. Actions need to move beyond simply 'encouraging' or 'nudging' people to change their behaviour. London is one of the leading cities in investing in public transport and in charging for car use in the central area. But even here there is a long way to go. Achieving deep CO_2 emissions reductions – up to 60, 80 and even 90 per cent – will be exceedingly difficult in the transport sector. Much of travel would need to be electric and clean (with a clean fuel source), and trip-making much more local, and/or involve higher levels of electronic interaction than at present. The likelihood of achieving this type of deep CO_2 reduction in transport seems very unlikely, based on current policy-making and investment, unless a radically revised policy approach is adopted.

We should remind ourselves of the thoughts of John Wyndham (1953, pp. 221–223):

> One day we walked down to Trafalgar Square. The tide was in, and the water reached nearly to the top of the wall on the northern side, below the National Gallery. We leant on the balustrade, looking at the water washing around Landseer's lions, wondering what Nelson would think of the view his statue was getting now [. . .] She took my arm, and we started to walk westward. Halfway to the corner of the Square we paused at the sound of a motor. It seemed, improbably, to come from the south side. We waited while it drew closer. Presently, out from the Admiralty Arch swept a speedboat. It turned in a sharp arc and sped away down Whitehall, leaving the ripples of its wake slopping through the windows of august Governmental offices.

Perhaps the gap between reality and unreality is closing – the near science fiction is becoming more believable. The increased frequency in the raising of the Thames Barrier indicates that we need to start to change the trends to a radical degree in transport. The business as usual projection in transport CO_2 emissions is not tenable, yet it seems very difficult to engender major changes in the political and public understanding of travel and its environmental impacts, of the required changes in investment programmes and in travel behaviours. The analysis within this chapter has not considered funding issues, and clearly these are critical, particularly in an era of financial constraints in countries such as the UK. Perhaps the more 'inexpensive' options, such as land-use planning, walking and cycling, smarter travel choices and legislative change (vehicle emissions) will become more attractive here; perhaps a much increased investment in public transport infrastructure can be used as a stimulus investment. There are also important issues to incorporate in the analysis beyond ground transport, including international air and shipping.

A critical issue remains in developing a greater level of engagement and involvement of policy-makers, businesses and the general public, at all levels of decision-making. This is essential. It is not just a question of whether challenging targets can be achieved through the creative combinations of policy packages. There is also a need to get all stakeholders to 'buy into' and 'own' changed future travel behaviours so that real progress can be made. Hence the development of the TC-SIM simulation and participation tool in the London analysis. Such tools can aim to raise awareness about the nature and scale of change required, and to facilitate the discussion of potential pathways. This can only become very important in future years. Ownership of solutions and future lifestyles will be critical, especially where 'trend-breaks' – significantly different to the norm – are being discussed.

The scenario analysis and backcasting approach offers a way forward to this extremely challenging future policy and lifestyle dilemma. London can provide a model for achieving deep transport CO_2 reductions in a Western industrialised, and modern, compact and polycentric city. But the huge challenge now is to develop a consensus around future pathways to carbon efficiency in the transport sector. And then – the difficult step – to enable and actually achieve a level of consumer and behavioural change consistent with the strategic ambitions.

Notes

1   The VIBAT-London study was led by Halcrow and University of Oxford, Transport Studies Unit with Space Syntax and funded by the UrbanBuzz programme, Higher Education Funding Council for England (HEFCE) and Department for Innovation and Skills (DIUS), 2007–09 (Hickman et al., 2009a).

2   Sir Patrick Abercrombie developed the County of London Plan (1943) (with J. H. Forshaw, then chief architect, at the London County Council) and the Greater London Plan (1944), which are both commonly referred to as 'The Abercrombie Plan'.

3   The population trend for London follows a U-shape, with a peak of 8.6 million in 1939, a decline to 6.7 million in 1988 with governmental policy explicitly encouraging low development densities and dispersal to areas beyond London. A rebound was experienced to the present day levels of 7.6 million, associated with a GLA encouragement of growth. Much of the growing population is located in East London.

4   Metro-land was revisited in 1973 by poet Sir John Betjeman in his famous TV documentary: 'A verge in front of your house and grass and a tree for the dog . . . in fact the country had come to the suburbs. Roses are blooming in Metro-land just as they do in the brochures.'

5   The Kyoto Protocol is a protocol to the United Nations Framework Convention on Climate Change (UNFCCC). As of July 2010, 191 states have signed and ratified the protocol, these include thirty-nine industrialised countries and the European Union (known as the 'Annex I' countries) who commit themselves to reduce their collective greenhouse gas emissions by 5.2 per cent from 1990 levels. The targets are cross-sectoral. Transport emissions are for ground-based, domestic transport only; hence do not include emissions by international aviation and shipping – see Chapter 1.

6   'Ground-based aviation', in the London context, is defined as all travel under 1,000 metres in height, including passenger travel and freight.

7   The modelling was provided by Transport for London and used the London Travel Survey strategic model (LTS) and a public transport model (Railplan). The runs were largely based on scenarios from T2025 – particularly the Reference Case, Scenario 1 and Full Programme, Scenario 4 as found in T2025.

8   TC-SIM London and the other simulation tools developed under the VIBAT series of studies can be accessed via www.vibat.org

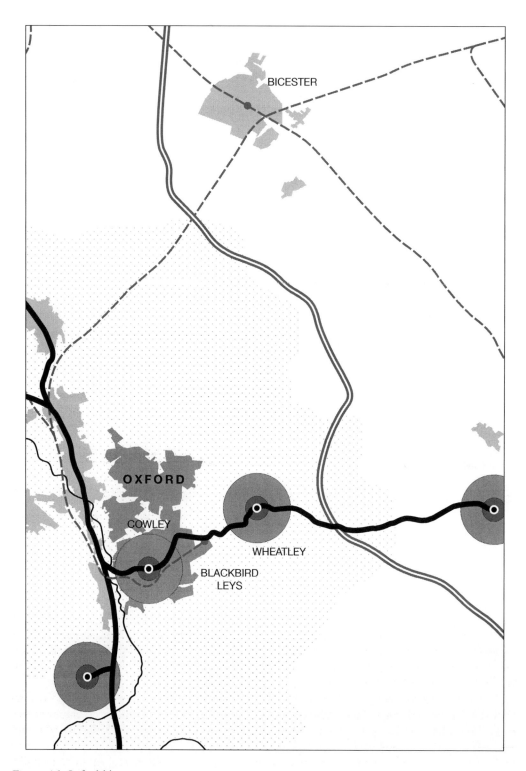

Figure 4.1 Oxfordshire
Source: Mapping by Bally Meeda and Urban Graphics.

4 Affluent rurality and car dependence (Oxfordshire)

There was only one catch and that was Catch-22, which specified that a concern for one's own safety in the face of dangers that were real and immediate was the process of a rational mind. Orr was crazy and could be grounded. All he had to do was ask; and as soon as he did, he would no longer be crazy and would have to fly more missions. Orr would be crazy to fly more missions and sane if he didn't, but if he was sane, he had to fly them. If he flew them, he was crazy and didn't have to; but if he didn't want to he was sane and had to. Yossarian was moved very deeply by the absolute simplicity of this clause of Catch-22 and let out a respectful whistle.

'That's some catch, that Catch-22,' he observed.

'It's the best there is,' Doc Daneeka agreed.

(Joseph Heller, *Catch-22*, 1961, p. 52)

Introduction

Oxfordshire, a county in the southeast of England, provides an example of a relatively sustainable central urban area (the city of Oxford), in urban mobility terms, but a car dependent rural hinterland (the remainder of the county of Oxfordshire). This reflects many factors, including high incomes and car ownership levels, the general poor provision and high cost of public transport, a relatively dispersed urban structure beyond Oxford, and also individual aspirations to own and use the private car. These issues combine to result in high transport CO_2 emissions, with growth projected. There is potential for developing a much greater emphasis on walking, cycling and public transport in future years, and also to make major progress in terms of using more low-emission vehicles. But there are major difficulties being experienced in reducing transport CO_2 emissions, of the Hellerian Catch-22 variety, particularly in the suburban and rural areas beyond the central urban area of Oxford. The public policy aspiration is to reduce emissions, and there is general agreement that much greater progress needs to be made; but the investment levels required are not available, and the public aspire to car usage. Even the more carbon efficient European cities – including the classic good practice examples such as Freiburg, Strasbourg, Amsterdam and Zurich – tend to have sustainable transport options in the central areas, but are often surrounded by relatively car dependent suburban and rural areas. This is also the case in Oxford and the surrounding county, and indeed in many other contexts.

This chapter considers these issues, assessing the potential policy measures and packages available within Oxford, and wider throughout Oxfordshire, and develops scenarios for reduced CO_2 emissions. The context is thus very different to London as it involves finding solutions for an affluent rural hinterland as well as a compact urban centre. People often choose to live in the rural town and village centres of Oxfordshire because of the perceived higher quality of life, of small and attractive local communities; and often large houses and open spaces;

Figure 4.2 St. John Street, Oxford. The quintessential historic university city – with a very high quality of life and beautiful built fabric in the central areas and inner suburbs.
Source: Harry Rutter.

with movement usually facilitated by the car. The level of funding available for transport investment is much reduced as compared to a metropolitan area. Policy interventions are also likely to have a diversity of impacts against other policy objectives (in addition to CO2) and their spatial impacts will also be very variable.

The methodology is therefore progressed, or at least considered from a wider perspective, to consider the impact of low CO2 scenarios relative to wider multi-criteria impacts. Low CO2 transport futures need to perform well against wider sustainability objectives (including the strategic and local environmental, economic, social and safety dimensions). This is a critical issue, but low CO2 transport strategies are in an early stage of development, hence the consideration of multiple goal achievement has rarely been considered. Certainly it is very difficult to develop 'optimised' strategies that perform well against multiple objectives, as policy objectives often act in competing directions. The analysis draws on work carried out in the INTRA-SIM Oxfordshire study (Hickman et al., 2010b).[1]

The county and city context

The county of Oxfordshire has a population of 653,800 (Office for National Statistics, 2012). It comprises the historic university city of Oxford – the 'city of dreaming spires' (Arnold, 1866) – with origins stretching back to the fifth-century Saxons. There are also a number of large towns (such as Banbury, Bicester and Didcot), several smaller towns (such as Chipping Norton, Wallingford and Henley), and rural villages and more remote rural areas. West

Oxfordshire is the most rural district in the county with a population of around 96,000, and the only town of size being Witney.

The city of Oxford itself has a population of 151,900 (Oxford City Council, 2011) and is a 'county town' that serves a wider sub-regional hinterland, referred to as 'Central Oxfordshire'. The ring of market towns and dormitory settlements is around 10–15 miles from the city. Settlements on the east and south sides of the county are very accessible to London (Oxford is around 60 minutes from London Paddington, and Didcot around 45 minutes, so within a daily commute). Neighbouring major urban areas include Reading, Swindon and Milton Keynes.

In terms of land-use planning history, the Oxford Green Belt was designated in 1956 and has led to a relatively effective containment of the Oxford urban area. So much so that the perceived problems now are in the constraint in housing supply within Oxford, particularly in view of housing affordability, and the longer travel distances involved in travelling into Oxford from beyond the green belt. Of course the counterfactual is seldom considered – a sprawling Oxford would have brought other problems in terms of reduced urban quality and

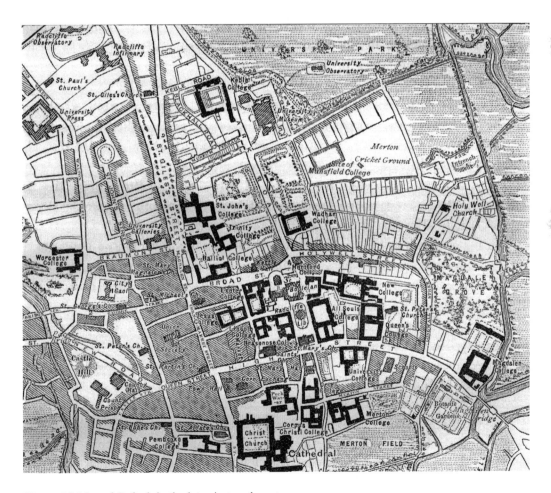

Figure 4.3 Map of Oxford, in the late nineteenth century
Source: From *Our Own Country*, published 1898/Private collection/Ken Welsh/The Bridgeman Art Library.

Figure 4.4 Woodstock. The rural areas within the county are home to some very attractive market towns and villages – many are overrun by cars.

potentially higher transport energy consumption and emissions. The first Oxfordshire County Structure Plan, developed in the 1970s and reflecting the then growth model for London, displaced growth to designated towns beyond the green belt, principally Banbury, Bicester, Didcot and Witney. This strategy can perhaps be viewed as a forerunner to PPG13 (Department of the Environment, 1994; Department of the Environment Transport and the Regions, 2001), where new residential development is encouraged in established urban areas (Headicar, 2009; 2010; Hickman et al., 2012b). It is in the urban areas that facilities can be accessed easily, where there are better prospects for local employment creation and higher levels of public transport accessibility. Sporadic development throughout the county has in the main been avoided, and there are some very attractive rural areas, villages and market towns.

An unanticipated problem resulting from the largely effective land-use planning regime has been that the level of self-containment within the designated growth towns has been low. Although 70 per cent of the commuting trips of residents in Oxford are 'short' (less than 5 miles), less than 35 per cent of trips from the expanded towns are in the same short-distance cohort. The majority of trips are in the 5–25 mile distance band, and most are made by car. Car driver distance per resident worker is 3.9 miles in Oxford relative to 8.5 miles in the expanded towns (Headicar, 2010). This 'many-to-many' origin and destination travel pattern creates difficulties for public transport provision throughout Oxfordshire, with many tangential journeys evident, as well as the more conventional radial journeys centred on Oxford. These types of movement are difficult to serve by conventional public transport. Sustainable transport initiatives still need developing in Oxford, but also throughout the outlying towns and villages. It is here that it is most difficult to reduce car dependency.

The local authorities, Oxfordshire County Council and Oxford City Council, are developing planning strategies and transport investment strategies with a fairly extensive forward look (often to 2021 and 2026), and they are both viewed as progressive authorities in transport and urban planning within the UK. The Oxford Local Development Framework (LDF), for example, has been prepared by Oxford City Council (2008, Core Strategy), and there are four other LDFs across the county (Cherwell, South Oxfordshire, Vale of White Horse and West Oxfordshire). Each was prepared within the context of the regional South East Plan (Government Office for the South East, 2009) and national planning policy guidance. Recent developments at the national level in land-use planning, with the current Conservative–Liberal coalition government less supportive of regional planning efforts, and the land-use planning system as a whole, means little strategic direction is being offered, and there is much confusion as to the most effective process for policy-making. The regional tier of planning has been abolished and the national level is also very weak, leading to an absence of strategic planning. The Oxfordshire Local Transport Plan (LTP3) (Oxfordshire County Council, 2011) involves a time horizon 2011–2030, with a 3- and 5-year investment programme. The longer term strategy is

Table 4.1 Oxfordshire – some statistics

Issue	Comment		
Demonym	Oxonian (an inhabitant of Oxford or member of the University of Oxford)		
Population			
Oxfordshire (2011)	653,800		
Oxfordshire (1801)	111,977		
Oxford (2011)	151,900		
Oxford (1801)	12,690		
Area (2007)	2,605 km^2		
Population density			
County	246/km^2		
City	3,331/km^2		
University students (2012)	University of Oxford, 21,000 students		
	Oxford Brookes University, 20,000 students		
Commuters	75% of Oxford's population works within Oxford; only 9% travel outside of the county to work; yet around 50% of Oxford's workforce lives beyond its boundary		
Mode share (2001)	*Oxfordshire*: Main mode for the journey to work: 62% car, 10% walk, 7% bus, 7% bicycle, 10% work at home, 2% rail.	*Oxford*: Journey to work: 42% car, 15% walk, 16% bus, 15% bicycle, 8% work at home, 2% rail.	*West Oxfordshire*: Journey to work: 67% car, 9% walk, 5% bus, 5% bicycle, 10% work at home, 2% rail
Travel cost, single bus ticket in Oxford (2012)	£1.80 (Two bus companies – Oxford Bus Company and Stagecoach)		
CO2 reduction target	None		
Total CO2 emissions (2008)	9.0 tCO2 per capita		
Transport CO2 emissions (2008)	3.0 tCO2 per capita		
Transport % of total	33%		

Source: Oxfordshire County Council, 2006; Oxfordshire County Council, 2007; Oxford City Council, 2011.

much less developed than the immediate programme, and this is a recurring problem with local transport planning – often the strategic issues fail to be tackled at the expense of short-term crisis management, with the focus on highway maintenance or similar issues such as 'congestion hotspots'.

There are no explicit county-wide or local CO_2 emission reduction targets, either cross-sectorally or for the transport sector. The nearest perhaps was a traffic growth target in LTP2 which seeks to limit the growth in overall traffic levels on Oxfordshire roads. A baseline is used of 10.9 million vehicle kilometres travelled in 2000; with a target of 'no more than' 12.2 million vehicle kilometres per day travelled in 2010. This equates to an approximate 1 per cent per annum maximum traffic growth target, against a projected 2 per cent per annum (Oxfordshire County Council, 2000). Although the development of sustainable transport initiatives has some history over the last decade or so, the development of low CO_2 transport strategies are less well-developed. There is a lack of clarity in strategic direction, insignificant funding, and little progress in terms of the scale of change in travel behaviours required to contribute to national CO_2 reduction targets. Only ad hoc progress appears possible in recent years.

Baseline and projections

Recent historic cross-sectoral CO_2 emissions are given for the districts in Oxfordshire in Table 4.2. Cherwell, South Oxfordshire and Vale of White Horse are associated with the highest emissions in the county. Cherwell has a total of 11 tCO_2 per capita, and 5 tCO_2 per capita in transport; 30–45 per cent of emissions are associated with the transport sector in some districts. Oxford is by far the lowest emitter, with a total of 6.9 tCO_2 per capita, and just 0.9 tCO_2 per capita in transport. The differences in emissions, even in a county as small as Oxfordshire, are thus large, with income levels and accessibility to public transport and central urban areas playing a large part (Brand and Preston, 2010).

The national UK target of an 80 per cent reduction in emissions by 2050 on 1990 levels can be applied to Oxfordshire. There are, however, data issues in that 1990 data do not appear to be readily available for the county. A 60 per cent reduction in emissions by 2030 can be derived on a 2005 base. This would mean a target for Oxfordshire as below:

- Total, 2005 = 5,880 $ktCO_2$ (9.4 tonnes CO_2 per capita)
- Transport, 2005 = 1,964 $ktCO_2$ (3.1 tCO_2 per capita)
- Total target, 2030 = 2,352 $ktCO_2$ (~3.8 tCO_2 per capita)
- Transport target, 2030 = 786 $ktCO_2$ (~1.2 tCO_2 per capita).

There are important issues here though in terms of target setting: different contexts have very different baselines and opportunities for changing travel behaviours, hence national targets will need to be differentially apportioned by area. Urban and rural areas will provide different possibilities. There is, however, very little analysis below the national levels concerning appropriate targets to be adopted. No population growth has also been assumed within the above per capita targets (this could also make the per capita targets more difficult to achieve depending on how they were conceived). As discussed in the previous chapter, budget allocations will also encourage early progress to be made in terms of investing in certain transport options, and progressing more quickly to end state targets.

As a comparison, Table 4.3 gives similar data for selected local authorities in England, and again the differences in emissions are very large. The affluent rural areas (Berkshire,

Figure 4.5 Oxfordshire is very car dependent, particularly beyond central Oxford and in the rural areas, leading to high transport CO2 emissions per capita

Figure 4.6 West Oxford floods, 2007: a sign of things to come?
Source: Harry Rutter.

Figure 4.7 West Oxford floods and cycling, 2007. Cycling can be difficult if the conditions are not quite
right.
Source: Harry Rutter.

Table 4.2 CO2 emissions by local authority in Oxfordshire

Local authority*	Year	Industry and commercial	Domestic	Road transport	Total	Population (000s, mid-year estimate)	Total per capita emissions (t)	Transport per capita emissions (t)	% transport
Cherwell	2005	570	354	688	1,632	137	11.9	5.0	42.2%
Cherwell	2006	571	360	692	1,642	138	11.9	5.0	42.1%
Cherwell	2007	544	352	695	1,611	138	11.7	5.0	43.1%
Cherwell	2008	513	351	664	1,548	139	11.2	4.8	42.9%
Oxford	2005	569	308	147	1,026	144	7.1	1.0	14.3%
Oxford	2006	581	302	142	1,026	144	7.1	1.0	13.8%
Oxford	2007	523	296	146	965	145	6.6	1.0	15.1%
Oxford	2008	577	296	139	1,014	147	6.9	0.9	13.7%
South Oxfordshire	2005	422	374	460	1,252	129	9.7	3.6	36.7%
South Oxfordshire	2006	444	378	452	1,277	129	9.9	3.5	35.4%
South Oxfordshire	2007	423	370	465	1,262	129	9.8	3.6	36.8%
South Oxfordshire	2008	432	370	445	1,252	130	9.6	3.4	35.5%
Vale of White Horse	2005	399	313	435	1,165	118	9.9	3.7	37.4%
Vale of White Horse	2006	403	317	432	1,168	118	9.9	3.7	37.0%
Vale of White Horse	2007	376	311	432	1,135	118	9.6	3.7	38.0%
Vale of White Horse	2008	406	311	415	1,148	118	9.7	3.5	36.1%
West Oxfordshire	2005	262	287	233	805	99	8.1	2.3	29.0%
West Oxfordshire	2006	251	297	229	797	100	8.0	2.3	28.7%
West Oxfordshire	2007	249	292	233	796	102	7.8	2.3	29.3%
West Oxfordshire	2008	242	292	223	779	102	7.6	2.2	28.6%
Oxfordshire Total	2005	2,221	1,636	1,964	5,880	628	9.4	3.1	33.4%
Oxfordshire Total	2006	2,250	1,654	1,946	5,911	630	9.4	3.1	32.9%
Oxfordshire Total	2007	2,114	1,622	1,970	5,770	632	9.1	3.1	34.1%
Oxfordshire Total	2008	2,171	1,620	1,885	5,740	636	9.0	3.0	32.8%

Note: * In local authority order.
Source: Department of Energy and Climate Change, 2010.

Table 4.3 CO2 emissions by local authority in England

Local authority	Year	Industry and commercial	Domestic	Road transport	Total	Population (000s, mid-year estimate)	Total per capita emissions (t)*	Transport per capita emissions (t)	Local transport %
West Berkshire	2008	587	439	809	1,841	151	12.2	5.3	43.9%
Derbyshire	2008	5,177	1,814	1,925	8,945	758	11.8	2.5	21.5%
Fenland, Cambridgeshire	2008	473	223	189	1,036	92	11.3	2.1	18.3%
Chester, Cheshire	2008	494	309	461	1,291	118	10.9	3.9	35.7%
Richmondshire, North Yorkshire	2008	135	133	268	537	51	10.5	5.2	49.9%
Wiltshire	2008	2,016	1,301	1,283	4,694	454	10.3	2.8	27.3%
Warrington	2008	749	463	706	1,934	196	9.9	3.6	36.5%
Harrogate	2008	478	431	587	1,533	156	9.8	3.8	38.3%
Oxfordshire	2008	2,171	1,620	1,885	5,740	636	9.0	3.0	32.8%
Doncaster	2008	862	761	897	2,546	289	8.8	3.1	35.2%
Shropshire	2008	868	812	732	2,509	291	8.6	2.5	29.2%
Kent	2008	5,123	3,250	3,568	11,879	1,402	8.5	2.5	30.0%
Hampshire	2008	4,090	3,184	3,515	10,834	1,284	8.4	2.7	32.4%
Milton Keynes	2008	809	510	594	1,920	233	8.2	2.6	30.9%
Devon	2008	1,941	1,976	1,834	6,096	747	8.2	2.5	30.1%
National (England)	2008	228,137	149,317	131,045	506,526	61,398	8.2	2.1	25.9%
Harlow, Essex	2008	366	172	106	645	80	8.1	1.3	16.5%
St Albans	2008	244	343	491	1,080	135	8.0	3.6	45.5%

Surrey	2008	2,418	2,919	3,252	8,574	1,101	7.8	3.0	37.9%
Cornwall	2008	1,358	1,523	1,052	4,131	529	7.8	2.0	25.5%
South East	2008	23,058	20,295	20,402	63,773	8,369	7.6	2.4	32.0%
Leeds	2008	2,080	1,728	1,647	5,465	779	7.0	2.1	30.1%
Stevenage	2008	257	171	131	560	81	7.0	1.6	23.4%
Stoke-on-Trent	2008	755	549	341	1,647	239	6.9	1.4	20.7%
Oxford	2008	577	296	139	1,014	147	6.9	0.9	13.7%
West Sussex	2008	1,847	1,929	1,667	5,368	789	6.8	2.1	31.0%
Newcastle upon Tyne	2008	791	622	474	1,890	278	6.8	1.7	25.1%
Manchester	2008	1,534	989	687	3,215	473	6.8	1.5	21.4%
Sheffield	2008	1,798	1,191	682	3,666	540	6.8	1.3	18.6%
Kingston upon Hull	2008	865	552	319	1,738	261	6.7	1.2	18.3%
Cambridge	2008	437	236	109	782	119	6.6	0.9	13.9%
Birmingham	2008	2,808	2,224	1,493	6,534	1,019	6.4	1.5	22.8%
Liverpool	2008	1,209	997	602	2,815	441	6.4	1.4	21.4%
Leicester	2008	954	628	341	1,925	304	6.3	1.1	17.7%
York	2008	444	436	296	1,182	195	6.1	1.5	25.1%
Nottingham	2008	821	615	370	1,806	297	6.1	1.2	20.5%
Greater London	2008	20,825	16,740	8,736	46,357	7,668	6.0	1.1	18.8%
Norwich, Norfolk	2008	399	267	128	794	137	5.8	0.9	16.1%
Plymouth	2008	586	486	336	1,414	256	5.5	1.3	23.8%
Bristol	2008	920	857	536	2,320	426	5.4	1.3	23.1%

Note: * Ranked in descending order by total per capita CO2 emissions (t).

Source: Department of Energy and Climate Change, 2010.

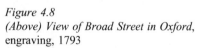

Figure 4.8
(Above) View of Broad Street in Oxford,
engraving, 1793

Source: Farington, Joseph (1747–1821)/London
Metropolitan Archives, City of London/The Bridgeman
Art Library.

Figure 4.9
(Left) Outside the King's Arms, Oxford, 2002 (oil
on linen)

Source: Hamel, Francis
(contemporary artist)/Private collection/The Bridgeman
Art Library.

Figure 4.10
All Saints Church, now the library of Lincoln
College, Oxford (w/c on paper)

Source: Casson, Hugh (1910–99)/Private collection/Hugh
Casson, RA, from *Hugh Casson's Oxford*, Phaidon Press,
1989/The Bridgeman Art Library.

Figure 4.11 St. Giles, Looking Towards St. Mary Magdalen (South), 1903 (colour litho)
Source: Fulleylove, John (1847–1908)/Private collection/The Stapleton Collection/The Bridgeman Art Library.

Figure 4.12 A View of Oxford (oil on millboard)
Source: Turner, William (Turner of Oxford) (1789–1862)/Yale Center for British Art, Paul Mellon Collection, USA/The Bridgeman Art Library.

Figure 4.13 Abingdon Bridge and Church, engraved by Robert Havell the Younger (1793–1878) published 1818 (aquatint)

Source: Havell, William (1782–1857) (after)/Private collection/The Stapleton Collection/The Bridgeman Art Library.

Figure 4.14 The Thames near Henley

Source: Parker, Henry (1858–1930)/Private collection/Photo © Bonhams, London, UK/The Bridgeman Art Library.

Cambridgeshire and Harrogate) are associated with relatively high per capita emissions, in cross-sectoral and transport terms, whereas the lower incomes areas and larger urban areas (London, Liverpool and Manchester), historic university cities (Cambridge, Oxford and York) and very remote urban areas (Plymouth and Norwich) have lower per capita emissions. Some of the low-income northern towns also have surprisingly high per capita emissions because of their high levels of car use (Warrington and Doncaster).

Available potential interventions and packages

There is a very wide range of potential interventions available for use in the Oxfordshire transport planning context that may affect transport CO_2 emissions, including various schemes and wider initiatives. The process used to narrow down the conventional 'long list' was to systematically 'sift' the potential options against agreed criteria (national and local objectives, deliverability and feasibility). This enables a focus on the options with most potential to score well against sustainability criteria, and was carried out with transport planners at Oxfordshire County Council. Policy packages (PPs) were derived, including a number of complementary measures. Each package typically has a level of 'applicability' – business as usual (BAU), low, medium and high. This may be viewed in terms of investment, policy support or initiative; there are also important issues of feasibility and deliverability. The following PPs are used within the Oxfordshire INTRA-SIM modelling:

- PP1 Rail
- PP2 Bus
- PP3 Walk
- PP4 Cycle
- PP5 Highway infrastructure
- PP6 Traffic demand management
- PP7 Pricing
- PP8 Parking management
- PP9 Park and ride
- PP10 Land-use planning
- PP11 Behavioural change
- PP12 Low-emissions vehicles
- PP13 Alternative fuels
- PP14 Slower speeds and ecological driving
- PP15 Freight
- PP16 Long-distance travel substitution.

Hence the coverage is again wide, covering the range of interventions likely to reduce transport CO_2 emissions and also perform well against wider sustainability criteria.

Developing scenarios

Scenarios are developed with a 'trilemma' approach, which is based around three dimensions using major trends and uncertainties affecting transport in Oxfordshire (Table 4.4). A workshop with local transport planning officers was used to help select the perceived three most important issues, in terms of uncertainty and likely impact. These are used to derive the 'possibility space' for future scenario development (Figure 4.15) and three contrasting scenarios have been designed within this space.

Table 4.4 Major trends and uncertainties affecting transport

Trends and uncertainties	Ranking
Economy and governmental	
Economic growth rate (e.g. GDP or other growth metric)	
Funding for transport investment and urban development	**1
Income levels, income inequality	
Tertiary education sector growth	
Socio-demographics	
Population growth	
Age profile (including an ageing population)	
Aspirations and culture – continued 'western consumption' model?	
Technologies	
Clean vehicle technologies	**2
Energy and power supply – renewable sources	
Environmental	
Major environmental shocks – changing climate, flooding, water supply	
Quality of environment and ecology	
Urban issues and transport planning	
Environmental issues – stewardship, extent of 'seriousness' given to them in policy making and implementation	**3
Urban design and built environment quality	
Extent of development and urban sprawl	
Level of sustainability in travel, investment in public transport, walking and cycling	

In Oxfordshire, and indeed much of the UK, funding levels are likely to be a severe constraint on efforts to achieve sustainable travel. The policy intention will, as ever, be there – the 'policy sections' of local transport plans or other transport strategies mostly read very well – but the implementation programme in terms of schemes and initiatives are usually very different to the objectives. Funding problems are evident in the short term, but also over the

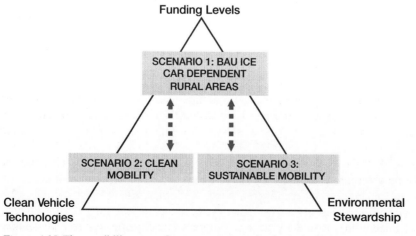

Figure 4.15 The possibility space for transport scenarios in Oxfordshire

Figure 4.16 Broad Street, Oxford. How do we progress towards strategic policy goals more effectively? Enabling sustainable travel is complex and difficult process, requiring infrastructure investment, urban planning, traffic demand management, cleaner vehicles; and also a strong and concerted governmental lead, public awareness, participation and engagement. Changing travel behaviours is complex societal problem requiring a complex and wide-reaching response.

longer term, and authorities find it difficult to progress significantly towards strategic targets such as reducing CO_2 emissions. Such barriers are linked to the centralised funding system, where the larger investments are controlled by the Department for Transport. This needs to change, with funding prioritised and even raised locally. There is also a wider problem in practice. There is a major aversion to innovation (and necessarily risk) in transport planning, and efforts to adopt the newer public transport options, or public realm, cycling and walking schemes are often lacking. Compare some of the practice in the UK to Copenhagen, Delft or Gröningen (cycling and walking); virtually any of the French cities, such as Strasbourg, Montpellier, Bordeaux (tram schemes and public realm); Bogotá and Curitiba (bus rapid transit); San Sebastian, Madrid or Barcelona (public realm); and Freiburg or Malmö (urban extensions); and we can see UK practice is failing to deliver the quality that has already been introduced elsewhere. The good practice has been around for years, and there are many advocates, but internationally leading practice in the UK is rare, and the reasons for this are often process or funding-based.

Nevertheless, despite the difficulties inherent in implementation, both at the city and the county level, three contrasting scenarios were constructed for Oxfordshire:

*   *Scenario 1 – Business as usual (BAU)*: a continuation of the current policy approach (and levels of implementation), with only ad hoc progress being made towards sustainable travel behaviours, no real strategic direction, and low funding levels.

- *Scenario 2 – Clean mobility or 'satisficing with technology'*: a marked change in terms of use of low-emission vehicles, but levels of mobility continue to rise and there are no coordinated efforts to invest in alternatives to the car.
- *Scenario 3 – Sustainable mobility*: here the focus is in developing public transport, walking and cycling options as well as clean vehicle mobility. Urban structure plays an important role in shortening trip distances, and there is a reduction in travel by private motor car. Funding levels change in terms of much higher investment in the non-car modes and the public realm.

Modelling approach

The scenarios are quantified by modelling the policy packages at each level of application. This utilises the Central Oxfordshire Transport Model (COTOM), which includes a Saturn-based transport model and Emme2 public transport model.[2] Other datasets used include vehicle/speed CO2 emission factors (Department for Transport, 2008b), modal CO2 emission factors (Department for Food and Rural Affairs, 2009) and spatial planning assumptions from the South East Plan (Government Office for the South East, 2009). For all policy packages and enabling mechanisms the multi-criteria outputs are calculated relative to the BAU reference case. This leads us to another important but often overlooked issue, namely that the definition of the BAU is critical to the results in quantified scenario analysis and can take various forms, including a projection of current trends, a modelled 'current policy approach', or variants in between. The current policy approach is modelled in the Oxfordshire context.

Appraisal framework

Each scenario is compared relative to its CO2 reduction potential, but also wider multi-criteria impacts. This is an attempt to show that low carbon transport pathways may have differential impacts against other policy goals. A multi-criteria appraisal (MCA) framework is thus developed (Table 4.5), with five main elements and the means by which each can be measured.

The core scenarios are explored below in more detail.

Scenario 2: clean mobility or satisficing with technology

This scenario attempts to illustrate the problem of a partial 'satisficing' approach, concentrating on the technological options of low-emission vehicles and alternative fuels. It assumes a very successful delivery of these to the mass market to deliver reductions in transport CO2 emissions. The scenario and results are outlined in Table 4.6.

The total CO2 reduction impact is 1,057,932 tCO2 per annum (a 37.4 per cent reduction relative to the BAU level in 2030). This represents around 2.5 tCO2 per capita in 2030, relative to a BAU of 4.1 tCO2 per capita in 2030 (and a 2005 transport baseline of 3.8 tCO2 per capita and target of 1.2 tCO2 per capita). If this level of technological penetration could be delivered the gains would be very high, but the assumptions are strong, particularly when compared to current progress in delivering low-emission vehicles in Oxfordshire.

An average vehicle fleet emission level of 95 gCO2/km means the average vehicle in the fleet by 2030 is similar to the current leading Toyota Prius type technology (89 gCO2/km). Similar emission gains are expected with LGVs and HGVs. The penetration of alternative fuels is also ambitious in assumption – 15 per cent alternative fuels (mix of LPG, electric, biofuel) in the car, 25 per cent in HGVs and 40 per cent in the bus. This strategy is thus sub-

Table 4.5 MCA framework

Environment (strategic)	Environment	Accessibility	Safety (local)	Economy
• Total CO_2 emissions by car, LGV, HGV, bus and rail**	• Population affected by noise • Number of households experiencing noise levels above 68db • Population perceiving a noise nuisance • Population experiencing vibration • Number of households experiencing vibration • Air quality index (by nitrogen dioxide, ozone, sulphur dioxide, particulates)	• Hansen measure of accessibility to town centres (by mode)** • Hansen measure of accessibility to hospitals • Hansen measure of accessibility to workplaces • 2026 households within 30 minutes of town centres • 2026 households within 30 minutes of hospitals • 2026 households within 30 minutes of workplaces	• Number of personal injury accidents (PIAs), based on Stats19 data (2007) • Number of accidents resulting in slight injury • Number of accidents resulting in serious injury • Number of accidents involving fatalities	• Journey time reliability • Junction delays** • Travel time on links, by mode • Access to jobs

Note: Only partial reporting is given in the following analysis, concentrating on the metrics as highlighted **.

Figure 4.17 The Time Machine, 1960, written by H. G. Wells, directed by George Pal. The time traveller journeys (from Richmond, Surrey) to the year AD 802,701, where he meets the Eloi, a society of small, child-like people. They live in small communities, doing no work with a frugal diet.They have descended from the leisured class, whilst the downtrodden working class has become the violent, Eloi-eating, but light-fearing, Morlocks: 'There is no difference between time and any of the three dimensions of space except that our consciousness moves along it.'

Source: British Film Institute Stills Collection.

Figure 4.18 The vehicle fleet in Oxfordshire needs to be made radically cleaner in terms of lower CO2 emissions. The policy and legislative responsibility lies with national government, and progress needs to be much quicker than at present – with a target for the total vehicle fleet of less than 95 gCO2/km by 2030.

optimal in risk terms, as it is too narrow in the options being considered, and wider measures need to be considered. However, the importance of achieving a low carbon vehicle fleet is very clear, as this is where the majority of emissions are found. In Oxfordshire this means that even with this level of technology, the targets will not be achieved. These types of calculations seem to be rarely carried out, and there seems to be an absence of serious discussion in national and local transport planning. There is much talk of reducing CO2 emissions in transport, but little evidence of significant reductions on the ground.

These types of implementation pathways will take major efforts from the motor manufacturers, responding to mandatory emission standards, which in turn would require UK governmental legislation. There are issues of remit and jurisdiction, and many actions are not taken at the local Oxfordshire level, but instead nationally, internationally, and by the market. Consumer purchasing choice would also need to change markedly, perhaps with subsidy in the early years to encourage mass market purchase of low-emission vehicles. Clearly the market does not have the 'incentive' to achieve this level of change. There is a clear problem in finding an alternative pathway to the current business model, which is to sell largely petrol or diesel cars, and ideally large and heavy vehicles (which cost more and allow a greater profit margin for the manufacturer). This clearly acts against societal environmental goals. All of this is, or should be, well known but there seems to be little debate and consideration of policy approaches which would help to navigate these problems. There is a critical role at the governmental level to better position the boundaries for commercial operation and consumer choice. This would mean setting up the rules of the market within which businesses can operate

Table 4.6 Clean mobility or satisficing with technology

Policy package	Level of application	Summary specification
PP12 Low-emission vehicles	High (car/LGV)	A total car/LGV fleet at an average of 95gCO2/km and HGVs (fully loaded) at 800gCO2/km.
	High (HGV)	
PP13 Alternative fuels	Medium	Increase in car dieselisation and much greater uptake of biofuels across modes – car 25% diesel (from 15%), 60% petrol, 15% alternative fuels (mix of LPG, electric, biofuel); HGV 75% diesel (from 100%), 25% alternative fuels; bus 60% diesel (from 100%), 40% alternative fuels. No hydrogen in 'medium' level application.

SCENARIO RESULTS (relative to BAU 2030)	Absolute change	Per cent
Climate: carbon dioxide (CO2) emission reduction (tonnes CO2)	–1,057,932	–37.4%
	2.47 tonnes CO2 per capita (2030) relative to BAU of 4.10 (assumed aggregate BAU in 2030 is 2,664,849 tonnes CO2)	
Accessibility: improvement in accessibility to town centres by rail (Hansen composite households)	0	0
Economy: daily junction delay (aggregate seconds)	0	0
Local environment: carbon monoxide (CO) (kgCO)	–4,281,762	–32.8%
Safety: road fatalities (number of fatalities)	0	0

Note: The modelling is based on individual model runs for each level of application of a policy package. MCA indicator impacts are derived from travel distance, mode share and speed outputs. Additivity is assumed between packages.

successfully, but where strategic societal goals can still be met, in this case, to move towards a low emission vehicle fleet. The current progress in moving towards low-emission vehicles in the mass market is much too slow. The low-emission vehicle package by itself achieves a major share of the potential reduction in CO2 emissions; hence it is extremely important to the strategic CO2 reduction goal achievement.

The spatial distribution of CO2 emission also varies across the county. The dominant impact of lower emissions from vehicles means that the largest relative reductions are seen in the non-urban areas, namely in the villages and rural areas surrounding Oxford, where car dependency is highest. Hence this is very much a policy scenario targeted at car users, and the areas where car users are located. This equity dimension is poorly understood and very much underplayed, as central government policy is currently primarily targeted at car users (and by proxy higher income groups) in terms of relying on them to purchase more carbon efficient vehicles. There is little significant wider investment in the non-car modes, which are primarily, but not exclusively, used by lower income groups.

The wider sustainability impacts of the scenario are limited, with the exception of an improvement in carbon monoxide (CO) (–32.8 per cent relative to BAU in 2030), largely due to the change in fuel mix and less reliance on petrol as a fuel for cars. There are no gains made against accessibility, economic or safety objectives, as captured in the multi-criteria appraisal framework. Hence the scenario can be viewed as positive in low CO_2 terms but it performs poorly against wider sustainability objectives. The use of MCA illustrates the complexity in decision-making, where seemingly simple policy choices can have very wide impacts if assessed against multiple criteria which often act in different directions.

Scenario 3: sustainable mobility

Scenario 3 gives a much more balanced approach to reducing transport CO_2 emissions, and achieves much more against the wider sustainability criteria. The scenario results are given in Table 4.7. A wide selection of the policy packages on offer is used, and the total CO_2 reduction impact is 1,365,697 tCO_2 per annum (a 48.3 per cent reduction relative to the BAU level in 2030). The end result is a figure of approximately 2.0 tCO_2 per capita transport emissions in 2030, and this compares to a BAU figure of 4.10 tCO_2 per capita (and relative to a 2005 transport baseline of 3.8 tCO_2 per capita and target of 1.2 tCO_2 per capita). The scenario represents a significant level of intervention, but it is still unaffordable under current funding regimes, and it is also insufficient against assumed targets. This is a major problem for decision-makers.

The scenario hence delivers a significant level of CO_2 reduction. The major CO_2 reduction impacts arise from the following policy packages, and they also include the two packages that were used in Scenario 2 (Clean Mobility), implemented at the same levels of severity:

- PP12 Low-emission vehicles (high): as in Scenario 2 a high level of application is envisaged. The total car fleet averages 95 gCO_2/km and HGVs (fully loaded) 800 gCO_2/km by 2030. This level of new vehicle technology penetration will be very difficult to achieve across the whole vehicle fleet. The levels (2006) for the current new car fleet are at around 165 gCO_2/km and heavy goods vehicles (HGVs) (fully loaded) at 1,100 gCO_2/km.
- PP13 Alternative fuels (medium): as in Scenario 2 there is an increase in diesel cars and a much greater uptake of biofuels across all modes – the figures for the different vehicle fuels in the total fleet are: car – 25 per cent diesel (up from 15 per cent), 60 per cent petrol, 15 per cent alternative fuels (mix of LPG, electric and biofuel); HGV – 75 per cent diesel (from 100 per cent) and 25 per cent alternative fuels; bus – 60 per cent diesel (from 100 per cent) and 40 per cent alternative fuels.
- PP14 Slower speeds and ecological driving (medium): this has a major impact, representing 20 mph speed limits in all major towns and 50 mph speed limits on all rural single-carriageway roads; lower speed limits are supported by variable signage and enforcement. There is also a targeted public education campaign concerning ecological driving skills. This package achieves a 5 per cent reduction in CO_2 emissions.
- PP15 Freight (medium): HGV freight movements represent over 20 per cent of traffic on key routes in Oxfordshire, particularly the A34 and M40, and the large and heavy vehicles are high CO_2 emitters. An assumed increase in rail freight capacity between the south coast ports at Southampton and the Midlands and North, together with advisory HGV routing, would reduce heavy goods vehicle traffic through the county. This package also achieves a 5 per cent reduction in CO_2 emissions.
- The other selected policy packages also have a direct impact on CO_2 emissions, but the scales of impact are less than the above. PP1 Rail (medium), PP2 Bus (medium), PP3 Walk (high), PP4 Cycle (high), PP6 TDM/Active traffic management (medium), PP7

Table 4.7 Sustainable mobility

Policy package	Level of application	Summary specification
PP1 Rail	Medium	Interchange improvements, mainline network frequency upgrades (Reading–Oxford–Midlands) and assumed new networks (Cotswold line upgrade; Evergreen 3, Oxford–Bicester–London Marylebone; and East–West rail, Oxford–Milton Keynes–Cambridge–Felixstowe), new Milton Park station.
PP2 Bus	Medium	Improved Premium Routes to main housing and employment sites; improved bus services between large towns and small towns; electric and hybrid buses in Oxford.
PP3 Walk	High	High-quality pedestrian environment and streetscape upgrades in Oxford, larger towns, smaller towns and villages, and connections to Rights of Way network.
PP4 Cycle	High	High-quality network improvements, integrated cycle parking in Oxford, larger towns, smaller towns and villages, cycle hire schemes in Oxford and large towns. New links from new developments.
PP5 Highway infrastructure	BAU	None
PP6 TDM/active traffic management	Medium	Access to Oxford programme, including HOV lane on A34; routeing measures from Transport Networks Review (TNR); Traffic Incident Management (TIM) programme; expansion of real-time monitoring systems across the county.
PP7 Pricing	Medium	Road pricing scheme across Oxfordshire and the UK, charging 20p per kilometre for all vehicles.
PP8 Parking management	Medium	Reduced parking supply in new developments and maximum standards applied, increased use of controlled parking zones.
PP9 Park and ride	Medium	Increase capacity at existing sites: Seacourt, Redbridge, Thornhill; new remote park and ride sites for Oxford on A34(s), A40(w) and A34(n)/A41 corridors, used for accessing Premium Bus Routes.
PP10 Land-use planning	Medium	Development located according to South East Plan but better strategic co-ordination and sustainability travel aspirations achieve 25% lower car trip rates in new developments.
PP11 Smarter choice behavioural measures	Medium	Enhanced travel planning (workplace and schools), widespread travel awareness campaign, including increased availability of pre-trip and en-route information, personalised travel planning in new developments, support for car clubs.
PP12 Low-emission vehicles	High (Car/LGV) High (HGV)	A total car/LGV fleet at an average of 95gCO2/km and HGVs (fully loaded) at 800gCO2/km.
PP13 Alternative fuels	Medium	Increase in car dieselisation and much greater uptake of biofuels across modes – car 25% diesel (from 15%), 60% petrol, 15% alternative fuels (mix of LPG, electric, biofuel); HGV 75% diesel (from 100%), 25% alternative fuels; bus 60% diesel (from 100%), 40% alternative fuels. No hydrogen in 'medium' level application.

Table 4.7 Sustainable mobility—*continued*

Policy package	Level of application	Summary specification
PP14 Slower speeds and ecological driving	Medium	20mph speed limits in all major towns and 50mph speed limits on all rural single-carriageway roads; lower speed limits are supported by variable signage and enforcement. There is also a targeted public education campaign concerning ecological driving skills.
PP15 Freight	Medium	Increase in rail freight capacity between the south coast ports at Southampton and the Midlands and North, together with advisory HGV routing.
PP16 Long-distance travel substitution	Medium	Improved coach/rail links to a range of major destinations, including London, Oxford and all London airports, and along major corridors – Birmingham/Manchester, Oxford–Southampton (M40/A34 road/rail corridor), Oxford–Bristol (via Swindon).

SCENARIO RESULTS (relative to BAU 2030)*	Absolute	Percentage
Climate: carbon dioxide (CO2) emission reduction (tonnes CO2)	−1,365,697	−48.3%
	2.0 tonnes CO2 per capita (2030) relative to BAU of 4.10 (assumed aggregate BAU in 2030 is 2,664,849 tonnes CO2)	
Accessibility: improvement in accessibility to town centres by rail (Hansen composite households**)	−3,111	−28.3%
Economy: daily junction delay (aggregate seconds)	−32,092	−20.8%
Local environment: carbon monoxide (CO) (kgCO)	−5,399,618	−41.4%
Safety: Road fatalities (number of fatalities)	22.6	−15.0%

Note: ** Hansen composite measures are well used in accessibility planning. They measure accessibility for a given sub-area (in this case Oxfordshire) to all other sub-areas (all town centres in Oxfordshire).

Pricing (medium), PP8 Parking management (medium), PP9 Park and ride (medium), PP10 Land-use planning (medium), PP11 Behavioural change (medium), and PP16 Long-distance travel substitution (medium), for example, all lead to limited CO2 emission reductions as expected impacts are often masked by other traffic filling up the space gained in network improvements. The major gains are made when car and freight emissions are tackled (the vast majority of emissions). The interpretation of these types of result needs careful consideration. This is not an argument for not investing in the non-car modes, simply a result of the dominance of car use relative to other travel modes. PPs 1–4, 6–11 and 16 lead to a level of CO2 reduction and they are also useful for non carbon issues, such as supporting the wider quality of life in urban centres.

The actual modelling assumptions are also critical to the appraisal. For example, the initial specification of road pricing (PP7) on the major strategic roads in Oxfordshire actually led to an increase in travel and emissions, as traffic was diverted onto the non-strategic highway (rural roads) and longer travel distances arose. This again provides a useful lesson in terms of process – INTRA-SIM and similar appraisal simulations allow a speedy comparison of

Figure 4.19 The public transport network, including rail and bus, and potentially bus rapid transit and/or tram, could be massively developed to provide a much better offer for public transport across Oxfordshire and the surrounding region.

Figure 4.20 Park and ride. There are already some progressive elements of a public transport strategy, such as Park and Ride around Oxford, but there needs to be much more support for public transport.

Figure 4.21 Market structure. There are some difficult decisions to be made: the market structure within which public transport has to operate does not assist in providing state-of-the art services, rather it leads to fragmented and patchy provision, spatially, temporally and in quality.

Figure 4.22 Park End Street, Oxford. Oxford is a beautiful city, but has been partly ruined by poor traffic engineering that fails to consider the importance of urban design. This is the route into the city from the station, and requires less priority given to the car and the associated traffic paraphernalia, with the public realm redesigned for pedestrians, cyclists and public transport.

Figure 4.23 'View from engineering'. Oxford is a compact and relatively high-density city, it has excellent levels of cycling, walking and public transport usage, but this is largely confined to Oxford. There needs to be a major investment in cycling, walking and public transport in the surrounding urban areas.

Figure 4.24 Gloucester Green, Oxford. There are some excellent new developments within Oxford; Gloucester Green providing an example of attractive, urban, mixed use infill, with residential, retail uses and an outdoor market, adjacent to the city centre and bus station.

Figure 4.25
(Above) Cycling. Oxford has a reputation as a cycling city, though there can be much more done to improve facilities, including segregated cycle lanes on key arterial routes, better parking facilities and even a cycle hire scheme. Cycling facilities also need to be developed beyond the city centre and in the surrounding towns.

Figure 4.26
(Left) The public realm. The public realm in Oxford is often of excellent quality, but the city and surrounding towns in particular, would benefit from large investment in urban design and the public realm.

likely outputs from a series of interventions. Unsuitable impacts (and hence intervention definition) can be revisited and remodelled. In this case, a distance-based charge for the complete network, and better still an emissions-based charge, would lead to a greater reduction in travel and emissions. The idea with the latter specification would be to charge vehicles by distance travelled and type of vehicle, so that the heavier, more polluting vehicles pay more. This orientates road pricing more to the goal of CO_2 emission reductions. Hence the transport planning process can be iterative, where interventions are redefined to optimise the achievement against objectives. This is a critical element of objectives-based strategy development.

Low carbon transport and wider MCA impacts

The wider sustainability impacts of low carbon transport scenarios are also of great importance, but seldom well understood. The spatial distribution of CO_2 emissions across the county again shows major CO_2 reductions are made in the rural and car dependent areas in Oxfordshire, relative to the BAU in 2030. Feasibly, some scenarios may be very beneficial in CO_2 reduction terms, but do less for social or economic objectives. INTRA-SIM allows us to 'read across' the different metrics. Just four of the available indicators are discussed here – daily junction delay (a proxy for the economy), accessibility by train (social), carbon monoxide (local environment) and road fatalities (safety):

- Daily junction delay: reduces in aggregate (by 32,000 aggregate seconds, or 20.8 per cent, relative to BAU in 2030), hence traffic is viewed as travelling more 'smoothly' with less delay at junctions.
- Accessibility by rail to town centres: much increased accessibility in the areas surrounding the mainline rail network (Reading–Oxford–Midlands) and assumed new networks (Cotswold line upgrade; Evergreen 3, Oxford–Bicester–London Marylebone; and east–west rail, Oxford–Milton Keynes–Cambridge–Felixstowe) with an increase in accessibility of 28.3 per cent relative to BAU in 2030.
- Carbon monoxide: reductions are made virtually across the whole county with the exceptions of clustered increases in some of the urban areas. There is a reduction of 5,399,618 kgCO, or 41.4 per cent, relative to BAU in 2030.
- Safety: road fatalities reduce by 23, or 15.0 per cent, relative to BAU in 2030.

The economic metric can also be viewed as problematic. Junction delay (and annual car time) is often used as a proxy to other economic indicators such as GDP growth. However, this is a simplistic and often flawed view, indeed using such a measure by itself may mean that measures to reduce CO_2 emissions are not viewed 'positively' in economic terms. INTRA-SIM has a wider variety of indicators available, but care is required in interpreting results, particularly where available indicators need refining and where the impacts are often indirect. Wider impacts can also be explored across the full MCA framework, but are not discussed here. It is likely that appraisal methods need to change if major gains in CO_2 reduction are to be delivered through policy measures such as slower travel speeds; currently these are often viewed negatively in time-savings calculations.

More radical interventions: towards a 60 per cent and deeper reduction

Scenario 3 delivers major gains in CO_2 reduction and wider sustainability benefits. However, it appears that reducing transport CO_2 emissions on an area-wide basis by anything more

Figure 4.27 High Street, Oxford. There are some efforts to manage traffic movement in the city centre, with cars not allowed on particular roads. However, this needs to be made more widespread, including across the surrounding towns wherever possible. This can be incorporated into a programme of 'smarter choices', including travel planning and traffic demand management measures. The experiences of the Sustainable Travel Demonstration Towns programme in the UK is extremely promising (Darlington, Peterborough and Worcester) and needs to be expanded as common practice across all urban areas.

than 20–30 per cent is likely to present difficult decisions. These difficulties will be increased by the current reductions in national funding levels. Scenario 3, although representing a large level of investment beyond current funding levels available, still only delivers an expected level of 2.0 tCO2 per capita in 2030, relative to a BAU of 4.10 tCO2 per capita, and a 2005 transport baseline of 3.8 tCO2 per capita, and target of 1.2 tCO2 per capita. The possibilities as determined here with a set of strong policy packages only gets halfway towards the target, and even this is difficult to actually achieve. The scale of intervention being considered, even in the innovative authorities such as Oxfordshire, is nowhere near enough to deliver the 'fair share' contribution towards a national CO2 reduction target.

The implication of this conclusion is not good news, and perhaps underlines many peoples' belief (including politicians) that CO2 reductions on the scale required are not feasible under the current governance mechanisms. In addition to innovative thinking, there is a need for commitment and leadership at all levels and from all stakeholders. This conclusion applies across the UK, but also in other contexts, including the high per capita transport CO2 emitting locations, such as in Australasia, North America and the Middle East. In these locations, the current average per capita transport CO2 emissions are much higher than those found in Oxfordshire. There is a global atrophy in terms of policy actions, commitment and the necessary levels of investment.

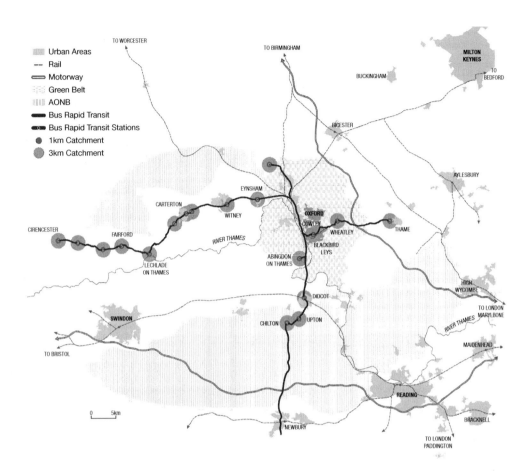

Figure 4.28 A future transport and urban planning strategy for the Oxfordshire Sub-Region
Source: Mapping by Bally Meeda and Urban Graphics.

Very deep reductions in CO2 emissions, and significant movement to wider sustainability goals, would require moving towards the 'high level' of application of the policy packagesas considered in Oxfordshire, and beyond. This may mean radical measures and initiatives, certainly in terms of the present day's debate. Key investments would include new local rail or quality public transport links. There is much potential in re-using disused railway lines, closed around the time of the Beeching cuts in 1963.[3] The routes of these lines are often still protected and preserved from development. For example, a new bus rapid transit (or light rapid transit or tram–train) network for Oxford and the sub-region could be developed, with four lines serving Reading–Abingdon–Oxford; Cirencester–Witney–Oxford; Woodstock–Oxford; and High Wycombe–Thame–Cowley–Oxford. New development could be purposively shaped around the stations on these routes, with increased densities and mixed uses in the surrounding pedestrian area catchments. Figure 4.28 gives an example strategy where transport investment is better linked to urban development. The public transport network is hence developed at the sub-regional level, linking the major urban areas, and helping the car dependent hinterland in rural Oxfordshire to have an attractive public transport option for some important journeys (Hickman et al., 2013). The projects would need to be implemented over a period of time due to the potential cost, but with consistent investment, say to 2030. There are, however, difficulties in pursuing such a project under the current project appraisal system in the UK: the cost–benefit ratio is likely to be low due to the lack of usage along 'dead running' sections (in the rural areas) relative to the project cost. This calculation ignores many of the potential wider benefits in terms of mode shift and effective city design, but these issues are not effectively considered in the current appraisal practice in the UK. The projects would also require some very effective strategic planning, an increase of densities around the interchanges in the urban areas along the route, and a forward-looking policy approach over 10–20 years. All of these areas remain difficult in the UK as the current transport and urban planning governmental framework is relatively weak.

In addition there can be a range of supporting measures: fare level changes; more extensive bus services in rural areas; better network planning and integration; taxi–bus type schemes for rural areas; a much improved public realm for pedestrians; cycle networks and hire facilities across the county; road pricing (at a high charge per kilometre); car-free developments, higher parking charges and restrictions in parking supply; much extended park and ride with 'remote' parking sites next to major routes; widespread, mass market smarter choice behavioural measures; and slower speed limits on all roads. International best practice in transport planning, as found in public transport in Zurich, Kassel, Freiburg, Strasbourg or Montpellier; and cycling facilities in Gröningen or Delft, needs to become standard practice. Despite the good intentions

Figure 4.29 'Heading home'. An effective process for transport and city planning would be to incorporate the principles of backcasting within strategy development and implementation: agree what we would like our travel behaviours and cities to be like in 2030, and develop a programme backwards to attempt to achieve this.

Source: Harry Rutter.

of many transport planners over the last 20 years, this has not happened. The effective transferability of good practice and a better understanding of the transitioning process towards sustainable travel behaviours must become a central concern, together with a real focus on the monitoring of progress against objectives and the iterative redefinition of strategy and programme if progress is not being made.

There are also wider issues involved in the transition to different travel behaviours. Improved networks, facilities and urban planning are only part of the rationale for travel, and the individual motivations and the wider workings of society are also critical. It is here that some of the emerging literature in transport planning sheds some light. There are important psychological and social and cultural dimensions to people's choice of travel. Lucas et al. (2011), for example, describe the motivations that may underlie individual choice processes, including needs and aspirations, social factors (identity and norms), beliefs, attitudes and values and behavioural intentions. These are also influenced by information and marketing, and of course interrelate with the networks, opportunities and urban form that are more conventionally the focus of transport planning. It is these types of factors that we tend to ignore when thinking about and modelling transport behaviours, and also when shaping policies and strategies for transport. This understanding can be taken further by considering the wider social and cultural context to life and travel, often brought together under the research around mobilities (Urry, 2000; Kaufmann, 2002; Sheller and Urry, 2006; Cresswell, 2006; Urry, 2007). This wider understanding of why people travel needs to be much more clearly understood and brought into the development of transport strategies at the local level. As yet we only have an emerging understanding of how these areas might combine, and, critically, the potentialities for change. These areas are further discussed in Chapter 8.

Conclusions: optimising strategies

The transport sector hence needs new approaches to demonstrate and discuss the potential pathways towards deep 'trend-break' reductions in CO2 emissions. This is more so in an era of very difficult funding constraints and antipathy towards strategic planning. The move towards sustainable travel behaviours needs to be progressive and area-wide; and low carbon targets also need to be consistent with wider sustainability objectives – this demands an effective, coordinated and consistent approach over time.

This chapter has compared different packages of measures within alternative future scenarios and examined these against wider sustainability objectives. The INTRA-SIM model particularly allows the exploration of the strategic policy choices in a transparent and participatory manner, with the role playing element allowing the different options to be tested by a range of participants. This makes explicit some of the tensions evident for decision-makers involved in local transport planning. The central arguments made are summarised below:

1   Oxfordshire provides a difficult case study but there are several lessons that can be drawn. There is a historic and compact central city, with good levels of walking, cycling and public transport, and a surrounding periphery that is much more dispersed and car dependent. This geography is common in many city sub-regions. Low carbon transport scenarios need an integrated package of measures and to be assessed against multi-criteria impacts. Depending on the composition of the scenarios considered, impacts are likely to vary substantially relative to economic, social and local environmental goals.

2   Wide-ranging scenarios are required to achieve deep reductions in transport CO2, and these should include low-emission vehicles, alternative fuels, rail, bus, walk, cycle,

behavioural change, slower speeds, freight planning, spatial planning, etc. An important issue here is remit. The interventions considered cover the responsibilities of Oxfordshire County Council and other key public and private decision-makers, including those at the national and European levels.

3   Policy options and schemes can be iteratively redefined to achieve the stated policy objectives through a different specification, changes in network routing, a tightening of legislation, or improvements in incentives. This stage of iteration and refinement is often overlooked in transport and urban planning. It also gives further opportunity to different stakeholders, if a transparent process is followed, to explore the possible implications of particular policy options and the progress against objectives.

4   Scenario costs (particularly in view of current funding constraints within the transport sector) would provide an additional dimension to the analysis, and are not assessed here, as would political and public implementability. Often the 'optimum theoretical' strategies fail because little consideration is given to deliverability issues, as illustrated by much of the experience in introducing road pricing regimes. Perhaps political and public acceptability should be considered first, and a consensus produced, before the technical work is undertaken, so that abortive work is avoided. Affordability issues are then tackled by programmes which work towards societal goals consistently over the long term.

5   Impacts across multiple indicators often work in different directions, and the use of a tool such as INTRA-SIM illustrates this well. Trade-offs will need to be made in putting together future strategies. For example, aggregate time savings (and junction delay/aggregate annual car time) become less important, as other measures of economic performance are refined (such as the economic performance and competitiveness of urban areas), and the achievement of CO_2 reduction, improvement in accessibility, safety and local air quality become more important. MCA also offers the potential to weight objectives and criteria, including changes in weighting over time, hence assisting in the achievement of the important strategic societal goals that are being adopted (Saxena, 2012; Hickman et al., 2010b).

Achieving deep reductions in transport CO_2 emissions is likely to prove very demanding, for example requiring a move towards the 'high level' of application of the policy packages considered in Oxfordshire, and beyond. These types of measures whet the appetite of many transport planners, yet are usually impossible to deliver in the current public and political context. This is the problem to be resolved in Oxfordshire and other similar contexts – how to develop and deliver more radical transport strategies that can lead to significant change. Castells (1978, p. 120) reminds us that:

> public transport becomes a synonym for discomfort, for congestion, for oppression, for compulsory timing [. . .] then one thinks only of escaping it, of autonomy, of the capacity of unrestrained autonomy; the 'need' is thus created and the market is there, all ready to satisfy the demand of the consumer – it is 'the reign of the car for individual freedom'. And once the cycle is begun, it is impossible to stop it.

The current level of debate, investment and implementation will not lead to significantly reduced transport CO_2 emissions in Oxfordshire. There needs to be a much greater focus on meaningful participation, and on preparing and selling a consensus over the key strategic and controversial decision points. It is perhaps here that new participatory tools can become important. Many of the younger, and next, generation of voters are used to conversing in a gaming and e-interaction world. Perhaps these new means of social interaction can be utilised to develop the 'strategic conversations' of Van der Heijden (1996) and others. This is critically required in transport planning, perhaps leading to a much widened participation in decision-making. Ultimately, much better progress in the implementation of supposedly radical measures can be achieved. Consensus building over transport futures hence becomes ever more important. Participatory scenario analysis and backcasting can perhaps help provide some of the answers, but of course we have a long way to go from our current problem of unrestrained autonomy.

Notes

1 The INTRA-SIM Oxfordshire study was developed by Halcrow and University of Oxford, Transport Studies Unit, and funded by Oxfordshire County Council, 2009–10. It includes the development of an INTRA-SIM model (Integrated Transport Appraisal, Decision Support and Simulation) that can be used to explore the major strategic investment choices available and their likely multi-criteria impacts (Hickman et al., 2010b).
2 SATURN and Emme are both travel demand software packages and well used in the UK.
3 The Beeching Report reviewed the need for an extensive railway network in Great Britain in view of increasing motorisation. It recommended that all lines should be run as profitable concerns, and that the financial losses being incurred by poorly used services should be reduced. The report started by quoting the prime minister, from 1960, to provide its overall aim: 'First, the industry must be of a size and pattern suited to modern conditions and prospects. In particular, the railway system must be modelled to meet current needs, and the modernisation plan must be adapted to this new shape.' Out of a total of 29,000 km of railway, Beeching recommended that 9,700 km, including commuter, industrial and rural branch lines, should be closed, and that some of the remaining lines should be kept open only for freight. Over 2,000 stations were recommended for closure. The report prompted much concern from local communities who were to lose their rail services, many of which had no other options for public transport, and to this day have since relied on either replacement bus services or usually use of the private car. Over 11,000 km of lines were removed in the period 1950–1974 (Beeching, 1963).

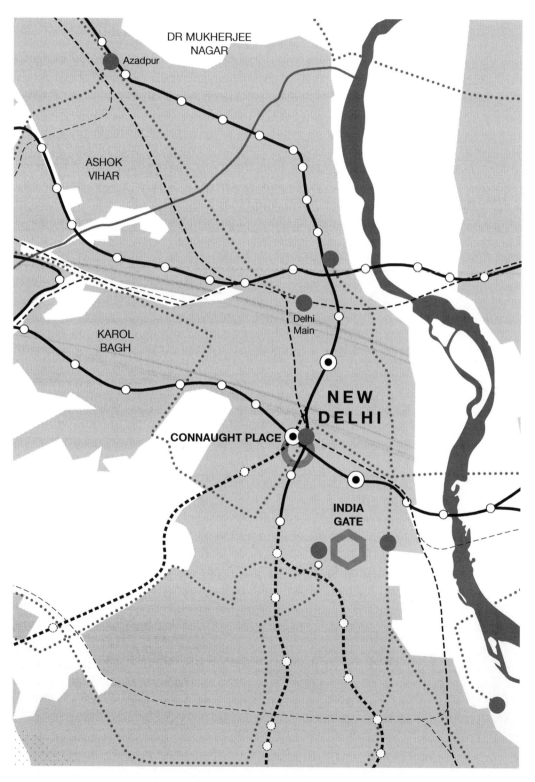

Figure 5.1 Delhi
Source: Mapping by Bally Meeda and Urban Graphics.

5   Breaking the projected trend (Delhi)

> The Emperor published an edict, commanding all his subjects, upon great penalties, to break the smaller end of their eggs. The people so highly resented this law, that our histories tell us there have been six rebellions raised on that account; wherein one Emperor lost his life, and another his crown [. . .]. It is computed, that eleven thousand persons have, at several times, suffered death, rather than submit to break their eggs at the smaller end.
>
> (Jonathan Swift, *Gulliver's Travels*, 1726, p. 44)

Introduction

Delhi is one of the world's largest megacities, rapidly growing over recent years, with a pattern of growth similar to a cluster of South Asian cities including Bangalore, Bangkok, Jakarta, Karachi, Lahore, Manila and Mumbai. All these cities face similar challenges in terms of urban transport. The dramatic projected rise in GHG and CO_2 emissions poses a major challenge for Asia, but also with global repercussions due to the scale involved. Population growth, increased urbanisation and sprawl, and increased average incomes and consumption, mean that travel demand is rising rapidly. The supply of transport funding and infrastructure to meet these challenges lags behind the growth in demand. Critically, there are limited funds available for investment, and this together with poor coordination and inertia in policy processes means that highway construction and motorisation are often the main elements of investment programmes. Naisbitt (1996, p. 10) sets the context and challenge: 'What is happening in Asia is by far the most important development in the world today [. . .] not only for Asians, but also for the entire planet'.

The choice of context within case studies is critical in 'bounding' or 'framing' the lessons that can be derived (Flyvbjerg, 2011; Dimitriou, 2006a), and cities in Asia, in particular, provide us with some very different understandings of the pathways towards sustainable mobility in view of the transport baselines and the opportunities. Urban traffic growth and congestion levels are at extreme levels in many parts of Asia, particularly in cities such as Delhi, Mumbai, Bangkok and Manila, with very long commute and journey times being part of everyday life for a significant cohort of the population. The urban transport problem in Asia has been considered since at least the 1970s, with various attempts to describe the 'malady' or difficulties in travel, essentially the immense growth in traffic demand, the resulting casualties, environmental pollution, poor conditions for cyclists and pedestrians, congestion, and poor public realm; and the differing strategies for dealing with these issues, often in the face of low funding levels (Thompson, 1977; 1983; Dimitriou and Banjo, 1990; Dimitriou, 1992; Schipper et al., 2000; Gwilliam, 2002; Asian Development Bank, 2009; Darido et al., 2009).[1] Barter (2000) describes the different developmental paths taken by selected cities in

Figure 5.2 View of the Jama Masjid (photo), Delhi, India. It is home to a rapidly growing population; but how does Delhi grow in developmental terms whilst also having a limited environmental impact?

Source: Photo © Luca Tettoni/The Bridgeman Art Library.

Asia, with the growth of the traffic-saturated bus cities (Bangkok, Jakarta, Manila) due to the rapid motorisation and low investment in transport infrastructure, and the eventual movement into congested conditions and gridlock. Other cities have developed from motorcycle cities (Hanoi and Ho Chi Minh City), but again increased levels of mobility have been overtaken by motorisation with similar effects (Figure 5.3).

The possibilities for the future seem to include the conventional model (1970s–2000s) of developing the motor car city (based on the US dispersed urban structure, or other similar variants from North America or Australasia). A major difficulty is that this cannot be afforded in terms of building the appropriate road infrastructure in cities with low income bases, and of course there are fundamental environmental, social and indeed economic difficulties in such an approach. Mumford (1968, p. 92) provides an early warning of the problems of planning for the private car, yet the same mistakes seem to be endlessly repeated on a global scale:

When Congress voted last year for a twenty-six-billion-dollar highway programme, the most charitable thing to assume about this action is that they didn't have the faintest notion of what they were doing. Within the next fifteen years they will doubtless find out. But by that time it will be too late to correct all the damage to our cities and our countryside [. . .] that this ill-conceived and absurdly unbalanced programme will have wrought.

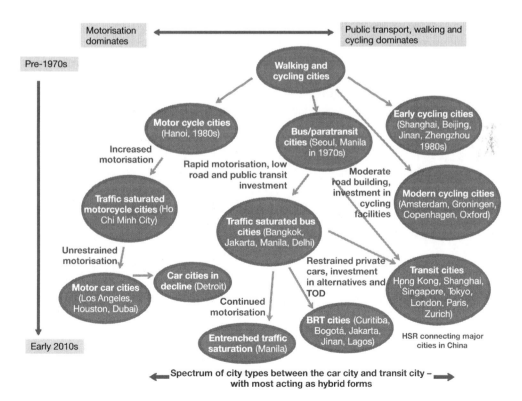

Figure 5.3 Developmental paths for transport in Asian cities
Source: Developing Barter, 2000.

There is often major public and civil society resistance to freeway building, yet, arguably, this remains the mainstream model within transport strategies and implementation in Asia. Traffic engineering, in practice, often reflects the traditional thinking from previous decades. The alternative, which is gaining great momentum, is in gradually developing the transit city (with examples in Seoul and Singapore) or indeed the bus rapid transit (BRT) city (Jinan and Jakarta). The BRT model has become very popular, inspired by the experience of Curitiba from the 1970s onwards (led by Mayor Jamie Lerner) and Bogotá in the 1990s (Mayor Enrique Peñalosa). BRT has become the central feature of transport strategies in an increasing number of cities in Asia, with a developing series of BRT schemes in cities such as Hyderabad, Pune, Taipei, Kunming, Beijing, Hangzhou and Dalian. There are now over 200 schemes in operation or being planned; BRT is affordable for many municipalities, and in terms of speed, capacity, and comfort is similar to many metro or tram systems (Wright, 2010; Hildago, 2009). India is central to much of this developing practice and it illustrates well the challenges, and efforts being made, in reducing the potential growth in motorisation (Tiwari and Jain, 2010).

India is the world's second most populous country, with 1.2 billion persons, and a greater population than Europe, Africa and the entire Western hemisphere. The population is likely to exceed that of China by 2030, with India becoming the world's most populous country. Some of the illustrations are very illuminating: Indian boys, or girls, below the age of 5 exceed 62 million (Haub and Sharma, 2006), marginally more than the total UK population. India is also noted as the largest democracy in the world and the seventh ranked country by its geographical area. The northwest of the country was home to the ancient Indus Valley civilisation (dating from the Bronze Age, 3300–1300 BC) and the first known settlements date back to 8,500 years ago (Reddy, 2003). India has a very diverse and distinct culture, with major religions playing significant roles, including Hinduism, Buddhism, Jainism and Sikhism (originating locally) and Christianity and Islam (arriving from overseas). In terms of modern history, the region was gradually annexed by the British East India Company from the early eighteenth century, and colonised as part of the British Empire. India became an independent nation in 1947, after a historic struggle led by Mahatma Gandhi and the Indian National Congress (Markovits, 2004).

The major urban areas within India are given in Table 5.1, with three megacities (over 10 million in metropolitan population) in Mumbai, Delhi and Kolkata, and a further ten cities with more than 2 million in city population. The rate of urbanisation is relatively low at 30 per cent, hence the rural villages and towns remain very important in demographic terms. Mahatma Gandhi noted that 'India lives in its villages', yet this is changing substantially over time.

Some of the key socio-demographic statistics for India are given in Table 5.2. Current population growth is at 1.3 per cent per annum, higher than a Western industrialised context, or that of China, but much less than found in India in previous decades. Gross national income (GNI) per capita is low at $1,220 per capita, less than half the levels in China. Gross domestic product (GDP) growth varies from 4 to 9 per cent per annum in recent years, which is high by global standards, but of course per capita GDP levels are low. Although India is a very important emerging economic power, only a fraction of Indians are benefiting from the growth. Material aspirations and consumption are both growing rapidly, but again from very low levels relative to industrialised country standards. Motorisation is at 15 vehicles/1,000 population, mobile phone subscriptions are at 30 per 100 persons and Internet use at 5 per 100 persons. All of these figures are substantially below the levels found in China. CO_2 emissions are also low at 1.3 tons per capita (2007/2008 data, World Bank, 2010a). But of course most of these metrics are rising rapidly, and because of the population base, aggregate levels are already

Table 5.1 India – major urban areas (city populations over 2 million, 2011)

No.	City	State	Urban metropolitan	City population
1	Mumbai	Maharashtra	18,414,288	12,478,447
2	Delhi	Delhi	16,314,838	11,007,835
3	Bangalore	Karnataka	8,499,399	8,425,970
4	Hyderabad	Andhra Pradesh	7,749,334	6,809,970
5	Ahmedabad	Gujarat	6,352,254	5,570,585
6	Chennai	Tamil Nadu	8,696,010	4,681,087
7	Kolkata	West Bengal	14,112,536	4,486,679
8	Surat	Gujarat	4,585,367	4,462,002
9	Pune	Maharashtra	5,049,968	3,115,431
10	Jaipur	Rajasthan	3,073,350	3,073,350
11	Lucknow	Uttar Pradesh	2,901,474	2,815,601
12	Kanpur	Uttar Pradesh	2,920,067	2,767,031
13	Nagpur	Maharashtra	2,497,777	2,405,421

Source: Census Organisation of India, 2011.

Table 5.2 India – World Development Indicators

Indicator	1990	2000	2005	2008	2009
Population, total	849,515,000	1,015,923,000	1,094,583,000	1,139,964,932	1,155,347,678
Population growth (annual %)	2.0	1.7	1.4	1.3	1.3
GDP per capita (current US$)	374	453	765	1065	1134
GDP growth (annual %)	5.5	4.0	9.3	5.1	7.7
Life expectancy at birth, total (years)	58.2	61.3	62.8	63.7	–
Fertility rate, total (births per woman)	4.0	3.3	2.9	2.7	–
Energy use (kg of oil equivalent per capita)	375	450	488	–	–
CO_2 emissions (metric tons per capita)	0.8	1.2	1.3	–	–
Motor vehicles (per 1,000 people)	–	–	15*	–	–
Mobile cellular subscriptions (per 100 people)	0.0	0.4	8.2	30.4	–
Internet users (per 100 people)	0.0	0.5	2.5	4.5	–

Note: * 2006 data; motor vehicles (passenger cars, buses, vans, lorries; not including two wheelers).

Source: World Bank, 2010a.

Figure 5.4 Traffic growth in Delhi. The potential traffic growth in Delhi could be huge – the very challenging task is to break the trend.

high. In aggregate terms, India is the world's fourth largest CO_2 emitting country, after China, the USA, and Russia (International Energy Agency, 2010b).

The choice confronting India represents the classic dilemma for the emerging countries in Asia, and indeed South America and Africa. The choice is over what levels of 'development' should be encouraged at the individual and national levels (including in income levels and economic growth), but at the same time providing this in an inclusive way, and through not adversely impacting the environment. Development is of course multi-dimensional, and it includes wide-ranging objectives as encapsulated in the Millennium Development Goals (MDGs).[2] The recent climate change issues have given an added impetus to the debate, with trend-breaking futures now required to help mitigate the likely impacts of global warming. The greatest adverse impacts, perversely, are likely to occur in those countries which have polluted least in historical terms. Again, the developing world gets the raw deal.

This chapter takes the problems of rapid traffic growth in Asia as its context and considers the possibilities for development within India, using the case study of Delhi. It is largely based on work carried out for the Asian Development Bank.[3] A baseline and projection for transport CO_2 emissions are developed to 2030, and consideration is given to appropriate future levels of emissions, with 'global equity' being used as the basis for target development. Scenario analysis is then used to develop different potential futures for transport in Delhi and a clear pathway towards sustainable transport is described.

The megacity context

Delhi is located on the River Yamuna (a tributary of the River Ganges) and has been continuously inhabited since at least the sixth century BC. It is the site of many important ancient
remains, for example, believed to be the site of Indraprastha (the City of Indra).[4] Delhi grew
as a political, cultural and commercial city and as centre of trade routes in northern India and
wider Asia. It has served as a capital of kingdoms and empires and has been invaded, ransacked
and rebuilt many times. The urban area, best described as polycentric, is effectively a cluster
of many cities spread across the wider urban area. The 'transport' rationale shaped the location
and growth of the city: in 1639 the walled city was built as the capital of the Mughal
Empire (1526–1857), which at the height of its power (around 1700) controlled most of the
Indian subcontinent, extending from Bengal in the east to Balochistan in the west, Kashmir
in the north, to the Kaveri basin in the south, and covered a population of between 110 and
150 million.

Delhi became the capital of India, superseding Kolkata, under the reign of George V in
1911, part of the British Raj (the colonial rule of India from 1858 to 1947). New Delhi was
built as the new capital city in the 1920s; the foundation stone of the city was laid in 1911.
It was planned by Sir Edwin Lutyens and Sir Herbert Baker, two leading British architects
of the time. New Delhi is known for its wide, tree-lined boulevards, of a very different style
to the rest of Delhi, and is home to many national institutions and landmarks. Connaught
Circus echoes Place de la Concorde in Paris, providing a central monument or display for the

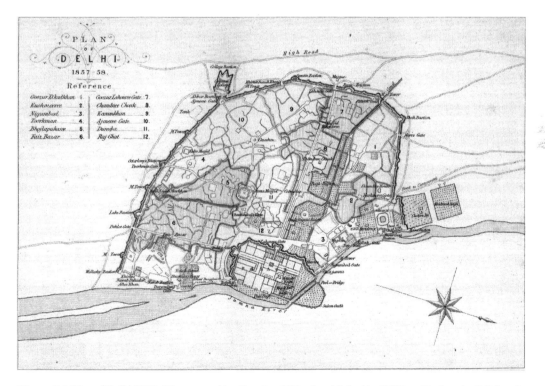

Figure 5.5 Plan of Delhi 1857–58, engraved by Guyot and Wood, published by William Mackenzie, Edinburgh,
c.1860 (coloured engraving), English School (19th century).

Source: Private collection/The Bridgeman Art Library.

Figure 5.6 Delhi (engraving), English School (19th century)

Source: Illustration from *The Age We Live In* by James Taylor (William Mackenzie, c.1870). Private collection/© Look and Learn/The Bridgeman Art Library.

Figure 5.7 Vehicle of a Rich Man in Delhi, 1874–76 (oil on canvas)

Source: Vereshchagin, Vasili Vasilievich (1842–1904)/Tretyakov Gallery, Moscow, Russia/The Bridgeman Art Library.

Figure 5.8
(Above) The Delhi Durbar, 1903
(oil on canvas)

Source: MacKenzie, Roderick
(1865–1941)/Private collection/The
Bridgeman Art Library.

Figure 5.9
(Left) The Tram, 1927–29
(w/c on paper)

Source: Burra, Edward (1905–76)/Private
collection/Photo © Lefevre Fine Art Ltd,
London/The Bridgeman Art Library.

Figure 5.10 The last journey: Gandhi's funeral in Delhi, 27 December 1948, held in Yamuna near New Delhi (b/w photo)

Source: Indian photographer (20th century)/Private collection/Dinodia/The Bridgeman Art Library.

Figure 5.11 New Delhi Railway Station, 1995 (w/c on paper)
Source: Fraser, Olivia (contemporary artist)/Private collection/The Bridgeman Art Library.

city (Hall, 1988). Following Independence and Partition in 1947, New Delhi was declared as the capital and seat of government. Imperial Delhi was therefore just one more overlay on a historic pattern of reconstruction and redevelopment, each with a new emphasis and focus, overwriting but never completely obscuring the previous history (Cox, 2010). Sivam (2003, p. 135) similarly describes the unique development of Delhi as: 'a kaleidoscope of old tradition and new forces'. Delhi was granted its own administrative identity as a full state in 1994, changing from the Delhi Union Territory (DUT) to become the National Capital Territory of Delhi (NCTD); the greater National Capital Region (NCR) including New Delhi and neighbouring cities such as Baghpat, Gurgaon, Sonepat, Faridabad, Ghaziabad, Noida, and Greater Noida.

The current urban population of Delhi is around 16.3 million (2011), with a projected growth of over 75 per cent to 26 million by 2030 (Table 5.3) – nearly three times the projected size of London in 2030. The population growth since the early 1900s has been remarkable, rising from around 400,000; and representing a fivefold increase in the size of the urban area since 1981 (Badami et al., 2004). The NCR has a current population of over 22 million, and there is a much wider sprawl of population and connected development beyond the city boundary. The growth in population is the result of internal city growth but also substantial levels of in-migration. Expansion has long outstripped the capacity of planned development. Whilst there is much planned new development there is also a legacy and contemporary growth

Table 5.3 Delhi – some statistics

Issue	Comment
Demonym	Dehli-ite
Population	
India (2011)	1,210 million
India (2001)	1,029 million
India (1900)	239 million[a]
India (1800s)	200 million
Delhi National Capital Region	22.2 million
Delhi urban area (2007)	14.8 million
Delhi urban area (1900)	400,000
Area (2007)	1,483 km^2
Population density (2007)	9,340/km^2
Income per capita (2007)	Rupees, Rs. 38,864 (£537)
Economic growth (2007)	GDP growth rate 9.9%
Cars per 1,000 persons	50
Motorcycles per 1,000 persons	74
Mode share by trips	Car (8%), motorcycle (14%), public transport (38%), bicycle and pedestrian (40%)
Metro network	Six lines commenced in 2002 with a total length of 190 km and 142 stations, 35 are underground. An average daily ridership of over 1.5 million commuters
Bus rapid transit network	Phase One (2005–10) has seven corridors and a route length of 116 km
Delhi/NCR Metro Fare	A minimum Rs. 8 (£0.11) to a maximum of Rs .30 (£0.42)
CO_2 reduction target	The Copenhagen Accord Pledge (2010) for India is to reduce their carbon intensity by 20–25% by 2020 on 2005 levels
Total CO_2 emissions (2008)	0.9 tCO_2 per capita
Transport CO_2 emissions (2008)	0.4 tCO_2 per capita
Transport % of total	46%

Note:

[a] India is representative of many poorer nations in having only incremental population growth until the early 1900s due to the high birth and death rates; once some of the major public health problems were tackled (including at birth and in childhood), life expectancy rose and aggregate population levels increased.

Source: Hildago and Pai, 2009; Government of National Capital Territory of Delhi, 2010; Thynell et al., 2010; Hickman and Banister, 2011; Dhamija, 2012.

in informal settlements. Formal housing, usually constructed within planning regulations, is principally aimed at the middle and upper classes, reflecting their ability to pay and the potential for the developer to make profit. The majority of the population growth has been in the informal sector, and nearly 50 per cent of the population lives in informal settlements of various types (Badami et al., 2004; Cox, 2010). GDP is expected to grow in the coming decade at up to 10 per cent per annum, continuing the current growth rate (2007) (Government of National Capital Territory of Delhi, 2010).

The principal strategic objective for Delhi, and common to almost all other cities, is to develop in a sustainable manner. This is narrowly interpreted, as principally facilitating economic growth whilst also improving the environment and social equity. From the 1980s onwards there have been concerns around severe air pollution, largely arising from the polluting vehicle fleet. Delhi was one of the world's most polluted cities in the 1990s, and in 1996 the Centre for Science and Environment started a public interest litigation in the Supreme Court of India, which ordered the conversion of Delhi's fleet of buses and taxis to be run on CNG and banned the use of leaded petrol in 1998 (Roychowdhury et al., 2006). This was very influential, and has led to a changed vehicle fleet and much improved local air quality. Reducing CO_2 emissions from transport has been much less of an issue for the city, but in recent years there has been increasing interest in climate change as a societal issue to be resolved. To an extent, though, CO_2 emissions have largely arisen from Western industrialised countries and this is certainly true when historical CO_2 emissions are considered. Consequently, it can be viewed as a Western (-induced) problem, and something that the developed countries should address.

India is becoming a much more significant producer of CO_2 emissions, with a rapid growth in consumptive lifestyles. As a consequence, there has been a rapid rise in cross-sectoral and transport CO_2 emissions, but from a very low base in per capita terms. India is currently the world's fourth largest fossil fuel CO_2 emitting country in terms of aggregate emissions. The government of India (Government of India, 2007) has prepared a White Paper on pollution in Delhi, and this has led to the establishment of the Environmental Pollution Control Authority with responsibility for reducing vehicular pollution. There is also a Masterplan for Delhi 2021 (Delhi Development Authority, 2010) (Figure 5.12), but the strategy seems largely about extending the area of development land, and there is little emphasis on polycentric growth or the development of new centres around the enhanced public transport network. A transport strategy based on demand management principles, integrated with the urban development vision, still seems a distant prospect.

Baseline and projection

Transport in Delhi is characterised by a large number of modes, a much wider range than that conventionally found in industrialised countries. These include the private car; a large proportion of government cars and taxis; two- and three-wheeler scooters, motorcycles and mopeds; bicycles, the cycle rickshaw and motorised rickshaw (usually the three-wheeler auto-rickshaw, commonly known as the tuk-tuk); informal bus; bus rapid transit; the Metro; and pedestrians. Data on travel in Delhi is very underdeveloped, as there are other priorities to spend scarce funding on. Hence, there is little robust understanding of movements across the city, or even car ownership levels, and GHG and CO_2 emissions are not known beyond broad estimates. The baseline position and future projections discussed below are all based on limited data availability, yet to an extent, this doesn't hugely matter. The scales of the projections and the required levels of change are very evident, even with uncertain data.

Delhi's urban area has grown dramatically in the last 25 years, and much of the urban development has been of low rise and low density form, with the exception of the informal settlements, which of course have high population densities. The increased urban area has resulted in increased trip lengths. But over 50 per cent of trips remain under 5 km in length, and hence there is considerable scope for continued use of walking and cycling (Mohan and Tiwari, 1999; Cox, 2010). There are current high mode shares for two- and three-wheelers, cycle rickshaws and buses. Table 5.4 gives an indication of vehicle numbers, though there is little understanding of walking and cycling levels in relation, and the variety in the numbers suggests some uncertainty in the actual trends. It seems certain, though, that two- and three-wheelers retain a major share of the market, followed by cars and jeeps, the latter of which

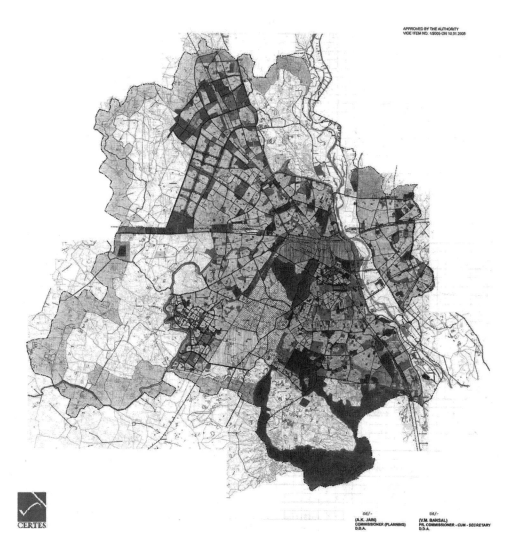

Figure 5.12 Land-use plan for Delhi 2021
Source: Delhi Development Authority, 2010.

are increasing rapidly in share. The numbers of auto rickshaws were affected by the introduction of compressed natural gas (CNG) and the clean air regulations, with a high level of substitution into scooters, motorcycles and cars (Roychowdhury et al., 2006). The informal settlements tend to develop around employment centres in the city and inhabitants tend to rely on walking (particularly females), bus or cycle for travel.

From the 1980s to the present day, Delhi, like much of the rest of India, has experienced a rapid rise in cross-sectoral CO2 emissions. Delhi has a slightly higher motorisation rate than the national levels, reflecting higher income and consumption levels. The projections for India

Figure 5.13 Vehicle fleet in Delhi. The vehicle fleet in Delhi is changing markedly year on year, with cars and jeeps gaining a much greater share in the last 10 years; scooters and motorcycles remain very popular.

Figure 5.14 Government cars and taxis. There are a large number of government cars and taxis.
Source: Carlos Pardo.

Figure 5.15 Walking and cycling remain very important modes of travel, particularly for the lower income
         groups.
Source: Santhosh Kodukula.

are for a rapid rise from around 40 vehicles[5] per 1,000 population in 2008 to around 240
vehicles/1,000 in 2035, representing a rise in the total vehicle population from 64 to 376
million. If the motorisation rate rises to North American or even European levels then the
space required, and the adverse impacts on the built environment and environment, will be
dramatic. This is the key transport problem facing cities in Asia: the potential for growth in
the motorisation rate multiplied by the large current and projective population. Continued
growth in motorisation is inevitable to a certain extent, and the symbolic value of the car is
very much evident. Many aspire to car ownership, but the rate of growth and level of 'saturation'
needs to be managed to avoid very large impacts on cities, energy consumption and emissions.
This is a difficult message for a population that generally aspires to the Western materialistic

Table 5.4 Vehicles in Delhi

Vehicle	1995/1996	1999/2000	2002/2003*	2003/2004
Auto rickshaw	79,011	86,985	15,567	20,893
Taxi	13,765	17,762	23,145	24,712
Bus	27,889	37,733	34,795	36,059
Cycle rickshaw	46,231	70,401	25,998	49,838
Car and jeep	633,802	869,820	1,214,693	1,314,672
Scooter and motorcycle	1,741,260	2,184,581	2,517,788	2,665,750

Note: * CNG regulation introduced.

Source: Kurosaki et al., 2007; Cox, 2010.

Figure 5.16 Dr Strangelove or: How I Learned to Stop Worrying and Love the Bomb, 1964, directed by Stanley Kubrick. Dr Strangelove explains the meaning of the Doomsday Machine and why it is essential that not only should it destroy the world in the event of a nuclear attack, but also destroy the world if anyone attempts to deactivate it: 'The whole point of the Doomsday Machine is lost if you keep it a secret. Why didn't you tell the world?'

Source: British Film Institute Stills Collection.

lifestyle, including the attractions of the motor car. This is similar also for the domestic Indian motor industry, strongly supported by trade organisations such as the Society of Indian Automobile Manufacturers (SIAM). The view is that the West has had a period of consumption that many in Asia would like to follow. The experience and mistakes of the West, however, can be noted and the lessons learnt, including that excessive use of the car leads to a poor urban fabric, low levels of quality of life in cities and very large per capita and aggregate CO_2 emissions.

The estimates from the available data are that the transport sector produces around 46 per cent of total CO_2 emissions and road transport contributes to 95 per cent of this (Dhamija, 2012). Passenger road transport CO_2 emissions in Delhi are expected to rise from around 6 $MtCO_2$ (2004) to over 26 $MtCO_2$ (2030) under a BAU projection (Table 5.4). This equates to 0.4 tonnes CO_2 per person (2004) rising to 1.0 tonnes CO_2 per person (2030). These numbers are, of course, estimates and are uncertain. Much of the growth is driven by rapid projected mobility growth, including rises in vehicle ownership and use (Hickman et al., 2008; Saxena, 2012). Current transport policies in Delhi do not attempt to limit the growth in vehicular traffic to any degree, though there are attempts to improve the quality of public transport provision with Metro and bus rapid transit.

Equity in target setting

No governmental targets have been adopted for reducing projected transport CO_2 emissions in India or Delhi.Under the Kyoto Protocol, India's commitments do not involve a numerical CO_2 growth limitation, simply an agreement to monitor emissions. The UN agreed to a set of a 'common but differentiated responsibilities', in that:

- The largest share of historical and current global emissions of greenhouse gases has originated in developed countries;
- Per capita emissions in developing countries are still relatively low;
- The share of global emissions originating in developing countries will grow to meet their social and development needs.

Hence India, and other developing countries including China, share only a 'monitoring' responsibility, alongside a more general agreed 'common responsibility' that all countries have a role to play in reducing emissions. The Copenhagen Accord Pledge (January 2010) for India is to reduce its carbon intensity. This refers to the amount of carbon emissions for each unit of economic output, measured in gross domestic product (GDP). The level of carbon intensity reduction is 20–25 per cent by 2020. This allows for economic growth, and reduces CO_2 output on a relative basis. The level of target reduction is smaller than China's commitment (40–45 per cent). Delhi's GDP is approximately US$58 billion in 2010, and assuming the GDP growth rate continuing at around 8 per cent, this means a GDP in 2020 of around US$125 billion. If the 25 per cent reduction in carbon intensity is met, this still means that transport emissions can rise from 2010 levels of around 8.5 $MtCO_2$ to 13.9 $MtCO_2$ (a growth of 162 per cent), assuming that transport plays a 'fair share' contribution against the intensity target. Hence in a rapidly rising economy, the intensity rate is fairly unrestrictive when translated into transport emissions. This has been the rationale behind India's choice of target metric. The country is rising from a very low level of emissions relative to Western levels, hence will be allowed to develop the economy, but at a slightly improved intensity level in terms of CO_2 emissions. Certainly an 'end state' target reduction in CO_2 emissions as found in London would be highly restrictive, and inappropriate in developmental terms. Transport CO2 emissions will rise in all plausible scenarios, and the scale of reduction against BAU becomes the important issue.

The argument from the Stern (2009) blueprint is slightly different in using per capita emission levels and equity as the basis for targets. Stern argues for a global reduction in cross-sectoral CO2 emissions of at least 50 per cent from 1990 levels (from over 50 GtCO2e now to 20 GtCO2e) by 2050 (see discussion in Chapter 1). For developed countries this means an 80 per cent reduction in CO2 emissions on 1990 levels, to around to 2 tonnes per capita per annum by 2050. If the transport sector accounts for 25 per cent of CO2 emissions, then this equates to around 0.5 tonnes per capita within transport. The richer countries and cities (e.g. London) are thus looking at major CO2 emission reductions, in the order of 60–90 per cent depending on their baseline. Cities such as Delhi are very different in that they can afford a substantial increase in emissions, at least on 1990 levels, to reach these equitable targets, as they are starting from lower baselines than the global blueprint target. The argument is very similar to that developed under the 'contraction and convergence' (C&C) framework developed by Meyer (2000) in that the equity principle is paramount, and everyone has an equal right to produce CO2 emissions. Meyer views per capita equality as possible by 2100, with an initial fall in emissions (contraction) and thereafter emissions would fall to reach 'safe' levels by 2100 (convergence) (Figure 5.17). The C&C framework was supported by countries such as China and India, largely because it was consistent with the 'developmental

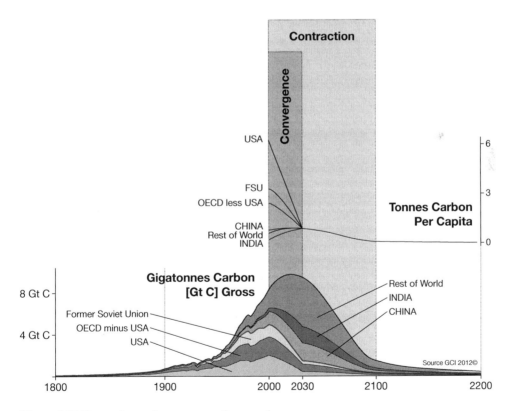

Figure 5.17 Contraction and convergence framework

Note: 450ppm and convergence by 2030.

Source: Aubrey Meyer, Global Commons Institute, 2013.

imperative' (Giddens, 2009). For the basis of our analysis, we take this 0.5 tC per capita figure as the 'best target' for the transport sector in Delhi as in all other countries. There are, of course, important issues around aiming for an equitable target internationally, with little else in 'consumption' terms as equitable across the world. But for the basis of comparing relative emissions and working towards broadly equitable futures, this is taken as a broad benchmark.

Developing scenarios

Despite the BAU projections and India's limited 'legal' requirements, much can be done to reduce transport CO_2 emissions in Delhi. The transport scenario analysis presented here draws mainly on the VIBAT India and Delhi scoping study, including discussions with IIT Delhi, other experts in Delhi and work from Wilbur Smith Associates (2008). There are a large potential number of trajectories for Delhi to follow in terms of future transport strategy. A number of major trends and uncertainties are evident in Delhi that can affect or indeed shape the future scenarios in transport. These trends include economic issues such as the GDP growth rate; the extent of globalisation; trade with the rest of the world and domestically; growth in manufacturing, employment and leisure sectors; technological progress; socio-demographic issues such as demographic change and rural to urban migration; cultural aspirations; and social inclusion. In addition there are environmental issues such as the extent and geographic impact of climate change, the level of protection given to the environment and urban and rural life, the level of technological change, and also governance issues such as the framework and effectiveness of governmental organisations and the role and influence of civil society.

Five of these key issues are used to represent the future 'possibility space' as a 'multilemma' – broadly based on the three pillars of sustainability, but also including technological issues and considering governance issues in terms of potential deliverability and public acceptability, as shown in Figure 5.18. Four scenarios are mapped against these six dimensions to show their different characteristics

A description of the core scenarios is given below:

Scenario 1: BAU   This future is an extension of existing trends over the next 20 years. There is some investment in public transport, limited change in the efficiency of the car stock and in the use of alternative fuels. There is a large projected growth in traffic, with an approximate 700 per cent increase in CO_2 emissions on 1990 levels. The scenario involves little technological change, and is likely to perform poorly against environmental, social inclusion objectives. In the long run, it may not be effective in delivering GDP growth. It is, however, easily delivered politically (there is little policy change relative to the current context). The scenario is ultimately not acceptable to the public as the adverse impacts on the built environment, environment and economy become evident over time.

Scenario 2: Low carbon mobility   This scenario relies on an ambitious implementation of new vehicle technologies, including low-emission vehicles, alternative fuels and smaller vehicle types.There is also an increase in rail use. Mobility levels increase, but much of it is carried out in clean vehicles. This would lead to an increase of over 500 per cent in CO_2 emissions on 1990 levels, and a per capita level of 0.76 tonnes. The scenario is designed to perform well against economic objectives (there is a new market in low-emission vehicles) and to be acceptable to the public (mobility growth). Even the progress against economic goals may be less than envisaged, as Delhi becomes highly motorised and congested, and a less attractive city to live and work in. There may be difficulties in political implementation, as clean vehicle

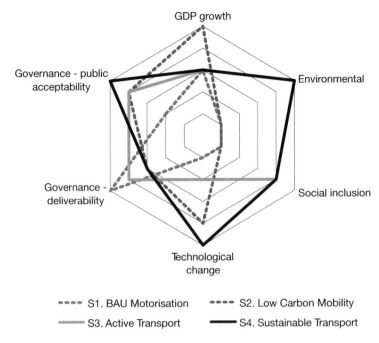

Figure 5.18 The possibility space

penetration rates are not easy to influence. There are few environmental benefits, as any gains in CO_2 emissions per vehicle are offset by increased mobility, or social benefits, as those without a car remain disadvantaged. The policy trajectory requires strong governmental legislation and enforcement, such as in mandatory lower emission motor vehicle standards and the acceptance and use of alternative fuels. The motor manufacturers would need to produce lower emission motor vehicles for the mass market, and substantial new patterns of consumer behaviour would be required so that these low carbon vehicles are bought.

Scenario 3: Increased active travel   In this scenario, a major change to present trends is assumed with a small increase in the distance walked and a more than doubling of the distance cycled. There is also a large increase in rail use and small increase in bus use. Critically there are substantial reductions in motorcycle use and only a slight increase in car use to 2030. There would still be a 300 per cent rise in transport CO_2 emissions from 1990 levels, and the per capita emissions levels are 0.49 tonnes.

The scenario is designed to be acceptable to the public, as more active travel is generally viewed positively, but it may perform less well against economic requirements (motor manufacturing is not supported to the same degree). This limitation is debatable, as there could be major employment possible around the emerging sustainable transport infrastructure, including the building of Metro, rail, bus rapid transit and cycling facilities. There is little requirement for technological change in private vehicles, but it is expected that environmental and social benefits are realised with much less reliance on car-based travel. Such a future would require a much greater prioritisation for pedestrians, cyclists and the use of cycle rickshaws and clean (CNG) auto rickshaws. There would need to be prioritisation of roadspace for non-motorised travel and effectively enforced restrictions on private car travel to ensure active travel is the safest and most convenient, pleasant, and quickest way to reach destinations. Reallocation of

Figure 5.19 Two- and three-wheelers. A low carbon mobility scenario in India could build on the current high proportion of two- and three-wheelers and small sized cars.

space could be promoted alongside high-quality streetscapes designed to meet the needs of pedestrians and cyclists.

Rather than active travel being the mode of necessity for those unable to afford motor vehicles, it would become the mode of choice, including amongst the higher income groups. Hence the Dutch model is followed, where cycling (including rickshaws) becomes the mode of choice for all since these modes are cheaper and quicker, and can provide an active and healthy means of travel. There is substantial investment in infrastructure designed for pedestrians and cyclists, perhaps also with road pricing, traffic demand management, restrictions for car parking and access, reduced speed limits, and behavioural change initiatives (e.g. marketing, raised environmental awareness and travel planning). To make major progress in mode shift there may be a need for carbon rationing or other form of 'currency' based around carbon use (Hillman and Fawcett, 2004).

Scenario 4: Towards sustainable transport This scenario seeks to successfully deliver both technological and behavioural elements of a sustainable transport system, including a major transition towards the use of low carbon emission vehicles and increased active transport. There would be a 203 per cent increase in CO_2 emissions from 1990, and the per capita levels would be around 0.36 tonnes. The scenario is designed to perform well against environmental and social objectives, as CO_2 emission reductions and mass access to active travel are central features. Public acceptability would presumably be high, with a focus on quality of travel and increased accessibility rather than an increasing quantity of motorised travel. This scenario might be difficult to implement politically, as it requires a high level of coordination and a much changed policy focus. Certainly civil society and government would need to work together to develop a progressive, forward-looking transport and city development strategy

Table 5.5 Transport CO2 emissions total and per capita levels

Baseline and projection		Transport emissions CO2 (tonnes)	CO2 emissions % increase on 1990	Population (millions)	Transport CO2 emissions per capita (tCO2/capita)
1990		3,121,711	0%	8.2	0.38
2004		6,146,650	97%	14.8	0.42
2010		8,574,411	175%	17.5	0.49
S1:	2030 BAU	26,298,176	742%	26.0	1.01
S2:	Lower carbon emission motor vehicles	19,711,039	531%	26.0	0.76
S3:	Increased active transport	12,629,030	305%	26.0	0.49
S4:	Sustainable transport	9,459,179	203%	26.0	0.36

Table 5.6 Travel distance per year (billion km)

Baseline and projection	Car	SUV	Bus	Rail	HGV	Walk	Bicycle	M/C 2-W	M/C 3-W	Total
2004	14.2	1.2	46.5	9.5	0.4	8.7	10.6	20.4	3.9	115.4
2010	22.8	3.2	50.1	10.2	0.6	9.4	11.4	30.0	5.5	143.0
2030 Scenario 1 (BAU)	97.3	19.5	74.4	37.9	2.7	12.0	10.1	74.4	6.8	335.0
2030 Scenario 2	97.3	19.5	74.4	37.9	2.7	12.0	10.1	74.4	6.8	335.0
2030 Scenario 3	32.4	1.6	84.4	50.7	1.8	16.0	44.6	32.7	6.8	271.0
2030 Scenario 4	32.4	1.6	84.4	50.7	1.8	16.0	44.6	32.7	6.8	271.0

Note: SUV = Sports Utility Vehicle; HGV = Heavy Goods Vehicle; M/C 2-W = Motor Cycle Two Wheeler; M/C 3-W = Motor Cycle Three Wheeler; Total = billion km per year.

for Delhi, being strong enough to outmanoeuvre the road and vehicle lobby, who would push for a much higher level of motorisation. There may be less economic gain, in terms of the narrow GDP definition, and there would need to be a redefinition of the understanding of 'societal growth'. The quality of life and promotion of individual capabilities and achievement all become much more central to the definition of progress than GDP growth or consumption (Jackson, 2009; Sen, 2009). Policy changes would need to be dramatic, requiring a 'high-intensity' implementation and effectiveness of all measures, including the monitoring and enforcement of the key measures. An effective governance framework is critical, moving away from the tendency for neo-liberalist support of vested interests in the motor industry and development sector towards one that promotes community values so that equity and environmental objectives can be met.

The key transport outputs for each scenario are illustrated in Tables 5.5 and 5.6 and also in Figures 5.20–5.22 (aggregate and per capita transport CO2 emissions; mode share by distance), all using a future year date of 2030.

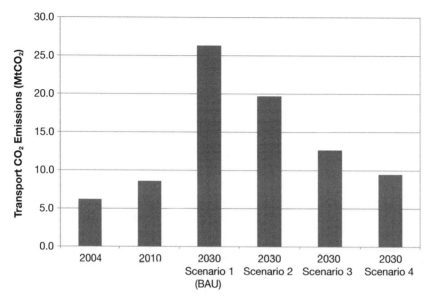

Figure 5.20 Aggregate transport CO2 emissions

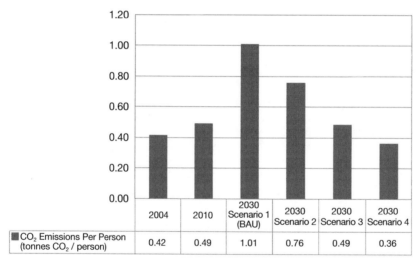

Figure 5.21 Per capita transport CO2 emissions

Exploring the 'optimised' scenario

Scenario 4 is most effective in reducing CO2 emissions and is described in more detail below. The scenario pushes extremely hard on all of the available policy levers and implements the technological and behavioural options to a 'high intensity level, achieving a 64 per cent reduction in transport CO2 emissions on BAU levels, but still representing a 203 per cent increase on 1990 levels. Car distance and vehicle gCO2/km are the most important features to resultant emissions. In Scenario 2 (and 1) overall travel distance increases markedly on current levels,

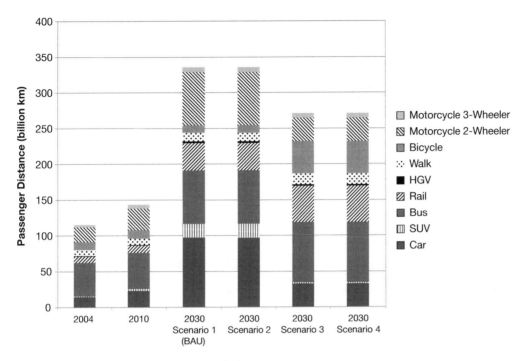

Figure 5.22 Mode share (billion passenger km)

but here, in Scenario 4, car distance increases only slightly on 2010 levels, with the difference taken up by a very large increase in bus (potentially a much wider Metro and bus rapid transit network, but also more extensive use of a clean bus fleet), rail and cycling. The larger vehicles in particular are restricted, for example SUV distance is restrained to below 2010 levels, so a major effort is required to ensure future vehicle mobility is in clean and small vehicles. Two- and three-wheelers also have most potential here, if fuelled cleanly (three wheelers are currently fuelled with CNG, but there are other fuel options as well). The following proportions are assumed in terms of market share by distance travelled by 2030 – car (12 per cent), SUV (1 per cent), bus (31 per cent), Metro and rail (19 per cent), HGV (1 per cent), walk (6 per cent), cycle (16 per cent), two-wheeler (12 per cent), three-wheeler (2 per cent). The subsequent paragraphs describe the range of possible measures within Scenario 4.

Metro, rail and BRT

Public transport can also be further developed in Delhi to provide a more attractive option for users. There are major efforts underway to develop a multi-modal transport system for Delhi. The building of the Delhi Metro commenced in 1998, and the first link opened in 2002, with Phase I being completed by 2006 with three corridors, a length of 65 km and around 13 km of the route underground. Phase II was completed by 2011, adding a further 53 km of line, 9 km underground. The design and construction was by RITES, the government-owned transport engineering company. The Metro has been expensive for Delhi, with a cost for Phase I and II at Rs.64,060 million and Rs.80,260 million (a total of around US$2.4 billion, 2004 prices) (Murty et al., 2006; Cox, 2010). This investment, however, is inexpensive relative to

Figure 5.23 Delhi Metro. The Delhi Metro has been expensive to build, but often this type of investment is the only way to move large volumes of passengers into the central urban areas.

Figure 5.24 Bus rapid transit (BRT) opening for the first time in Delhi in 2008
Source: Santhosh Kodukula.

Figure 5.25 Bus rapid transit (BRT) system design. There have been some system design problems, but these are likely to be improved over time and with more extensive networks.

Source: Santhosh Kodukula.

Figure 5.26 Urban structure. A major difficulty for running public transport services in Delhi is the urban structure, which tends to be relatively low density with few distinct centres.

Figure 5.27 Connaught Place. Even the main central area in the city has only a limited concentration of employment, retail or other attractions.

transport infrastructure prices in the West. There have been some concerns that network coverage has been limited and it directly benefits only a minor proportion of the city's population, given that fares are also expensive for many residents (Mohan, 2006). Also, the routing has often been guided by development opportunities, with the Delhi Metro Rail Company becoming a major property developer in its own right. There has been a policy of rapid clearance of informal settlements, with many difficulties in resettlement. With the more extensive network under Phases III and IV, the Metro will cover many of the remaining parts of Delhi, and even extend into the neighbouring states, with a total length of over 180 km. Current average daily ridership is around 1.8 million commuters. The Metro serves a large section of the travel market and makes a very important contribution to travel movements around an important global city such as Delhi. In parallel, the current heavy rail network in Delhi is vastly under-utilised, with the railways catering for only 1 per cent of local traffic, and here again there is much potential for improvement and investment in upgrading the network.

A bus rapid transit (BRT) system is also being developed in Delhi, with high-capacity buses using segregated lanes. But it is limited in design relative to the systems seen in Curitiba or Bogotá, where there are fuller exclusive busways, express and local services, smart card technology to improve boarding, high frequencies, ease of transfer, and supportive urban planning. The system has been designed by RITES and TRIPP (the Transportation Research and Injury Prevention Programme at the Indian Institute of Technology (IIT), Delhi (RITES, 2008). Bus lanes are generally inserted along the central part of the highway, with the first 5.6 km pilot phase opening in 2008. There were vociferous complaints in the media, largely from the perspective of reduced road capacity for private cars and increased congestion at junctions. Certainly, the limited design and scope of the initial system has made it difficult to appreciate the benefits of a city-wide system, but this may come with further extensions and the development of a network of routes that link in effectively with the Metro.

Under Scenario 4, there are significant shifts to public transport, including major investment in a more extensive Metro network and BRT system to 2030. Critically, the development of major transport corridors and interchanges is closely coordinated with urban planning, with higher densities and mixed-use centres developed around the interchanges. Such integrated development will encourage greater ridership potential. This integrated urban structure and transport planning is not occurring to any great extent in the current plans.

Walking and cycling

Walking and cycling can continue to be very important modes of travel in Delhi, but there needs to be significant investment in infrastructure. These two modes are critical to the mobility of the majority of Delhi's population, as more than 50 per cent of the population cannot afford any other means of travel unless heavily subsidised (Mohan, 2006), but the attraction of walking and cycling is being rapidly diminished as more space is given to motorised transport. Traffic casualty rates in the city are amongst the highest in the world, with pedestrians, cyclists and rickshaws often the most vulnerable.

Under Scenario 4, there is major investment in walking and cycling facilities. Bicycles and cycle rickshaws can be given segregated lanes away from vehicular traffic, and the pedestrian environment and public realm in key urban centres would be enhanced. Pucher and Buehler (2008) advise on extensive cycle networks being developed, alongside intersection treatments (to make cycle usage easier), traffic calming in residential areas and urban centres, coordination with public transport, effective parking facilities and legislative changes, including protection for cyclists in accidents (legally the motorist is assumed to be at fault in all collisions). Cycling ideally needs to be separated from other forms of transport, using segregated routes, as this is a key determinant of use. Amongst less confident cyclists, it is the perceived safety when travelling with traffic that is the difference between cycling or not cycling. Part of any new investment would be cycle training, cycle promotion and even the development of mass cycle hire facilities, similar to those being developed in China and Europe.

The practice of cycle provision in the Netherlands, Germany and Denmark can provide some guidance for the means by which successful implementation can take place. A major effort (and investment) must be made in terms of developing appropriate schemes for the Delhi context. Cycling, above all modes, seems to offer an equitable and inexpensive travel option for all in Delhi, yet attitudinal issues are perhaps most difficult – to change the perception of cycling from an option for the poor into one of travel for all, including the high income groups, where cycling gives the quickest and healthiest choice for active travel. Ideally cycling in Delhi will become fashionable, similar to trends in many European cities.

Urban planning

Strategic and local urban planning is seen as central to Scenario 4 so that the most value is obtained from transport investments, such as the proposed Metro and BRT networks, and also to facilitate more walking and cycling. This means an effective location of development at the strategic level, with most new development located around the new public transport interchanges, increased densities and the creation of mixed use centres around interchanges, and improved neighbourhood design to facilitate walking and cycling. Hence, urban planning is used to 'retrofit' the Delhi urban structure to more closely integrate with the planned public transport investments. Major efforts are made to develop the polycentric structure of Delhi, including strengthening the central area around Connaught Place with a much greater level of employment and retail development. All major urban centres could be connected by Metro and/or BRT. Figure 5.28 gives an indication of a potential future integrated transport and urban planning strategy to 2030. The city is of such a size (a projected 26 million population by 2030) that polycentric concentration, served by Metro, BRT, walking and cycling, is the only real choice for shaping development and travel in the city. Private vehicular travel will, of course, still be required in some cases, but this is only in low-emission vehicles. Again, there are difficulties in implementing such a strategy – the higher densities around public transport nodes seem difficult to deliver in Delhi, which is a relatively low density city. New development is planned in the west of the city, but as yet there is no effective shaping of the development around the public transport network to make the most of the transport networks. This should be possible in areas of new development, easier than retrofitting existing development, and including large, new employment centres and a series of supporting, smaller urban centres. Local neighbourhood design similarly needs to be much enhanced, favouring walking and cycling and local trip patterns. The green belt surrounding Delhi can be much enhanced, perhaps designed similar to the Copenhagen 'finger plan', with new development being shaped alongside the public transport connections.

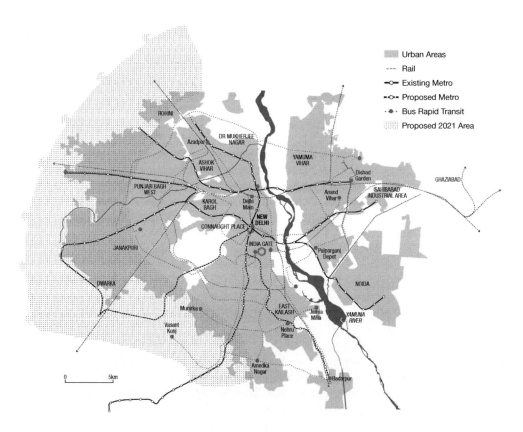

Figure 5.28 Proposed integrated transport and urban structure in Delhi Metropolitan Region
Source: Mapping by Bally Meeda and Urban Graphics.

Low-emission vehicles and alternative fuels

Private car ownership and use will grow in future years in Delhi, and it will be critical to ensure CO2 emissions from vehicular usage are as low as possible. Low-emission vehicles achieve reduced fuel consumption and emissions through innovative engine design, including hybrid petrol vehicles, diesel and electric engines. In the Delhi context, this technology is still novel and expensive, but globally, hybrid cars are available. Scenario 4 assumes much of the vehicle fleet is based on the current best international hybrid technology, or diesel technology, with a total car/van fleet average of less than 100 gCO2/km. This is a very strong level of technology penetration based on current patterns of take up in India, even though the current vehicle is typically small, and this also helps in limiting emissions. There is, however, a current focus in vehicle development on inexpensive, 'older' technology small car options. There are plans for hybrids to be made available in India, including the Honda hybrid Civic Sedan, Mahindra Industries' hybrid SUV, and TVS and Bajaj Auto are developing a hybrid three-wheeler. Import taxes mean that non-Indian produced vehicles are prohibitively expensive. There is a 100 per cent import duty for vehicles, with some discount for hybrids. Improved fuel economy standards are required; the motor vehicles sold in India (four wheels or more) are not particularly fuel efficient by international standards. Currently there are no voluntary or mandatory standards in India, manufacturers are only required to publish fuel economy figures, and there are no agreed test cycles (Hickman et al., 2008).

In addition, there are a number of possible alternative fuels on the market, many of which have lower carbon content than petrol and diesel, and including biofuels. Ethanol and biodiesel are perhaps most suited to use in India. Scenario 4 assumes a rising blend of biofuels in petrol and diesel, reaching around 30 per cent by 2030, and the use of a significant proportion of

Figure 5.29 Two- and three-wheelers. Many of the two and three-wheeler vehicles now run on CNG.
Source: Pongnarin Petchu.

Figure 5.30 Compressed natural gas supply. However, there have been problems in providing enough supply.

Figure 5.31 Cycling. A great challenge for Delhi is to develop a transport system which is useable by all and that doesn't dominate the urban fabric. Cycling perhaps has a larger (and continued) role than previously envisaged.

Source: Santhosh Kodukula.

electric and compressed natural gas (CNG) vehicles. The Government of India has already introduced a programme of 5 per cent ethanol in petrol (in 2003). There may be difficulties in implementing this level of biofuel use in terms of land take and infrastructure requirements, and there are ongoing concerns over lifecycle costs. Second- and third-generation biofuels may provide more opportunities in future years, and Jatropha, in particular, has potential for biodiesel production in India (Hickman et al., 2008). There is some precedence in changing fuel types in relatively short timescales, for example the Supreme Court of India ruling which led to buses and taxis to be run on CNG in 1998.

In future years the intelligent car or automated personal transit may become central to movement in the city, with near zero emissions as they would be powered by (clean) electricity, but there are other technological developments which aid safety issues or the comfort of driving. These types of technologies may be developed in India and China, where the car markets are in their infancy, the domestic motor manufacturers are looking for new 'niches' in the market, and they are also free to experiment in their production processes. Human qualities are already being appropriated into the car, as computers increasingly have 'memory', 'language' and 'intelligence'. At the same time, people are embracing the car as 'the living machine', developing 'networks' and 'interfacing' with others (Thrift, 2004). New hybrid forms may develop, where the use and governance of the car (and much of the discretion involved in driving) is taken out of the hands of the driver, so that the level of usage is raised. Cars can be driven at optimum speeds and 'stacked' to improve throughput or reduce emissions, and safety enhanced

Figure 5.32 Two children playing in the River Yamuna flowing beside the Taj Mahal, Agra, India. What would they want policy makers to do on transport and climate change?

Source: Omniphoto/ UIG/The Bridgeman Art Library.

with automated vehicle control. The Google self-driving car can already drive at speeds up to 40 mph and navigate obstacles, stop at street lights and traverse parts of San Francisco and California. Perhaps we will achieve the Latourian future: 'First, it has been made by humans; second it substitutes for the actions of people and is a delegate that permanently occupies the position of a human; and, third, it shapes human action by prescribing back' (Latour, 1992, p. 235). The challenge of course is to channel the myriad possibilities in technological developments to achieve societal goals, such as improved safety or environmental performance, rather than to simply introduce new features and interest, and sell more vehicles.

Wider 'behavioural' interventions

The European approach would also be to focus on 'traffic demand management' behavioural options, including pricing regimes (perhaps greater fuel taxes or vehicle registration schemes, with hypothecated funds for public transport and walking, cycling improvement), measures for restricted parking and higher charges (where applicable), the introduction of ecological driving and slower speeds, and travel planning. Information and communication technologies (ICT) could also be widely used, including high levels of broadband access, to encourage flexible working, home retailing, and electronic social interaction. The use of these measures needs careful thought and application in the Delhi context, as some measures are applicable and others are less suitable.

Conclusions: avoiding the BAU

The BAU trends for transport in Delhi, and elsewhere in Asia, are very problematic in terms of the speed and scale of growth in travel. Even though it is generally accepted that trend-based futures are unsustainable, it is proving difficult to develop and implement strategies of a sufficiently progressive nature to significantly reduce the projected growth in transport CO_2 emissions. However, even in cities and countries that are experiencing severe pressures for very substantive increases in travel demand, it is possible to explore the means by which low energy and carbon futures can be addressed. Workable, attractive models of low carbon transport lifestyles need to be demonstrated and debated, and this can be done by highlighting the good practice that is emerging and the potential for a more consistent application across a greater number of cities.

Scenario 4 for Delhi seeks to successfully deliver a multi-modal system for the city, based largely on an extended Metro, BRT, and use of clean two- and three-wheelers, walking and cycling, and some growth in the use of the clean private car. Hence there is a real focus on the behavioural elements (higher non-car mode shares) of a sustainable transport system, as well as the technological areas (new vehicle technologies) that tend to gain most emphasis. The modelling is uncertain to a degree, as there is little available data, but under Scenario 4 there would be an approximate 200 per cent increase in CO_2 emissions to 2030 from 1990, and the per capita levels would be around 0.36 tonnes CO_2 per capita, with a clear objective to hold this latter figure to below 0.5 tonnes CO_2 per capita over time. This implies large increases in public transport usage, clean two- and three-wheelers, and walking and cycling relative to levels in 2010.

International good practice in transport planning, such as found in Bogotá, Curitiba, Singapore, Shanghai and elsewhere, is instructive in demonstrating how public transport options and active modes of travel can be developed, how CO_2 emissions can be reduced and cities improved (Wright, 2010; Hickman et al., 2011). The increasing speed of good practice dissemination and knowledge transfer via the Internet offers new opportunities in terms of speeding up the strategy development and implementation process in a wide number of cities. In particular, the historical and discredited transport planning practices of the 1950s–1980s (but still continuing in some contexts), based on the old road building agenda, including the urban flyovers, increased road capacities, rapid motorisation and urban dispersal, can be replaced with the sustainable mobility approach. In Delhi, a city with low income levels, BRT and cycling in particular offer equitable and socially just travel options. The successful implementation of vehicle efficiencies and alternative fuels to the mass market is also critical, but this is currently not happening at the levels required. There are clear opportunities in encouraging low emission, small size and low price vehicle technologies, potentially using lean burn technologies. Financial incentives may be required here, including linking vehicle import duty to emissions in the short term. Some technological policy measures appear to be more limited in potential as they undergo closer examination (e.g. biofuels). There are wider traffic demand management possibilities, which can also be debated and developed over time, including pricing regimes (perhaps via a carbon tax or increased fuel duty), and travel planning for particular cohorts of the population.

International air, shipping emissions and freight have not been included in the analysis, as the focus has been on surface-based, passenger movements. The analysis has also looked at the city 'in isolation' and not in terms of its linkages with the rest of the world through travel (aviation), trade (shipping), and e-communications. The shorter distance travel within cities makes it easier to creatively look at a range of different options, individually and in combination, and it is possible under different scenarios to achieve substantial reductions in carbon emissions. But, when the wider picture is examined, there are fewer options in terms of both the technologies available and in the alternative means by which business and leisure trips can be undertaken. The globalisation of the economy and the long supply chains needed to provide food, energy, goods and materials for cities have not been considered here. These important international CO_2 emissions sources are outside of the international agreements at present, but they still remain important sources of CO_2. It is difficult to see how they can be included as the scale of emissions, their spatial distribution and allocations, the monitoring of target achievement and the individual responsibilities for action, all make the problems of sustainable mobility in the city look a relatively easy problem to resolve. These long-distance travel modes provide a real challenge for research over the coming years. It would then be important to convince both politicians and the public that the options available to reduce carbon emissions are acceptable and that strong levels of implementation are needed.

Institutional and funding issues will remain difficult for urban transport planning. However, this only reinforces the need for a strategic, forward-looking, progressive, coordinated and integrated policy approach, delivered at the city scale, and supported where necessary at the national, pan-Asian and international scales. There are important issues concerning how the necessary finance can be raised, and there will need to be changed governmental structures, new regulations, clearer enforcement, new financial instruments, and huge commitment among politicians, industry, communities and other individuals to deliver a sustainable transport strategy for Delhi. The Delhi context is particularly interesting in demonstrating the importance of grassroots organisations, civil society and NGOs in demanding a different transport future for the city, with groups competing and struggling against each other to be heard, and governmental action following, albeit often in an ad hoc and uncoordinated manner (Cox, 2010). The current and immediate challenges are in providing an effective institutional framework for more consistent strategy making and investment, with a more effective linkage between urban planning and transport investment, and a much greater focus on forms of transport planning that are inclusive. Strong action in the short term is the key to achieving radical change in the longer term.

Notes

1   There is also some useful wider literature, including Fouracre and Maunder, 1987; Bulman, 1988; Allport et al., 1998; Ng and Schipper, 2005; Dimitriou, 2006b; Hickman et al., 2008; and Darido et al., 2009.
2   The MDGs seek to encourage development by improving the social and economic conditions of the world's poorest countries. There are three major areas in terms of: improving human capital, improving infrastructure, and increasing social, economic and political rights. Much of the focus is on increasing basic standards of living. The MDGs were developed by the United Nations, with Jeffrey Sachs, and adopted in 2000.
3   The VIBAT-Delhi study was developed by Robin Hickman, Sharad Saxena and David Banister for the Asian Development Bank (with Jamie Leather) in 2008.
4   Indraprastha was the capital of the kingdom led by the Pandavas in the *Mahabharata* epic, one of the two major Sanskrit epics of ancient India, alongside the *Ramayana*, dating from before the third century BC.
5   'Total vehicles' includes passenger cars, buses, coaches, vans, lorries; but not two- or three-wheelers.

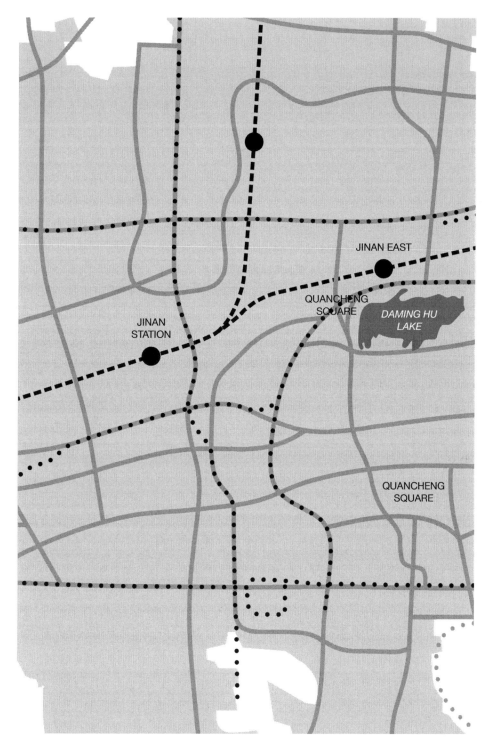

Figure 6.1 Jinan
Source: Mapping by Bally Meeda and Urban Graphics.

6   Building a new world (Jinan)

You must picture the consternation of our little town, hitherto so tranquil, and now, out of the blue, shaken to its core, like a quite healthy man who all of a sudden feels his temperature shoot up and the blood seething like wildfire in his veins.

(Albert Camus, *The Plague*, 1947, p. 13)

Introduction

The first urban settlements in the People's Republic of China emerged some 4,000 years ago,[1] ranking as one of the earliest civilisations globally. The area around the Yellow River was the cradle of Chinese development, with a written history emerging as early as the Shang Dynasty (1700–1046 BC) and the origins of Chinese culture, literature and philosophy developed during the Zhou Dynasty (1045–256 BC). In the years since there have been successive waves of dynasties, immigration, expansion and assimilation; innovation and cultural development; and huge change in terms of lifestyles and travel (Ma, 2009). Many Chinese cities are now developing rapidly. In terms of transport they are suffering from severe and worsening transport problems, including congestion, increasing energy use and emissions, a lack of mobility for excluded groups and an increasing casualty rate. This urban transport crisis results from continuing population growth, suburban sprawl, rising incomes and increased motorisation and use (Pucher et al., 2007).

Achieving sustainable mobility in urban areas in China is one of the most challenging problems facing international city development. The scales of growth in the Chinese economy and the resulting developmental aspiration and migration are unprecedented; the economy is the fastest growing in the world, and alongside there is a huge growth in motorisation. There are therefore important Camus-like questions of the human condition and how to improve this within the domain of transport and city planning. There are many irrationalities in the trends, some adverse impacts seem inevitable, and perhaps we have less control than we imagine or would like.

China is experiencing a rapid expansion of existing cities and development of new cities. Table 6.1 shows the level of urbanisation in China, with eleven cities currently at over 5 million population (at the urban area level), and three of these at over 10 million – Chongqing, Shanghai and Beijing. The wider metropolitan populations are even larger. An additional 300 million Chinese rural dwellers are likely to move to cities over the next 20 years, meaning that up to 75 per cent of the population will live in urban areas. The scale of urban development in China is hence much larger than that being considered elsewhere, with important transport implications again due to the scale. The urban developmental experience is also unique in

Figure 6.2 Transporting ceramics (painted silk), Chinese School (15th century)
Source: Topkapi Palace Museum, Istanbul, Turkey/Giraudon/The Bridgeman Art Library.

China, with components of population growth, migration and 'nation building' (Ma, 2009). Today China's CO_2 emissions are largely industrial, the by-product of an industrial power on the rise, similar to a Manchester or London in the 1800s (Glaeser, 2011). Only a tenth of China's CO_2 emissions come from the transport sector, but if this rises to the levels found in the US (40 per cent and upwards), the rise in emissions will be even more dramatic.

Some of the key socio-demographic statistics for China are given in Table 6.2. Population growth in China remains limited at 0.5 per cent per annum, but of course this is on a large existing population of 1.3 billion persons. The level of urbanisation is at 46.6 per cent in 2009 and, in recent years, growth is mainly a result of migration from rural areas. The urban population growth rate is at around 2.5 per cent. Gross national income (GNI) is relatively low at just over US$3,350 per capita (22,000 Chinese yuan, CYN), with much variation nationally. Gross domestic product (GDP) growth is averaging around an incredible 10 per cent per annum in recent years, but this level has reduced to about 8 per cent per annum (2012). The middle classes and consumption are both growing rapidly. For example, mobile phone subscriptions are at over 50 per 100 persons and Internet use at 29 per 100 persons. CO_2 emissions are still relatively low at 5 tons per capita, but rising rapidly. In aggregate terms China is the world's largest CO_2 emitter (World Bank, 2010a; China National Bureau of Statistics, 2010). The enormous challenge for China, also with global implications, is in developing a society that allows 'development' at the individual and national levels, including in income levels and economic growth, but is also inclusive socially and does not adversely impact on the environment.

Figure 6.3 Shanghai, China. Some of the world's leading cities are emerging in China, with 5 cities now with urban area populations of over 11 million.

Similar to other contexts, the transport sector is perhaps the most difficult sector in China in terms of achieving greater carbon efficiency. The large current and projected population, combined with a current small absolute number of vehicles, means an enormous and rapid growth in vehicle ownership and use. These will result in huge strains on urban infrastructure, energy use and CO_2 emissions (Ng and Schipper, 2005).

China has a unique opportunity and urgency to tackle and provide a response to sustainable mobility aspirations – on the grand scale – creating unique pathways towards sustainability. These can act as models for international application, across Asia and also in the West. Transport in most cities in China is still dominated by public transport (mostly the bus), two- and three-wheelers, walking and cycling. Many of the larger cities have good transport systems, including some metro systems, local rail and bus rapid transit, often extending across the surrounding metropolitan regions. Virtually all inter-city travel is by rail or air. The average Chinese person travels around 1,000 kilometres per year, compared with 15,000 km per year for Europeans and over 24,000 km for North Americans (Ng and Schipper, 2005) – many of the levels of walking and cycling, in mode share terms, are much higher than the best European benchmarks. But, of course, the growth in motorisation is dramatic over recent years.

The potential levels of motorisation pose serious difficulties. China has just over 100 million vehicles, with most concentrated in the larger urban areas. This is a relatively low level, but the projections rise to over 400 million vehicles in 2035. This can be viewed as still being modest, as the motorisation rate will rise from the current levels of less than 50 vehicles per 1,000 population (vehicles/1,000p) to around 300 vehicles/1,000p. If the motorisation rate

Table 6.1 The urbanisation of China (2009, millions)

Urban scale	City	Urban area	Metropolitan area
3 'Mega' cities (population above 10 million persons within urban area	Chongqing	15.43	32.76
	Shanghai	13.32	14.01
	Beijing	11.75	12.46
8 'Super large' cities (population 5–10 million within the urban area)	Tianjin	8.03	9.80
	Guangzhou	6.55	7.95
	Xian	5.62	7.82
	Nanjing	5.46	6.30
	Chengdu	5.21	11.40
	Wuhan	5.15	8.36
	Shenyang	5.12	7.17
	Shantou	5.03	5.11
114 'Large' cities (population 1–5 million persons within urban area)	Jinan	3.48	6.03

Note: Municipalities and prefecture-level cities are administrative units comprising, typically, an urban area core (the city) and surrounding metropolitan area including rural or less-urbanised areas usually many times the size of the central city.

Source: China National Bureau of Statistics, 2009.

Table 6.2 China – World Development Indicators

Indicator	1990	2000	2005	2008	2009
Population, total	1,135,185,000	1,262,645,000	1,303,720,000	1,324,655,000	1,331,460,000
Population growth (annual %)	1.5	0.8	0.6	0.5	0.5
GDP per capita (current US$)	314	949	1,731	3,414	3,879
GDP growth (annual %)	3.8	8.4	11.3	9.6	9.1
Life expectancy at birth, t otal (years)	68.1	71.3	72.6	73.1	–
Fertility rate, total (births per woman)	2.3	1.8	1.8	1.8	–
Energy use (kg of oil equivalent per capita)	760	865	1,296	1,616	1,687
CO2 emissions (metric tons per capita)	2.2	2.7	4.3	–	–
Motor vehicles (per 1,000 people)	4.8	12.7	24.2	38.4	47.1
Mobile cellular subscriptions (per 100 people)	0.0	6.8	30.2	48.4	52.4
Internet users (per 100 people)	0.0	1.8	8.6	22.5	28.8

Note: Motor vehicles (passenger cars, buses, vans, lorries; not including two wheelers).

Source: World Bank, 2010a; China National Bureau of Statistics, 2010.

Figure 6.4 Wheelbarrow taxi in the 1850s, China

Source: Engraved by Alfred Louis Sargent (b. 1828) from *Le Tour du Monde*, published in Paris, 1860s (engraving), French School (19th century)/Private collection/Ken Welsh/The Bridgeman Art Library.

Figure 6.5 A Chinese Mandarin; A Visit to the Chinese Collection (engraving), from *Pictorial Times*, 8 April 1843

Source: Prior, William Henry (1812–82)/Private collection/© Look and Learn/Peter Jackson Collection/The Bridgeman Art Library.

Figure 6.6
(Above) Classic propaganda poster: *The Workers Have Spirit and Achieve Self-Renewal to Found the New Business*, printed by the Shanghai People's Publishing Co., 1973 (colour litho)

Source: ChineseSchool (20th century)/Private collection/DaToImages/The Bridgeman Art Library.

Figure 6.7 From the Cultural Revolution in 1966: *Destroy the Old World, Build a New World*, 1967, unknown artist. The worker crushes the crucifix, Buddha and classical Chinese texts with his hammer. Perhaps there are some parallels to be made in the transition to a low carbon transport future – at least in the scale of ambition required, as this is huge.

Source: ChinesePosters.net and IISH/Stefan R. Landsberger Collections.

rises to North American levels (up to 800 vehicles/1,000p) then the space required and environmental consequences will be on a scale not seen anywhere before in the world (CAI-Asia et al., 2009). Continued growth in motorisation is almost inevitable, but the rate of growth and level of saturation can vary markedly according to policy direction. A massive slowdown in urban highway investment is required if environmental and city liveability goals are to be achieved. The decision-making process in China is strongly centralised and major innovations can take place in a relatively short period of time. The opportunity for China to lead the rapidly developing countries in a new direction that embraces sustainable transport is possible, but that opportunity needs to be taken.

The Chinese car manufacturing industry is one of the most rapidly growing in the world, largely serving domestic consumption, and includes leading firms such as FAW-Volkswagen (First Automotive Works), Shanghai Volkswagen, Shanghai GM, Chery, FAW Toyota, Dongfeng Nissan, and Guangzhou Honda. An increasing number of the emerging Chinese middle class would like to adopt the lifestyles and travel behaviours that are high in energy consumption and CO_2 emissions, consistent with the 'industrialised' model. The current and potential scale of growth is, however, very different to the West, as more new vehicles are sold in China than anywhere else in the world. China has overtaken the US to become the biggest car market in the world, with the sale of nearly 20 million vehicles in 2010. This is a primary driver for China's increasing demand for oil; over half of China's oil consumption is currently imported, and this could rise to 75 per cent by 2030 (Zhao, 2011).

Motorisation has resulted from population and income growth, and been supported by economic reforms, with private vehicle usage growing at rapid rates. Motor traffic in Shanghai, Beijing, Guangzhou and other large cities is already severely congested. Non-motorised transport was unfortunately discouraged in the 1990s and early 2000s, with walking and cycling viewed as 'out-dated' modes of travel. The Economic Planning Ministry announced in the 1990s that it planned to see 'a private car for every family in China', reminiscent of the earlier Fordist vision in the West. In Beijing the tree-lined median strips, which used to separate bicycle paths from the motorised vehicle lanes, have been removed to make space for additional vehicle lanes (Hook and Replogle, 1996), and this is symptomatic of attempts to support motorisation. However, in recent years, there have been major efforts to introduce more sustainable transport initiatives, particularly in cities such as Shanghai, including the development of an extensive subway and other public transport systems. There is also increasing investment in walking, cycling facilities and mass cycle-hire schemes; urban planning based on 'eco-town' principles; and traffic management such as vehicle registration schemes and the use of fuel economy standards. Beijing remains a much more car dependent city than Shanghai, so there are different developmental paths being followed, but even in Beijing there are major investments in public transport being considered and implemented. The projected growth in motorisation, however, remains rapid across all major urban areas in China. Avoiding the move towards carbon intensive travel – based on the ICE petrol and steel car – will be extremely difficult.

Some of the trends are explored below (and illustrated in Figure 6.8). Within major urban areas in China, overall trips are growing at over 5 per cent per annum, higher than population growth and just below income growth. Vehicle km travelled is increasing at around 10 per cent per annum, with some cities experiencing higher growth (Beijing and Shanghai at over 15 per cent per annum). Non-motorised travel continues to decline in favour of public and private motorised travel. All of the major cities still have large mode shares for cycling by trip, Jinan at around 40 per cent, but the shares are declining rapidly. There are large implications related to this dramatic change in mode, particularly if viewed in terms of the loss, or at least change, in travel practices and behaviours in the city (drawing on De Certeau, 1984; De Certeau, 2000; Thrift, 2004): 'If the city is a language spoken by walkers, then a post pedestrian city not only has fallen silent but risks becoming a dead language, one whose colloquial phrases, jokes, and curses will vanish, even if its formal grammar survives' (Solnit, 2000, p. 213). Hence travel can be fundamental to the experience of the city, realised differently by different modes, and a move to increased motorisation will mean that the distinct vitality of the urban areas suffers.

Vehicle ownership differs much by city, with Shanghai having a level of vehicle ownership less than one third that of Beijing, and this is directly affected by the different policies introduced in the two cities, as well as the income levels. In Beijing until recently, there were no restrictions on car purchase or use, but the numbers of new vehicles in Shanghai have been restricted by quotas and a bidding system (Xiaohong and Zhang, 2012). The trends in aggregate transport CO_2 emissions and emissions per capita also show much variation, with Beijing experiencing high growth and aggregate transport CO_2 emissions at just under 1,400 kg per capita; Shanghai has much lower transport CO_2 emissions at 600 kg per person. The level of reduction in bicycle use over a short timescale is remarkable, from over 60 per cent to under 40 per cent of trips in Jinan (1998–2005), with similar levels in Beijing, and to a lesser extent in Shanghai. Related to these trends is China's transition to a market economic system (post-1978) and state-sponsored capitalism. This has been associated with enormous economic growth, urban expansion and also changed travel behaviours. It has included cultural change, including a less restrictive hukou system,[2] the breakup of the danwei system[3] and the long-term land-leasing system. The result in terms of travel behaviour, for example, is that many urban Chinese residents no longer live near to their workplaces, and this results in longer commutes and other trip trips (Darido et al., 2009).

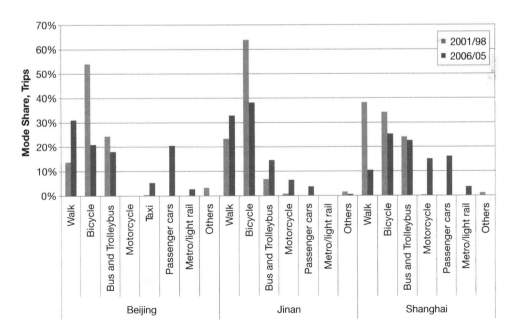

Figure 6.8 Change in mode share by city
Source: From Darido et al., 2009.

Figure 6.9 Code 46, 2003, directed by Michael Winterbottom. It is the not-
too-distant future, the population is divided between those who
live 'inside', in high-density cities physically separated from the
'outside', where the poor underclass lives.

> *Maria*: You'd never been to Shanghai before. It was all
> new to you.

Source: British Film Institute Stills Collection.

The emerging provincial city context

The case study used to illustrate the transport issues associated with the rapidly growing urbanisation in China is the city of Jinan. Jinan is a sub-provincial city, located on the east of the country, 400 km south of Beijing, and 200 km from the east coast.[4] Jinan is the provincial capital of Shandong and in recent years it has evolved into a major administrative, economic and transportation centre, with a population of 6.4 million and average annual GDP per capita of US$9,800 (64,000 CYN). The city is booming economically, with a current GDP growth rate of 17.7 per cent (China National Bureau of Statistics, 2009). The modern-day name of Jinan derives from 'south of the Ji' (waters), referring to the old Ji River that flowed to the north of the city. The Ji River disappeared in 1852 when the Yellow River changed its course to the north.

Like many Chinese cities, Jinan is currently undergoing rapid urbanisation. The city's urban area has expanded from 24.6 km² in 1949 to 295 km² in 2008 (Jinan Statistics Bureau, 2009). Jinan's population has increased over time primarily due to the migration of the agricultural population and young graduates. Jinan has a monocentric and irregular sprawl pattern, with direct jurisdiction over six urban districts (Lixia, Licheng, Huaiyin, Tianqiao, Changqing and Shizhong), one county-level city (Zhangqiu), three counties (Pingyin, Shanghe and Jiyang), and over 6 million people under its jurisdiction. With growth to the south constrained by hilly topography and to the north by the Yellow River, Jinan's 2004–2020 Master Plan proposes

Figure 6.10 Traffic congestion is becoming a large problem, as the road capacity cannot keep up with the demand for road space

Figure 6.11 Spring Waters. The central area of Jinan is very attractive, with a historic centre based around the Spring Waters.

Figure 6.12 Quancheng Square (Spring City Square). A new and attractive central pedestrianised centre has been created in Jinan with the removal of an area of housing. Redevelopment is often easier in China than in countries such as the UK.

to expand eastward, with the urban area expanding to the third ring road. This will increase the urban area to 410 km^2 by 2020.

The area around Jinan is one of the oldest urban centres in China; it was known during the Zhou Dynasty (1045 BC–256 BC) as the city of Lixia; and Lixia is now the name of one of the city's central districts. Marco Polo, the well-known Venetian explorer who travelled to China in the thirteenth century, visited the area and described it as Chingli. When the Ming Dynasty (1368–1644) created Shandong province, Jinan became its capital. Jinan is also known as the 'City of Springs', due to the artesian springs found in the urban centre and surrounds, many of which converge into Daming Lake. Jinan was developed around textile and flour milling and also a machine-building industry. By the early 1970s Jinan had become one of the main centres of China's car manufacturing industry, developing a wide range of heavy trucks and earth-moving machinery. Jinan is the cultural centre of the region of Shandong, with agricultural, medical, and engineering colleges and several universities, notably Shandong University, founded in 1901. The surrounding area has many well-known sites, including Mount Tai, a designated UNESCO World Heritage site (from 1987) (Encyclopedia Britannica, 2010).

Table 6.3 Jinan – some statistics

Metric	Comment
City tree and flower	Chinese willow and the lotus
Metropolitan area (2009)	8,177 km^2
Population	
Jinan Urban Area (2009)	3,482,000
Metropolitan Area (2009)	6,032,700
Jinan Metropolitan Area (1949)	3,052,000
Population density	738 persons/km^2
Selected political history	The Cultural Revolution[a] apparently started in Jinan in 1966 with an article in the *Jinan Evening News* denouncing the vice-governor
GDP per capita (2009)	Jinan: US$9,800 (64,000 CYN); China: US$3,350 (22,698 CYN)
Economic growth (2009)	Jinan 17.7%; China 9%
Mode share (2009)	21% car, 10% walk, 43% bus, 24% bicycle, 2% taxi
Bus rapid transit network	6 routes – 112 km, with 35 km as dedicated routes, and 55 BRT buses. A flat fare of 10p
CO2 reduction target	The Copenhagen Accord Pledge (2010) for China is to reduce carbon intensity by 40–45% by 2020 compared to 2005 levels
Transport CO2 emissions (2010)*	0.51 tonnes CO2 per capita

Notes:

* Including car, bus, motorcycle, taxi and non-motorised modes within Jinan metropolitan area, but not freight or international travel.

[a] The Cultural Revolution was led by Mao Zedong, Chairman of the PRC from 1949 to 1959 and of the Communist Party from its establishment in 1949 until his death in 1976. The Cultural Revolution followed the 'Great Leap Forward' and aimed to remove liberal elements in the Party and society at large. It resulted in widespread persecution, death, and the destruction of historical sites and culture. It included an (unsuccessful) attempt to reverse the meaning of the red traffic light to 'go'! (Encyclopedia Britannica, 2010).

Source: China National Bureau of Statistics, 2009; Encyclopedia Britannica, 2010.

Jinan is positioned at the intersection of two major railway routes – the Jinghu railway runs from Beijing to Shanghai as the major north–south route, and the Jiaoji railway connects Jinan to the seaport of Qingdao on the east coast. Major highways include the national Highways 104, 220 and 309. Jinan Yoaqiang International Airport is 33 km northwest of the city centre.

Baseline and projections

Data to estimate the current baseline and likely business as usual (BAU) trajectory for transport movement in Jinan are very limited. Table 6.4 gives the baseline data used in the Jinan analysis, including person trips per capita, trip distance and occupancy (Darido et al., 2009). This is combined with other sources, including data from the Jinan local authorities and a travel survey carried out in Jinan.[5]

Targets for CO2 reduction

A target for transport emissions reduction in Jinan can be derived to help explore the likely required scales of change. Target definition for China is usually made on an intensity basis (CO_2 emissions per unit of GDP), hence is different to the absolute and budgetary targets developed in Western countries such as the UK.[6] In 2009, as a participant in the Copenhagen

Table 6.4 Jinan – baseline statistics

Year	2005	
Population	6,422,500	
Car ownership	72 per 1,000 population	
Person-trips per capita per day	*Trips/person/day*	
	Total	2
	NMT	1.4
	Motorcycle	0.1
	Taxi	0.05
	Bus	0.3
	Car	0.1
	Other	0.05
Average trip distance	*km/trip*	
	Total	37.6
	NMT	4.5
	Motorcycle	5
	Taxi	6
	Bus	13.6
	Car	8.5
Occupancy	*Persons/vehicle*	
	Motorcycle	1
	Taxi	1.2
	Bus	15
	Car	1.2

Source: Using data from Darido et al., 2009; Jinan Statistics Bureau, 2010.

Table 6.5 Transport CO2 emission reduction targets (Jinan)

Metric	Data
CO2 1990	658,601 tCO2 (0.12 tCO2 per capita)
CO2 2030 Business as Usual (BAU)	9,580,235 tCO2 (1.16 tCO2 per capita)
GDP 1990	Chinese Yuan (CYN) 141.79 billion (US$ 21.65 billion)
Growth rate @7%, GDP 2030	CYN 2123.23 billion (US$ 324.18 billion)
CO2 Intensity (CO2/GDP), 1990	4,644.91 tCO2/billion CYN
CO2 Intensity (CO2/GDP), 2030 BAU	4,512.11 tCO2/billion CYN (2.9% reduction on 1990)
TARGET 50% reduction in CO2 intensity to 2030 relative to 1990 levels	2,256.10 tCO2/billion CYN (0.58 tCO2 per capita)

Note: 1 CNY = 0.152683 US$ (March 2011).

Accord, China pledged to reduce its economy's carbon intensity by 40–45 per cent by 2020 compared to 2005 levels. This allows economic growth, but reduces CO2 intensity, a relative decoupling. Jinan's potential transport CO2 intensity calculations are shown in Table 6.5, based on an equivalent levels to the national targets. The Chinese government has not developed an absolute national reduction target, but there have been some estimates of the 'peak time' for CO2 emissions in China, either between 2025 and 2030 (Energy Research Institute, 2009) or 2030 and 2040 (UNDP, 2010). The VIBAT-Jinan modelling, developed in consultation with Jinan officials, assumes a peak year for transport CO2 emissions for Jinan in 2025 and a reduction of 5 per cent in 2030 compared to 2025. The intensity target is very difficult to reach due to the huge expected increase in transport emissions, far outreaching even an assumed 7 per cent increase in GDP per annum. The BAU intensity in 2020 is a 230 per cent increase relative to 2005. A 45 per cent CO2 intensity reduction target would require a much increased GDP growth rate and/or reduction in transport CO2 emission growth rate.

Developing scenarios

Future scenarios can be generated in view of likely trends and uncertainties, and can be used to help assess progress against targets. Trends and uncertainties for Jinan are given in Table 6.6, covering issues likely to affect transport and urban development within the city, and ranked according to uncertainty and impact. The prioritisation of impacts was carried out in coordination with transport planning experts from Jinan.[7] The most important potential 'black swans' (high uncertainty and high impact) are given scores of 1 and 2. These are migration rates and level of environmental stewardship.

China's economy has grown rapidly with an 8–11 per cent annual growth rate during the last two decades. It is likely to continue to grow but the rate may slow. The Chinese government has set a target of 8.7 per cent for 2011, down from 10.3 per cent in 2010, while international banking forecasts estimate that China's economy will grow by 8.4 per cent in 2012. China's twelfth 5-Year Plan assumes an economic growth target for this period (2011–2015) of 7.0 per cent annually. China seeks to address rising inequality and to create an environment for

Table 6.6 Trends and uncertainties

Trends and uncertainties	Ranking
Economy and governmental	
Economic growth rate (GDP)	
Political stability (national and local)	
Globalisation, international trade and movement	
Income levels, income inequality	
Employment and manufacturing sector growth, including motor vehicle manufacturing	
Tourism and leisure industry growth	
Socio-demographics	
Rural to urban migration and population growth	**1
Age profile (influenced by 'one child' policy and ageing population)	
Household size	
Aspirations and culture – 'Western consumption' or 'other' model	
Social equality, social welfare, urban–rural balance	
Social stability	
Technologies	
Technological innovation	
Clean vehicle technologies	
Energy and power supply – renewable sources	
Environmental	
Climate change	
Major environmental shocks – earthquake, drought, flooding, water supply	
Improvement in environmental quality	
Urban issues and transport planning	
Environmental issues – stewardship, extent of 'seriousness' given to them in policy making and implementation	**2
Urban design quality	
Extent of urban sprawl	
Aspirations towards sustainable travel, level of investment in public transport, walking and cycling	
Extent of car dependency	
Inter-city movements	

more sustainable growth by prioritising more equitable wealth distribution, increased domestic consumption, and improved social infrastructure and social safety nets. China requires local governments to set a lower target for economic growth, and Jinan's GDP growth rate is assumed at 11 per cent annually for the next 5 years, which is higher than the national average growth rate (Jinan Municipal Government, 2011). In addition, in Jinan and in China, economic development has entered a transition period, perhaps increasingly dependent on domestic demand, innovation-driven industries and modern services.

Population projections are an important component of CO_2 emission scenarios. China is likely to continue its family planning policy and has set a national population target of 1.39 billion by 2015. There are other important demographic issues, as the Chinese population is rapidly ageing due to a lower mortality rate and the one child policy. The country had 169 million people over age 60 in 2010, comprising 12.5 per cent of the country's total population. This is projected to reach 31 per cent by 2050, leading to a pension problem for the Chinese government, and this may reduce China's ability to compete economically in the future. This will also represent challenges to the future transport system in terms of different requirements and abilities in accessing activities. Ageing will affect household structure and there are uncertainties in terms of household formation and urbanisation rates, and likely impacts on transport infrastructure requirements and CO_2 emissions (He, 2010). China's urbanisation will continue due to the increase of the existing urban population and rural-to-urban migration. The twelfth 5-Year Plan suggests an urbanisation rate of 51.5 per cent by 2015. Jinan's population growth rate has been relatively slow, averaging 0.28 per cent for the past 5 years and is planned to be less than 0.5 per cent for the next 5 years. Jinan's population within the metropolitan area is expected to reach 6.2 million and an urbanisation rate of 75 per cent by 2015 (Jinan Municipal Government, 2011). Urbanisation in Jinan is rapidly growing, but relies to a certain extent on infrastructure upgrading to improve people's living standards, happiness and social harmony (Jinan Municipal Government, 2011).

In terms of environmental goals, China's twelfth 5-Year Plan devotes considerable attention to energy and climate change and establishes a new set of targets and policies for 2011–2015. While some of the targets are largely in line with previous publications, other aspects represent more dramatic moves to reduce energy consumption, promote low carbon energy sources and restructure China's economy. Key targets include:

- 16 per cent reduction in energy intensity (energy consumption per unit of GDP);
- Increasing non-fossil energy to 11.4 per cent of total energy use from the current 8.3 per cent;
- 17 per cent reduction in carbon intensity (carbon emissions per unit of GDP).

There is increasing international pressure for addressing GHG reductions in China, particularly on an absolute reduction basis, but perhaps this is a Western agenda rather than something that will be taken up in China. The intensity targets allow economic growth, and unless GDP growth greatly outweighs the growth in transport CO_2 emissions, there is still also a need to decarbonise the transport sector to a large degree. Shandong has established its energy intensity target for 2015 as 17 per cent, higher than the national target; Jinan will follow the province's 17 per cent target.

The two key uncertainties are used to generate the two axes in a classic scenario dilemma (Figure 6.14). There are different potential scenarios for Jinan according to migration rate and population growth and the level of environmental stewardship. There are also important issues around path dependency (Mahoney, 2000; Arthur, 1994), wherein social phenomena are explained in terms of historical events influencing the future. These path dependency issues are usually viewed as negative, but can in theory also be positive, and are evident in all the scenarios. Scenario 1 (BAU), for example, suffers from adverse 'lock-in' to car and oil dependency as investment is made in a motorised society. A high motorisation level and high transport CO_2 emission level is contingent on earlier road building, an investment in car manufacturing, the development of a dispersed urban form, and poor investment in public transport, walking and cycling. Any later development of public transport is effectively foreclosed, or at least greatly inhibited, as a supportive urban form has not been developed.[8] Thus, the resultant travel behaviour is 'inefficient' in CO_2 emission terms. In contrast, Scenario 4 aims to use path dependency in a more positive fashion, gradually building up the investment in public transport to provide a detailed network across the city, developing walking and cycling facilities, and supporting this with a compact urban form.

Figure 6.13 Electric bicycles. E-bikes and bicycles remain popular.
Source: Carlos Pardo.

Motorisation v. sustainable mobility

Two of the dilemma scenarios are outlined in more detail below, illustrating what a continuation of the current, largely BAU, trajectory ('High Motorisation') might involve, and also a different policy trajectory reflecting high investment and high environmental stewardship ('Good Intentions'). The other two futures (Scenario 2 and Scenario 3) seem to be less suitable for development in Jinan, as one might involve a breakdown of society in the city ('City Failure') and the other is based on severe limitations on migration and growth in the city ('Plan B'), and this would be politically unacceptable. When developing future scenarios with representatives from the city authorities, it is advisable to focus on positive futures rather than the less attractive alternatives, but it should always be remembered that uncertainties and weak decision-making may lead towards undesirable futures. Again the scenario alternatives were developed and selected in conjunction with planners and government officials from Jinan and Shandong province.

Scenario 1: 'high motorisation'

The 'high motorisation' scenario (S1) assumes substantial levels of increased motorisation, along the lines of the 'North American' model. Scenario 1 is based on a high level of migration, development and transport (mainly highway) investment, but also lower levels of environmental stewardship. The conventional petrol car dominates, with little or no attempt to constrain

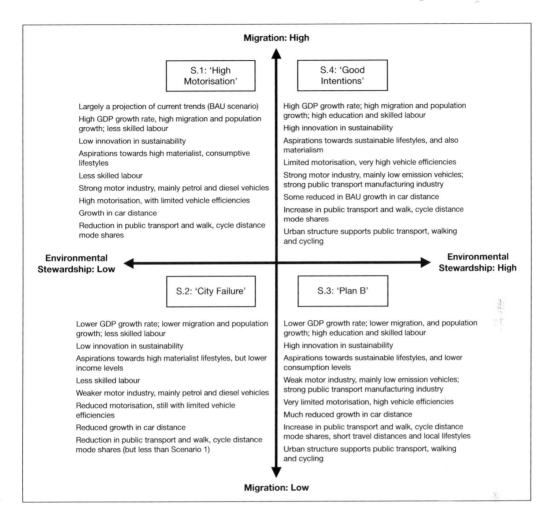

Figure 6.14 Scenario matrix

traffic growth, and few gains are made in vehicle efficiencies. There are no road pricing mechanisms and public transit investment is low. To a certain extent, the current policy approach in Jinan has already superseded this approach, with a relatively high level of current and planned public transport investment. However, it is useful within the scenario analysis to consider likely impacts of high investment in road building and low effectiveness of fuel efficiency policies, which are often part of the route to high motorisation, and indeed there are parts of this in the current approach in Jinan.

The targets and budgetary CO_2 analyses are shown in Table 6.7 and Figure 6.15. Within this scenario, transport CO_2 emissions rise from 1.42 million tonnes CO_2 (MtCO2) in 2005 to 16.27 MtCO2 in 2030 – this represents over a tenfold increase. These assumptions are representative of a high level of motorisation, moving from 72 vehicles/1,000 population (2005) to 590/1,000 population (2030), around an 8 per cent growth per annum in motorisation (2000–2030). This would result in a very high level of motorisation, nearly reaching current USlevels (675/1,000 population) in 20 years. The result would be large increase in per person

Table 6.7 Scenario 1 CO2 outputs

Scenario	Car	Bus	Motorcycle	Taxi	NMT	All
1990 (tonnes)	89,913	206,037	180,246	155,621	–	631,818
1990 per capita (tonne/person)	0.02	0.04	0.03	0.03	–	0.12
2005 (tonnes)	524,900	345,100	306,400	246,900	–	1,423,300
2005 per capita (tonne/person)	0.08	0.05	0.05	0.04	–	0.22
2010 (tonnes)	2,441,233	484,400	246,914	285,284	–	3,457,830
2010 per capita (tonne/person)	0.36	0.07	0.04	0.04	–	0.51
BAU 2030 (tonnes)	15,212,371	259,621	416,388	384,615	–	16,272,995
BAU 2030 per capita (tonne/person)	1.85	0.03	0.05	0.05	–	1.98
BAU 1990–2030 aggregate (tonnes)	230,906,958	13,593,463	11,757,124	11,214,220	–	267,471,764
Proportion of 2030 budget used by 2010					10%	26,604,791

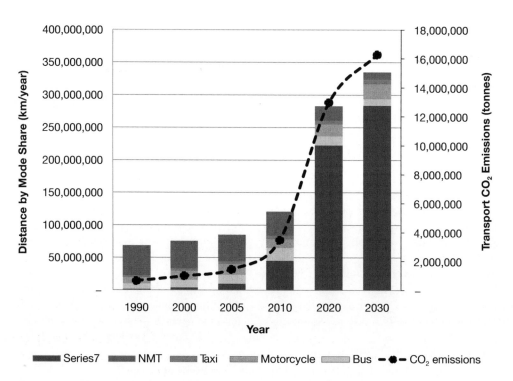

Figure 6.15 Transport distance by mode and CO2 emissions in Jinan (Scenario 1)

transport emissions, from 0.22 tonnes/person in 2005 to 1.98 tonnes/person in 2030. Car travel rises from 11 per cent to 85 per cent of all distance travelled, bus declines from 16 per cent to 3 per cent, and NMT declines from 48 per cent to 3 per cent (2005–2030). Car emissions are assumed to reach 139 gCO2/km by 2030, relative to 178 gCO2/km in 2005. This means that emissions per km driven are 22 per cent less in the future projections, but this reduction is outweighed by the huge increase in car travel. This scenario is of course very sensitive to assumptions, hence a lower motorisation rate, growth in distance travelled or improved vehicle efficiency would reduce the growth in emissions significantly.

A parallel can be made to the experience of Beijing, demonstrating what might happen under this type of high motorisation future. Beijing has undergone a massive transformation in urban transport, in supply and demand terms, in under 20 years. Short trips by bicycle and foot historically dominated mode share, but car ownership has recently become extremely attractive to the middle class, in terms of status, image and utility, as lifestyles are becoming orientated around car use. Motor vehicle growth is well over 10 per cent per annum, and even higher at 15 per cent for private cars. Car ownership in Beijing exceeded 4 million (2009), an increase of one million in just 31 months. Ownership is growing by half a million a year, which is more than 10,000 a week (*China Daily*, 2010). Road capacity has been massively

Figure 6.16 Dodge Hybrid. Though there are some low-emission vehicles emerging in the Chinese market, availability is certainly not widespread. The huge growth in vehicle numbers, distance travelled and vehicle sizes means that transport CO2 emissions are rising rapidly.

Source: Low CVP.

expanded, and Beijing has built its sixth ring road at 15–20 km from the city centre. Land development pressures have followed, with much greater demand for development in outer areas, and trips have become longer and less focused on the radial commute. Over one-third of trips are now taken by car, with a dramatic decline in cycling, even though bus use remains largely unchanged. A changed policy approach was partly developed prior to the 2008 Olympics, as several new metro, light rail and BRT lines were built. Traffic demand management has become more important, and during the Olympics a license plate scheme was used to restrict 50 per cent of vehicles from travelling in central areas (i.e. the commute by car was only allowed on alternate days). There is popular and political support to extend the scheme, but as a one-day-a-week variant (a 20 per cent regime), similar to that used in Mexico City and São Paulo (Darido et al., 2009).

Some important lessons, and also lessons, can be drawn from experience in Japan, where the rise in car mobility has been managed in a different way to the conventional US and, to a lesser extent, the European model. Domestic consumption of the private car was controlled until the national motor vehicle manufacturing industry was in a position to capture the majority of market. General Motors and Ford were forced to leave Japan in 1939, and thereafter economic nationalism and the promotion of domestic firms translated into policies supporting rail and subway infrastructure. These tended to be domestically manufactured, and relied on hydropower and coal which were domestically supplied (oil was 98 per cent imported). The large *keiretsu*[9] firms also had real-estate interests in the urban centres, which would have been devalued if urban dispersal was encouraged, and no interests in the motor industry. As late as 1956, the road between Tokyo and Osaka remained unpaved in sections. In the 1970s a concerted effort was made by the Ministry of International Trade and Industry to encourage motor manufacturing and the keiretsu became involved. Government investments and subsidy increased markedly, including three ring roads around Tokyo alone, and motorisation increased rapidly (Hook and Replogle, 1996). In contrast, in the USA and Europe the development model was to encourage motorisation as part of the auto–industrial complex, including the motor industry, road construction companies, oil companies and development industry (Freund and Martin, 1993).

Mobility infrastructures and ensuing travel patterns are associated with a complex process of policy development, and can be shaped in various directions according to strategic objectives. It is not by coincidence that some countries and cities are associated with car-based mobility patterns and others with public transport, walking or cycling or hybrid forms. We should perhaps remember the scale of the automotive industry internationally:

> if counted like a country it would be the sixth largest economy in the world, with an equivalent turnover of US$2 trillion, supporting an estimated nine million direct jobs and 50 million supplier jobs, and contributing US$400 billion to governments in tax.
>
> (Wells et al., 2012, p. 127)

In view of this scale, perhaps it is unlikely that a few well-meaning environmentalists, academics, politicians and interested members of the public can be sufficiently organised to catalyse major change in the transport system unless the industry is in support of this. The lessons for China are that motorisation can be managed, and public transport, walking and cycling encouraged, but only by a very clear and strong policy approach. A strong motor manufacturing industry, which is already a reality in China, is likely to lobby for the success of their business model. This is likely to be similar to the lines of the auto–industrial complex in the West, encouraging dispersed urban structure, low vehicle tax bases and fuel prices, and

Figure 6.17 Who Killed the Electric Car? 2006, directed by Chris Paine. The story of the development of the engine and battery technology, but also the purposive limited commercialisation and subsequent demise of the battery electric vehicle in the US, with the General Motors EV1 playing the central character. Are we about to repeat history, or is the timing better now? 'Who writes the history? Um, well . . . The guy with the biggest club.'

Source: British Film Institute Stills Collection.

aggressive vehicle marketing. Even a relatively well-organised environmental lobby in the West has failed to slow the trend towards motorisation. Jinan, and China more generally, needs to consider how they might get around this problem of powerful, vested interests. Motorisation can be developed in China, but it has to be managed in a way that supports city life, and it has to be of the low-emission vehicle variety for environmental reasons. This still provides a business model for the domestic car manufacturing industry, and can also be combined with wider sustainable mobility measures (Banister, 2008).

As a final comment, the current trends from Jinan are perhaps salutary. Between 2006 and 2010, Jinan's economy grew very quickly, with a 13.9 per cent annual average growth rate, higher than the 13 per cent target. Similar to many cities in China, motorisation has developed rapidly. By 2010, Jinan had 730,000 vehicles, of which 610,000 were privately owned, an increase of 24 per cent relative to 2009. Jinan has not formulated policies to manage the increase in vehicle population, such as in Shanghai and Beijing. In Jinan's twelfth 5-Year Plan, the automotive industry, along with the electronic and information sector, and mechanical equipment sector, are viewed as the three 'pillar industrial sectors' that are to be supported (Jinan Municipal Government, 2011). Scenario 1 (or a limited variation of this) provides a probable future for Jinan, where vehicle ownership is likely to continue to increase at a rapid rate.

Scenario 4: 'good intentions'

The 'good intentions' scenario assumes a much reduced level of motorisation, with a high level of migration, development and investment, including a very high level of environmental stewardship. The conventional petrol car is much less dominant, with a highly effective and wide-ranging policy approach to reduce potential traffic growth. Public transport, walking and cycling investment is high, with pricing mechanisms used to reduce the use of the private car. Car use is restricted to clean and small, light vehicles. Target and budgetary CO_2 analysis is shown in Table 6.8 and Figure 6.18. Within this scenario, transport CO_2 emissions rise from 1.42 $MtCO_2$ in 2005 to 4.47 $MtCO_2$ in 2030 – there is still an increase in emissions, but much less than in the BAU scenario. Motorisation rates are much lower, moving from 72 vehicles/1,000 population (2005) to 260/1,000 population (2030), less even than European levels. The result would be a reduced increase in per person transport emissions, from 0.22 tonnes/person in 2005 to 0.54 tonnes/person in 2030 (and relative to 1.98 tonnes/person under BAU). Mode share distance travelled by car hence rises more slowly, from 11 per cent to 38 per cent, bus rises slightly from 16 per cent to 20 per cent, and NMT declines to a lesser degree from 48 per cent to 38 per cent over the period 2005–2030. Car emissions are assumed to reach 92 gCO_2/km by 2030, relative to 178 gCO_2/km in 2005, and motorcycle usage is also much cleaner at 8 gCO_2/km from 50 gCO_2/km in 2005, largely consisting of e-bikes and motorcycles. There has been a major effort to make motorised travel much cleaner.

This very ambitious scenario still does not achieve the 45 per cent reduction in intensity target. Relative to 2005 levels, CO_2/GDP intensity rises by 31.7 per cent. Hence again we can see the difficulty of achieving the target, as this would require an even higher GDP growth rate and/or a more formidable reduction in transport CO_2 emission growth rate.

Shanghai provides more of a model for this type of high growth, high environmental stewardship future, with commonalities also found in some of the progressive European cities. Since the early 1990s Shanghai has experienced tremendous developmental growth and infrastructure investment. The registration of new vehicles (cars and trucks) has been capped at 50,000 annually since 1998. The registration of mopeds (under 50 cc) has also been capped since 1996, and scooters and motorcycles (over 50 cc) have been banned from the city centre. Two-wheelers powered by batteries are unrestricted. From 1991 to 1996 nearly 15 per cent of the city GDP was spent on infrastructure, an unprecedented amount, amounting to over £10 billion and including a new ring road, two major bridges and the first line of a metro system. Car ownership is limited by keeping the acquisition of a driving licence expensive. A driving school costs US$500 to attend, which is expensive for residents, involving classroom sessions, behind the wheel training and three road tests. A typical car also costs around US$10,000, with a 10 per cent sales tax and, historically, a large registration fee at US$20,000 per vehicle. This latter fee was scrapped in 1998, and a vehicle registration auction created (with a fee of US$2,500) which is used to limit the number of new vehicles, similar to the scheme in Singapore. New road infrastructure has also been limited, but there is a dense urban structure conducive to walking, cycling and public transport usage (Zhou and Sperling, 2001; Darido et al., 2009).

Even though Jinan continues to focus on rapid economic growth in 2011–2015, it also stresses innovation and environmental sustainability in economic development. Jinan is one of the pilot cities that encourages battery and hybrid vehicles in public transport. In 2010 there were 200 hybrid and battery buses in operation in Jinan and five battery charging stations. Jinan added 800 battery buses and public vehicles in 2011, and 1,610 in 2012. By the end of 2015, Jinan is expected to have 100,000 battery or hybrid public vehicles in operation.

Table 6.8 Scenario 4 CO2 outputs

Scenario	Car	Bus	Motorcycle	Taxi	NMT	All
1990 (tonnes)	89,913	206,037	180,246	155,621	–	631,818
1990 per capita (tonne/person)	0.02	0.04	0.03	0.03	–	0.12
2005 (tonnes)	524,900	345,100	306,400	246,900	–	1,423,300
2005 per capita (tonne/person)	0.08	0.05	0.05	0.04	–	0.22
2010 (tonnes)	2,441,233	484,400	246,914	285,284	–	3,457,830
2010 per capita (tonne/person)	0.36	0.07	0.04	0.04	–	0.51
S4 2030 (tonnes)	1,835,418	1,277,284	1,035,962	323,717	–	4,472,381
S4 2030 per capita (tonne/person)	0.22	0.16	0.13	0.04	–	0.54
S4 1990–2030 aggregate (tonnes)	70,202,861	23,111,032	15,425,203	10,547,189	–	119,286,285
Proportion of 2030 budget used by 2010					22%	26,604,791

Note: These two scenario visions for Jinan in 2030 give contrasting views of the potential pathways that can be followed, one based on BAU (High Motorisation) with transport-related emissions levels reaching nearly 2 tCO2 per person and the other (Good Intentions) reaching a level of 0.54 tCO2 per person. These differences are substantial and demonstrate the potential for a decarbonisation of the transport sector at the city level, even in situations where huge growth is taking place in levels of personal mobility. To keep CO2 emissions at these lower levels requires a continuous and committed set of policy actions across a wide range of sectors, including transport, land use and development, technology and pricing. The options available, together with comments on the scale and timing needed for effective implementation, are now presented.

Jinan is also investing in public transport. It has one of the most extensive BRT networks in China and will add six more lines to the current BRT network, with plans for a 50-km network. Jinan aims to have 20 buses per 100,000 persons, and a mode share for public transport of 30 per cent by 2015 (Jinan Municipal Government, 2011). Further policy options can also be used in Jinan, including economic policy instruments such as differentiating parking fees, congestion charging, and policies to encourage the purchase of electric and hybrid cars for private users, investment in public transport and facilities for cycling and walking. The plans are for Jinan to become a model city focusing on electric vehicles, public transport, walking and cycling, and this will require a very strong policy-making approach, with a clear future vision, and the leadership and resources necessary for effective implementation.

Policy interventions and assumptions within Scenario 4

Some of the important policy interventions within Scenario 4 are explored in more detail below, grouped into a number of policy areas or packages, but within each of these are many individual measures. It is acknowledged that individual policies will have only limited impact when challenging CO2 reduction targets, and it is only when they are combined in mutually supporting packages that they will have any real impact. The policy packages themselves need to be grouped together to maximise their effectiveness (Banister et al., 2000; Hickman et al.,

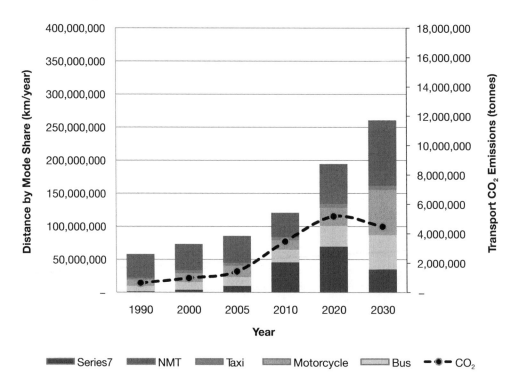

Figure 6.18 Transport distance by mode and CO2 emissions in Jinan (Scenario 4)

2010a). In future scenarios, it is important to understand the implications of the expected changes in travel distance, the relative efficiencies of the different modes of transport, and the significant changes in modal shares for each form of transport. This is an important point that is often overlooked – the extent to which policy interventions can affect behaviour. Perhaps in China the likely impact of governmental actions are much greater than in other contexts. The purpose below is to identify the likely range of measures available and how best to group them in packages, and to comment on the scale of implementation.

Bus rapid transit

China has been investing huge amounts of money in transport infrastructure, including in public transport. The National Energy Policy for China (2004) suggests that public transport should be the main access method for large cities, with inter-city rail, and personal cars (and bicycles) being used as supporting modes (Ng and Schipper, 2005). Many of the larger cities are developing bus rapid transit (BRT) networks, including Beijing, Shanghai, Chongqing and Tianjin.

Jinan is developing a relatively extensive BRT network and this system is likely to be the mainstay of the public transport system in the city, due to the cost-effectiveness of building the system relative to a metro system. There are currently six routes and fifty-five BRT buses, with a route length of 112 km, of which 35 km are dedicated lanes. Fares are low at around US16 cents per trip for use of the whole network. By 2020 the BRT network is to be extended to total 200 km, covering most of the major routes in Jinan. There are also plans to develop a metro, but there are concerns over impacts on the famous springs in Jinan.

Scenario 4 assumes a large increase in distance travelled by public transport (+270 per cent on 2010 levels by 2030), delivered mainly by an extensive BRT system and a limited metro system. Jinan currently has 3,500 buses and 4,000 bus stops with an annual travel distance of 155 million km (Jinan Statistics Bureau, 2009). The existing bus capacity cannot meet the increasing demand of Jinan city, but the conventional bus network can also be much enhanced, with newer and clean vehicle technologies and traffic priority measures, improved integration between services and other modes, through ticketing and integrated fares. Information and communication technology (ICT) can also provide more information about public transport services, and traffic conditions. The integrated smart card (IC) can be used on the public transport system and a discount to normal ticket pricing can be introduced to encourage the increased use of public transport.

Urban form

Chinese urban cities are built at relatively high densities, certainly in the inner areas, and this fits well with efforts to encourage the use of walking and cycling and public transport. The likelihood is that they will remain fairly compact and well planned. However, there is a danger in the developing urban sprawl as increased development is accommodated. More and more cities are suburbanising, replicating the dispersed structure of North American cities. Residents are relocating to the suburbs, moving away from the central area congestion. They are searching for more living space (usually mid- to high-rise towers in isolated superblocks), and employment sites are also being developed away from central locations, resulting in longer commuting distances (Cervero and Day, 2008).

There is much interest in sustainable city form, or the development of eco-cities, as part of efforts to decarbonise city life. For the moment, progress with eco-cities remains limited, with only a few examples being developed, usually as joint ventures between Chinese land and investment companies and overseas developers and consultants. Examples such as the Dongtan, Tianjin (China–Singapore) and Cao Fei Dian eco-cities remain limited in size, and they are often remote from the neighbouring city. Most have experienced difficulties in implementation, and any resulting ecological credentials have been queried (Wu, 2012).

China's urban form is the result of a very particular historical trajectory. Urbanisation was extremely limited during the 15 years of the Cultural Revolution (ending in 1979). Public investment in urban transport and housing infrastructure was minimal, with a greater focus of effort on rural areas. Rural–urban migration was tightly restricted by laws and government control over employment locations. Market reforms were introduced in 1979, and rural–urban migration picked up again, and recently this has accelerated rapidly. Urban land and housing markets have been introduced. Previously there was no private mechanism for farmers to sell land to developers, hence cities remained compact (Hook and Replogle, 1996). In recent years, cities have been promoted by central government as 'engines of growth' for national and regional economies. Cities, for example, are allowed to annex suburban areas and develop them as city districts. Large foreign capital revenue streams have been attracted from Hong Kong, Taiwan and elsewhere internationally, and new industries, commercial organisations and services have appeared. With increasing exports from China, and the manufacturing sector now acting as the 'world's factory', a significant middle class has emerged that consumes material goods, including homes, cars and other products. New spaces of 'differentiation and marginalisation' have developed, exemplified by the rise of exclusive gated communities and also poor migrant enclaves, and an increase in income inequality. At the same time urban life has been enriched for the new middle classes, with a greater range of cultural activities, entertainment, fashion, consumerism, literature and personal interactions. A 'multiplex urbanism' has been described, with urban centres as centres of production for the nation as well as the world, and money directed towards municipal government via taxes and business fees (Ma, 2009).

Within Scenario 4, the Jinan urban structure is purposively designed to support the use of public transit (largely BRT) and walking and cycling. Clusters of high-density development are developed along key axes, around an enhanced public transport network. Sprawl is contained on the edge of the urban area, and the public realm is much improved for pedestrians and cyclists. Jinan's 5-Year Plan (2011–2015) makes a start in focusing development in three new districts, extending the existing urban area into a new western district, new eastern district and to the river bank area in the north. The existing urban area is planned to become the centre of the spring waters, together with the protection of historical and cultural sites, and it will also act as the centre for retail, finance, education, research and health care. These three new districts are currently suburban areas or rural areas under the administration of Jinan. The construction of the BRT and railway will form the spine to these areas.

The areas will each have a different focus: the new western district will include higher-end business and financial services, exhibition, cultural, creative and travel and leisure industries, taking advantage of the close proximity to the high-speed rail hub and the cultural and educational resources in the urban centre. The new eastern district is envisaged as an area of high-technology industries, high-end manufacturing, strategic and emerging industries and business exhibition, administrative offices, culture and sports. The National Games were held in Jinan in 2009 in the eastern district, with many sport facilities and exhibition facilities constructed; Jinan has also moved its municipal government offices to this area. To the north of the existing urban area, along the Xiaoqing River, Jinan plans to build a river bank district with leisure and tourism facilities, commercial and residential buildings and logistics uses. In the years after 2015, Jinan is likely to expand further in these three directions into current rural areas administered by Jinan. The transport network will develop from the existing urban centre, to the southwest, east and north, hence there is a 'public transport spine' for all the new development plans and existing urban centre (Figure 6.19).

High-speed rail

China has the world's most extensive high-speed rail (HSR) network with about 8,358 km of routes in service (as of January 2011), including 2,197 km of rail lines with top speeds of 350 km/h.[10] There are plans for the HSR network to reach 13,073 km by the end of 2011, and 45,000 km by the end of 2015 (Figure 6.25), but these plans have been delayed following the HSR accident near Wenzhou in July 2011. Even though there is controversy over the necessity of having an expensive HSR system, the Chinese government believes that the system can promote economic growth by increasing the transport capacity and linking labour markets. The view is that HSR stimulates the growth of urban centres and limits sprawl, alleviates oil dependency, and reduces GHG emissions by shifting from oil to electricity, in particular electricity generated by renewable energy. It also reflects the rapid modernisation of the Chinese national transport system.

The Beijing–Shanghai HSR runs at an average speed of about 300 km/h, cutting the journey time between the two cities to less than 5 hours. Currently, a rail trip on the 1,318-km route can take up to 18 hours. Jinan is an important station along this route[11]; the journey

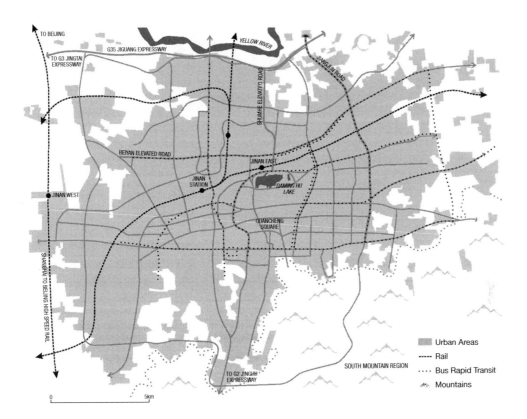

Figure 6.19 An integrated transport and urban strategy for Jinan Urban Area
Source: Mapping by Bally Meeda and Urban Graphics.

time between Jinan and Beijing reducing to just 1.5 hours from up to 7 hours previously, while the trip between Jinan and Shanghai is now 3.5 hours, down from as much as 15 hours. The rail line also enhances the transport links and cuts the journey time between Jinan and Hebei, and Anhui and Jiangsu provinces. The (proposed) metro in Jinan will have a major interchange with Jinan West railway station, hence providing a link between high-speed rail and the metro to the city centre.

There is considerable potential for Jinan to develop as an axial city, as the HSR station is located in the Western New District. High-density mixed-use development can be concentrated around the new HSR station, as this provides the most accessible public transport location in the city. The centre of gravity within Jinan moves to the west, but this will be compensated for by the new metro link to the existing city centre. This local axis will be matched by a regional axis to the east, as Jinan is linked by another HSR link to the port city of Qingdao (population of 2.75 million) some 200 km away, with intermediate stops at Zibo (2.79 million) and Qingzhou (1.35 million), giving a total regional population of over 20 million in the corridor.

Figure 6.20 Bus rapid transit as the framework for new development form, with high density development along the route network and particularly at interchanges

Figure 6.21 New BRT vehicle fleet, comfortable inside and pleasant to use

Figure 6.22 Real-estate development is booming around the BRT stops
Source: Carlos Pardo.

Figure 6.23 Jinan West rail station. A new HSR station at Jinan West provides a stop on the high-speed line
from Beijing to Shanghai, and again is built at a huge scale. A new western district is in
development around the station, to be linked to the existing city centre by bus rapid transit.

Figure 6.24 High-speed rail in China. China has the world's longest HSR network, with state-of-the-art and often luxurious train systems and interchanges.

Motorised two-wheelers and paratransit

The growth in use of motorised two-wheelers in China has been on a very large scale and rapid, from only 200,000 in 1981 to over 50 million in 2002 (Pucher et al., 2007). Two-wheelers now account for the vast majority of motorised vehicles in China. They provide an increasing middle class with affordable, flexible and quick transport, even though there are still serious problems in terms of congestion, traffic safety and casualty rates. Policy-makers are concerned about the speed of electric bikes, fearing that they are either too fast to operate safely in the bike lanes or too slow and dangerous to operate in the motor cycle lanes. A number of Chinese cities have banned the use of motorcycles, hence electric bikes and scooters have become even more popular. Motorcycles are typically allowed if they are light and have small engine capacities. Electric bicycles are gaining market share due to the faster speed than conventional bicycles, and they are much less expensive than cars (Cherry et al., 2009).

Urban trip distances have risen due to rapidly expanding cities, encouraging faster, longer range bicycles. The Chinese population bought 21 million e-bikes, compared with 9.4 million cars, in 2009. China has about 65 million electric bicycles and scooters. Even some who can afford cars are replacing them with electric two-wheelers to avoid traffic congestion and expensive gasoline. E-bikes are likely to continue to replace motorcycles, and this may lead to further electrification of China's transport sector (Weinert et al., 2008). Paratransit modes, including taxis, motorised rickshaws, minivans and minibuses, also provide essential public transport services, often along routes and journeys that are not well served by conventional public transport options. Many paratransit vehicles tend to be old and polluting, and they often have a poor safety record.

Scenario 4 envisages that new vehicle technologies are introduced, providing a new, clean paratransit vehicle fleet, with improved driving standards. Scenario 4 assumes a large increase in motorised two-wheelers on current levels, and they are all electric. E-bikes have uncertain environmental impacts depending on power supply and their use of the old lead-acid battery technology. E-bikes should be encouraged to the extent that they displace car or motorcycle use, but the majority of e-bikes tend to belong to previous bus or bicycle users, so there are some unintended mode shifts.

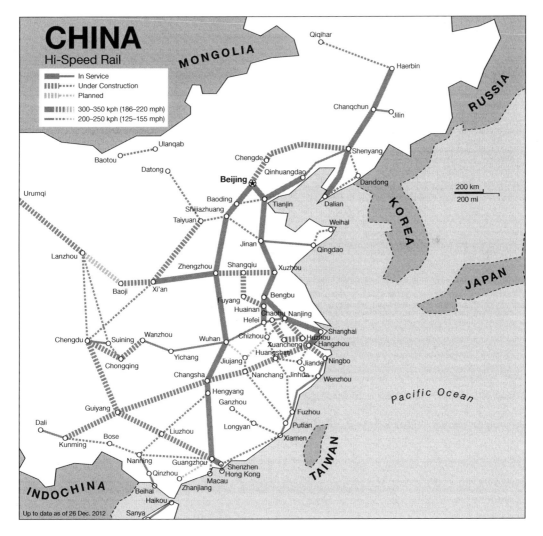

Figure 6.25 High-speed rail network map, China
Source: Yonah Freemark and Thetransportpolitic.

Cycling and walking

For many decades, transport in Chinese cities was dominated by bicycles, with extensive cycle paths and cycle parking provision. The mode share for cycling was typically higher than anywhere else in the world, with cycling and walking trips accounting for over 90 per cent of total trips in some of the major cities. Cities tended to be dense at the centre, facilitating movement by cycling and walking. (Hook and Replogle, 1996).With minimal public investment in roads and public transport, the mass transport option in Chinese cities became the bicycle. Bicycles were affordable and, until recently, subsidised by employers. Low average incomes meant that ownership of a motorcycle or car was out of reach for the vast majority of people. One-third of road space was typically reserved for cycles and one-third for pedestrians. Before the economic reforms, owning a bicycle in China was a privileged position. Bicycles were rationed to favoured employees, and only one person in four or five had a bicycle. The vast majority of the rest of the population, except very high-level Party officials and foreigners, travelled by public transport. The bicycle was hence seen as a high-status consumer good, helping to avoid use of the crowded buses. In the 1980s and 1990s the use of the bicycle grew rapidly with a more ubiquitous usage. In major cities bicycle congestion and chaotic bicycle parking became problematic. In the 1990s in Beijing more than 50 per cent of people commuted to their jobs by bicycle, with 70 per cent in Tianjin and 40 per cent in Shanghai (Hook and Replogle, 1996). More recently, the bicycle was often been perceived as an outdated mode, and usage not encouraged to the same extent as private motorisation, with some active discouragement. Many cycle lanes and pedestrian facilities have been narrowed or removed to accommodate the car.

Cities such as Shanghai and Tianjin have been the most progressive in terms of encouraging cycling, and most of the major cities now have extensive cycle hire schemes, developed as larger scale versions of the Paris Vélib' system (launched in 2007) and pioneering La Rochelle system (developed in the 1970s). Cycle rickshaws, with two- and three-wheeler variants, are also popular in Chinese cities. As fuel was rationed primarily to state enterprises at highly subsidised prices, light goods vehicles were expensive, hence the tri-shaw became the mode of choice for small businesses, particularly for suburban farmers selling produce. The flatbed of the tri-shaw also served as housing for some of the estimated 50 million 'floating' population, the most recent rural migrants to urban areas (Hook and Replogle, 1996).

Under Scenario 4, Jinan is planned to aggressively support the use of cycling and walking, with an assumed large increase in distance travelled by non-motorised modes (+270 per cent on 2010 levels by 2030). To achieve this level of increase necessitates a large investment in infrastructure, including a dense network of dedicated cycle lanes, developing some of the existing routes. There can also be further cycle parking provision, cycle hire, pedestrianisation in retail districts, and a much improved public realm. The Netherlands can be used as a model for further cycle provision; whilst some of the public realm design found in the centre of Jinan is of high quality, and can be extended across the city where there is expected to be a high level of pedestrians and social interaction. These types of facilities can be provided at a fraction of the cost of highway investment. A compact, polycentric urban form can support the use of cycling and walking. Safeguarding the existing space for cyclists and monitoring the use of bike lanes are important to encourage the public to use bicycles. Such actions avoid the vicious circle of cycle mode share decline, with some cities such as Beijing opting to use bicycle space for vehicle lanes and parking space, and then having to reallocate space for cyclists to encourage cycling again.

Further complementary policy measures aimed at reducing the growth in motorised travel and CO_2 emissions can include the development of flexible working and lifestyles (working

Figure 6.26 Shanghai cycle hire. In Shanghai cycle hire schemes have
been developed at the residential end of the trip, to allow a
wide catchment to the rail and Metro stations. These schemes
are often very large and popular and can be extended across
the wider city area including in the central urban area.

and shopping at home) to reduce travel distance and traffic congestion, and thus CO2 emissions.
Ecological driving and slower speeds also have the benefit of CO2 reduction. Lower speeds
need to be combined with awareness programmes and the use of better driving techniques to
reduce fuel use. The comprehensive implementation of all these measures will mean that,
under Scenario 4 ('good intentions'), Jinan will come close to achieving the absolute targets
set for reducing carbon in transport. The more detailed modelling work required to give
accurate estimates of the scale of change needed for each of the measures has not been
undertaken, nor has the sensitivity analysis that would be required to determine the linkages
between changes in carbon intensity and GDP output. But the measures have been discussed
with the local policy-makers and academics in China to determine the feasibility of the policy
interventions in achieving carbon emissions reductions, hence there is a level of robustness
built in to the future strategy.

Figure 6.27 Segregated cycle provision in Jinan

Figure 6.28 Attractive public realm in the central area

Figure 6.29 Urban highways. Jinan has also built many urban highways in recent years, at a cost to the quality of the urban realm, and also facilitating greater traffic volumes and transport CO2 emissions. These types of highways are very expensive and the money can be much better spent on other transport investments.

Vehicle emission profiles and fuel efficiency

Low-emission vehicles, if they become readily available and taken up by the mass market, could make a very large impact on projected CO2 emissions. An and Sauer (2004) outline the potential and relative progress in vehicle-emission profiles by country (Figure 6.30). Fuel economy standards were introduced in China in 2004, and are based on fuel intensity, the weight of the vehicle and the type of transmission. For passenger vehicles weighing less than 750 kg, the maximum new fuel vehicle intensity for a manual transmission is 7.2 litres/100 km[12] and 7.6 litres/100 km for automatic transmission. Permitted fuel intensity rises as the vehicle weight rises. The current vehicle mix in China is relatively heavy, with a large share of imported large cars and sports utility vehicles (SUVs), though an increasing number of smaller vehicles are being purchased by middle-class households (Ng and Schipper, 2005). China is thus seeking to move from a fleet with relatively high emission levels of 210 gCO2/km (2002) to the lower level of 170 gCO2/km (2009). It is not yet clear whether these profiles have been achieved, but this would still represent poor progress relative to Japanese or European standards. There is substantial potential for reducing carbon emissions from the vehicle fleet relative to international best practice.

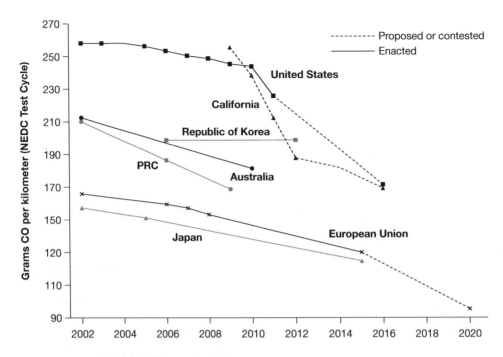

Figure 6.30 Vehicle fuel efficiency standards

Note: NEDC = New European Driving Cycle.

Source: An and Sauer, 2004; CAI-Asia and ICCT, 2009.

The assumed vehicle-emission profile, as used in the Scenario 4, is shown in Table 6.9. The projected progress is ambitious in aiming for a target below 100 gCO2/km by 2030, but there is a risk here in relying too heavily on vehicle technology improvements, as there may be difficulties in implementation, but such targets provide an opportunity for demonstrating the steps that need to be taken. Hybrid car technologies are becoming available in China's vehicle market. FAW, for example, has started building the Prius in association with Toyota (available from 2006), and compressed natural gas and electric vehicles both have considerable potential. Jinan is one of the New Energy Vehicle Pilot Cities, and it is building a number of electric vehicle charging stations, so is beginning to provide the necessary low emission vehicle infrastructure.

Jinan follows the national standards for fuel efficiency and does not have particular local regulations. Privately owned vehicles account for more than 80 per cent of total vehicles and this is likely to continue to increase. Restricting vehicle ownership through vehicle registration (following the Shanghai or Beijing model) can be used to control the rapid increase in vehicle population in Jinan. Car rental and sharing schemes have not developed in Jinan, but can provide another approach to reducing the total vehicle population and the use of vehicles.

Table 6.9 Assumed vehicle-emission profiles (car/taxi, gCO2/km)

2005	*2010*	*2015*	*2020*	*2025*	*2030*
178.2	169.5	145.5	125.0	107.3	92.2

The means of car ownership is also assumed to change over time in Jinan, with less use of the conventional model (private ownership) and a greater use of rental and shared ownership schemes. These can be developed as part of car-free or low-car developments. Building on the success of cycle hire schemes, Paris now offers an *autolib'* car sharing programme with around 4,000 small electric cars available for the public's use. This type of scheme can act as a model for development in Jinan. A third approach is the use of the 'yellow tag' for high emission and low fuel efficiency, usually older, vehicles. The vehicles with yellow tags are restricted to run in suburban areas, and not in the urban centre. Over time, the city government can phase out the older vehicles and encourage the use of more efficient vehicles.

Battery and plug-in hybrid vehicles

China is investing heavily in research and development and commercialisation of cleaner vehicles, such as battery vehicles and hybrids, and fuel cell vehicles (Ni, 2008; Sperling and Gordon, 2009). In the past 10 years, the Chinese government has allocated more than 10 billion yuan (US$1.52 billion) to research and development in energy conservation and emissions reduction technologies, of which 2 billion yuan has been invested in electric vehicles, involving over 500 research projects.[13] Since 2009, a 'Ten Cities, a Thousand EVs' plan has been implemented. This programme aims to select ten cities each year and promote 1,000 demonstration vehicles. So far twenty-five cities and fifty-four automobile manufacturers have been involved in the national programme.

The programme initially focused on buses and other commercial vehicles, but since 2010 a pilot programme has been developed in five cities (Shanghai, Hefei, Hangzhou, Shenzhen and Changchun) to subsidise the purchase of electric cars, involving up to 60,000 yuan (US$9,160) off the price of a battery car and 50,000 yuan (US$7,634) off plug-in hybrids. The subsidy is paid directly to the car manufacturers, who then reduce the vehicle price accordingly. Individual buyers of electric vehicles can also get a 3,000-yuan (US$458) subsidy from dealers.

The Chinese government has an ambitious plan to invest 100 billion yuan (US$15.2 billion) in electric and hybrid vehicles over the next 10 years, and it has set a target for 1 million electric cars on its roads annually, beginning in 2015.[14] Hence the policy objectives are ambitious in terms of electric vehicles, but perhaps the focus is weak in terms of reducing motorisation growth (albeit this is likely to be a cleaner fleet). The adverse impact of a large vehicle fleet on congestion and the urban fabric cannot be reduced by clean vehicles, but the clear intention to support the motor manufacturing industry seems to override these problems. Jinan is one of twenty-five cities selected to promote cleaner buses and commercial vehicles and building infrastructure for battery charging, and it is drafting its low carbon development plan. Jinan is not one of the five cities which promote battery and plug-in hybrid cars through subsidy, but it is promoting its automotive industry sector through the construction of cleaner vehicle manufacturing.

TDM and pricing regimes

Increased charging for car use is also critical to make the relative marginal cost of using public transport (and cycling and walking) more attractive and to help restrict the expected growth in car ownership and use. There are a number of levers that can be used, including taxation and pricing regimes:

- Vehicle taxes in China are currently charged on an annual basis, with the amount varying by type of vehicle.Vehicle consumption tax is also charged based on engine size, with higher taxes for large-engine vehicles. Scenario 4 assumes vehicle taxation is differentiated by vehicle type, with the high-emission vehicles having a higher level of taxation. The level of taxation is high, relative to income levels, at around US$1,000 per annum.
- Fuel is taxed at a higher level than at present under Scenario 4, similar to European levels (e.g. the UK and the Netherlands), and this is important alongside vehicle taxation in contributing to the variable costs of car travel, hence influencing distance travelled. The current levels of vehicle taxation in China are at 99 US cents/litre, above the US (56 cents/litre), but below the higher taxation countries such as the UK (144 cents/litre) and the Netherlands (163 cents/litre). In comparison, the base price for oil at $48 dollars/barrel is 30 cents/litre (GIZ Deutsche Gesellschaft für Technischer Zusammenarbeit, 2008).
- Road pricing on an area-wide basis is also assumed within Scenario 4, covering the built up area of Jinan, and charged on a distance and emissions basis (again according to vehicle type). The revenue raised is 'hypothecated' into public transport, walking and cycling facilities, and public realm improvements. This reflects the experience in London, Singapore and elsewhere, but is carried out on a wider basis and different specification. A cordon-based congestion charge might prove to be a useful first step towards an area-wide scheme.

The Jinan municipal government is seeking to increase and charge parking differentially based on location, such as at the airport, train and bus stations, tourist facilities, the city centre, and those areas with serious traffic congestion, with the intention of increasing costs from the current 2 yuan/hour to 8 yuan/hour. Free or low fees can be charged for electric vehicles in order to promote their use in Jinan. These types of measures could be adopted as part of a wider TDM strategy and implementation.

Figure 6.31 *2046*, 2004, directed by Wong Kar-wai. A huge rail network connects the planet, but the world is a vast dystopia; lonely souls try to reach a mysterious place called 2046. In the world of 2046 nothing ever changes, so there is never loss or sadness. No-one has ever returned from 2046 except the protagonist: as the story begins, Tak is on a long train ride returning from 2046: 'Whenever someone asked why I left 2046, I always gave them some vague answer. It was easier.'

Source: British Film Institute Stills Collection.

Conclusions: accommodating the growth

Transport and city building in China have important implications globally, largely because of the huge size of the population, but also the scale of the travel and CO2 emissions involved, and increasingly in the innovations that are being developed. Building a low carbon transport system in China is an immense task, but also a great opportunity. At one level China can learn the lessons from experience in the West, but maybe the Chinese will simply prove more effective strategists, with a greater focus on societal gain, and also have the available funds to implement major projects. The history of urban development in China suggests that once again new and leading practices may emerge, that urban reconstruction can occur at the grand scale, with a strong administrative lead, often involving breathtaking speed and involving great economic and social complexity (Ma, 2009). Strategic urban planning may be pursued more strongly, and become more progressive in approach, in the coming years in China relative to countries such as the UK, New Zealand (see the following chapter), or in the US, where the neo-liberal approach to governance has become strong, and efforts to control the location and form of development are somehow framed as 'anti-competitive'.

Scenario analysis provides us with an indication of what futures might be possible given current trends and potential uncertainties (Table 6.10). Scenarios, with a quantitative underpinning, take us beyond the generic policy objectives in sustainable transport to show the potential changes possible in distance by mode, vehicle emissions, motorisation rates and resulting transport CO2 emissions under different intervention strategies. Significant growth is expected in car ownership and use in Jinan, and the mode share by distance of bus and NMT is likely to fall from current levels. However, an effective sustainable transport strategy is also likely to include the following features over the period 2010–2030:

- Car distance travelled remains at levels similar to those found today (Scenario 4) rather than a potential increase of over 500 per cent (Scenario 1) on current levels; bus and NMT distance each increase by around 170 per cent and e-bikes by 400 per cent or more.
- Motorisation levels are kept to under 250 vehicles/1,000, rather than the US-type levels of 600+/1,000, with use of vehicle registration and pricing mechanisms (such as increased cost of car ownership and use) and car parking supply restraint.
- Private car use, where used, is clean with average car emissions at below 100 gCO2/km.
- Mode shares for NMT are maintained at around 20 per cent, bus at 20 per cent and e-bikes at 20 per cent, with the car below 40 per cent.
- Transport emissions increase to the threshold of 0.5 tonnes CO2 per capita by 2030.

To achieve the aspirations of Scenario 4 will mean the building of an extensive BRT system, and the building of an urban structure with higher densities around the public transport network. Sustainable travel is possible if the transport investments are combined with a polycentric style of development undertaken within Jinan but also regionally across Shandong province, with connections by HSR to the main cities in China. There is also likely to be some form of restriction of vehicle ownership and use (either through a registration scheme or pricing) and substantial investment in the e-bike and walking and cycling environment. The motor industry also has a critical role in designing and supplying low-emission vehicles at a market price that is cheaper than the petrol equivalents. These types of futures can help overcome associated problems with congestion, traffic safety and local air pollution.

It is important to achieve changed travel behaviours that do not follow the North American and to some extent the Beijing model (Scenario 1). Flexible and positive outcomes need to

Figure 6.32 Increasing highway capacity to accommodate the projected growth in traffic is now very outdated as an approach in transport planning, and needs to be superseded by large investments in
public transport, walking and cycling and urban planning, supported by a clean vehicle fleet

be achieved, together with self-reinforcing adaptive strategies and synergies or 'increasing returns'. The institutional framework that promotes sustainable mobility needs to be established, seeking to deliver increasing benefits, seen here as societal goals. With respect to Scenario 4, which follows the Shanghai model more closely, and to some extent the European pathway, the transition is complex as it involves many different drivers of change and a wide range of policy options.

There are critical points, such as the initial development of bus rapid transit and the urban structure being pursued in the master-planning of Jinan's development, and these will influence the direction, scale and speed of change. All of these opportunities need to be considered in the composite approach adopted in the policy packaging. The institutional framework is present to allow such a system to be financed and introduced, together with the supporting policy packages (electric vehicle subsidy and promotion; clean fuel sourcing for electricity; public transport and bicycle infrastructure; policies for parking and congestion, TDM and ICT, etc.).

Chinese cities are likely to move centre stage over the next 10–20 years in terms of their tremendous growth, but also in their potential for leading the promotion of innovative strategies for city development and transport investment, and there is a clear opportunity for them to demonstrate best practice in the design and operation of the sustainable city. Unless the

Figure 6.33 Maglev. Similarly, some public transport investments can be poorly targeted, sometimes as 'prestige' projects. The Maglev (Magnetic Levitation) airport connection in Shanghai was built in 2004 at a cost of US$1.2 billion for just 33 km of line. It runs at around a fifth full, requires large operating subsidies in spite of a high fare (US$6 one way), and has virtually no practical use for daily travel in Shanghai (Pucher et al., 2007). Transport investment needs to be much more carefully planned, with a consideration of the effectiveness of spending across modes relative to likely societal impact.

Table 6.10 Summary scenario metrics

Baseline	Car	Bus	All
2005 (tonnes CO2)	524,900	345,100	1,423,300
2005 per capita (tonne CO2/person)	0.08	0.05	0.22
2010 motorisation	72 vehicles/1,000 population		
2005 car gCO2/km	178		
2010 mode share, distance (km)	*Car* 11%	*Bus* 16%	*NMT* 48%

2030 Projection	Scenario 1: High Motorisation			Scenario 4: Good Intentions		
	Car	Bus	All	Car	Bus	All
2030 (tonnes CO2)	15,212,371	259,621	16,272,995	1,835,418	1,277,284	4,472,381
2030 per capita (tonne CO2/person)	1.85	0.03	1.98	0.22	0.16	0.54
2030 motorisation	590 vehicles/1,000 population			244 vehicles/1,000 population		
2030 car gCO2/km		139			92	
2030 mode share, distance (km)	*Car* 85%	*Bus* 3%	*NMT* 3%	*Car* 38%	*Bus* 20%	*NMT* 38%

projected growth in motorisation is avoided and public transport, cycling and walking are positively encouraged, there will be huge increases in CO2 emissions. The environmental stewardship of the globe is dependent on Chinese and wider Asian cities achieving low carbon mobility, together with more progressive policy-making in the Western industrialised countries. For Jinan, the objective must be to effectively achieve the transition to sustainable transport at a much faster rate than has been achieved in the West, and to avoid the wasteful period of carbon-dependent motorisation fuelled by oil. In the face of widespread aspiration for car ownership amongst the public this is a difficult task, but there is great progress being made and this offers us hope.

Notes

1   The early Chinese towns emerged during the Longshan period (3000–2000 BC) in the central plain in modern Henan province, and also the Shandong peninsula, mid-Yangzi River Valley and Inner Mongolia. They were known as *chengbao* (walled fortresses), and included signs of state formation, urban planning and complex societies with social stratification and product specialisation (Ma, 2009).

2   A *hukou* refers to the system of residency permits, which dates back to ancient China. A household registration record officially identifies a person as a resident of an area and includes information such as the name, parents, spouse and date of birth. In 1958, the Chinese government modified the hukou system to control the movement of people between urban and rural areas to ensure some structural stability. After the Chinese economic reforms in the late 1970s, it became possible for some to unofficially migrate and gain employment without a valid permit. The system has undergone further relaxation in the mid-1990s and again in the early 2000s. Rural residents can buy temporary urban residency permits to work legally. By 2004, the Chinese Ministry of Agriculture estimated that over 100 million people registered as 'rural' were working in cities. However, these reforms have not fundamentally changed the hukou system. Instead, reforms have only decentralised hukou control to local governments. It has been argued that the system will have to be further relaxed in order to increase availability of skilled workers to industries.

3   *Danwei* was the name given to a place of employment in China prior to the economic reforms introduced by Deng Xiaoping, although it is still in use today. The danwei work unit acted as part of the hierarchy, linking each individual with the central Communist Party infrastructure, and assisted in implementing party policy; they are typically based around a factory, state agency or university. Workers were bound to their work unit for life, with each creating their own housing, child care, schools, clinics, shops, services, post offices and other facilities. Work-unit housing was usually built to common space standards and building styles. The danwei had much influence, for example permission had to be obtained for under-taking travel, marriage or having children. The move from a socialist ideology to 'socialism with Chinese characteristics' has weakened the danwei system – in 2003 it became possible to marry or divorce without needing authorisation.

4   Much of the analysis reported in this chapter draws on the Visioning and Backcasting for Transport in Jinan study (VIBAT-Jinan). This was carried out by Robin Hickman, David Banister, Jimin Zhao and Jian Liu, at the University of Oxford's Transport Studies Unit, as part of the Future of Cities Programme, 2010–11.

5   A model of transport movements was developed for Jinan with a baseline 1990–2010 and projections to 2030 by mode distance, vehicle fleet and CO2 emissions. Different policy scenarios can be tested to 2030 and transport CO2 emissions estimated.

6   China, similar to India, is classified as a 'non-Annex I' country under the Kyoto Protocol. This means they are not obligated to reduce emissions under the Protocol. They have only a 'monitoring' responsibility, alongside a more general agreed 'common responsibility' recognising that all countries have a role to play in reducing emissions.

7   A workshop was held in Oxford and used to develop the trend and uncertainty issues and scenario matrix. This included transport planners, urban planners and other government officials from Jinan and Shandong, and also academics from the University of Oxford and other transport planning experts from the UK.

8   There are many examples of persistent inefficient technologies, including the QWERTY typewriter keyboard, video recorders, electricity supplies, railway gauges and computer programming languages, all contradicting the expectations of neoclassical theory (Mahoney, 2000).

9 The *keiretsu* is a uniquely Japanese form of corporate organisation – a grouping or family of affiliated companies working in alliance towards each other's mutual success. They often include a main bank, common shareholding, and seconded/common directors, and cover most of the parts of the economic chain. 'Horizontal' keiretsu are headed by the major Japanese banks and include the Mitsui and Mitsubishi groups. 'Vertical' keiretsu are industrial groups, connecting manufacturers and suppliers, wholesalers and retailers, such as Toyota, Nissan, Honda, Hitachi, Toshiba and Sony.

10 High-speed rail in China refers to any commercial train service with an average speed of 200 km/h (120 mph) or higher.

11 For more information see http://en.wikipedia.org/wiki/Beijing-Shanghai_High-Speed_Railway

12 As a comparator, 200 gCO_2/km equates to 8.7 l/100 km; 150 gCO_2/km equates to 6.5 l/100 km; 80 gCO_2/km equates to 3.5 l/100 km if petrol conversion factors are used. Conversion factors are as follows: gCO_2/km = 22.961 _ petrol l/100 km or gCO_2/km = 26.05 _ diesel l/100 km. Actual average fleet figures are uncertain due to issues with fuel sales data and real world fuel economy, as opposed to test cycle.

13 'China to add 12 cities to green vehicle subsidy pilot program', available at http://autonews.gasgoo.com/china-news/china-to-add-12-cities-to-green-vehicle-subsidy-pi-100917.shtml

14 'China's new energy vehicle goals dwarf the US', available at www.energyboom.com/yes/chinas-new-energy-vehicle-goals-dwarf-us

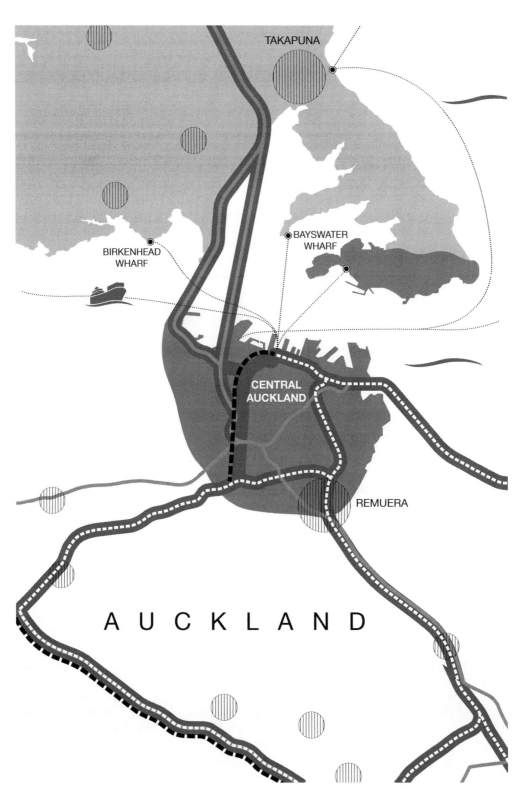

Figure 7.1 Auckland
Source: Mapping by Bally Meeda and Urban Graphics.

7 Urban dispersal and high motorisation (Auckland)

> The creature walked round the flat today for the first time. Laughed in the corridor after looking at the electric light. Then, accompanied by Philip Philipovich and myself, he went into the study. Stands firmly on his hind (deleted) . . . his legs and gives the impression of a short, ill-knit human male.
>
> Laughed in the study. His smile is disagreeable and somehow artificial. Then he scratched the back of his head, looked round and registered a further, clearly pronounced word: 'Bourgeois'. Swore. His swearing is methodical, uninterrupted and apparently totally meaningless. There is something mechanical about it – it is as if this creature had heard all this bad language at an earlier phase, automatically recorded it in his sub-conscious and now regurgitates it wholesale. However, I am no psychiatrist.
>
> (Mikhail Bulgakov, *The Heart of a Dog*, 1925, p. 64)

Introduction

Auckland, known as the 'City of Sails', has a beautiful setting with a central business district overlooking Waitemata Harbour, and beyond to the South Pacific Ocean. The city is New Zealand's major commercial centre and home to a third of the country's population; the metropolitan area includes a residential population of over 1.4 million (Auckland Regional Council, 2010). Auckland's population is expected to grow to 2.1 million by 2040. The main urbanised area lies between the Hauraki Gulf of the Pacific Ocean to the east, the low Hunua Ranges to the southeast, the Manukau Harbour to the southwest, and the Waitakere Ranges and smaller ranges to the west and northwest. The central part of the urban area occupies a narrow isthmus between the Manukau Harbour on the Tasman Sea and the Waitemata Harbour on the Pacific Ocean[1] (Hickman et al., 2012a).

New Zealand itself has a population of over 4 million, growing at around 1 per cent per annum. GDP per capita, at just under US$30,000, is low relative to Australia (US$42,000) or the United Kingdom (US$35,000), but there has been high growth in the last 10 years. The motorisation rate is very high at 720 vehicles per 1,000 population, one of the highest national figures in the world, less than the US (820), but more than Australia (671) or the UK (517) (Table 7.1). CO_2 emissions per capita and energy use are hence high, even for an industrialised country.

In terms of international climate agreements, New Zealand is a signatory (in 2002) to the Kyoto Protocol. The international agreement is to reduce the total GHG emissions of developed countries (and countries with economies in transition) to 5 per cent below 1990 levels. New Zealand has committed to 'reduce its greenhouse gas emissions to 1990 levels on average over the 2008–2012 commitment period, or take responsibility for any emissions over these levels'.[2]

Figure 7.2 The Auckland waterfront and ferry terminal

Table 7.1 New Zealand – World Development Indicators

Indicator	1990	2000	2005	2008	2009
Population, total	3,448,000	3,857,800	4,133,900	4,268,900	4,315,800
Population growth (annual %)	1.5	0.6	1.1	1.0	1.1
GDP per capita (current US$)	12,907	13,336	26,846	27,599	29,352
GDP growth (annual %)	0.0	2.4	3.2	−1.4	–
Life expectancy at birth, total (years)	75.4	78.6	79.9	80.2	–
Fertility rate, total (births per woman)	2.2	2.0	2.0	2.2	–
Energy use (kg of oil equivalent per capita)	3859	4360	3966	–	–
CO2 emissions (metric tons per capita)	6.9	8.5	8.1	–	–
Motor vehicles – (per 1,000 people)	–	720	–	–	
Mobile cellular subscriptions (per 100 people)	1.6	40.0	85.4	108.2	–
Internet users (per 100 people)	0.0	47.5	62.4	71.4	–

Source: World Bank, 2010a.

At Copenhagen (COP15, 2009), New Zealand agreed to reduce GHG emissions by 10–20 per cent below 1990 levels by 2020, subject to an international agreement on limiting temperature rises to not more than 2°C and developed countries making similar efforts to New Zealand. There was also agreement to pursue a longer term target of a 50 per cent reduction in emissions below 1990 levels by 2050. The latest Net Position Report (Ministry for the Environment, 2009), however, reveals the difficulties in that emissions continue to rise and that reducing emissions requires more than target setting. In 2007, New Zealand emitted 75.6 million tonnes of carbon dioxide equivalent[3] (MtCO2e), an increase of 22 per cent from 1990 levels. New Zealand has quite weak targets relative to the UK, which seeks to reduce emissions by 12.5 per cent under Kyoto, by 10–20 per cent below 1990 levels by 2020 at COP15 (at the EU level) and has a national target of an 80 per cent reduction in emissions below 1990 levels by 2050 (Climate Change Act, 2008).

The motorised city context

Auckland offers a high quality of life for many of its residents. Much of this quality of life is based on the dispersed city model, which can be viewed as a variant of the Broadacre City (Lloyd Wright, 1935), where large plot sizes and largely two-storey detached housing predominate. This includes some high-quality neighbourhoods, with access to a higher density urban centre, and also surrounding city parks, coastline, beaches and open spaces. Movement around Auckland is facilitated by use of the motor car and perhaps the form of the city reflects its major growth period in the 1950s and 1960s, when planning around the motor car was more fashionable. There are three urban motorways feeding into the city centre near Waitemata Harbour (the Northern, Southern and Auckland–Kumeu motorways). 80 per cent of Aucklanders travel to work by private car, and only five per cent as pedestrians and one per cent by cycling. Six per cent of Aucklanders travel to work by public transport (2006 Census), and use of public transport for non-work trips is also marginal. The average resident makes forty-one public transit trips per year. These levels are similar to those found in Los Angeles (5 per cent public transport for the LA census area; and forty-nine public transit trips per year). Public transit patronage has suffered a large decline since the 1950s; in 1954, public transit accounted for 58 per cent of trips and the car less than a third, whilst public transit averaged 290 trips per year (Utley et al., 2011; Hickman et al., 2012a).

Mees (2010) recounts the story of public transit usage in Auckland collapsing over four decades, as the result of direct planning for motorisation, but not particularly related to the lobbying influence of a motor industry. The city's transport planners deliberately adopted a transport policy based around the car. In 1950, a consultancy report from William Halcrow and Partners recommended the electrification of the suburban rail system, the construction of a central city tunnel, and the reorganisation of bus services to act as feeders to the rail system. A new multi-modal public transit agency would provide coordination, and spending on urban roads was to be curtailed. Auckland's city engineer, however, opposed the strategy, especially the plans to restrict spending on the roads, and he argued that the roads should take priority.

The national transport minister of the time, W. S. Goosman, famously said to a journalist at the opening of a section of New Zealand's first motorway, 'My boy, the future of Auckland is with the motor car.' The then head of geography at the University of Auckland also called the railway scheme a 'potential white elephant', one that 'may prejudice the chances of improvement to the highway system'. In 1954, the City Council voted with the city engineer's recommendation to reject the consultant's report, and in 1955 agreed an alternative transportation master plan for Metropolitan Auckland, cancelling the rail scheme and diverting funding into a motorway network. A single public transit authority was also rejected. The 'critical juncture' was made, largely reflecting the 'progressive' transport planning views of the time, and the pathway towards motorisation commenced.

The progress to motorisation was rapid. By 1963, public transit's share had fallen to only 22 per cent, less than half that of 9 years previously. This change in travel behaviour is instructive in highlighting how important the chosen policy approach can be to the resulting travel behaviours, and perhaps also how the dominant views of the time can also become so difficult to move away from, as they become embedded in the city culture and widespread beliefs, namely that car ownership is important to living in Auckland. McLuhan writes in the context of the US, but the message is important also for cities such as Auckland:

> With the coming of the horse-drawn bus and streetcar, towns developed housing that was no longer within site of the shop or factory [. . .] the railroad next took over the development of the suburbs, with housing kept within walking distance of the railroad stop. Shops and hotels around the railroad gave some concentration and form to the suburb. The automobile, followed by the airplane, dissolved this grouping and ended the pedestrian, or human, scale of the suburb. Lewis Mumford contends that the car turned the suburban housewife into a full time chauffeur. Certainly the transformations of the wheel as expediter of tasks, and architect of ever-new human relations, is far from finished, but its shaping power is waning in the electric age of information, and that fact makes us more aware of its characteristic form as now tending to the archaic.
>
> (McLuhan, 1964, pp. 196–197)

Figure 7.3 Auckland, 1853 (w/c on paper)
Source: Hatton, W. (fl. 1853)/Museum of New Zealand Te Papa Tongarewa/The Bridgeman Art Library.

Table 7.2 Auckland – some statistics

Issue	Comment
Demonym	Aucklander
Early settlement	c.1350, settled by Māori
	1840, settled by Europeans
Population (Auckland urban area)	
2006	1.4 million
1864	12,400
1841	1,500
Area (2011)	482.9 km²
Population density (2011)	2,900/km²
Mode share (2007–11, trip stages)	80% by car or van driver
	15% pedestrians
	1% cycling
	3% public transport
Cars per household (at least one)	92.6%
Travel cost, single bus ticket, Browns Bay (a North Shore suburb) to Auckland University (central city)	NZ$6.80 (£3.47)
CO2 reduction target	A reduction in CO2e emissions by 50% on 1990 levels by 2040 (RLTS)
Total CO2 emissions (2006)	8.6 tCO2e per capita
Transport CO2 emissions (2006)	3.7 tCO2e per capita
Transport % of total	43%

Source: Auckland Council, 2006; Auckland Regional Council, 2010; Statistics New Zealand, 2011; Ministry of Transport, 2012.

In recent years there have been attempts to reduce the scale of motorisation in Auckland, acknowledging the problematic nature of high car usage in environmental and city design terms, but this has been of a limited scale. There has been a greater investment in public transport, but the city remains largely wedded to private car usage, with access to the car seen as an integral part of the attractive lifestyle on offer. The Auckland Plan (Auckland Council, 2012), Auckland Transport Plan (Auckland Regional Transport Authority, 2009) and Auckland Regional Land Transport Strategy (Auckland Regional Council, 2010) set the spatial planning and transport policy framework for the region, but there is of course a long way to go in investing in public transport, in walking and cycling facilities, and perhaps most difficult, in creating an urban form that supports use of the non-car modes.

Baseline and projections

The scale of change required against the BAU projection is quite dramatic in Auckland due to the high level of motorisation. By 2050 BAU transport emissions are expected to be just over 8 MtCO2e (Maunsell, 2008; Maunsell, 2009),[4] whereas a 20 per cent reduction target would require emissions at around 1.9 MtCO2e in 2020, and a 50 per cent reduction to 1.2 MtCO2e in 2050, all on 1990 levels (Figure 7.4). The rising BAU is due to an increasing

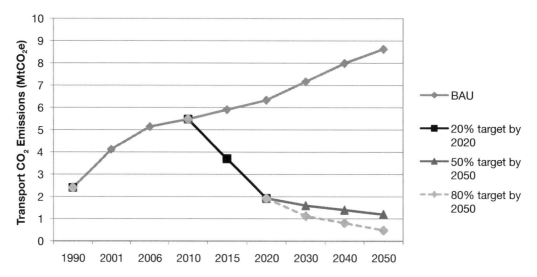

Figure 7.4 Transport CO2 emissions, Auckland
Source: Based on Maunsell, 2009.

Figure 7.5 View of Queen Street, Auckland (oil on canvas)
Source: Carabain, Jacques (1834–p. 1889)/Private collection/Photo © Christie's Images/The Bridgeman Art Library.

Figure 7.6 Map of Auckland, circa 1902

Source: Encyclopedia Britannica/UIG/The Bridgeman Art Library.

motorisation rate, vehicle miles travelled, a low rate of improvement in fuel economy and a high mode share by car.

The transport sector is also very important relative to total emissions; 43 per cent of emissions in 2006 are associated with transport in Auckland, which is a very high level for New Zealand and also internationally.[5] The reasons for this are in the high level of car usage and also the relatively low prevalence of agricultural activities and high use of renewable energy in 'stationary' activities (hydro-electric power accounts for more than 50 per cent of electricity usage). Within the transport sector again the major share of emissions is for the road, with car accounting for 51 per cent and road freight 31 per cent. As in all contexts, there are also issues here with carbon budgets (the 'area under the line'). It is the total amount of CO2 in the atmosphere that is important more than targets or snapshots in time, and this means that the pathways taken are of crucial importance.

Figure 7.7 Auckland from Ponsonby, 1905 (silver gelatin print)

Source: Moodie, George (1865–1947) and Muir, Thomas Mintaro Bailey (c.1852–1945)/Museum of New Zealand Te Papa Tongarewa/The Bridgeman Art Library.

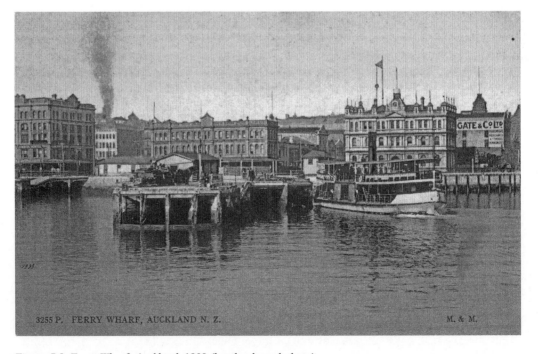

Figure 7.8 Ferry Wharf, Auckland, 1909 (hand-coloured photo)

Source: Moodie, George (1865–1947) and Muir, Thomas Mintaro Bailey (c.1852–1945)/Museum of New Zealand Te Papa Tongarewa/The Bridgeman Art Library.

Figure 7.9 General View of Auckland, 1909 (hand-coloured photo)

Source: Moodie, George (1865–1947) and Muir, Thomas Mintaro Bailey (c.1852–1945)/Museum of New Zealand Te Papa Tongarewa/The Bridgeman Art Library.

Figure 7.10 Shelly Beach, Ponsonby, Auckland, 1910 (b/w photo)

Source: Moodie, George (1865–1947) and Muir, Thomas Mintaro Bailey (c.1852–1945)/Museum of New Zealand Te Papa Tongarewa/The Bridgeman Art Library.

Figure 7.11 The dispersed urban structure in Auckland: the suburban plot of land is in great demand

Figure 7.12 The urban centre is denser, with an attractive retail, entertainment and cultural offer and high
levels of employment

The current mode share in the Auckland region (2007–11) is a major contributor to the high levels of CO_2 emissions, even when considered in terms of trip stages rather than main mode, as 80 per cent of travel is by car or van driver (including 26 per cent by car or van as a passenger), 15 per cent pedestrians, one per cent cycling, and three per cent public transport (Ministry of Transport, 2012). Expected traffic growth to 2041 is also significant, with some difficulty in maintaining existing service levels, let alone improvements, unless transport investment is made. If projected demands, reflecting an increased population and urban dispersal, are loaded onto a 2006 network, it is expected that daily trips by car will rise by 153 per cent, public transport by 240 per cent and active travel trips by 157 per cent. Vehicle km travelled would rise by 142 per cent (Auckland Regional Transport Authority, 2009).

Achieving the national CO_2 reduction targets in Auckland (and by implication achieving deep reductions in CO_2 emissions in New Zealand) hence seems a long way off in the current context. This is similar, of course, to experience in many other cities and countries. The 'conditions' for the national target of a 20 per cent reduction in CO_2 emissions by 2020 are instructive. Global agreement must set the world on a pathway to limit a temperature rise to not more than 2°C, and developed countries must make comparable efforts to those of New Zealand, with major emitting countries taking action that is fully commensurate with their respective capacities. All of these factors imply that New Zealand is unlikely to act unless all countries do, at least those in the industrialised West. Countries are very wary of unilateral action, mindful that they may somehow reduce their 'economic competitiveness'. Yet continued inaction is surely to prove more expensive in the long run, and not only in financial terms.

The UN expert review team reports that there is no plan for achieving at least two thirds of the stated national target for New Zealand (Utley et al., 2011; United Nations Framework Convention on Climate Change, 2011). The scale of change required in travel behaviours hence is not being appreciated, and waiting for international agreement or coordinated action is unlikely to bear fruit. For many contexts such as New Zealand and Auckland, the targets being adopted are little more than 'aspirational', even where supposed (and well-reading) 'strategies' are seemingly in place.

Developing scenarios

A number of scenario development studies have been developed for Auckland, and indeed more widely for New Zealand; for example, those from Oram (2009) and Landcare Research (2007). The scenarios developed tend to be for society as a whole, and not particularly transport-focused. Hence, for the purpose of examing what might happen in the transport sector, transport-specific scenarios for Auckland are developed below. These follow the classic approach, based around likely trends and uncertainties. They cover economic, socio-demographic, environmental and technological issues, and there is some overlap in the issues with previous case studies: many of the factors that are likely to affect travel behaviours are common across contexts. The main trends and uncertainties for Auckland were identified in dicussion with local academics and policy officers, so there is a level of participation in deriving the key issues, and these are as listed below. The most important issues for Auckland were seen as the potential emergence of new vehicle technologies, levels of funding available and priorities taken in investment (translated as investment in sustainable modes), and continued extent of car dependence.

Key trends and uncertainties

- Population growth and immigration;
- Economic growth rate (GDP);
- Globalisation, international trade and movement;
- Income levels, income inequality;
- Tourism and leisure industry growth;
- Age profile (ageing population);
- Social equity, inclusion of minority groups;
- Energy and power supply – renewable sources;
- Climate change;
- Major environmental shocks – earthquake, drought, flooding, water supply;
- Improvement in environmental and urban quality;
- Environmental issues – stewardship, extent of 'seriousness' given to them in policy-making and implementation, levels of funding for non-road;
- Urban design quality; extent of urban sprawl;
- Clean vehicle technologies, electric vehicle penetration rate (#1);
- Progress towards sustainable travel, level of investment in public transport, walking and cycling (#2);
- Continuing extent of car dependency (#3).

A central scenario

The perceived key issues are used as the polarities of the 'trilemma' as given in Figure 7.13, which shows the possiible space within which the scenarios can be developed. There is a similar emphasis in the Auckland scenarios to those used in the Oxfordshire context, perhaps reflecting the high level of car usage in both contexts. The scenario axis and labelling, however, are slightly different, reflecting a different discussion in the workshop sessions.

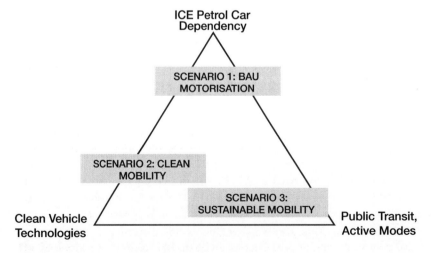

Figure 7.13 Future scenario 'trilemma'

Towards sustainable mobility

Below the two potential 'non-BAU' scenarios (Scenarios 2 and 3) are developed in more detail, with example impacts considered against CO2 and also across a wider MCA framework.

Scenario 1: BAU motorisation

This scenario is a continuation of current historical trends, a 'business as usual' projection, with motorisation levels continuing at current levels, and little progress being made in moving towards a low emission vehicle fleet and limited investment in public transit, walking and cycling.

Scenario 2: clean mobility

The 'clean mobility' scenario (Table 7.3) envisages very radical progress to be made in the vehicle fleet, with much reduced car and LCV (light commercial vehicle) emissions, though mobility levels are not reduced, indeed continue to increase. The average private car vehicle fleet emits around 95 gCO2/km by 2041, hence around the level of the current best hybrid and diesel vehicle technologies. More progress could be made by 2041. For example, the King Review (2008) in the UK recommends a target of 100 gCO2/km in the EU new car fleet by 2020. The vehicle fleet in New Zealand is, however, relatively old, including a large number of second-hand cars from Japan. Hence this scenario would represent a major step forward in new vehicle technology penetration into the vehicle fleet, and much less reliance on a

Table 7.3 Scenario 2 'clean mobility'

Policy package	Level of application	Summary specification	
PP1 Low-emission vehicles	High	95 gCO2/km average car fleet, relative to the current average car fleet of 235 gCO2/km; and 800 gCO2/km average HCV fleet, relative to the current average HCV fleet of 1,100 gCO2/km	
PP2 Alternative fuels	Low	Minimal use of alternative fuel, car and LCV (80% petrol, 20% diesel), HCV (95% diesel, 5% LPG), bus (95% diesel, 5% biofuel)	
SCENARIO RESULTS (relative to BAU 2041)*		*Absolute*	*Percentage*
Climate: carbon dioxide emission reduction (tonnes CO2)		–2.84 MtCO2	–34.6%
		2.4 tonnes CO2 per capita (2041) relative to BAU of 3.8 tCO2 per capita (assumed aggregate BAU in 2041 is 8.03 MtCO2)	
Economy: daily junction delay (aggregate seconds)		No change	No change
Local environment: particulate matter		No change	No change
Safety: road fatalities (number of fatalities)		No change	No change

Note: * Modelling results, 2012. The modelling is based on individual model runs for each level of application of a policy package. MCA indicator impacts are derived from travel distance, mode share and speed outputs, and are illustrated with the INTRA-SIM Auckland simulation model. Additivity is assumed between packages. Clearly this omits potential super-additivity (synergy) and sub-additivity (double counting) effects. This is an area for further research by the study team in terms of developing approaches to optimising the packaging process. Initial thoughts on synergies are given in Hickman et al. (2009b).

Figure 7.14 The vehicle fleet is relatively old, hence has a high average level of CO2 emissions

Figure 7.15 Hybrid taxis. There are some hybrid vehicles, but largely in the taxi fleet.

Figure 7.16
Second-hand car fleet. Many of
the vehicles are second-hand
cars from Japan.

second-hand fleet. The results show that CO2 emissions might be reduced by around 35 per cent relative to the BAU in 2041, or 2.4 tCO2 per capita relative to 3.8 tCO2 per capita under BAU.

The spatial pattern of CO2 reduction is also interesting, if assessed using INTRA-SIM Auckland, in that the greatest reductions (relative to the 2041 BAU) are found on the North Shore and Manuwera, i.e. where car dependency and travel distances are longest, and where vehicle technologies would make a large difference to emissions.

Scenario 3: sustainable mobility

The 'sustainable mobility' scenario envisages very radical progress to be made with a fuel efficient vehicle fleet, with much reduced car and LCV vehicle emissions, but also much lower levels of vehicle use relative to the BAU projection. In terms of cars, the average fleet emits around 95 gCO2/km by 2041, hence below the level of the current best hybrid and diesel vehicle technologies. There is heavy investment in public transit, walking and cycling, and the urban structure is developed to help support the use of non-motorised travel.

Public transit investment is critical for the future development of sustainable travel behaviours in Auckland, with a current network and patronage levels well below what can be expected for a city of this size. Patronage has dropped consistently since the 1950s, though there has been a recent increase in boardings (Abusah and de Bruyn, 2007). There are complications in terms of the ownership of transit services (contracted and commercial), which make improving service provision difficult. Recent discussions about improving farebox recovery also seem to ignore the wider city liveability, social, economic and environmental benefits of public transit investment. Public transport needs to be viewed as an essential part of the sustainable transport solution, not just as a cost-effective means to provide a minimal service for those without a car.

Providing for effective public transit in low-density urban areas such as Auckland is difficult, but there are options (Pharoah and Apel, 1995; Mees, 2010). Zurich, for example, shows how high-quality transport, usually only found in dense urban centres, can be extended into the low-density urban areas, suburbs and even rural areas. Public transport networks are reconfigured to serve cross-city, off-peak (as well as the conventional peak) and even recreational trips. The network effect means people can easily transfer, 'pulse' scheduling improves connections, and public transport becomes possible beyond the usual key radials. Levels of walking and cycling also increase in support of a high-quality public transport service.

Mees (2010) illustrates how effective public transport can work even where the urban structure doesn't particularly help. The network approach is important in providing the 'anywhere to anywhere' service, allowing passengers to travel between all parts of the city by transferring from one line to another, just as motorists navigate on a road by turning at junctions. The interchange becomes critical, with the transfer viewed as an opportunity rather than a penalty. The transfer has to be free, resulting in a multi-modal and integrated system. Network and timetable design is also important in allowing random frequent service transfer (a maximum 15-minute headway, such as Zurich trams in the central urban area, Paris Metro, Toronto Subway, and London Underground) and timed infrequent service transfer (Zurich trams in the suburban area and Swiss National Rail). This latter approach allows a move away from the costly high frequencies at all times, with networks laid out on a hub-and-spoke pattern rather than the usual grid. The 'pulse' of service integration can occur at regular intervals, say every 10, 15, 30 or (in rural areas) 60 minutes, but this requires very effective service planning and optimisation. Regular clockface timing (repeated every hour) can also assist in service legibility. Cross-subsidy is required, with the popular services funding the less popular, but even in the remote areas high occupancies need to be ensured. Networks in rural areas tend to be simple and legible, but sparse, allowing higher frequencies, and move us beyond the common bewildering 'tangle' of low-quality lines. Services can also act as 'trunk and feeder', along the lines of Curitiba, where the main routes use high-capacity vehicles. Hence the objective: 'our customer wishes to set off from a place of his own choosing, travel quickly, comfortably, cheaply, and in safety to his destination, and arrive there at a time set by himself; nothing else will do' (Brändli, 1990, cited in Mees, 2010).

The current policy approach in Auckland is to develop a rapid transit network (RTN), providing high-speed, high-frequency services connecting regional areas to the CBD; a quality transit network (QTN), including buses and ferries to regional centres, assisted by prioritisation measures to reduce congestion; and a local connector network (LCN) providing wider coverage over the city. New Zealand's first dedicated busway opened in 2008, offering fast access to Auckland's CBD from the North Shore. Future RTN services will include: a 3–5 minute headway, which allows 'turn up and go' travel; smart card ticketing, real-time travel information, high-quality rolling stock (potentially including metro-style underground rail), stations located

Figure 7.17 The Britomart. Auckland's CBD public transport hub – the Britomart – opened in 2003, with bus and rail interchanges at two levels, housed in a former Edwardian post office and new extension.

Figure 7.18 The bus and wider public transport mode share, however, remains very low; services are often poor and uncoordinated

in and integrated with commercial areas, and maximum 3–5-minute waiting times for connecting services (Auckland Regional Council, 2010). Clearly a much more extensive public transport network needs to be established that provides the fine grain accessible network of services, operating on exclusive rights of way, so that it is attractive and affordable to all users.

Active travel modes (walking and cycling) are very under-utilised in Auckland, with cycling accounting for just 1 per cent of journey to work trips (2.3 per cent nationally) and walking 4.6 per cent (6.5 per cent nationally) (Tin Tin et al., 2009); over recent years their use has been on the decline. Recent national policy has tried to reverse these trends, with a strategy to encourage walking and cycling (Ministry of Transport, 2005), including a programme of long-distance cycle routes, but generally provision for cycling is absent. There is much potential for greater use of walking in cycling in Auckland, with most trips below 7 km in length. The Auckland Regional Land Transport Strategy seeks to complete the planned 938 km regional cycle network by 2026 and to improve active mode share from 16 per cent of all trip legs to 35 per cent (Auckland Regional Council, 2010).

Experience elsewhere, such as in the Netherlands or Denmark, offers much needed lessons for Auckland. Segregated cycle ways are used along arterials, and high-standard complete networks are very common in urban areas (Pucher and Buehler, 2008). Some towns experience very high levels of trips by cycle, around 30–40 per cent of all trips made in Gröningen are by cycle (Pharoah, 1992; Pharoah and Apel, 1995). Cycle hire schemes, of course, have also become popular in Europe, with popular schemes in Lyon (Vélo'v), Paris (Vélib') and London. Some very large cycle hire schemes have been recently developed in China. Much more extensive cycling and walking facilities, including a fine network of segregated and on-road facilities, an extensive cycle hire scheme, parking facilities, and supporting ancillary measures can all be developed. Though there is little current cycling culture (at the mainstream level) in Auckland, and although the topography of the city is very hilly, the sporting and 'outdoor' nature of the population is quite similar to Vancouver or the Netherlands, Sweden or Denmark. Hence cycling can become an important mode for the city. Policy-makers simply need to become much more adventurous in their cycling and public realm strategy development and infrastructure investments, intially targeting 10 per cent of trips by cycle and five per cent walk, with consequent short trip reductions by car.

The sustainable mobility scenario results (Table 7.4 and Figure 7.24) show that CO_2 emissions might be reduced by around 70 per cent relative to the BAU in 2041, or 0.6 tCO_2 per capita relative to 3.8 tCO_2 per capita under BAU, if this type of future could be delivered. Sustainable transport means rebalancing the over-emphasis on the narrow economic efficiency associated with faster travel (and more CO_2 emissions) with the wider social and environmental benefits of slower travel over shorter distances by a wider range of modes.

If the spatial pattern of CO_2 reduction is considered using INTRA-SIM Auckland, it can be seen that there are more reductions (relative to the 2041 BAU) in the central urban area of Auckland as well as the northern and southern hinterland, hence the distribution is more evenly spread.

A critical part of the future strategy for cities like Auckland is likely to be the implementation of low-emission vehicles. This will also be the case in many other contexts where there is a high level of motorisation, the urban structure is dispersed, and the public are supportive of future private car usage. Sperling and Gordon (2009), for example, tend to emphasise the importance of the 'technological fix' in the Californian context. These types of vehicles will be the only way to reduce CO_2 emissions in many parts of the dispersed city. They may also be effectively combined with autonomous vehicle technology (i.e. driverless vehicles). Google is currently testing a fleet of these in California and the results are impressive insofar as few

Figure 7.19 An improving public realm in the city centre

Figure 7.20 Cycling facilities. It is surprising how few cycling routes and facilities there are available – there is much room for improvement here.

Figure 7.21
(Above) Car-free days. Festivals and car free days can be used to demonstrate the attractions of walking, cycling and socialising, adding to the vitality of the city.

Figure 7.22
(Left) Highway over-provision. The city centre still has huge over provision for highways – valuable space can be used for cycle routes or bus or tram lanes, with fewer lanes for cars.

Figure 7.23 Urban motorways. Some of the urban motorways can also be removed. There is no need for
fast highway access into the city centre – this is to be provided by public transport and cycling,
and the severance and environmental impacts can be much reduced.

accidents are occuring. In the longer term, the potential is to reduce traffic accidents altogether,
or at least significantly, as virtually all human error can be removed from the system. Perhaps
these vehicles may contribute more to suburban sprawl, with the longer distance commute
becoming more bearable as the driver no longer has to drive and can work or be otherwise
active on the way (*The Economist*, 2012). Ironically, the automated car becomes more similar
to public transport – where the driving function is replaced – hence perhaps there will be
some merging of the modes in future years.

There is an interesting and critical decision that now needs to be made for Auckland. This
is similar to an earlier juncture in policy-making, namely the Gooseman master plan decision
of 1955. This decision concerns whether the 'North American model' is followed, and private
car mobility is still encouraged, but with clean technologies, or whether the 'European model'
is pursued, with a much broader range of policy measures, including higher levels of public
transport investment, traffic demand management and urban structure changes. From the policy
documentation being developed, it seems there is some support for a range of policy measures,
and some acceptance that relying solely on vehicle technologies can only reduce emissions
by so much, with many of the gains offset by the subsequent increases in traffic volumes.
But, of course, this remains largely at the level of conjecture, or at best, at the level of strategy
development. There still needs to be a great deal of effort in persuading the politicians and
public that much greater use of public transport, walking and cycling is an attractive future
for travel in Auckland, and for investment priorities in transport planning to change markedly

Table 7.4 Scenario 3 'sustainable mobility'

Policy package	Level of application	Summary specification
PP1 Low-emission vehicles	High	95 gCO2/km average car fleet, relative to the current average car fleet of 235 gCO2/km; and 800 gCO2/km average HCV fleet, relative to the current average HCV fleet of 1,100 gCO2/km
PP2 Alternative fuels	Medium	Use of alternative fuels in the vehicle fleet; car and LCV (80% petrol, 20% diesel), HCV (95% diesel, 5% LPG), bus (95% diesel, 5% biofuel)
PP3 Ecological driving and slower speeds	Medium	30 km/h zones across all residential areas and ecological driving training. Assumed 5% improvement in fuel efficiency and 5% reduction in speeds.
PP4 Traffic demand management	Medium	Application of intensive behavioural change measures, including walking school bus and school travel plan programmes, community road-safety projects, personalised travel planning and area wide travel planning. There is also a tightening of the parking regime by 2041, with a 50% increase to the charge level and a subsequent increase in the number of people paying charges from 30% to 50%.
PP5 Public transit	High	Complete current passenger rail programme including the CBD rail tunnel and frequency increases, CBD loop, completion of the planned rapid transit network (RTN) using buses, extension of North Shore RTN, more tangential connections, new routes such as Auckland International Airport access, higher frequencies on the quality transit network (QTN), QTN reconfigured to better serve the new RTN (RLTS 2009 WP21 SO2 transit component plus additions). Reduction in fares, by 50%, to encourage mode shift. Significant efforts to improve network planning and timetabling
PP6 Walking and cycling	Medium	Complete regional cycle network and finer network of segregated and on-road facilities, extensive cycle hire scheme, parking facilities, and supporting ancillary measures. Encourage greater walking and cycling through widespread measures such as reduced speed limits for cars, cycle priority, reallocated road space, improved signage and mapping (targeted 10% of trips by cycle and 5% walk, with consequent short trip reductions by car).
PP9 Freight	High	Improved load factors, including intensity per tonne-km, reduced empty running, changed mode share and other operational factors; fuel efficiency; land use and location of facilities; consumption and production patterns, including local sourcing; and infrastructure, traffic restrictions and regulation. Some reduction of trips to the port of Auckland, to and from Onehunga, Southdown and Westfield, and the wider network, reflecting improved vehicle logistics and reduced empty running

Table 7.4 Scenario 3 'sustainable mobility'—*continued*

SCENARIO RESULTS (relative to BAU 2041)*	Absolute	Percentage
Climate: Carbon dioxide emission reduction (tonnes CO2)	–6.72 MtCO2	–72.7%
	0.6 tonnes CO2 per capita (2041) relative to BAU of 3.8 tCO2 per capita (assumed aggregate BAU in 2041 is 8.03 MtCO2)	
Accessibility: Improvement in accessibility to town centres by public transit (**)	N/A	N/A
Economy: Annual car time (aggregate minutes)***	–19,477 million	–43.9%
Local environment: Affected population noise nuisance	–14,466 people	–20.5%
Health: Vehicle road casualties by vehicle pollution (number of fatalities)	–4.6 people	–43.8%

Notes: * Modelling results, 2012. ** Accessibility modelling not developed for this model version. *** Annual car time reduction is very high here. This reflects the modelling approach for the cycling package. There is no cycle (and walk) model available in Auckland, hence future cycle movements were based on mode shift from a proportion of vehicle movements under 10 km in length.

The modelling is based on individual model runs for each level of application of a policy package. MCA indicator impacts are derived from travel distance, mode share and speed outputs.

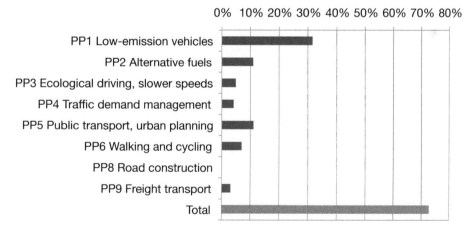

Figure 7.24 Components of Scenario 3 sustainable mobility

away from road building. This will involve much cultural change, and this is an area that is difficult to tackle.

Closely tied to this will be the future role of urban planning. This, in itself, is a controversial area for Auckland, with the bounds of the discussion largely limited to reducing the BAU sprawl, debating what proportion of new development should be in or outside of the current urban boundary, rather than attempting to radically increase densification and mixed uses in the parts of the urban and surburban area, shaped around a more extensive public transport system. New Zealand is well known as the 'quarter-acre pavlova paradise' (Mitchell, 1972),[6] and the strength of feeling for a large plot of land in the suburbs largely remains. Perhaps attitudes are changing a little, as apartment-based inner city living or smaller lot housing is becoming a little more popular, certainly for the younger age cohorts (typically the 20–30 age bracket) but perhaps also wider groups such as 'empty-nesters'. Most people would like to live within walking or cycling distance of local shops, parks, schools and employment, so the 'urban living' aspiration is perhaps not too uncommon. There may well be a significant latent demand for high quality denser urban living, in the attractive older suburbs and also new developments, but the supply of this type of housing is currently limited at affordable prices (Preval et al., 2010).

Figure 7.25 Playtime, 1967, directed by Jacques Tati. Monsieur Hulot attempts to navigate a futuristic Paris, or 'Tativille', constructed of modernist straight lines, glass and steel high-rise buildings, and multi-lane elevated roads; the architecture is viewed as obstructive to daily life and problematic to natural human interaction.

Source: British Film Institute Stills Collection.

In addition, the public transport system, if well integrated along the lines of Zurich and other similar cities, may be less dependent on increased development intensification than usually envisaged. In a future where oil prices are dramatically higher than the present day, then a reliance on only a limited use of public transport, and a stronger usage of hybrid cars, is a vulnerable position if oil remains the main transport fuel. By 2041, the urgency of the climate change and oil scarcity problem will be much more evident to the public and to politicians, and urban structural change will become a reality. But of course the retrofit is always much more difficult than the shaping of new development. This will mean that some seemingly difficult decisions, in the context of 2012, need to be taken. Figure 7.26 illustrates what might be possible in terms of developing the uban structure more effectively around a public transport network, drawing on the vision in the current Auckland Plan (Auckland Council, 2012). Many of the areas around the key public transport interchanges can be densified, even in the suburbs, and perhaps also – much more controversially – the areas that remain poorly accessible to public transport could be returned to open space provision. This means that areas where public transport accessibility is poor are not developed and don't become reliant on car usage. This latter position would take us well beyond the current frame of the urban planning debate in Auckland and similar examples of the dispersed city. Auckland, however, needs to become much more progressive in implementing its strategic planning vision – and it is this area that represents the greatest problem: how to develop a changed awareness and approach to sustainable travel in politicians and the public.

Transition possibilities

Moving from the current level of motorisation in Auckland to more sustainable travel behaviours is a huge step and it will involve a complex range of interventions, covering infrastructure, pricing, demand management, the built environment and cultural change. This can be viewed in socio-technical transition terms (Kemp, 1994; Geels, 2002), including a range of issues such as technological innovation and progress, behavioural change and also governmental initiative. Hence the system in question, in this case automobility, can be seen as occurring at multiple levels, covering issues of:

- Landscape (the city, infrastructure, political ideology, the media, macro-economic trends, societal values and beliefs);
- Regime (activities of transport users, firms, transport planners, engineers, politicians, the motor industry, prevailing habits and norms);
- Niche (a new practice, technology or policy measure).
(Geels and Schot, 2007; Geels, 2011a)

The transition approach has been criticised in terms of the structuring of the factors involved in transition, in the over-emphasis on technological innovation, and lack of focus on agency (individual change), power and politics, and the cultural dimension (Geels, 2011b). Nevertheless, it does provide an improved understanding of the complexity of the problems faced and potential solutions that can be employed, and is useful to contexts such as Auckland in highlighting the extent of change required. There are no simple and effective measures that are available that will make a significant difference by themselves, and no direct causalities between intervention and outcome; rather, a complex package that needs to be developed and tailored to the context. Infrastructure design and investment levels remain important, but efforts are also required in changed governance systems and enhanced attempts to influence the cultural

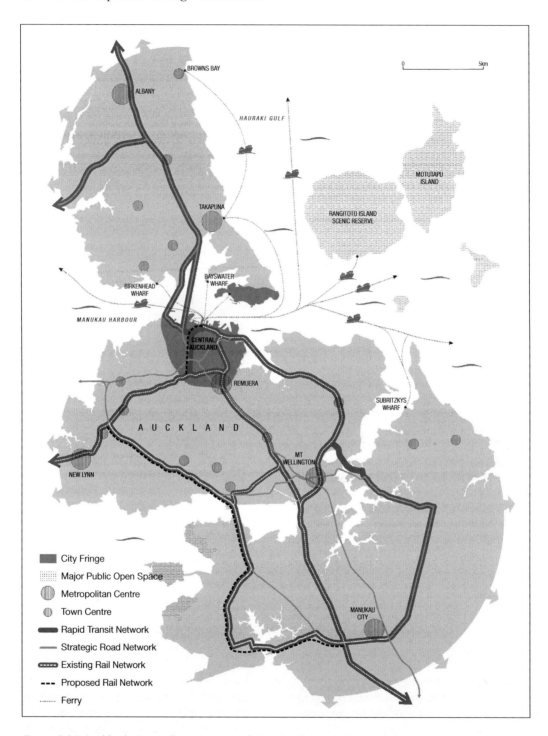

Figure 7.26 Auckland Metropolitan Area: retrofitting the dispersed urban structure?
Source: Based on Auckland Council, 2012. Mapping by Bally Meeda and Urban Graphics.

discourses associated with travel and the 'embeddedness' of travel within everyday life and society (Geels, 2011a). Hence an evolutionary and systemic view is taken, where the transport system can be seen as: 'a semi-coherent configuration of mutually aligned elements, including technology, industry, markets, consumer behaviour, policy, infrastructure, spatial arrangements and cultural meaning'. A multi-actor based approach can be developed with issues of 'framing, perceptions, actions and interactions' between transport users, of different modes, transport planners, politicians, various other 'stakeholders' and the public (Kemp et al., 2012, p. 16).

For Auckland, this means that reducing transport CO_2 emissions is a very complex process, with interventions required at multiple levels, including at the landscape, regime and niche levels. There is also an additional and critical difficulty, in that there is already a high level of motorisation, and a city and culture based around, or at least facilitated by, use of the private car. Some emerging factors, of course, are more 'malleable' than others. The city authorities are pushing for sustainable transport (to an extent), yet the political ideology, media, societal values and beliefs remain fairly fixed, at least in the short term. Transport planners and engineers may seek to build sustainable transport systems, yet prevailing habits and norms amongst the travelling public remain 'sticky'. New niches remain very slow to progress, at least in terms of low-emission vehicles. There may be some signs of the 'older' niches – of public transport usage and cycling – becoming fashionable again, and it is perhaps here that there is great hope. The niches don't always have to be 'new' innovations but also can be effective reinventions of old technologies.

There are many potential forward trajectories, or future pathways, including a 'transformation' where landscape developments exert pressure on the regime, so that 'reconfiguration' takes place where niche innovations are well developed and exert pressure on the regime. Alternatively 'technological substitution' is found where tensions in the regime allow a niche development to break through, or 'de-alignment and re-alignment' may occur where major landscape pressures lead to a disintegration of the regime and niche innovations take advantage of the new space (Geels and Schot, 2007). The change process may develop from within the existing automobility regime, with an adoption of new travel practices, technologies and rationalities. But it is perhaps more likely that the current automobility regime will become 'stranded' by change beyond its control, and a new system of travel will develop. Important here would be that the external costs of the regime outweigh the benefits, and the ability of the regime to resist or absorb change. There may even be some hybrid version of both (Wells et al., 2012).

Conclusions: a radical transformation?

This chapter has explored some of the issues that are difficult in terms of reducing transport CO_2 emissions in Auckland, and it also considers, to a limited extent, some of the wider MCA impacts that might be associated with low carbon transport futures. The current Auckland transportation system is heavily dependent on the motor car, and the internal combustion engine fuelled by petrol or diesel. This is a very vulnerable position for Auckland in terms of many issues, including climate change, oil scarcity, potential rapid rises in future oil prices, and also energy security. Dependence on motor vehicles, and the associated infrastructure this entails, has an adverse impact on the local community and urban fabric, health, economy and local environment. These are all major issues with the current 'path dependency' in carbon intensive travel behaviours in Auckland.

There are potential policy pathways for Auckland in moving to a much more efficient transport system in CO_2 emission terms, and some of these are being tested at the policy level

Figure 7.27 Auckland quality of life. Auckland and the surrounding areas offer a fabulous quality of life –
the great challenge is to radically reduce the environmental impacts.

through the current metropolitan transport strategy and spatial plan. However, the implementation difficulties will be large for all pathways that reduce emissions significantly. For
significant reductions in transport CO_2 emissions, there needs to be a significant governmental
effort, affecting change at multiple levels, along the lines of the MLP understanding of
landscape, regime and niche innovation. Almost all governmental strategies underestimate this
complexity.

What is resolutely clear is the need to break the business-as-usual projected trends. Auckland
has a very high baseline in transport CO_2 emissions as a starting point, with continued high
projected growth.The weak strategic direction at the national level does not help the efforts
in Auckland. New Zealand has only 'partially' responded to climate change at the national
level (relative, for example, to the more progressive approaches taken in the UK and London,
where an 80 per cent reduction in CO_2 emissions on 1990 levels has been adopted – Climate
Change Act, 2008). There is an opportunity for cities to lead the way in developing carbon
efficient travel and less carbon intensive lifestyles, particularly in view of the recent difficulties
in finding a consensus for change at the international level. Cities can certainly push a more
radical agenda than seems possible at the international level. But, in many contexts, we are
again confronted by issues relating to implementation and the scale of required change. The
latter is universally underestimated.

There are also likely to be large economic and social equity dimensions in the policy
trajectories chosen, as low carbon transport futures are likely to have large differential impacts
spatially. Environmental equity considerations should be an essential part of the development

of sustainable transport strategies. Almost all strategies, however, take a limited view on this aspect, considering at best CO_2 emission reductions, perhaps through the lens of economic impact and some limited cost–benefit analysis, but ignoring the wider social impacts (Feitelson, 2002). Many of these issues remain to be explored, in Auckland and elsewhere.

So we need to move beyond the current debate, where public transport is offered as a solution to only a limited degree, but much of the investment is still on highway development. Further difficult decisions include the old and polluting car fleet and poor penetration of low-emission vehicles into the fleet; the very poor levels of cycling provision in Auckland, and the current dispersed urban structure, which makes the greater use of public transport difficult. Generally, the reliance on dispersed suburban living, dependent on private car usage, is much too great. Auckland is in a critical situation, and largely has its 'head in the sand'. But, the current automobility regime is becoming severely outmoded, the costs of high motorisation are increasingly outweighing the advantages, and this will only become ever more evident over time. In future years, the only result is a radically changed system, one that is much less reliant on CO_2 emissions, with a much changed vehicle fleet, and a much higher public transport and non-motorised mode share, utilising higher density and mixed use centres at highly connected nodes. The only significant question is which pathway is taken to this different future, including how the city develops spatially.

The emerging picture of sustainable mobility

There are many good examples of transport projects and initiatives from cities around the world, and each of these will help in the transition towards sustainable mobility. Over the next 10–20 years a strong case needs to be made to give priority to investment in these types of projects and initiatives, and for their profile to be monitored in terms of contributions to the carbon targets set. Hence these investments need to be massively 'scaled up' to cover a much wider range of cities and urban areas, including in suburban areas, and to be aware of the potential for the new innovations (including the positive 'black swans') that will help us achieve progress at a much quicker rate.

It is not the lack of good ideas or visioning about different more sustainable transport futures that seems to be difficult, but it is the slow momentum in terms of the implementation. Many of the larger cities have elements of developing good practice in sustainable transport, but this remains very ad hoc and inconsistent spatially. Even in the 'good practice' cities in the West, the suburbs are usually car dependent; whilst the high levels of walking and cycling in many Asian or South American cities are the result of low income levels rather than positive choice. The emerging lessons – from Amsterdam, Barcelona, Bogotá, Cambridge, Curitiba, Frankfurt, Freiburg, Lisbon, London, Lyon, Madrid, Manchester, Oxford, Paris, Seville, Shanghai, Singapore and Zurich, and many others – can, however, all prove inspirational, and offer a pathway forward towards a more positive future. It is becoming very clear that the current approach to transport analysis and decision-making is not working, even in its own terms, and it is certainly not contributing to wider social and environmental goals. As a means to introduce the last chapter in this book, we illustrate some of the cities where transport projects and initiatives are being developed that might emerge as the mass market sustainable mobility systems of the future.

Notes

1   Much of the analysis reported in this chapter draws on work carried out in the Visioning and Backcasting for Transport in Auckland study (VIBAT-Auckland). This was carried out by Robin Hickman, Olu Ashiru and Catherine Seaborn at the Halcrow Group, David Banister at the Transport Studies Unit, University of Oxford; and Tricia Austin, Megan Howell and Tanya Utley at the School of Architecture and Planning, Auckland University.

2   The Kyoto Protocol includes 'flexibility mechanisms' to allow excess emissions. These are: International Emissions Trading, Joint Implementation, and the Clean Development Mechanism. Developed countries can purchase emissions units from other developed countries or from emissions reduction projects implemented in other countries and use these for compliance with their Kyoto Protocol obligations. Hence a country such as New Zealand can comply with its target even though its domestic emissions may exceed its assigned levels. This is a typical fudge by the international community, and only seeks to allow the industrialized countries to continue to emit more than their fair share of emissions, transferring the burden (of not emitting) to the emerging countries. The qualifier, of course, is that there may be an income stream for emerging countries to use in building sustainable transport options.

3   New Zealand's and Auckland's CO_2 emissions tend to be calculated in terms of CO_2e (carbon dioxide equivalent), hence we use this metric in this chapter to be consistent with wider work in Auckland. This is based on the Global Warming Potential (GWP) – the impact that a particular gas has on 'radiative forcing' (the additional heat/energy which is retained in the Earth's ecosystem through the addition of this gas to the atmosphere). The GWP varies by type of gas and the time period under consideration. CO_2e is a weighted measure of the collective GWP of a range of greenhouse gases expressed relative to CO_2. For example, comparisons are: CO_2 = 379 ppm; CO_2e(Total) = 375 ppm (Chamberlin, 2012).

4   There is some discussion over the level of transport CO_2 emissions in Auckland, with varying estimates (Utley et al., 2011).

5   Relative to ~22 per cent in London and ~33 per cent in Oxfordshire.

6   Mitchell celebrated life in New Zealand as 'heaven on earth': the 'quarter acre' referring to the ubiquitous suburban plot of land on which most New Zealanders built their homes; and the 'pavlova' as the popular meringue-based dessert (itself named after the Russian ballerina Anna Pavlova).

Plate 7.1
Osaka, Japan
Source: Lloyd Wright.

Plate 7.2
(Below) Miami, USA

Plate 7.3 Liverpool, UK

Plate 7.4 San Sebastian, Spain

Plate 7.5 Singapore
Source: Carlos Pardo.

Plate 7.6 Seoul, South Korea
Source: Manfred Breithaupt.

Plate 7.7 Nice, France

Plate 7.8 Copenhagen, Denmark
Source: Harry Rutter.

Plate 7.9
(Left) Melbourne, Australia

Plate 7.10
(Below) Manchester

Plate 7.11
(Left) Amsterdam, Netherlands

Plate 7.12
(Below) Rio de Janeiro, Brazil
Source: Carlos Pardo.

Plate 7.13 Delft, Netherlands

Plate 7.14 Oxford, UK

Plate 7.15 Beijing, China
Source: Manfred Breithaupt.

Plate 7.16 Hanoi, Vietnam
Source: Manfred Breithaupt.

Plate 7.17 Breda, Netherlands

Plate 7.18 Freiburg, Germany

Plate 7.19 Camel trail, Cornwall, UK

Plate 7.20 Amsterdam, Netherlands

Plate 7.21
(Left) Seville, Spain

Plate 7.22
(Below) New York, USA

Plate 7.23 Curitiba, Brazil
Source: Manfred Breithaupt.

Plate 7.24 Bogotá, Colombia
Source: Shreya Gadepalli.

Plate 7.25
(Left) Bangkok, Thailand
Source: Santhosh Kodukula.

Plate 7.26
(Below) Ahmedabad, India
Source: Abhijit Lokre.

Plate 7.27 Jakarta, Indonesia
Source: Manfred Breithaupt.

Plate 7.28 Grenoble, France

Plate 7.29 Strasbourg, France

Plate 7.30 Montpellier, France

Plate 7.31 Bilbao, Spain

Plate 7.32 Seville, Spain

Plate 7.33 The Randstad, Netherlands

Plate 7.34 Melbourne, Australia

Plate 7.35
(Left) Ørestad, Copenhagen, Denmark

Plate 7.36
(Below) Kuala Lumpur, Malaysia
Source: Manfred Breithaupt.

Plate 7.37 Vancouver, Canada

Plate 7.38 Beijing, China
Source: Manfred Breithaupt.

Plate 7.39 London, Liverpool Street Station, UK
Source: Halcrow Group.

Plate 7.40 Paris, France

Plate 7.41 Berlin Hauptbahnhof, Germany
Source: Manfred Breithaupt.

Plate 7.42 King's Cross St. Pancras, London, UK
Source: Eurostar International Ltd.

Plate 7.43
(Left) Eurostar High Speed Rail
Source: Eurostar International Ltd.

Plate 7.44
(Below) Delft Station Masterplan, Netherlands
Source: Mecanoo.

Plate 7.45 Rotterdam Central Station Masterplan, Netherlands
Source: Team CS.

Plate 7.46 Malmö Central Station, Sweden

Plate 7.47 Nanjing, China
Source: Andreas Rau.

Plate 7.48 Singapore
Source: Carlos Pardo.

Plate 7.49
(Left) Delft,
Netherlands

Plate 7.50
(Below) Hammersmith,
London, UK

Plate 7.51 Low-emission bus, London, UK

Plate 7.52 Electric bus, Cannes, France

Plate 7.53 Mahindra Reva electric car, Oslo, Norway

Plate 7.54
Honda Civic
hybrid car
Source: Low CVP.

Plate 7.55 Peugeot biofuel car
Source: Low CVP.

Plate 7.57 Sexy Green Car Show, UK, 2007
Source: Low CVP.

Plate 7.56 Mercedes Bluetec, Shanghai Challenge
Bibendum, China
Source: Low CVP.

Plate 7.58 Citroën Berlingo electric van
Source: Low CVP.

Plate 7.59 Autolib' electric car sharing, Paris, France

Plate 7.60 City Car Club, London, UK

Figure 8.1 Fahrenheit 451, 1966, written by Ray Bradbury, directed by François Truffaut.
In a future where the masses are hedonistic, anti-intellectual and critical
thought through reading is outlawed, Guy Montag is employed as a 'fireman'
(which, in the future, means 'bookburner'). Anyone caught reading or
possessing illegal books is confined to a mental hospital while the books are
burned – at Fahrenheit 451 – by the firemen: 'time has fallen asleep in the
afternoon sunshine'.

Source: British Film Institute Stills Collection.

8   Sustainable transport and the city

Alice laughed: 'There's no use trying,' she said: 'one *can't* believe impossible things.'

'I daresay you haven't had much practice,' said the Queen. 'When I was your age, I always did it for half an hour a day. Why, sometimes I've believed as many as six impossible things before breakfast.'

(Lewis Carroll, *Through the Looking-Glass*, 1871, pp. 210–211)

Thinking about the future

Perhaps Arthur C. Clarke (1999, p. 33) can help us to draw together our discussions about transport, the car, and its possible future use in the city:

> The car is an incredible device, which no sane society would tolerate [. . .] millions of vehicles, each a miracle of (often unnecessary) complication, hurtle in all directions, at very close quarters, under the impulse of a few hundred horsepower. Many of them are the size of small houses, with incredible sophistication, yet carry only one person. They can travel at over 100 miles per hour, but usually at no more than 40 mph. In one lifetime they have consumed more energy than the whole previous history of mankind [. . .] the casualties are on the scale of a large war (every year).

Yet, despite the appalling expense, our civilisation appears to be largely dependent on the use of the private motor car, or to aspire to car usage. Perhaps the attraction of the current transport system, and the private car dominance, will fade, as we begin to realise there are other very positive alternatives in travel – ones that can be more attractive to the individual and to society. There are certainly 'cracks' appearing in the system of motorisation; and perhaps the 'halcyon days of the car' are coming to an end (Heinberg, 2003; Dennis and Urry, 2009; Gilbert and Perl, 2010; Geels et al., 2011). This may only be apparent at present with a gradual improvement in CO2 efficiency of cars; some cities successfully supporting public transport, walking and cycling usage; and there is a clear awareness about the need to reduce carbon-based energy sources. But perhaps the change in technologies will also lead to wider changes in the practices of mobility.

Climate change, and the need to use resources more responsibly, supported by moves to achieve active and healthy lifestyles and quality in the urban fabric and urban life, all mean that we are starting to enter a new era for transport. Over the past 40 years there have been many efforts in seeking to achieve sustainable transport in cities, from Buchanan (Ministry of Transport and Buchanan, 1963) onwards, and even though there are good examples in many cities, there is little consistency in really tackling the key issues or in terms of measurable, area-wide impacts. Even the classic good practice city examples often fall down in the suburbs and in the urban sprawl on the edge of the metropolitan area, where the car becomes the major mode of choice. The increasing price of fuel, together with the apparent reducing availability of conventional oil supplies, have all acted as a focus for debate, but even here the addiction to oil is difficult to break. The evidence suggests that more, not less, oil is being used in transport globally. The large potential volume of unconventional oil resources, in oil sands and shale, provides a resource for future mobility growth, but this is hugely problematic in terms of the potential CO_2 emissions this implies.

The substantial growth in traffic volumes has had an enormous impact on the city and city life, over only a very limited time period. This speed of change has been underestimated and many cities seem to be 'sleepwalking' into the high energy, carbon dependence of mass car ownership and usage. It is easy to think that the car and its associated systems and infrastructure have been around for centuries because of its dominance in the urban environment and because of its centrality to many people's life. A walk through almost all of the cities in the world quickly demonstrates its dominance. The motor car, usually with an internal combustion engine and powered by petrol or diesel, has become the core technology for mobility; it has become a central part of modern life and often facilitates the activities undertaken (Urry, 2007).

However, as a counter, the unsustainability of the increased motorisation trend is also remarkable. The world received its billionth car in 2011, and is on the pathway to 2 billion cars by 2020 (Sperling and Gordon, 2009; Schäfer et al., 2009). The reality or even hyperreality of the current situation has formed a central theme within this book. We have sought to understand the car in its use value and in motorisation as a symbol of modernity and success. This draws on the thoughts of Mannheim (1936, p. 74):

> an ideology that cannot, in the long run, continue its upward trend. We anticipate that its expansion and diffusion will lead to a juncture at which it is no longer possible for the trend to be justified and maintained. Inadvertently, we will move to a new stage in the analysis of thought.

Hence our transport systems may be entering this transition stage, where the key actors – governments at various levels, civil society, the motor industry, the wider supporting auto–industrial complex and the public – start to confront the problem of the inherent instability of the current system and seek new directions for the future. As noted above, although there is good practice emerging in sustainable transport, the scale and speed of action is not sufficient to respond to the requirements for global reductions in carbon emissions and more resource efficiency in transport. There is too much inertia in the system, too much caution in ways of thinking about the problems being faced, and too much convention in the nature of investment decisions. There is a tendency to think that good practice will snowball and a sufficient momentum for change will happen organically, but this is likely to be wishful thinking. The reality is that there is no global, concerted action to address the problems, and many national governments are not committed to carbon reduction targets or resource efficiency, and it is clear that markets have not worked for carbon or energy. The question here is that thinking needs to go beyond the art of the possible to thinking about the impossible. Again, the world of Borges offers inspiration, perhaps illuminating the unreality of our present situation, the changes that are possible in our understanding (and travel behaviours) if sustainable travel is to be developed in the mainstream:

Things become complicated in Tlön; they also tend to become effaced and lose their details when they are forgotten. A classic example is the doorway which survived so long as it was visited by a beggar and disappeared at his death.[1]

(Borges, 1961, p. 39)

The central approach in this book has been the development of scenarios in transport for various contexts, and to demonstrate that the impossible can become possible through concerted action from all stakeholders and through clear and consistent policy packages. Scenarios are widely used at all levels of decision-making, particularly as they relate to climate change and energy use, and common messages can be summarised from the previous chapters:

1   In terms of definition, scenario analysis is often conflated with option analysis, but we have used scenarios in the tradition of Herman Kahn, incorporating wide-ranging issues into images of very different futures that affect transport planning at the city level. There is a large difference here to the use of option analysis in transport planning, where many options are often considered, such as route alignments and pricing changes. We have been concerned with strategy development at the strategic level, and the possible choices in direction to be taken.

2   The scenarios used have usually numbered between two and four, and it is better not to generate too many in a strategic decision-making process. Scenarios should also represent very different futures, and many studies end up with two more extreme alternatives and some sort of compromise in between. All scenarios need to be distinctive and represent plausible futures, but of course they are unlikely to result in blueprints for any particular future.

3   The scenario analysis process works well if it is explicitly participatory, and this should include experts and wider stakeholders. Historically, experts have been used as the main source of guidance, but this can lead to a narrow frame of understanding and innovation, and perhaps also limit the ultimate acceptability of the scenarios as developed. The participation should occur at many different stages in the process and should include a wide range of views, including experts, wider stakeholders and ideally the public, so that a diversity of views can be obtained, including some of the more radical options.

4   The expectations from participants must be realistic, and within the appropriate time frames, but the debate must also allow for the opportunity to break out of conventional thinking. A question here is whether it is better to achieve more modest objectives, rather than fail against more ambitious ones, but certainly the strategic policy issues we face demand innovative responses.

5   A range of different timelines have been used in the case studies presented here. The future should not be too close, as this reduces the opportunity to think about trend-breaking futures, but it should also not be too far in the future, as indeterminacy will increase. With the rapidly changing cities, a shorter timescale may be more appropriate as change is happening very quickly. In more well-established cities a longer term horizon might be effective, but with intermediate time points when certain objectives need to have been reached.

6   It is helpful if the likely impacts of scenarios are quantified in some way, so that the scales of change can be assessed. This can be against CO_2 or indeed any metric(s) that is (are) deemed important. As part of each scenario, there should be clear milestones and achievable targets so that progress in the direction anticipated can be monitored, and

changes made if necessary. This latter iterative element is often omitted from transport analysis. Scenarios should not be rigid and inflexible, but they should be adaptable to external and other changes such as innovations (Eriksson and Weber, 2006). The label attached to each scenario is also important to improve resonance. These need to be memorable, and perhaps inspirational, and the details of each scenario should help demark the differences in each potential future.

7   There are many different approaches to scenario building, and its methodological flexibility is a real strength. Many societal problems can be examined by combining suitable elements of the basic approaches outlined previously.

The underlying rationale we have used for examining longer term futures through scenario building is the need to tackle climate change and sustainability in its widest context. There is a fundamental dilemma between increasing the complexity of the problem and the need to communicate simplicity in the message if changes are to take place that are acceptable both politically and publicly. Hence the concentration on the CO_2 reduction target in London, Delhi and Jinan, and a richer, more complete set of climate change and sustainability objectives in Oxfordshire and Auckland. As in all planning strategies, there is a balanced judgement to be made between the need to be aware that progress against one indicator (such as CO_2 reduction) may lead to adverse problems, or knock-on effects, against other indicators. This is a central problem in sustainability, as the three pillars (economic, environmental and social; and sometimes governance and cultural objectives are also added) very often lead in different directions. This tension, and the framing of the discussion, is central to effective communication between the participants, their engagement and the ownership they might take over the implementation of the necessary actions.

It is also very difficult to convey the message about the immediacy and the need for substantial actions now. Both the timing and scale of the climate change imperative have been underestimated, and there is still a strong belief in technological solutions to what are essentially social problems. Scenarios are successful in getting people to think about the longer term issues and the consequences of taking (or not taking) actions, and many of the key actors are prepared to take an active role in thinking about the 'desirable' future city. Understanding the city in 2030 or 2050 is an important step, but the pathways are also crucial. There needs to be a timeline that traces when particular decisions need to be taken and by whom, so that the pathway from the present situation to the future is mapped out. This pathway is likely to change over time, but it is necessary so that important decisions are taken with a sufficient lead time. Part of the new thinking is that difficult decisions that have a major impact on the future patterns of low carbon mobility should be taken quickly, rather than postponed. Carbon budgets and interim targets, alongside end state targets, can help here. In the past too much thinking has been focused on the short-term future and the resolution of more immediate problems, rather than thinking more prospectively over a longer term. Policy-making hence tends to be incremental and avoids issues that are deemed 'difficult'.

In addition, transport investment has to be much more supportive of city design than it has in the recent past, and it needs to be much more explicitly linked to supporting the city more generally through contributing to its viability (economy), vitality (environmental) and vibrancy (social). Many of these issues are not unique to sustainability and futures studies, as they illustrate a fundamental problem in the way in which scientific research engages with policy actions and outcomes (Banister, 2008; Schwanen et al., 2011). At present there is a major 'implementation gap'. The means by which knowledge is translated into policy measures is extremely weak. It is left to the decision-makers, many of whom are unaware of the latest thinking, or are comfortable with doing things in a particular way, or are not prepared to take the risks (and opportunities) for innovation through the implementation of new ideas and new knowledge.

Political leadership is often not visible and it is also very inconsistent, certainly in the Western democratic context, where the typical UK Secretary of State for Transport is in office for one or two years, then moves on to a 'more rewarding' set of responsibilities. The next minister then takes several months to get up to speed on the issues, and this reduces continuity and the effectiveness of decision-making. Much greater consistency in approach is necessary, and this would include much more effective links across the ministries, so that a more coordinated approach to policy-making is created that can really address the important longer term issues facing society in the twenty-first century.

More generally, in risk terms, we often 'distance' ourselves from the more difficult issues. For example, we have a sense of invulnerability to climate change as a 'distanced risk-group' (Joffé, 1999). If these types of problems remain, progressive policy-making and risk aversion results, and there is only a small chance that effective change will take place. There needs to be a new dialogue and process in decision-making, a more effective transfer of knowledge, and an openness and consistency in working relationships between researchers, practitioners and politicians.

Figure 8.2 Mad Max, 1979, directed by George Miller. 'The last law in a world gone out of control. Pray that he's out there somewhere.' Surely we can think our way around a future such as this? Though many would say this is already materialising in the rush for the remaining oil fields (Dennis and Urry, 2009).

Source: British Film Institute Stills Collection.

This final extended chapter elaborates on some of the means by which this ambitious and radical agenda can be realised. It covers the broader issues of climate change, and the centrality of the sustainability debate, not so much in its definitional sense, but in looking at the ways to 'get things done', and it uses the material from the case studies to illustrate the scale of change needed and the difficulties involved. There are three additional substantive contributions: the first covers the adaptive backcasting approach that has been developed as a flexible means to identify sustainable transport futures and to use the dynamics of change to enhance outcomes. Second, the critical importance of urban form and the structure of cities is restated as one means to reduce the need for car-based transport and through the potential for shorter journey lengths. Third, there is a commentary on the implications of achieving different scenarios in transport, and in making progress on a variety of related themes. These include more thoroughly understanding the rationales for peoples' travel, the role of transport in society, the modelling problems and the importance of different forms of governance (the means of implementing scenarios). Finally we restate the criticality of imaginative thinking in futures analysis, both in the immediate term and over the longer term. Returning to the inspiration of Herman Kahn: we need to start thinking   and achieving – the (currently) unthinkable in our future travel behaviours.

Meta narratives in transport

Climate change, in Goffman's (1959) phraseology, has become 'frontstaged'. Alongside oil scarcity, wider energy depletion, traffic casualties and impacts on city design, climate change has become a central concern for decision-makers in transport planning and city planning. Still, too much time has been spent on forecasting against historic trends, 'improving' modelling methodologies and assessing transport impacts at the local level, such as modelling how much traffic can be fitted through a junction, or a particular network. These are important issues in specific locations, but relative to the strategic policy concerns of climate change and oil scarcity, support for the macro economy, and achievement of improved quality of life and well-being, they seem much less important. Sustainable transport remains largely an unresolved policy area. There is still debate over its definition, the direction of change, and the type of investments and innovations required to significantly reduce CO_2 emissions and to concurrently achieve wider environmental, social and economic objectives in transport.

Cities in the industrialised West are often very CO_2 intensive in their travel patterns; the cities in Asia and elsewhere usually much less so. There are very different baselines between cities and within cities (in terms of the inner areas, outer suburbs and hinterlands). This large difference in CO_2 emissions within cities and city regions is under-appreciated and largely overlooked when international, national and city-based targets are set. It is at these different levels, however, that the transport investment, the city structure, and any gains, can be made in implementation terms. The different baselines and opportunities require very different strategies. For example, the emerging cities face very different realities to those in the industrialised West. They often have much lower per capita incomes (and tax receipts) at the national and city levels. GDP growth rates would need to be maintained at high levels for decades to make up the difference, hence transport investment is limited. The focus here, therefore, has to be on the less expensive and more inclusive modes, which means walking, cycling and bus rapid transit – akin to the Curitiba and Bogotá models. Metro systems are potentially unaffordable in many cities. The exception here might be the major cities in China, and perhaps also in a smaller number of cities in India, or major cities elsewhere. In addition, many cities are limited in terms of the actions that they can take, as decisions on issues such as fuel duties, subsidies and prices are all taken by national governments; vehicle fleets may be imported from overseas markets; and many of the environmental standards are set by international agencies. Cities that are extended or built almost from scratch can be constructed in ways that are much less transport intensive. The way cities are built and retrofitted – including the walking and cycling provision, levels of public transport and provision of parks and open space – will determine people's travel behaviours for decades to come (Peñalosa, 2011). Hence, transport planning becomes critical to the achievement of sustainability at the city level.

The previous case study chapters have attempted to explore these issues, with an emphasis on long-term change, the potential for the development of innovative scenarios, the discussion, and in the end achievement, of desirable low carbon futures. There are multiple future pathways, even within each city or jurisdiction, but perhaps there are some 'meta narratives', that effectively capture some of the major directions possible. All of the case studies used workshops with local experts and wider stakeholders to develop their understanding of local trends, problems, opportunities, and potential future scenarios. They examined similar timescales, either to 2030 or 2041. The elaborations of scenarios were different in detail, but often covered common ground. The analysis had a different emphasis to the Foresight Programme Intelligent Infrastructure Systems (IIS) study (Department for Trade and Industry and Office of Science and Technology, 2006) in that technological developments were not the central focus of attention. We utilised a very wide range of policy measures that may affect travel in future years, including the development of low-emission vehicles and alternative fuels, but also larger investments in public transport, walking and cycling, the built environment and also traffic demand management measures. A key message is of the importance of the integrated approach – relying on a narrow set of policy measures does not result in any significant reduction in transport CO2 emissions. The case study scenarios are brought together in Figure 8.3 with common dimensions – of technological change and environmental stewardship – to highlight the common choices that many contexts face.

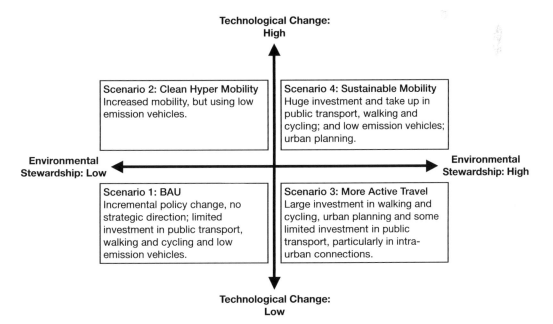

Figure 8.3 Meta narratives in transport

A key argument is that technological change may not be as forthcoming as many protagonists imagine, and, perhaps more likely, that it may not be particularly well-tailored to the environmental imperative; as it may even encourage more travel, with a large rebound effect, even though per km travel is less resource consumptive. The techno-optimist approach holds great store that Moore's Law[2] will apply in transport (i.e. in rapidly lowering vehicle emissions and improving fuel efficiency), similar to the trends experienced in computer hardware design. But the evidence is not supportive, as the curve of technological progress, and particularly market take up in vehicle technologies, is not exponential and never seems to fully deliver against societal expectations. There is always a 'complexity brake'[3] or unexpected directions are taken, and the transport system is one that is slow to react to change. Technological developments are rarely targeted at solving the problems of city life, or travel behaviours, as might be intended, and they can often act to accentuate them. Innovations are more usually driven by the profit motive in organisations and there are often mismatches between any requirements to address broader societal objectives.

Relative to the IIS scenarios, environmental stewardship is seen as a more important dimension to emphasise. The case studies hence more explicitly explore the importance of reducing mobility (particularly by car, petrol- or diesel-based), the level of stewardship in governance terms, and the implications of this for individual and societal behaviours. This highlights the critical question in low carbon transport analysis: whether mobility can continue along the same pathway as now and simply travel by cleaner modes of transport (the dominant governmental line), or whether levels of mobility also have to be reduced. Again this seems a fairly fundamental problem to address, yet it is not well understood, largely because the political implications of widespread demand management. The effective management of traffic growth and of realising traffic reduction are rarely on the agenda. This dichotomy is thus very revealing, yet it is also a little disingenuous, as technological change and behavioural change (and environmental stewardship) are very closely linked, as illustrated by the availability of new car technologies and ways in which consumers might purchase and make use of them.

Marguerite: Sometimes you have a dream. And you get involved, you believe in it, you love it. In the morning, when you open your eyes, the two worlds are still confused. The brilliance of the light blurs the faces of the night. You'd like to remember, you'd like to hold them back. But they slip between your fingers, the brutal reality of day drives them away. What did I dream about you ask yourself? What was it happened? Who was I kissing? Who did I love? What was I saying and what was I told? Then you find you're left with a vague regret for all those things that were or seemed to have been. You no longer know what it was that was there all around you. You no longer know.

King: I no longer know what was there all around me. I know I was part of a world, and this world was all about me. I know it was me and what else was there, what else?

[. . .]

The disappearance of the windows, the doors and the walls, the King and the throne must be very marked, but happen slowly and gradually. The King sitting on his throne should remain visible for a short time before fading into a kind of mist.

Eugène Ionesco, *Exit the King*, (1967, pp. 89, 95)

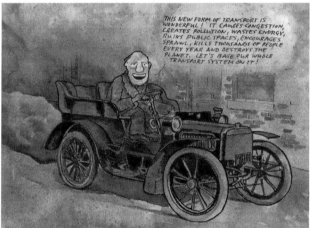

Figure 8.4 Definition and meaning
Source: Cowan, 2010.

Pathways to the future

In the case studies, the 'meta narrative' scenarios have been broadly applied to each of the five case studies, with of course large differences in application by context. The policy measures, though within similar scenarios, are very different in that certain policy measures are suited to particular context-specific problems and opportunities. Figures 8.5 and 8.6 bring together the results in absolute and per capita terms. For each city seven different sets of comparable values are given for city related transport CO_2 emissions and for per capita levels. These represent historical emissions (1990), the current baseline (one of 2004, 2005, 2006, 2010), future BAU (2030 or 2041), the three different future scenarios (2030 or 2041) and an equity target where the same aspiration for per capita emissions is used. The main comments on the findings are:

Overall (absolute) emissions

- CO_2 emissions in 1990 and 2005 show the high levels of London (at around 10 MtCO2), as a large industrialised city with relatively high levels of car ownership and use. The other case study contexts are fairly low in emissions, either due to small populations (Oxfordshire, and to a lesser extent Auckland) or low levels of car ownership and use (Delhi and Jinan).
- As time progresses to 2030, the BAU scenarios show CO_2 emissions changing markedly. London increases marginally (nearly 12 MtCO2), but Delhi grows rapidly (over 26 MtCO2) and Jinan (over 16 MtCO2). Auckland approaches 8 MtCO2 and Oxfordshire nearly 3 MtCO2.
- The future scenarios reduce emissions significantly relative to BAU, particularly under Scenario 4, where low-emission vehicles are delivered at the mass scale and behavioural change is strong.

Per capita emissions

- The per capita data show a very different story, as the impacts of large populations are removed, and the focus is, to a greater extent, on the level of car ownership and use. Auckland (3.7 tCO2) and Oxfordshire (3.1 tCO2), for example, have very high transport CO_2 emissions per capita in 2005, relative to London (1.3 tCO2), Delhi (0.4 tCO2) and Jinan (0.2 tCO2), resulting from current high levels of car dependency.
- The BAU projections to 2030 extrapolate the historic trends, including estimated population growth, motorisation and mode share, but are modified by the current policy approach which tends to include some traffic demand management, in the industrialised countries at least. Auckland (3.8 tCO2) and Oxfordshire (4.1 tCO2) remain high, with some increase in per capita levels, relative to London remaining steady (1.4 tCO2), Delhi increasing nearly to London per capita levels (1.0 tCO2) and Jinan increasing at a rapid rate (2.0 tCO2).
- Again, the future scenarios reduce per capita emissions significantly relative to BAU, particularly under Scenario 4.

The end goal is perhaps a 2050 equity target in transport, where all contexts 'contract and converge' to a common level of emissions of around 0.5 tCO2 per capita, drawing on the framework developed by Meyer (2000), and taken up by the IPCC (2007) and Stern (2009).

But as yet it has not been directly applied to the transport field. Such targets may be desirable as end points, but obtaining international agreement on such tough targets is almost impossible, as illustrated in the rather 'soft' CO2 targets achieved in the Kyoto Protocol (1997), which in themselves have not been reached by many of the signatory states. It also ignores the legacy that the developed countries have as the major polluters in the past. For many developing countries, the climate change problem is seen as a Western industrialised country problem (Saxena, 2012). Yet, sadly, CO2 emissions are unlike local air emissions, in that they do not remain local. The impacts of a largely Western-induced climate problem are felt globally, and the consequences will be most apparent in the developing world. An equitable or equal shares approach to climate change policy-making provides one means to address the geopolitical issues of fairness, even though it doesn't address the historical responsibilities for CO2 emissions. Alternatively, there could be two (or three) levels for emission targets, with higher ones for developing countries and lower ones for developed countries in recognition of the legacy, and a possible intermediate one for countries in the transitional stage.

Despite very different geographical and development contexts, similar types of scenarios can be built for each of the different situations, even though the policy options must be adapted to the particular local situation. The types of futures (clean mobility, limited change, and sustainable transport) all have the same generic roots, and they are often constructed on similar dimensions (e.g. market-based or more interventionist, planning-based policies, and different levels of technological innovation). The differences concern the specifics of the policy measures (or packages) being implemented in each location, the levels of application (investment and wider initiative), and the timeline (pathways) over which the changes take place. In addition

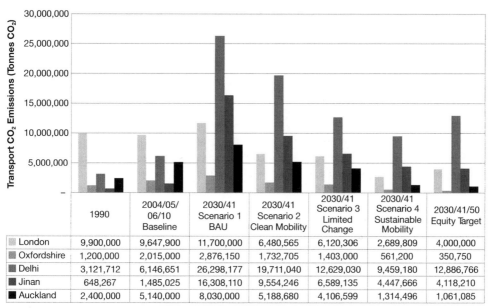

	1990	2004/05/ 06/10 Baseline	2030/41 Scenario 1 BAU	2030/41 Scenario 2 Clean Mobility	2030/41 Scenario 3 Limited Change	2030/41 Scenario 4 Sustainable Mobility	2030/41/50 Equity Target
London	9,900,000	9,647,900	11,700,000	6,480,565	6,120,306	2,689,809	4,000,000
Oxfordshire	1,200,000	2,015,000	2,876,150	1,732,705	1,403,000	561,200	350,750
Delhi	3,121,712	6,146,651	26,298,177	19,711,040	12,629,030	9,459,180	12,886,766
Jinan	648,267	1,485,025	16,308,110	9,554,246	6,589,135	4,447,666	4,118,210
Auckland	2,400,000	5,140,000	8,030,000	5,188,680	4,106,599	1,314,496	1,061,085

Baseline and Scenarios

Figure 8.5 Comparative transport scenarios, CO2 emissions absolute

Note: Different base years are used in the case studies dependent on what data was required and used in the original research studies. For example, the baseline is 2004, 2005, 2006 or 2010 and the future scenarios are developed for either 2030 or 2041.

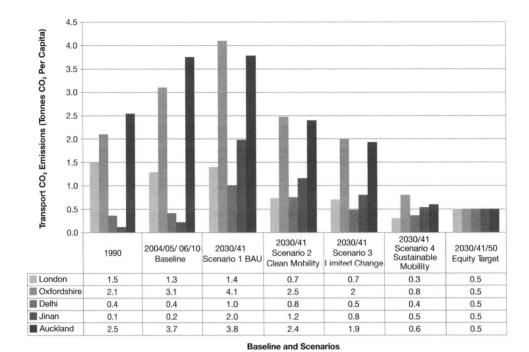

	1990	2004/05/ 06/10 Baseline	2030/41 Scenario 1 BAU	2030/41 Scenario 2 Clean Mobility	2030/41 Scenario 3 Limited Change	2030/41 Scenario 4 Sustainable Mobility	2030/41/50 Equity Target
London	1.5	1.3	1.4	0.7	0.7	0.3	0.5
Oxfordshire	2.1	3.1	4.1	2.5	2	0.8	0.5
Delhi	0.4	0.4	1.0	0.8	0.5	0.4	0.5
Jinan	0.1	0.2	2.0	1.2	0.8	0.5	0.5
Auckland	2.5	3.7	3.8	2.4	1.9	0.6	0.5

Baseline and Scenarios

Figure 8.6 Contraction and convergence in transport (CO2 emissions, per capita)

there are the differences in the priorities allocated by the decision-makers at various levels of government, the key roles that the different actors play in influencing the policies, and the awareness, role and influence of the public. All of these variables have a clear impact on the levels of CO2 reduction. Some of these issues are tackled within the scenario process through participation and debate over the policy options, and perhaps even through the multi-criteria analysis carried out to give priorities and weightings to the decision-making. But a major part also relates to the role that transport has in everyday life, the political process, and the understanding of the limitations under which decision-makers operate. Good intentions and strong commitment to radical change do not necessarily lead to strong action and the achievement of large scale change necessary for sustainable transport.

Adaptive backcasting

In this book, and this concluding chapter, a wide-ranging discussion has covered the practical and the methodological issues concerning the use of scenarios in sustainable transport. One of the overriding messages has been that the scale and speed of action needed for substantial CO2 reduction (on BAU) has been totally underestimated. For example, in the Delhi case study, there is a possibility to reduce the rate of increase in CO2 emissions under the BAU 2030 future by two-thirds, and this can be achieved through less travel distance (a reduction of 20 per cent) and through the use of more efficient (and healthy) forms of transport. International experience (such as found in Bogotá) is helpful in illustrating what can be done, as there has been a major effort in terms of developing BRT and walking and cycling facilities to achieve a better urban environment and a sustainable transport system. In a city with low income levels, bus rapid transit and cycling offer equitable (and healthy) travel options for all. In Delhi, there will be a substantial increase in both travel and CO2, but this is explained by the growth in population (nearly +50 per cent 2010–2030) and the existing low levels of CO2 emissions, both in aggregate and per capita terms.

Achieving climate change targets in all cities is both possible and desirable, and as noted here it helps achieve much more than carbon reduction in policy terms. This is only one of many important policy objectives, and such a limited approach focusing on carbon could be called reductionist in that it over-simplifies the policy objectives of sustainability in cities. But it does help to focus the discussion. A fuller interpretation of the issues relating to climate change and the implications for mobility requires a vision of the city that would include an assessment of its viability (in terms of its economic rationale), its vibrancy (in terms of its social and cultural rationale), and its vitality (in terms of its environmental and health rationale). In this context, the role of transport can then be implemented as an integral and supportive part of city design. In recent years, conventional transport investment (e.g. in highways and flyovers) has often had an adverse impact on the quality of the city, and there has been a discontinuity between transport planning and city design.

With respect to the methodological issues raised here, scenario analysis provides a rich background against which to think about city futures and how they can actively respond to climate change. Table 8.1 uses four key descriptors to describe the underlying rationale for scenario building. Many of the scenario studies overlap and do not fall conveniently in any one category, and elements of several different approaches have been used or adapted to particular applications. This is a key strength of the general scenario building approach.

Table 8.1 The rationale for scenario building

---

(1) *Shaping and adapting*: Focus of scenario building is directed at specific issues, often with others being discarded or not given much attention. All interested parties should be included in the discourse at all stages, and the role of experts needs to be limited. Shaping takes place in a specific direction, and uncertainties and contingencies are often underestimated. Robust processes (see below) need to be adaptive to changing internal and external situations. This means that options must be kept open and the agenda should not be single issue or exclusive.

(2) *Single futures or multiple futures*: Single visions of the future provide powerful images and they are useful in building coalitions and setting agendas. Multiple approaches, often based in socio-technical scenarios, are less prescriptive and allow space for thinking about alternative courses of action. This greater flexibility may have advantages for decision-makers as it keeps more options open.

(3) *Normative or exploratory*: The more normative single vision driven future, often used in backcasting, has a strong element of what is desirable, and this is helpful if there is a clear overriding imperative. Exploratory scenarios can deal more easily with the unexpected, but increasingly they also have to become more normative when producing policy recommendations. Perhaps the two approaches ought to be combined, as an Adaptive Foresight scenario building process, where more normative elements are central to the exploratory scenarios and where more explicit but divergent normative futures can be addressed.

(4) *Robustness and adaptability of policy portfolios*: Options need to be maintained in terms of the normative objectives, but they also need to respond to the changing external environment as portrayed in the exploratory scenarios. Robustness is really a measure of whether the policy options being considered are beneficial under all alternative scenarios, whilst the adaptability relates to the ease with which unexpected events (risks and opportunities) can be included.

Source: Based on Weber, 2004; Eriksson and Weber, 2006; Eriksson and Weber, 2008.

Table 8.2 Adaptive backcasting

Phase 1:	Initial analysis and reviews, including retrospective analysis, the identification of focal issues and the analytical boundaries.
Phase 2:	Drafting exploratory framework scenarios through workshop(s) that identify external drivers, inductive storylines and more deductive scenarios based on two dimensions of uncertainty, as in the UK Foresight Programme example. These scenarios should be relevant, plausible and challenging.
Phase 3:	Specification of exploratory framework scenarios to sharpen the driving logic and to ensure ownership by participants.
Phase 4:	Formulation of collective visions and objectives to be debated and to identify the dimensions for policy options.
Phase 5:	Identification of challenges associated with each of the framework scenarios, with a workshop involving structured brainstorming on the risks and opportunities.
Phase 6:	Identification of shared pathways (multiple backcasting) so that the best variant of each framework scenario is highlighted together with the means to move strongly in that direction. Action and intervention windows are needed to take advantage of opportunities when they occur.
Phase 7:	Identification of collective strategies (portfolio analysis) so that robust and adaptive options can be found in the scenarios. This will help to avoid negative effects and encourage the exploitation of the positive opportunities.
Phase 8:	Identification of individual objectives, roles and options.
Phase 9:	Identification of individual strategies.
Phase 10:	Realisation and coordination, including implementation and learning through monitoring and feedback.

Source: Based on Eriksson and Weber, 2006.

A recent trend in futures studies has been to move away from forecasting the potential impacts of science and technology alone, and to enlarge the discourse to include economic, social and environmental factors, so that there is a more fundamental understanding of socio-technical change (Quist et al., 2011). This requires the involvement of all interested parties in a fully participatory process, so that consensus can be reached. If a consensus is not possible, then the participating parties can at least understand the different perspectives on the issues being discussed. Such involvement leads to a greater ownership of the policy measures and a greater likelihood that outcomes will match up with expectations in a fully transparent debate that highlights the risks and the opportunities. The result is that the scenarios help shape the future, but do not control or predict it (Eriksson and Weber, 2008). The key question here is whether the development of shared views, collective actions and responsibilities is sufficient to really bring about change. The process is summarised in a series of phases (Table 8.2).

The interest in this examination of the process of scenario building is that it moves the thinking forwards, by presenting a framework within which different examples can be placed, and it also cuts across the different types of scenarios outlined in the case study chapters. For example, the Delhi study (Chapter 5) uses an adaptive backcasting approach that combines a BAU (forecasting) stage with more exploratory analysis of alternative futures. But it is primarily a visioning process, with extensive use being made of participatory methods to debate targets, comment on the visions of the future, discuss the policy packages, and assemble them in a series of mutually supporting clusters together with detailed implementation pathways. It covers Phases 1, 2 (in part), and 4, 5, 6 and 7, in the schema above, but it places a far greater emphasis on participation and discussion throughout the process. It includes an educational and learning function, as well as a more pragmatic normative policy objective.

Components of the future

There are no easy answers to the question of what form our mobility should (or even will) be in 2030 or 2050. But certainly we should attempt to develop storylines and strategies, which provoke debate over the key issues, and can be discussed as part of the 'strategic conversation' in each city. These can help us look backward from where we would like to be, to where we are at present, and then to develop the pathway(s) in between. Well-structured implementation programmes can be developed, progressing consistently towards the strategic goals, with a phased sequence of interventions, helping to achieve a consensual, or at least widely agreed, future. The potential conflict here is that to achieve a consensual view often requires a weakening of the policy interventions. In the case of carbon reduction this should not be the way out, as weak implementation would result in little or no improvement, and this is where leadership and a clear understanding of the importance of the issues must form the basis of any agreement. If travel can be made much more sustainable at the city level – in all of the major cities internationally – then the impact on global emissions will be significant.

The backcasting form of scenario building is a normative method, and it provides an effective approach to measure, analyse and intervene in transport and city planning. It also has the potential to become the dominant approach in transport planning, particularly where the need is for a longer term outlook or where there exists a future of great uncertainty. Quantum change is an essential part of effective action, and mere incrementalism is not even worth discussing. Central to the achievement of sustainable transport is progressive, consistent, and long term commitment to action.

Drawing on the inspiration of Hall (1963; 1989), and even earlier luminaries in 'looking backward' such as Bellamy (1888), we can ask what our travel behaviours might look like in 2030 or 2050, and what might be generic to cities. There are many questions evident: will transport and movement be a positive experience? Will the affective dimensions of travel be improved (the quality of the journey and interaction)? Which types of transport and travel will become less used or obsolete? Are some journey types less useful and more suitable to demand management? In the end, how can transport best contribute to the sustainable city?

There will, of course, be a much smaller global environmental footprint for transport than at present. In the leading cities in 2030, and the majority of cities by 2050, much of travel will be local, using walking and cycling as important modes of travel, supported by extensive networks of well integrated and clean (in terms of CO_2 emissions) public transport. Low-emission vehicles are used, but only where the use of other modes is not possible. Private cars are not the first choice of travel for most people. The travel patterns of the Netherlands, Germany, Denmark and Sweden in 2010 have been replicated internationally, with cycling infrastructure and public transport improvements seen as critical, and the first option for transport investment in the sustainable city. The mode share benchmark of at most 20–30 per cent of trips by car (and these by low-emission vehicles) is seen in almost all urban areas internationally. The ownership of vehicles will change markedly, with a much greater share of car rental and leasing. Transport policy and investment will be geared to achieving this headline figure. The share of walking, cycling and public transport varies by area according to opportunities and aspirations, but there are two main models that are sought after: the public transport city model such as found in London (40 per cent of trips by public transport, 20 per cent walk, 10 per cent cycle, 30 per cent low emission car); and the Copenhagen cycle city model (20 per cent of trips by public transport, 10 per cent walk and 40 per cent cycle, 30 per cent low emission car). Some cities may do 'better' than this – with a lower mode share for the car. There are many future pathways, but perhaps the commonalities (in 2030) include the following six key elements:

1. Urban structure: has become a critical policy tool in transport planning. It is shaped, at the regional, city and local levels, to ensure that public transport and cycling is possible, with high density and mixed use clusters developed along key public transport routes. Almost all cities have been, or are being, redeveloped, including their outer areas, to support use of walking, cycling and public transport. Higher density clusters of development are found around all public transport interchanges. Interchange locations are developed as activity hubs. There are many more people living and working in the city and other urban areas, with 'high people intensity' uses such as employment located in the highly accessible areas. The amorphous sprawl of development in the suburbs has been replaced with carefully re-planned polycentric clusters of development. Growth area boundaries (e.g. green belts) are used to restrict development spreading into rural areas, though the focus is on corridors of growth, centred around public transport interchanges, rather than a simple encircling of urban areas. The confidence to strategically plan development at the regional and urban level has been rediscovered in places such as the UK, and the practice has spread internationally.

A key element here is the reallocation of scarce road space in cities to the most appropriate use, and this varies by the time of day and the day of week. New networks of routes for people, cycles and public transport mean less space for cars, and certain areas (e.g. parts of city centres, particular residential areas and locations of high people activity) have no cars. Achieving car-free areas, or areas where cars are restricted in their movement, is seen as an important policy goal in all cities. The reticence of earlier years to develop such progressive policy approaches has become very outdated. The quality of local facilities reduces the need to travel and allows more multi-purpose activities, and the range of 'green' modes of transport has reduced the need to own a car.

Reduced levels of car ownership in the city means that even more space can be reallocated to other uses, and this new open space is often transformed into green space. This urban quality changes attitudes to living in cities and the means of travel whilst there. Urban living is a primary choice for many, and housing quality has been much improved, as there is more supply and so housing is cheaper. Neighbourhoods are vibrant and there are opportunities to access multiple employment, educational, social, entertainment and cultural activities. Hence urban living is popular amongst many age cohorts: the 20–35 year group, but also those with families and 'empty nesters' and the retired. All seek and value the better access to activities that urban living offers. Private car ownership and use in the city is also very different to previous years. Where one is needed, it is hired, shared or even borrowed, but this is usually only when public transport or walking or cycling doesn't provide an option. Rather than the city being organised around the car, the car has to adapt to the city, and eventually the city, or large parts of it, flourishes without the car.

Many of the inaccessible areas in and around cities (inaccessible to public transport), including the areas beyond the urban boundary, are used in ways that are less people- and car-intensive, such as growing local agricultural produce, so that car dependency becomes less of a problem. Also the need for long distance freight is reduced through increased local sourcing.

2. Walking, cycling facilities and the public realm: There has been a huge investment to make cities more liveable and useable for pedestrians and cyclists, with extensive networks of segregated pedestrian and cycle routes, cycle parking and cycle hire schemes. The progressive cycling practice in the Netherlands and Denmark has spread around Europe, and internationally. There are extensive networks of segregated and on-road cycle routes in all cities, together with large cycle parking provision, hire and repair facilities. Cycling is now a very popular means of travel, including for commuting; people are very aware of the health benefits of active lifestyles. Road space is reallocated away from the private car, and packages of these smaller walking and cycling schemes are now seen as 'major projects' in transport, rather than viewed as 'Cinderella' schemes. There are no districts zoned for single uses, or where only one type of people live or work. There are many small, interconnected streets, lined by mixed uses. Electric bikes (two- and three-wheelers) are also very important in many contexts, including in Asia, but also Europe and North America, and particularly in the suburbs.

3. Public transport: There has similarly been huge investment in public transport, of all modes, including metros in larger cities (following the London, New York, Paris and Shanghai models), extensive BRT networks (the Curitiba and Bogotá model), tram systems (the French city model), tram–train systems, feeder bus networks and other variants. All cities have an extensive and mixed portfolio of public transport networks, including one or more different modes. For inter-urban travel, high speed networks have largely replaced short haul air, and slower speed networks have been electrified.

There is a revolution in the production and use of renewable energy; local generating facilities (solar, wind, biothermal, biodigester, wave and tidal power, and algae ponds) produce electricity or fuel, to be used in public and private transport, and by households and industry. All buildings are clad with photovoltaic panels, designed to use natural light and heat, and rooftops are green.

4. Traffic demand management measures: There is much greater utilisation of TDM measures, and a much greater acceptance that these are necessary elements of a sustainable transport strategy. Measures include road pricing, parking restraint and behavioural measures. For example, road pricing in the UK is charged at 15 p per mile (or more). Local business are also subject to a transport and public realm tax (following the French city model), which is used for local transport improvements. In London, for example, this has funded extensive public transport, cycle and public realm improvements, including tram schemes in the suburbs. Many urban motorways have been redeveloped to reduce traffic capacity, reallocating road space to public transport and walking and cycling priority.

5. Low-emission vehicles: The average total vehicle fleet (new and old vehicles) in all fleets internationally is less than 90 gCO2/km in 2030, meaning that many vehicles are electric or hybrid electric, and the use of petrol and diesel has been replaced with locally produced biofuels. City vehicles are also small and low speed, which again radically improves their efficiency, and has additional benefits of reducing accidents and the space needed for parking. Much of this progress has been achieved with the setting of mandatory emissions standards in all countries. Car ownership levels are still relatively high in European countries, and growing in Asia and other emerging countries, but usage patterns are very different. Clean vehicles (below the 100 gCO2/km threshold) now account for the vast majority of vehicles, including the larger size and specification vehicles. There are many vehicles, including the electric options, with significantly lower gCO2/km. There have been similar improvements in freight vehicles, with low-emission vehicles now used in all light and heavy goods vehicles. Average distance travelled per vehicle has reduced, with much less use for local and city-based journeys. The means of ownership has also changed dramatically, with a much great use of hire schemes and car clubs. Individuals tend to pay for vehicles at the time of use rather than as an upfront cost.

6. Information and communications technology: The potential for ICT to transform lifestyles has become a reality, and this in turn has also made many people reconsider their priorities, away from the necessity to always travel, and to own a car, towards a much more flexible use of transport, space and time in cities. New forms of communication have also changed perceptions of all forms of transport; including mass use of teleconferencing (replacing a significant level of business travel), working at home (where the employment activity allows), home retailing and even types of educational access and social interaction. Public transport has become much easier and attractive to use, as real-time information is available, time spent on the journey is seen as 'productive' for work, education, socialising and entertainment access. Public transport has a great advantage over private car usage here, as people can do other things whilst on the journey, hence the feeling of 'wasted time' in travel has reduced. For example, using the Internet or mobile phone, tickets can be bought on a door-to-door basis, even for multi-mode and international journeys (rather than buying individual tickets by each operator and journey link). This includes the hiring of bikes or shared taxis, etc., at each end of the public transport journey.

Transport investment is focused on improving the quality of the journey experience, and of life more generally, as the affective begins to outweigh the instrumental value of travel. ICT facilitates the 'seamless' public transport journey, a new level of information allowing journey times, interchanges and delays to be checked; the access of news, reading material and other forms of entertainment, or booking activities at the destination, often as 'augmented reality'[4] whilst on the move. The journey is no longer seen as 'wasted time' or something to be 'reduced in time', but it becomes an integral part of the day, allowing productive work and entertainment on the go. The new technologically based innovation means that greater flexibility can be introduced; movement is not just provided on the basis of cheapness and speed, but in terms of a positive experience. For example, route guidance for cyclists and walkers can take place according to individual priorities; say to avoid traffic, or dangerous locations, or to follow green space.

The long (and hyper) distance commute would become very difficult as the cost of private transport is much more expensive. Oil is priced at over $200 a barrel, and it is priced differentially for essential and luxury uses, with the remaining (cheaper) oil being used for the most important functions, such as in health provision. The popularity and frequency of international air travel has also been reduced, as this is seen as a luxury use of oil and as there has been no real progress in the development of alternative fuels for air travel. People tend to fly internationally only occasionally, the cost is high, and long-distance trips are used to combine multiple activities, such as a business trip and a holiday, or the visit of family and friends. Business meetings and conferences are often carried out by teleconference or through the smart phone; overseas holidays are usually made by high-speed rail.

Sustainable transport has been attained by many of the leading and progressive cities in 2030, and by 2050 a majority of urban areas have become sustainable in transport terms. Improvements in networks and facilities have been carried out over a long time period, with much greater consistency in effort and funding. Though the particular policy measures differ greatly according to the individual city, there is a common objective of delivering a much higher mode share of walking, cycling and public transport. All of these suggestions made above under each of these six headings are available now and do not depend on expectations about technological innovation. Most are not expensive and encourage safer, healthier and more community-based lifestyles. An obvious question is why these measures have not been introduced already.

The critical role of urban structure

Looking in more detail at the role that urban structure has to play in the overall future of urban transport, we see this policy area as a critical enabling element to many of the other package components. Each of the future scenarios in the case studies utilises urban structure to various degrees, using the strategic location of development, density, mix of use, local neighbourhood and layout to encourage more sustainable travel patterns. Urban structure is hence viewed as a critical element of the sustainable mobility vision, working alongside and assisting investment in public transport, walking and cycling. Low-emission vehicles are only used where private car and freight vehicle use is necessary or preferred. This builds on the theory as developed over the last 30 years by a range of authors, and discussed previously. The recent self-selection debate is seen as important insofar as highlighting the important influence of attitudes to location and travel, and their relationship to the urban structure and travel nexus, but again it is likely that attitudes are modified according to urban structure and other contextual possibilities (Banister and Hickman, 2012).

Urban structure provides the means by which sustainable transport can be achieved in the city, and the need for efficiency in terms of the space occupied, the energy used, and the numbers of people carried. An important dimension is the space question – typically, about a quarter of the ground-level urban area is used for car-based mobility, in the form of streets and parking (Vasconcellos, 2001). This seems a very inefficient use of land, particularly where land is valuable and can be employed for other uses, which can be much more supportive of urban vitality and design aspirations. In many of the largest and rapidly developing cities this figure decreases substantially.[5] All cities were, of course, not designed for the levels of mobility that are currently being experienced – as predicted years ago by Buchanan (Ministry of Transport and Buchanan, 1963) – as street space is limited and there are many other uses apart from traffic movement (e.g. as markets, social space or work space). There is an important time element here – cities that were developed extensively before the 1950s–1980s motorisation period (such as London) have tended to be based around public transport; those that were developed in the motorisation age (Auckland) have reflected those aspirations in their design. Many cities in Asia have very ineffective, often absent, land-use planning systems, hence have very limited tools for guiding the location of development.

The sustainable mobility paradigm (Banister, 2008) promotes the case for urban spatial structure being central in determining transport mode and distance travelled, as it links the spatial distribution of population, jobs and other activities within the city to the pattern of trips. Higher density cities encourage more walking and cycling to take place, particularly if space is allocated for exclusive rights of way. This means that the available street space in cities can be optimised for the highest number of users, giving both environmental and social benefits. Urban structure evolves over time, often with 1–2 per cent being replaced each year, through new construction and the replacement of existing buildings (Banister, 2005). In addition, there is an increasing amount of refurbishment taking place, as the reuse of existing buildings (e.g. warehouses and industrial buildings) can result in much greater change over a much shorter period of time. Many cities in developing countries are also growing rapidly, mainly driven by inward migration, and so it is important to provide homes and jobs for

Figure 8.7 Sun on Prospect Street (Gloucester, Massachusetts), 1934 (oil on canvas). This type of car-based development needs to be halted – it is ubiquitous, in various forms, across the world, but it is incompatible with the sustainable mobility aspiration.

Source: Hopper, Edward (1882–1967)/Cincinnati Art Museum, Ohio, USA/The Edwin and Virginia Irwin Memorial/The Bridgeman Art Library.

Figure 8.8 Under the El (oil on canvas). The city, with development orientated around an extensive public transport system, becomes the dominant form of development.

Source: Fiene, Ernest (1894–1965)/Private collection/Photo © Christie's Images/The Bridgeman Art Library.

Figure 8.9 Sunday. 7 Across: Stationery, 2004 (oil on card). Of course, some problems remain – our international flying and freight patterns need to be seriously reconsidered. Solving the surface-based transport CO2 emission problem is of little use if long-distance travel is not managed in some way. Yet demand management in air travel remains beyond the political debate. Perhaps an individual carbon rationing system will be required here (Hillman and Fawcett, 2004).

Source: McLaughlin, Ben (contemporary artist)/Private collection/Wilson Stephens Fine Art, London/The Bridgeman Art Library.

migrants that keep travel distances as short as possible. Peripheral sprawl needs to be discouraged, and limited, as it uses valuable agricultural land, it increases the distances that need to be travelled, and makes the provision of public transport more difficult. The arguments for high urban densities are strong for both transport and land take reasons, and all cities should be encouraged to build upwards (higher densities) and not outwards (suburban sprawl) (Glaeser, 2011), but of course there needs to be a good integration with transport provision.

There are various spatial forms that can be taken up, with point, linear and dispersed variants. First, the classic city form is a monocentric structure with a radial pattern of transport links into the centre, where most of the jobs are located (e.g. Oxford, Cambridge). Densities are highest in the centre and the system can support both public transport and non-motorised transport, as distances are relatively short. As cities grow larger, more complex structures are needed (London, Paris, New York and Jakarta). Second, polycentric cities have several centres and develop a hierarchy of functions that can result in more local activities being carried out at the smaller centres, and higher function activities in the major centre (Rio de Janeiro and Mexico City). Oxfordshire, and perhaps even Delhi, match up to the polycentric pattern, albeit in Oxfordshire's case, in a more spatially disperse format at the regional level, with lots of open space. Non-motorised modes can be important at the local level, but a high-quality public transport system is needed so that travel to the major centre and between the minor centres can be undertaken. There is an increasing complexity in all travel movements – with multiple origins and destinations – which means that the quality and density of the public transport network (including interchanges) has to be of a high order.

Third, the axial city has developed where there are two major cities joined by high-speed rail, or two or more major centres in a city joined by a major public transport corridor. For example, in China, development has taken place at the two 'end' cities (Jinan and Qingdao), but also at the intermediate stations along the route that are accessible to the high-speed rail link (Zibo and Qingzhou). Jinan is also being shaped internally as a linear city, with growth in the traditional centre linked by BRT to the new centre around the high-speed rail station. In all cases it is important to develop around the highly accessible public transport nodes, so that the attractiveness of these new transport development areas is fully realised. Development needs to be of mixed use, including housing, employment, schools, shops, health facilities and recreational opportunities. This now the major development form being pursued in most master plans internationally, certainly in the central parts of most cities. Even the former motorised cities (including Auckland, and even some of the dispersed cities in the US such as Los Angeles) are now being retrofitted with public transport options, to the extent that is possible with unsupportive urban forms. The level of urban structural change, however, remains limited, with strong opposition often found against increasing densities. In the progressive cities, public transport interchanges can become the new commercial hubs for cities, acting as 'superhubs' where a major international interchange is involved. Examples are King's Cross St. Pancras (London), Berlin Hauptbahnhof (Berlin) and Shin Yokohama (Yokohama) (Hall et al., 2013).

A fourth possibility is the satellite city where new towns are built around an existing centre (Seoul, Shanghai, and to an extent London), with good-quality links to the central city. The intention with satellite towns is that each should be relatively self-sufficient, with a balance between jobs and housing, so that the daily travel would be carried out locally. The difficulty here is that this option can result in high levels of commuting between the satellite town and the central city, and often this can be car-based.

In the introduction, the original thinking of Michael Thomson was discussed, in particular how he categorised the different city structures. Figure 8.10 attempts to revisit the city typologies of Thomson (1977), and to a degree Wegener and Fürst (1999), in the light of recent and potential future developments in transport and city planning, and in view of the case studies as discussed. It should be remembered that the Thomson categorisation reflected the time when oil was cheap and plentiful, and when there were few concerns over supply or resource constraints, and when the potential effects of climate change were not known. We can see that most cities or jurisdictions have developed as 'hybrids' of the given typologies, with one or more of 'full motorisation', 'weak centre', 'strong centre', 'low cost' and 'traffic limitation' attempted, certainly when considered across different parts of the city. Indeed, perhaps there is coalescence in strategies, with a large investment in public transport now in many cities, and some form of traffic demand management and polycentric growth. Similarly, in the case studies presented in this book, each has developed different supporting strategies according to the baseline behaviours, problems and opportunities. Strategy development in transport has become much more refined in all contexts, with integrated and tailored packages of measures, some very progressive, being implemented.

London has changed from a traffic limitation city (1977) to what might be labelled a modern low carbon transport city, whilst Auckland has switched from being heavily motorised (1977)

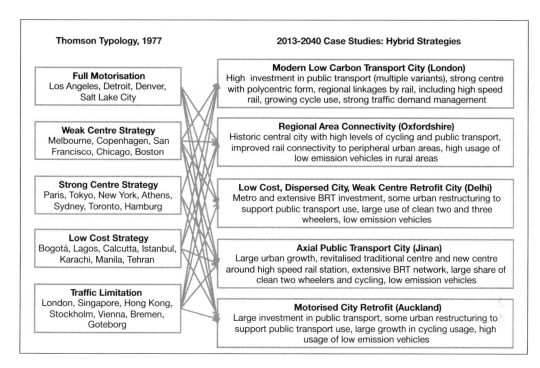

Figure 8.10 Emerging city strategies

to a modified version that now includes increasing low carbon transport options. Delhi maintains its position in the low cost strategy (1977), but is developing improved public transport networks and a clean three-wheeler fleet. Jinan is an example of a rapidly growing urban form, with axial development based on public transport, two-wheelers and cycling. Oxfordshire is a little different as a county with a more dispersed pattern of development and activities, but the potential to develop a much improved sub-regional public transport network.

The policy imperative has changed since Thomson's time (1977), and the importance of climate change and oil scarcity has come to the fore. There is much more potential for the vehicle fleet to be clean in CO_2 emission terms, yet the progress in reducing average vehicle fleet emissions remain frustratingly slow. All cities may eventually converge in strategic policy approach in terms of the key problems that they must face, and as noted here the range of options are similar, and this means that cities can and should learn from each other. There is no single future for transport world-wide, as each city will have a very different transport system. Transport planning, over time, can learn the importance of context and change over time: 'People do not produce history and places under conditions of their own choosing, but in the context of already existing, directly encountered social and spatial structures' (Pred, 1985, p. 8).

Thinking the unthinkable?

Achieving significant reductions in transport CO_2 emissions will take a major effort, and will require us to consider and implement some of the policy measures that may be considered too difficult to deliver. The scenario process can help us think through the varied possibilities,

Figure 8.11 Manhattan, 1979, directed by Woody Allen. 'Well, all right, why is life worth living? That's a very good question. Well, there are certain things I guess that make it worthwhile. Uh, like what? Okay. Um, for me . . . oh, I would say . . . what, Groucho Marx, to name one thing . . . and Willie Mays, and . . . the second movement of the Jupiter Symphony, and . . . Louis Armstrong's recording of 'Potatohead Blues' . . . Swedish movies, naturally . . . 'Sentimental Education' by Flaubert . . . Marlon Brando, Frank Sinatra . . . those incredible apples and pears by Cézanne . . . the crabs at Sam Wo's . . . Tracy's face . . . (and cycling on your bike in the city).'

Source: British Film Institute Stills Collection.

and to develop a debate around them. Some of these areas may even seem unpalatable in 2013, but we should include them in the strategic conversation – in Herman Kahn's words to help think the unthinkable.

Perhaps in 2030 and 2050 we will experience great surprise in looking back at the way people used to live and travel (in 2013). The car-dominated society of the late twentieth century and early twenty-first century might seem very anachronistic. How we used oil as if it was an infinite resource, how we ignored the problems of climate change and the impact of transport on the city. But to get there we need much imagination in the process of strategy development, participation and implementation. Bellamy (1888, pp. 6–7) describes society and the process of capitalism as follows:

> A prodigious coach which the masses of humanity were harnessed to and dragged toilsomely along a very hilly and sandy road. The driver was hunger, and permitted no lagging, though the pace was necessarily very slow. Despite the difficulty of drawing the coach at all along so hard a road, the top was covered with passengers who never got

down, even at the steepest ascents. The seats on top were very breezy and comfortable. Well up out of the dust, their occupants could enjoy the scenery at their leisure, or critically discuss the merits of the straining team. Naturally such places were in great demand and the competition for them was keen, everyone seeking as the first end in life to secure a seat on the coach for himself and to leave it to his child after him. By the rule of the coach a man could leave his seat to who he wished, but on the other hand there were so many accidents by which it might at any time be wholly lost. For all that they were so easy, the seats were very insecure, and at every sudden jolt of the coach persons were slipping out of them and falling to the ground, where they were instantly compelled to take hold of the rope and help to drag the coach on which they had before ridden so pleasantly. It was naturally regarded as a terrible misfortune to lose one's seat, and the apprehension that this might happen to them or their friends was a constant cloud upon the happiness of those who rode.

There are perhaps great parallels here with the current system of motorisation. The car users, for example in SUVs or high-specification cars, are usually very aware of the privileged position they occupy, and this seems attractive to many in society internationally. Those driving in congested conditions often wish that others would get public transport or walk, or not make the journey at that particular time – but of course not themselves. The manner in which we have designed our cities, and indeed set up society, often perpetuates the motor car system. Yet, for all but the most ardent drivers, there are large concerns over the problems of climate change, of what will happen when the oil supplies dwindle or become even more expensive, of the problems in extracting non-conventional oil supplies, the huge toll in traffic accidents, and the impacts of traffic on the city.

The development and discussion of alternative scenarios is a very necessary first step in the transition to more sustainable transport futures. Yet, without the achievement of different travel behaviours, this is likely to result in wasted effort. This, of course, takes us beyond the pioneering thinking of Kahn, Wack, Schwartz and Van der Heijden, who comment that scenarios are used as a method to improve thinking around future options. They go no further than this, and indeed advise against choosing preferable futures. Although improved thinking around future possibilities is certainly required in transport, it is also useful to consider how we can most effectively change practice and delivery.

We discuss this problem at three levels. The first two gain only cursory commentary, and are being developed elsewhere as emerging research areas in transport. The third issue is considered in more detail, but again requires much more research and consideration than has yet been developed. The first area is to further understand why people travel and the role of transport in society; second is to consider the implications of different transport scenarios for the practice of transport planning, modelling and appraisal; and third, the means of governance in transport. All of these are seen as emerging research areas in transport, as very necessary to the achievement of different scenarios in transport, but they remain 'in development', as open-ended and under-researched. They are ripe for much further research, discussion and debate, building on the initial efforts being made.

As an early step, it is useful if we can further understand the social and cultural 'embeddedness' of the private car for many people, and perhaps why others are less reliant on the car. The use of the car is associated with both instrumental and affective emotions (which are often interlinked), and it is these latter issues that are perhaps the least well understood in empirical terms. In all likelihood, they will be critical factors in the design of future successful transport systems. This means that the journey is designed to improve the quality of the experience rather than the speed of the trip from A to B. Much of the current analysis, policy development, the investment and implementation in transport planning, does not reach these issues or the 'the routines of practice' (Sheller, 2004; Sheller and Urry, 2004; 2006; Urry, 2007; Shove, 2010; Aldred and Tepe, 2011). This may be an important reason in that the mobility regimes appear to be much more difficult to change than has previously been thought. Societal values and travel cultures need to be well understood before change is likely to happen. This wider appreciation can complement and assist the conventional approaches to achieving greater sustainability in transport, such as investing in infrastructure, redesigning the built environment, changing the pricing levels and encouraging cleaner vehicle technologies (Banister et al., 2011).

In parallel, there are major changes that need to be made in terms of the development of the theory and practice of transport planning, including in strategy development, modelling and appraisal. The use of theoretical approaches[6] to help understand transport and travel behaviour has been very limited in transport planning, certainly when compared to the progress made in related disciplines. There is, however, some recent progress insofar as critiquing the current practice and applying approaches from other disciplines to the transport planning domain (Banister et al., 2011; Schwanen et al., 2011). This is perhaps a useful avenue to developing the theory in transport planning, where consideration has been given to the theoretical approaches used elsewhere and translating them in terms of a stronger ontological basis for transport planning.[7] This is, however, again an emerging body of work, and there is much to be done in developing our understanding. Transport, and travel behaviour, is often viewed from the domain of natural science, and it is this that can often prove problematic. The difference in subject content, but also approach and aspiration, between the natural sciences and social sciences is important.

The important social science perspective is often overlooked within transport, as it is still firmly entrenched in an engineering, economic and mathematics tradition. Engineering is used to design and build transport systems, and the latter two to evaluate and model them. Natural science considers the behaviour of physical objects, while social science considers the behaviour of humans. These, of course, tend to be much more complex (Giddens and Dallmayr, 1982; Flyvbjerg, 2001). Giddens (1984) develops a 'theory of structuration', whereby society is based on social structures, such as rules, institutions and frames of meaning, and individual factors such as identity, sense of self, and action (or 'agency'). All of these, in combination, are important in determining the workings of society. Transport, as analysed from this angle, is very different to the natural sciences, which largely ignore the human complexity. There is no 'self-interpreting' entity or frames of meaning, simply the movement of physical objects. This reliance on the natural science perspective, on the simplistic utilitarian theoretical framework, becomes increasingly critical, not so much when the main task is to build a highway network and develop car ownership and use (yesterday's problems), but when behaviours need to be understood and changed, so that transport more effectively supports sustainability goals and city life (the problems of today and tomorrow).

Similarly, the neo-classical framework, which extends into transport modelling and appraisal, and indeed provides the conceptual underpinning for much of practice, seems very simplistic and outdated. The practice of calculating time savings and comparing relative to the cost of the transport investment, often the basis of transport appraisal, seems to analyse only part of the debate. Comparing options between a road widening delivering 5 minutes of time savings for 1,500 commuters in the morning peak, at a cost of £35 million; or a new motorway delivering 30 minutes of time savings for 5,000 commuters, at a cost of £150 million; or a new regional public transport scheme for 20,000 commuters, at a cost of £2 billion; and using the highest cost–benefit ratio to guide investment, seems to be giving undue emphasis to the natural science perspective and ignoring major issues concerning the climate and built fabric. But this is the basis of much of our decision-making, and of course is the subject of millions of pounds' worth of engineering, planning and economic analysis. The so-called 'intangibles' are often the most important factors, and they include the impact on travel distance, traffic volumes, mode share, development patterns, CO_2 emissions and casualties. In much of the current analysis they are all perceived very much as secondary issues, even within a supposed 'systematic' and wide-ranging multi-criteria analysis, particularly if particular issues cannot be quantified effectively.

There are fundamental implications in a changed view of transport behaviours and costs, of incorporating uncertainty, and the need to achieve different futures, and these are only beginning to be thought through. Different approaches need to be developed, with a reduced focus on extrapolation of existing trends and observed behaviour, and a greater emphasis on understanding why people travel by particular modes, how this might change, and how transport can contribute to the sustainable city (Table 8.3).

Hence there are many complexities to think through. We can try to understand why people might not rationalise their travel choices in a manner that we would expect. People are not fully informed, they are inattentive to information and they do not perfectly discriminate between options. We often fail to understand the importance of context, judgment, practice, habit, trial and error, experience, common sense, intuition and bodily sensation. All of these are excluded in our analysis of 'rational' travel behaviour (Flyvbjerg, 2001; Schwanen et al., 2012). This causes many problems within the conventional application of transport planning, and provides a great challenge to transport planners, including in re-conceiving strategy development, transport appraisal and implementation. How many projects have been built that are overused or underused relative to the original forecast? Why does car use prove so attractive to the majority of people? Why is it so difficult to reduce the use of the car? Why does transport investment fail to support urban design, or progress towards societal goals? How can we better deliver alternative transport futures, with a greater use of public transport, walking and cycling? All of these are questions requiring fundamental rethinking of conventional approaches to transport in a resource-constrained world. Hence:

> By taking seriously how people feel about and in cars, and how the feel of different car cultures elicits specific dispositions and ways of life, we will be in a better position to re-evaluate the ethical dimensions of car consumption [. . .] only then can we consider what will really be necessary to make the transition from today's car cultures (and the automotive emotions that sustain them) to more socially and environmentally 'responsible' transportation cultures.
>
> (Sheller, 2004)

Finally, in addition to the concerns over why people travel and new social science based methods, there is the issue of governance, in terms of how we might deliver new and more attractive transport futures. Foucault (1966; 1991) develops a critique of convention, and of mainstream thought, through the concept of exploring discourse. This might help us to understand how issues can be thought through differently. Foucault, for example, considered how the means of government (the bureaucracy that governs), the governance (what the government does), and the governmentality (the art of government) might change to help address issues in a different manner. Two broad concepts, in particular, were developed:

Table 8.3 Changing approaches in transport planning

The conventional transport planning and engineering	The emerging sustainable mobility
Premised on abundant supplies of energy that can be reduced through greater efficiency is use	Premised on the need to reduce resource consumption in transport, particularly the dependence on oil
Market mechanisms (e.g. prices) can lead to efficiency in transport	Strategic planning and investment is required to help shape the rules of the market
Travel decisions as a choice, framed within rational decision making	Travel decisions seen as more complex assemblages of routines, habits and constraints
Traffic and mobility focus, particularly on increasing vehicle volume and throughput	Travel as important to social activity, improvements to accessibility, improvement to the quality of the journey experience, multi-modal
'Predict and provide' approach to analysis	Traffic demand management, improving the journey experience, slowing movement down where appropriate
Concern over the main transport mode, rather than the total journey	Concern over the door to door travel – improving the entire journey experience
Street as a road	Street as a space with multiple users
Motorised transport	All modes of transport, often in a hierarchy with pedestrian and cyclist at the top and car users at the bottom
Focus on major schemes, mainly road	Integrated strategies and packages of complementary measures
Accept trends and examine transport issues over the shorter term	Concern about achieving the desirable city over the longer term and the role that transport should play
Transport planning disregarding context	Strategic and local urban planning as a central element in achieving sustainable transport
Demand forecasting, mainly traffic-based with some public transport	Visioning and scenario analysis, benchmarking for cities and transport
Social and environmental objectives given less weight than economic	All three pillars of sustainability considered important – and, in addition, the importance of cultural context and political and public acceptability
Economic evaluation, quantitative analysis given most importance	Multi-criteria analysis to take account of environmental, social and implementability concerns; quantitative and qualitative analysis given equal balance
Travel as a derived demand, instrumental factors important	Travel as a valued activity as well as a derived demand – instrumental and affective factors, often interlinked
Traffic to be speeded up, journey time to be minimised	Concepts of slower travel, reasonable travel time, and reasonable energy use in transport
Segregation of pedestrians and traffic	Integration of pedestrians, cyclists and traffic

Source: Developing Marshall (2001), Banister (2008).

- The reversal of the traditional interpretation of an event, or a system, looked at from a different angle, as not an 'essential thing', but a 'constructed reality' and concept in accordance with the social atmosphere of the current society.
- Discontinuity, rejecting the traditional notions of history as progressive and causational, looking for ruptures and shifts in the traditional narrative.

There are, of course, multiple ways to govern society, including how to invest in transport and city development. Many would argue that the dominant governance approach in recent years has been one of 'muddling through' or 'incrementalism'. This approach struggles to deliver radical policy change, as carefully planned strategic steps become 'ordinarily impossible' (Lindblom, 1979). Governance is limited to consideration of alternative policies, all of which are only incrementally different to the status quo. There is a limitation in the analysis to a few somewhat familiar policy alternatives, a greater analytical preoccupation with problems to be remedied rather than with positive goals to be sought; a sequence of trial, error and revised trial; and exploration of only some of the consequences of alternative approaches (Lindblom, 1979). This all seems very familiar in the transport planning field. Instead we have strongly argued for a 'quantum change', as this is the new order of change that is required, and marginal changes in the transport system will not achieve sustainable mobility.

Foucault similarly would demand a new framing of the debate, looking very differently at how issues in transport are understood, discussed and delivered – including whether the existing governance structures, the participation of the public, and even the focus of consumption and capitalism need to change markedly to attain sustainable transport futures. As Hajer (1995, p. 2) comments: 'Policy making is not just a matter of finding acceptable solutions for pre-conceived problems. It is also the dominant way in which modern societies regulate social conflicts.' How these issues and relationships need to play out is not clear, and they are not being debated to any serious degree, but certainly the process of implementing the currently 'politically difficult' policy measures needs to be hugely improved. The development of our knowledge, understanding of issues and rationales for travelling around, are all essentially framed by experience, language and images. The terms and boundaries of this understanding often are, or can be, set by government; hence there can be much scope for influence depending on the approach taken.

The most recent forms of governance and governmentality, at least as developed over the last 30 years in the USA, UK and much of Europe, have been heavily influenced and characterised by neo-liberal beliefs. Individual freedoms, 'rights' and 'choice' are championed over the 'excessive intervention' of the state (Foucault, 1991; Lupton, 1999; Harvey, 2005). The mechanism of governance has been developed in a particular manner, often to avoid 'shaping' individual behaviours, and to avoid policy measures that are deemed as acting against 'choice' in the mode of travel. Alongside, however, there has been strong support for the use of the car (road building is seen as investment, public transport as 'subsidy'), often the motor industry is heavily subsidised as a central feature of the economy, and mass market advertising of the motor car shapes aspirations in the public. The response to climate change has been technocratic, framed in economic terms, and in the end it is unlikely to deliver large reductions on transport CO_2 emissions. The problems of current travel behaviours are much more complex than can be understood in these terms.

Modern political institutions as currently framed are not particularly well-equipped and ultimately do not have a functional purpose of addressing diffuse and long-term environmental problems (Beck, 1992). The climate change problem is fundamentally difficult in that it is very closely linked to lifestyles and consumer behaviour. Many of the policy approaches being considered, and implemented, are having little impact against the strategic targets being set at the city level. This conflict is often hidden in the initial definition of the problem, in the issues discussed and those that remain undiscussed. A particular framing of the debate makes certain elements seem 'fixed' and inappropriate, others are viewed as 'problematic', and some much easier to discuss and 'deliver'. In transport, policy measures such as road pricing, reducing space for the private car, increasing densities in suburban areas, reducing the growth in international air travel, carbon rationing, etc., are all seen as 'politically difficult' and usually remain beyond the mainstream debate. These are seemingly 'technical' positions, but of course conceal a normative stance, supported by the institutional arrangements (Hajer, 1995). A 'weak state tradition', say in the United States, or perhaps increasingly in New Zealand or the UK, means that policy tools are generally chosen from the least controversial part of the spectrum, such as voluntary emission standards, labelling schemes or limited media campaigns on 'travel awareness'. Regulation on businesses and individuals results in hostile responses and intense lobbying and 'watering down' of original proposals. Increasing taxes, for example, is almost viewed as 'legalised extortion' (Dunn and Perl, 2010). The contest between the suitability of different policy approaches and measures, and wider issues such as development and sustainability is often, however, an ideological one, rooted in fundamentally different value systems and worldviews (Wheeler, 2012) – and this is where the intractability of the problems remains. Progressive transport planning becomes almost impossible in practice – there is a huge gap between the few examples of good practice and the widespread implementation on the ground. The current emphasis on neo-liberal policy-making creates a reliance on the individual as the agent of change (Giddens, 1991) but, of course, when the individual is largely unaware of the problems of their current travel choices there is little likelihood of significant changes being made in travel behaviours. As Foucault (1991, p. 100) advises: 'The population [. . .] is the subject of needs, of aspirations, but it is also the object in the hands of the government, aware, *vis-à-vis* the government, of what it wants, but ignorant of what is being done to it'.

If society is to move beyond the hyperreality of car dependency – realising that the costs of mass motorisation, on the environment, in the number of casualties in traffic accidents, and also the impact on the city fabric, massively outweigh the benefits in individual mobility – then many of these difficult governance and governmentality issues need to be tackled. Transport and city planning becomes critical to the status of the human condition. How might these changes come about? Like Plato's (2007) *Allegory of the Cave*, we have not noticed that there may be better ways of developing transport systems and of travelling around our cities. Wide-ranging debates on future travel possibilities should be possible in all cities and jurisdictions. This will involve a better understanding of why people travel and the role of transport in society. It will involve changes to our strategy development, our approaches to modelling and project appraisal. The framing of the debate in transport can therefore be much wider. Achieving sustainability in travel is not about marginal change; instead it requires very different thinking – a huge change in mindset across a range of approaches in transport planning – perhaps much more than we realise. This will involve a reshaping of the governmental frameworks and mechanisms to better achieve sustainable mobility, and a greater participation by the public in developing their own travel futures:

> One-dimensional thought is systematically promoted by the makers of politics and their purveyors of mass information. Their universe of discourse is populated by self-validating

hypotheses which, incessantly and monopolistically repeated, become hypnotic definitions of dictations.

(Marcuse, 1964, p. 14)

We have previously ascribed forms to the car-based lifestyle: that it brings freedom, status and expression, but in reality many of these are not real, and not as valuable as we imagine (or are sold). There are many hugely adverse impacts that can no longer be ignored. The first step is to realise that there are much more attractive travel behaviours and lifestyles on offer; we just need to look outside to the sunshine.

Towards the day-after-tomorrow

Time is our great hope, but we are also running out of time. The expectation is that new generations will learn to think and live very differently, that the dominant beliefs of today will soon begin to seem difficult to maintain, and eventually to appear untenable. The dual problematic of climate change and resource scarcity might mean we have to develop our thinking more rapidly than we now imagine. But perhaps the transition will not be as dystopian as often envisaged. The best practice in 2013 is already achieving, or close to achieving, the mode share levels suggested for 2030 and 2050. Low-level car usage in some cities is already possible, and the travel behaviours and lifestyles on offer in parts of many urban areas are often much more attractive than the car dependent variants. Echoing Orwell, probably when we get there, the sustainable mobility future (for almost all) will perhaps not be so dreadful as we feared, indeed will be more attractive than where we are now.

Certainly we need to understand the factors affecting our social systems before we can hope to change them. All of us are situated in multiple overlapping social systems, which influence and are influenced by the individual. All are influenced, to a greater or lesser degree, by the contemporary media and advertising. This is increasingly shaping people to aspire to the same or similar lifestyles, internationally. Drawing on the inspiration of Foucault (1991), we can argue for a reversal in our understanding of travel, initiating 'strategic conversations' and an alternative discourse in many more cities, so that the search for different futures that might help substantially reduce transport CO2 emissions in the city can begin.

Similarly, the understanding developed from transition theory offers a way forward, thinking through complex strategies for change that cover myriad interventions, including new infrastructure, vehicle technologies, urban planning, the political mechanisms to deliver effectively, and changes to public beliefs and norms. The private car has been an incredible invention, popular with the public and important to the growth of national economies. But, we need to consider the nature of the car's irrationalities and to start to break some of the boundaries in the contemporary system of motorisation. This can take many forms, but it must include reflection on the institutions and organisational structures that are central to cities and transport, asking whether they are still appropriate in a resource-constrained world, when new political priorities are emerging. In addition, much more creativity is needed in deciding what measures are employed, how they are packaged in a complementary manner, how social regulation and control are used, and the actions of the electorate or members within society are shaped.

Governance can be used in a much more progressive manner than at present to help achieve the futures that we would like to live within. This will help us avoid 'the March of Folly': where governments persistently pursue policies contrary, in the long run, to their own interests (Tuchman, 1984). Urry (2011) argues for the 'resource turn', whereby societies should be

Figure 8.12 Being John Malkovich, 1999, directed by Spike Jonze.

Craig Schwartz: 'There's a tiny door in my office, Maxine. It's a portal and it takes you inside John Malkovich. You see the world through John Malkovich's eyes.' Perhaps the scale of change required is beyond our current understanding and the current political system. How do we engineer the metaphorical portal?

Source: British Film Institute Stills Collection.

examined through their use of resources, in pattern, scale and character. This can be a central element in the judgment of progress and success in transport and city planning; with metrics such as the resource footprint, alongside the quality of the journey and well-being, becoming central to strategy development and project modelling and appraisal.

Perhaps a great hope is the Internet and the revolution we are experiencing in terms of information dissemination and knowledge transfer. At the heart of any democratic society, and also other forms of government, is the notion of an informed public, and one that is willing and able to participate in decision-making, at least indirectly through electing, supporting or giving tacit approval to officials. This participation demands at least a basic understanding of the issues at hand (Cacciatore et al., 2012). The sharing of good practice is something that can radically change over time, to help disseminate good practice, and to challenge the advertising and marketing representing the powerful vested interests. Transport planners, for example, in Jinan or London can easily be aware – indeed many are – of the emerging practice globally, of what is developing in Delhi, Hyderabad, Shanghai, Strasbourg, Vancouver and Zurich, simultaneously. The recent spread of investment in bus rapid transit system building is perhaps symptomatic of this process. Starting with limited development in South America, in Curitiba and then Bogotá, from the 1970s onwards, there has been an incredible proliferation of system development in recent years. There are now approaching 200 bus rapid transit systems internationally, and this process gives us great hope. Similar can be seen with high-speed rail, public realm improvements and cycling provision.

Of course, we are blighted by the problem of indeterminancy, and of ineffectiveness and narrow aspect in our working:

> The car as vehicle [. . .] will go the way of the horse [. . .]. Had the infant automobile industry, in 1910, seen fit to call a conference to consider the future of the horse, the discussion would have been concerned to discover new jobs for the horse and new kinds of training to extend the usefulness of the horse. The complete revolution in transportation and in housing and city arrangement would have been ignored. The turn of our economy to making and servicing motorcars, and the devotion of much leisure time to their use on a vast new highway system, would not even have been thought of. In other words, it is the framework itself that changes with new technology, and not just the picture within the frame.
>
> (McLuhan, 1964, p. 238)

The scenarios developed for London, Oxfordshire, Delhi, Jinan and Auckland illustrate that different futures are possible, and that the 0.5 tCO2 per capita target can be achieved in different contexts. However, this assumes that a 'sustainable mobility' scenario is deliverable, that governance is far reaching and effective, and that the (petrol and diesel) private car can be disassociated from use in everyday life. This is very positive thinking, and we should remind ourselves that changing travel practices are associated with fundamental change at the societal level. But these are the problems that now need to be resolved.

Dennis and Urry (2009) ask us to envisage life 'after the car', and it is very likely that a new pathway will begin, and is beginning, to emerge. What will travel look like in a world with very expensive oil and with limited energy resources? We perhaps don't know how society will respond as yet, but in the not-too-distant future we will need to travel in ways that require much less oil. The convention of facilitating increased mobility, of relentless consumer novelty, and supporting GDP growth in the economy may recede. It may be replaced by a new approach, perhaps premised on a better and fairer social logic where cities, travel and the quality of life are developed to make a positive contribution to well-being, livelihoods and capabilities (Sen, 2009; Jackson, 2009). This will require a very different basis for transport and city planning, internationally, but there is much to be gained from a new approach. Central to this will be the informed public; like Debord (1967) we hope we can 'wake up the spectator who has been drugged by spectacular images'.

We have sketched only the barest outlines of potential transport futures at the city level. We have left many loose ends, but perhaps some of these can be developed, and we hope to have begun a serious discussion of the possibilities for changing travel behaviours at the city scale. Mobility is critical to social relations, it is important to the human condition, and very often this is currently delivered by the petrol or diesel private motor car. This latter social construction, however, can – and must – be changed. Progress must be made now, but not incrementally. A 'quantum change' is required that involves composite actions that are flexible but mutually supporting, so that a new direction is initiated that can be consistently followed over a period of time. Thus the direction of policy is not towards any one societal goal, but many, and the pathway is not fixed, but will be iteratively changed over time as we understand what progress is being made.

We hope to have begun a serious debate about the possibilities for changing the relationships between transport, climate change and the city, and that the scale and immediacy for action have both been made very clear. But in thinking about utopian or dystopian futures, we should consider a final warning (More, 1516, p. 118): 'there are many features of the Utopian commonwealth that I can more easily wish for in our own societies than hope to see realised'. Dystopian, inequitable and unsustainable futures loom large if we fail to plan for and deliver radical changes to our travel and city futures. But the final message must be optimistic, namely that the present dependence on the car and carbon can, should and will, be substantially reduced in cities internationally as we progress to 2030 and beyond.

Notes

1   Borges discusses the mysterious country called Uqbar, where a conspiracy of intellectuals imagine (and thereby create) a world known as Tlön. The people of Tlön deny the reality of the world, including most of what would usually be considered common-sense reality.

2   Moore's Law (named after Intel co-founder Gordon Moore): the observation that, over the history of computing hardware, the number and performance of transistors on integrated circuits doubles approximately every 18–24 months. If Moore's Law applied in transport, we would 'drive to the city centre in one car, and they would be so cheap we would pick up a new one to drive home. Your first tank of petrol would be your only refill in each car. The only problem is, each car would be so small that you would never be able to find them' (Gelsinger, 2002; cited in Department for Trade and Industry and Office of Science and Technology, 2006b).

3   The 'complexity brake': borrowed from the world of artificial intelligence and the debate around the potential for 'The Singularity' – where artificial intelligent 'agents' become more powerful than their human equivalents (Kurzweil, 2005). The complexity brake, however, is found as we go deeper into our understanding of natural systems, and typically find that we require more and more specialised knowledge to characterise them, forcing the continual expansion of our scientific theories in more and more complex ways. This seems to apply in transport – the 'silver bullet' of the clean vehicle never arrives, due to difficulties in design and production, and delivery to the mass market; and indeed in understanding the complex rationales for travel and vehicle purchasing patterns.

4   Augmented reality (AR) is a live view of a real-world environment, where the elements are augmented by computer-generated content such as sound, video, text or graphics, facilitated by GPS positioning of the user. It is related to mediated reality, in which reality is modified (perhaps diminished as well as augmented). The technology functions by changing the current perception of reality. In contrast, virtual reality replaces the real world with a simulated one. The possibilities are endless in informational, entertainment or educational terms.

5   Note that the area devoted to streets gives a distorted view as density is not controlled for. So a city with low density can have a low per cent of land allocated to streets, whilst a city of high density can have a higher per cent of land allocated to streets. For example, the San Francisco peninsula has a population density of 17,166 persons per sq mile and 26 per cent of land is devoted to streets; the corresponding figures for Downtown Dallas are 4,339 and 13 per cent and the core of Shanghai 17,728 and 7 per cent. In many rapidly growing cities, there are high densities and low per cent of land allocated to streets, thus exacerbating the problems of movement.

6   Theory derives from Ancient Greek (*theoria*) meaning 'looking at, viewing, beholding', and refers to contemplation or speculation, as opposed to action or 'practice' (*praxis*). In the social sciences, theory is seen as illuminating the 'concrete processes of human life' (Giddens, 1984). For example, in transport, theory would seek to understand the reasons behind travel, whilst transport practice seeks to move people around more effectively. In transport planning, theory has been most developed in transport modelling, often in mathematical terms, in attempting to more effectively model the real world. There are relatively few attempts to understand why people actually travel, and how they might be encouraged to travel in different ways.

7   Ontology: the philosophical study of the nature of 'being, existence, or reality', as well as the basic categories of being and its relations to others. In the transport domain: what is the nature of travel, what are its essential properties, and hence why do feel we need to travel? These types of questions should be addressed before we plunge into the engineering of transport networks.

Annex

Best-selling motor cars globally
(to 2010 . . . and counting)

Rank	Model	Country*	Years in production	Sales (million)
1	Toyota Corolla	Japan	1966–	32.0
2	Ford F-series	USA	1948–	30.0
3	VW Golf	Germany	1974–	25.0
4	VW Beetle	Germany	1938–	22.3
5	Ford Escort	Great Britain	1968–2000	20.0
6	Honda Civic	Japan	1972–	17.7
7	Ford Model T	USA	1908–1927	16.5
8	Honda Accord	Japan	1976–	15.8
9	VW Passat	Germany	1973–	14.1
10	Chevrolet Impala	USA	1958–	14.0
11	Ford Fiesta	USA	1976–	12.5
12	Opel/Vauxhall Corsa	Spain	1982–	12.0
13	Oldsmobile Cutlass	USA	1961–1999	11.9
14	Chrysler Voyager	USA	1984–	11.7
15	Toyota Camry	Japan	1983–	10.5
16	Mazda 323	Japan	1963–2003	10.4
17	Opel/Vauxhall Astra/Kadett	Germany	1991–	10.0
18	BMW 3-series	Germany	1977–	9.8
19	Fiat Uno	Italy	1983–	9.2
20	Renault Clio	France	1991–	8.9
21	Renault 5	France	1972–1996	8.8
22	Ford Mustang	USA	1964–	8.3
23	Renault 4	France	1961–1992	8.2
24	Fiat Punto	Italy	1993–	6.9
25	Ford Taurus	USA	1986–	6.8
26	BMC Mini	Great Britain	1959–	6.7
27	Opel/Vauxhall Vectra	Germany	1988–2008	6.5

Rank	Model	Country*	Years in production	Sales (million)
28	Chevrolet Cavalier	USA	1982–2005	6.2
29	Peugeot 206	France	1998–2007	6.1
30	Buick Le Sabre	USA	1959–2005	6.0
31	Nissan Sunny/Sentra	Japan	1966–	5.9
32	Ford Explorer	USA	1991–	5.7
33	Mitsubishi Galant	Japan	1969–	5.6
34	Ford Focus	Germany	1998–	5.5
35	Ford Crown Victoria	USA	1980–	5.5
36	Toyota Land Cruiser	Japan	1953–	5.3
37	Peugeot 205	France	1983–1998	5.3
38	Ford E-series	USA	1961–	5.2
39	Ford Ranger	USA	1983–	5.1
40	Chevrolet Camaro	USA	1967–2002	4.8
41	Fiat 126	Italy	1973–2000	4.7
42	Opel Ascona/Vauxhall Cavalier	Germany	1970–1988	4.4
43	Ford Model A	USA	1927–1931	4.3
44	Ford Cortina/Taunus	Great Britain	1962–1982	4.2
45	Pontiac Grand Am	USA	1973–2005	4.0
46	Citroen 2CV	France	1948–1990	3.9
47	Fiat 500	Italy	1957–	3.9
48	Fiat 127	Italy	1971–1983	3.8
49	Peugeot 504	France	1968–2005	3.7
50	Peugeot 405	France	1988–1997	3.5

Note: * Country denotes where the car was originally developed or produced, although many of the models have been built in several countries.

Source: Motortrend Forum, 2010.

References

Abram, S. 2000. Planning the public: some comments on empirical problems for planning theory. *Journal of Planning Education and Research*, 19, 351–357.

Abusah, S. and De Bruyn, C. 2007. Getting Auckland on track: public transport and New Zealand's economic transformation. Working Paper. Wellington: Ministry of Economic Development.

Ackroyd, P. 2003. *Illustrated London*, London: Chatto and Windus.

Adams, J. 1981. *Transport Planning. Vision and Practice*, London: Routledge and Kegan Paul.

Aditjandra, P., Cao, X. and Mulley, C. 2012. Understanding neighbourhood design impact on travel behaviour: An application of structural equations model to a British metropolitan data. *Transportation Research Part A: Policy and Practice*, 46, 22–32.

Åkerman, J. and Höjer, M. 2006. How much transport can the climate stand? Sweden on a sustainable path in 2050. *Energy Policy*, 34, 1944–1957.

Albers, G. 1974. Modellvorstellungen zur Siedlungsstruktur in ihrer geschichtlichen Entwicklung. In *Akademie für Raumforschung und Landesplanung: Zur Ordnung der Siedlungsstruktur*, Hannover: Jänecke, 15.

Aldred, R. and Tepe, D. 2011. Framing scrappage in Germany and the UK: from climate discourse to recession talk? *Journal of Transport Geography*, 19, 1563–1569.

Allaire, Y. and Firsirotu, M. 1989. Coping with strategic uncertainty. *Sloan Management Review*, Spring, 7–16.

Allen, W. 1979. My speech to the graduates. *New York Times*, 10 August.

Allport, R., Key, G. and Melhuish, C. 1998. *A New Approach to Setting the Future Transport Agenda*, Manila: Asian Development Bank.

An, F. and Sauer, A. 2004. *Comparison of Fuel Economy and GHG Emission Standards*, Arlington, VA: Pew Center.

Anable, J. 2005. 'Complacent car addicts' or 'aspiring environmentalists'? Identifying travel behaviour segments using attitude theory. *Transport Policy*, 12, 65–78.

Anable, J. and Bristow, A. 2007. Transport and climate change. Supporting document to CfIT. London.

Anable, J. and Gatersleben, B. 2005. All work and no play? The role of instrumental and affective factors in work and leisure journeys by different travel modes. *Transportation Research Part A: Policy and Practice*, 39, 163–181.

Anderson, K., Bows, A. and Mander, S. 2008. From long term targets to cumulative emissions pathways: reframing UK climate policy. *Energy Policy*, 36, 3714–3722.

Arnold, M. 1866. *Thyrsis*, line 19, 'And that sweet city with her dreaming spires'. *Macmillan's Magazine*.

Arthur, W. 1994. *Increasing Returns and Path Dependence in the Economy*, Ann Arbor: University of Michigan Press.

Asian Development Bank 2009. *Changing Course. A New Paradigm for Sustainable Urban Transport*, Manila: ADB.

Auckland Council 2006. *Monitor Auckland*, 2006 Census. (http://monitorauckland.arc.govt.nz) (Accessed October 2012). Auckland: Auckland Council.

—— 2012. *The Auckland Plan*, Auckland: Auckland Council.

Auckland Regional Council 2010. *Auckland Regional Land Transport Strategy 2010–2040*, Auckland: Auckland Regional Council.

Auckland Regional Transport Authority 2009. *Auckland Transport Plan*, Auckland: ARTA.

Badami, M., Tiwari, G. and Mohan, D. 2004. Access and mobility for the urban poor in India: bridging the gap between policy and needs. *Forum on Urban Infrastructure and Public Service Delivery for the Urban Poor*, New Delhi.

Ballard, J. G. 1973. *Crash*, London, Cape.

Banham, R., Barker, P., Hall, P. and Price, C. 1969. Non-plan. An experiment in freedom. *New Society*, 20 March.

Banister, D. 2005. *Unsustainable Transport: City Transport in the New Century*, London: Routledge.

—— 2008. The sustainable mobility paradigm. *Transport Policy*, 15, 73–80.

—— 2011. The trilogy of distance, speed and time. *Journal of Transport Geography*, 19(4), 950–959.

Banister, D. and Hickman, R. 2006. How to design a more sustainable and fairer built environment: transport and communications. *Intelligent Transport Systems, IEE Proceedings*, 153, 276–291.

—— 2012. Transport and energy: planning beyond incrementalism. Expert Review Paper, ESPRC Retrofit 2050 Project.

Banister, D., Watson, S. and Wood, C. 1997. Sustainable cities, transport, energy and urban form. *Environment and Planning B*, 24, 125–143.

Banister, D., Stead, D., Steen, P., Akerman, J., Dreborg, K., Nijkamp, P. and Schleicher-Tappeser, R. 2000. *European Transport Policy and Sustainable Mobility*, London: Spon.

Banister, D., Anderton, K., Bonilla, D., Givoni, M. and Schwanen, T. 2011. Transport and the environment. *The Annual Review of Environment and Resources*, 36, 247–270.

Barter, P. 2000. Urban transport in Asia: problems and prospects for high density cities. *Asia-Pacific Development Monitor*, 2, 33–66.

Baudrillard, J. 1981a. *For a Critique of the Political Economy of the Sign*, St Louis, MO: Telos Press.

—— 1981b. *Simulacra and Simulation*, Ann Arbor: University of Michigan Press, 1994 (originally published in 1981, Editions Galilée).

—— 1983. *Simulations*, New York: Semiotext(e).

—— 1988. *America*, London: Verso.

—— 1998. *The Consumer Society: Myths and Structures*, London: Sage.

Beck, U. 1992. *Risk Society: Towards a New Modernity*, London: Sage.

Becker, H. and Van Houten, D. 1982. *Manual for Designing Scenarios*, the Netherlands: Utrecht University Press.

Beeching, R. 1963. *The Reshaping of British Railways*, London: British Railways Board, HMSO.

Bellamy, E. 1888. *Looking Backward, 2000–1887*: Oxford, Oxford University Press (2007).

Berger, J. 1972. *Ways of Seeing (Based on the BBC Television Series with John Berger)*, London: British Broadcasting Corporation; Harmondsworth: Penguin Books.

Berger, P. and Luckman, T. 1966. *The Social Construction of Reality: A Treatise in the Sociology of Knowledge*, New York: Anchor Books.

Bishop, P., Hines, A. and Collins, T. 2007. The current state of scenario development: an overview of techniques. *Foresight*, 9, 5–25.

Bohte, W., Maat, K. and Van Wee, B. 2009. Measuring attitudes in research on residential self selection and travel behaviour: a review of theories and empirical research. *Transport Reviews*, 29, 325–357.

Bonsall, P. 2009. Do we know whether personal travel planning really works? *Transport Policy*, 16, 306–314.

Borges, J. 1960. On exactitude in science. In *The Aleph and Other Stories*, London: Penguin.

—— 1961. Tlön, Uqbar, Orbis Tertius. In *Labyrinths*, London: Penguin.

—— 1976. *Doctor Brodie's Report*, London: Penguin.

Bourdieu, P. 1972. *Outline of a Theory of Practice*, Cambridge: Cambridge University Press (Originally published as *Esquisse d'une théorie de la pratique*, by Libraire Droz, Switzerland, and reprinted in English in 1977).

Bows, A. and Anderson, K. 2007. Policy clash: can projected aviation growth be reconciled with the UK government's 60% carbon-reduction target? *Transport Policy*, 14, 103–110.

Bradfield, R., Wright, G., Burt, G., Cairns, G. and Van der Heijden, K. 2005. The origins and evolution of scenario techniques in long range business planning. *Futures*, 37, 795–812.

Brand, C. and Preston, J. 2010. '60–20 emission': the unequal distribution of greenhouse gas emissions from personal, non-business travel in the UK. *Transport Policy*, 17, 9–19.

Breheny, M. 1992. The contradictions of the compact city: a review. In Breheny, M. (ed.) *Sustainable Development and Urban Form*, London: Plon.

—— 1997. Urban compaction: feasible and acceptable? *Cities*, 14, 209–217.

Bristow, A. and Nellthorp, J. 2000. Transport project appraisal in the European Union. *Transport Policy*, 7, 51–60.

Bruegmann, R. 2006. *Sprawl: A Compact History*, Chicago: University of Chicago Press.

Bruton, M. 1980. Public participation, local planning and conflicts of interest. *Policy and Politics*, 8, 423–442.

Bulgakov, M. 1925. *The Heart of a Dog*, London, Vintage Classic (2009) (first published in English by Harvill Press in 1968).

Bulman, J. N. 1988. Urban transport in developing countries. *Habitat International*, 12, 169–172.

Cacciatore, M., Scheufele, D. and Corley, E. 2012. Another (methodological) look at knowledge gaps and the internet's potential for closing them. *Public Understanding of Science*, 12 June 12 (online version), 1–19.

CAI-Asia, Asian Development Bank, Segment Y and International Energy Agency 2009. *Motorization Rate and Vehicle Population*, Manila, Philippines: CAI-Asia.

CAI-Asia and International Council on Clean Transportation 2009. *Review of Fuel Efficiency Standards*, Manila, Philippines: CAI-Asia.

Cairns, S., Sloman, L., Newson, C., Anable, J., Kirkbride, A. and Goodwin, P. 2004. *Smarter Choices: Changing the Way We Travel*, London: Department for Transport.

Camus, A. 1947. *The Plague*, London: Penguin (1960).

Cao, X., Mokhtarian, P. and Handy, S. 2009. Examining the impacts of residential self-selection on travel behaviour: a focus on empirical findings. *Transport Reviews*, 29, 359–395.

Carroll, L. 1871. *Through the Looking Glass*. In *Alice's Adventures in Wonderland* and *Through the Looking Glass*, Ware: Wordsworth Classics (2001) (Originally published by Macmillan).

—— 1893. *Sylvie and Bruno Concluded*, Whitefish, MT: Kessinger Publishing (2009) (Originally published by Macmillan).

Carson, R. 1962. *Silent Spring*, London: Penguin Books in association with Hamish Hamilton (1999).

Castells, M. 1978. Collective consumption and urban contradictions in advanced capitalism. In Castells, M. and Susser, I. (eds) *The Castells Reader on Cities and Social Theory*, Oxford: Blackwell (2002).

—— 2000. *The Rise of the Network Society*, Oxford: Blackwell.

Castro, C. 2004. Sustainable development: mainstream and critical perspectives. *Organization and Environment*, 17, 195–225.

Census Organisation of India. 2011. *India Census 2011, City Populations* (Online). Available: www.census2011.co.in/city.php (Accessed January 2013).

Cervero, R. 1989. Jobs–housing balancing and regional mobility. *Journal of the American Planning Association*, 55, 136–150.

—— 1996. Jobs–housing balancing revisited. *Journal of the American Planning Association*, 62, 492–511.

Cervero, R. and Day, J. 2008. Suburbanization and transit-oriented development in China. *Transport Policy*, 15, 315–323.

Cervero, R. and Kockelman, K. 1997. Traffic demand and the 3Ds: density, diversity, and design. *Transportation Research Part D*, 2, 199–219.

Chamberlin, S. 2012. Dark Optimism website. www.darkoptimism.org/2008/09/03/the-climate-science-translation-guide/ (Online). (Accessed October 2012).

Chappell, M. 2006. Delphi and the Homeric Hymn to Apollo. *Classical Quarterly*, 56, 331–48.

Cherry, C., Weinert, J. and Yang, X. 2009. Comparative environmental impacts of electric bikes in China. *Transportation Research D*, 14, 281–290.

China Daily 2010. Traffic growth in Beijing (The Standing Committee of the Beijing Committee of the Chinese People's Political Consultative Conference). 10 June. www.chinadaily.com.cn/cndy/2010-06/10/content_9959101.htm (Accessed 22 July 2013).

China National Bureau of Statistics 2009. *China Statistical Yearbook*, Beijing: National Bureau of Statistics.

—— 2010. *China Statistical Yearbook*, Beijing: National Bureau of Statistics.

Clark, C. 1957. Transport: maker and breaker of cities. *Town Planning Review*, 28, 237–250.

Clarke, A. 1999. *Profiles of the Future*, London: Victor Gollancz.

Committee on Climate Change 2008. *Building a Low-Carbon Economy:- The UK Contribution to Tackling Climate Change*, London: TSO.

Courtney, H. 2001. *20/20 Foresight: Crafting Strategy in an Uncertain World*, Boston: Harvard Business School Press.

Courtney, H., Kirkland, J. and Viguerie, P. 1997. Strategy under uncertainty. *Harvard Business Review*, 75 (November–December), 67–79.

Cowan, R. 2010. *Plandemonium*, Tisbury: Streetwise Press.

Cox, P. 2010. *Moving People: Sustainable Transport Development*, London: Zed Books.

Cresswell, T. 2006. *On the Move: Mobility in the Modern Western World*, London: Routledge.

Darido, G., Torres-Montoya, M. and Mehndiratta, S. 2009. *Urban Transport and CO2 Emissions: Some Evidence from Chinese Cities*, Washington DC: World Bank, ESMAP, AusAID.

De Certeau, M. 1984. *The Practice of Everyday Life*, translated by Steven Rendall, Berkeley: University of California Press.

—— 2000. Walking in the city. In Ward, G. (ed.) *The Certeau Reader*, London: Blackwell.

Debord, G. 1967. *Society of the Spectacle*, Eastbourne: Soul Bay Press (2009) (first published as *La société du spectacle* by Buchet-Chastel).

Delhi Development Authority 2010. *Masterplan for Delhi, 2021*, New Delhi: DDA (http://delhi-masterplan.com) (Accessed December 2012).

Dennis, K. and Urry, J. 2009. *After the Car*, Cambridge: Polity.

Department for Food and Rural Affairs 2008. *Synthesis Report in the Findings from Defra's Pre-Feasibility Study into Personal Carbon Trading*, London: DEFRA.

—— 2009. *Modal CO2 Emission Factors*, London: DEFRA.

Department for Trade and Industry and Office of Science and Technology 2006. *Intelligent Infrastructure Systems: Project Overview*, London: DTI and OST.

—— 2010. *Land Use Futures: Summary Report*, London: DTI and OST.

Department for Transport. 2007. Gillian Merron's letter to chief executives on the success of the Sustainable Travel Towns (Online). Available: www.dft.gov.uk/pgr/sustainable/demonstrationtowns/ (Accessed March 2010).

—— 2008a. *Delivering a Sustainable Transport Strategy (DaSTS)*, London: The Stationery Office.

—— 2008b. *Vehicle/Speed CO2 Emission Factors*, London: Department for Transport.

—— 2009. *Low Carbon Transport: A Greener Future*, London: The Stationery Office.

—— 2011. *Creating Growth, Cutting Carbon: Making Sustainable Local Transport Happen*, London: The Stationery Office.

—— 2012. Website for Transport Analysis Guidance (WebTAG) (Online). (Accessed May 2012).

Department of Energy and Climate Change. 2010. *Local and Regional CO2 Emissions Estimates for 2005–2008 for the UK* (Online), London: AEA and DECC. (Accessed March 2010).

Department of the Environment 1976. Transport policy: a consultation document. London: HMSO.

—— 1994. Planning Policy Guidance Note 13, London: HMSO.

Department of the Environment Transport and the Regions 2001. Planning policy guidance note 13: Transport (PPG13), London: The Stationery Office.

Department of Transport 1989. *Roads for Prosperity*, London: HMSO.

Dhamija, P. 2012. *Climate Change Agenda for Delhi, 2009–12*, Delhi: Government of Delhi.

Diamond, J. 2005. *Collapse: How Societies Choose to Fail or Survive*, London: Allen Lane.

Dimitriou, H. 1992. *Urban Transport Planning: A Developmental Approach*, London: Routledge.

—— 2006a. Urban mobility and sustainability in Asia and the power of context. China Planning Network 3rd Annual Conference, Ministry of Construction. Beijing, PRC.

—— 2006b. Towards a generic sustainable urban transport strategy for middle-sized cities in Asia: lessons from Ningbo, Kanpur and Solo. *Habitat International*, 30, 1082–1099.

Dimitriou, H. and Banjo, G. 1990. *Transport Planning for Third World Cities*, London: Routledge.

Dimitriou, H., Ward, J. and Wright, P. 2012. *OMEGA Project: Summary Report*, London: OMEGA Centre, University College London.

Dodgson, J., Spackman, M., Pearman, A. and Phillips, L. 2009. *Multi-Criteria Analysis: A Manual*, London: DCLG Publications.

Dreborg, K. 1996. Essence of backcasting. *Futures*, 28, 813–828.

Dreborg, K. and Steen, P. 1994. A Swedish transportation futures study. Working paper, Stockholm University.

Drucker, P. 1968. *The Age of Discontinuity*, New York: Harper and Row.

Dunn, J. and Perl, A. 2010. Launching a post carbon regime for American surface transportation: assessing the policy tools. World Conference on Transport Research, Lisbon.

Echenique, M. and SOLUTIONS Consortium 2009. *SOLUTIONS Final Report*, Cambridge: University of Cambridge.

Encyclopedia Britannica 2010. *The New Encyclopedia Britannica*, London: Encyclopedia Britannica.

Energy Information Administration. 2010. Total carbon dioxide emissions from the consumption of energy (Online). Available: www.eia.gov/cfapps/ipdbproject/iedindex3.cfm?tid=90andpid=45andaid=8andcid=regionsandsyid=1980andeyid=2010andunit=MMTCD (Accessed December 2012).

Energy Research Institute 2009. *2050 China Energy and CO2 Emissions*, Beijing: ERI.

Environmental Audit Committee 2008. *Personal Carbon Trading*, 5th Report of the EAC, London: The Stationery Office.

Eriksson, A. and Weber, M. 2006. Adaptive foresight: navigating the complex landscape of policy strategies. Proceedings of the 2nd International Seville Seminar on Future-Oriented Technological Analysis: Impact of FTA Approaches on Policy and Decision Making. Seville, Spain.

Eriksson, A. and Weber, M. 2008. Adaptive foresight: navigating the complex landscape of policy strategies. *Technological Forecasting and Social Change*, 75, 462–482.

Ernst, J. 2011. Environmental challenges of urban transport: the impacts of motorization. In Dimitriou, H. and Gakenheimer, R. (eds) *Urban Transport in the Developing World: Perspectives from the First Decade of the New Millennium*, Cheltenham: Edward Elgar.

EU POSSUM 1998. *POSSUM: Final Report: Policy Scenarios for Sustainable Mobility*. European Community Fourth Framework Programme. University College London; Free University of Amsterdam; National Technical University of Athens; Environmental Strategies Research Group, Stockholm; EURES, Freiburg; VTT, Helsinki; Warsaw University of Technology; and Ministry of Transportation of the Russian Federation, Moscow. Submitted to EC DGVII Strategic Research, Brussels, December.

Ewing, R. and Cervero, R. 2001. Travel and the built environment. *Transportation Research Record*, 1780, 87–114.

—— 2010. Travel and the built environment: a meta analysis. *Journal of the American Planning Association*, 76, 265–294.

Fawcett, T. and Parag, Y. 2010. An introduction to personal carbon trading. *Climate Policy*, 10, 329–338.

Feitelson, E. 2002. Introducing environmental equity dimensions into the sustainable transport discourse: issues and pitfalls. *Transportation Research Part D: Transport and Environment*, 7, 99–118.

Flyvbjerg, B. 2001. *Making Social Science Matter: Why Social Inquiry Fails and How It Can Succeed Again*, Cambridge: Cambridge University Press.

—— 2011. Case Study. In Denzin, N. and Lincoln, S. (eds) *The Sage Handbook of Qualitative Research*, Thousand Oaks, CA: Sage.

Flyvbjerg, B., Holm, M. and Buhl, S. 2002. Underestimating costs in public works projects: error or lie? *Journal of the American Planning Association*, 68, 279–295.

Flyvbjerg, B., Bruzelius, N. and Rothengatter, W. 2003. *Megaprojects and Risk: An Anatomy of Ambition*, Cambridge, Cambridge University Press.

Foucault, M. 1966. *The Order of Things: An Archaeology of the Human Sciences*, London: Routledge 2002 (first published in 1966 as *Les mots et les choses*).

—— 1991. Governmentality. In Burchell, G., Gordon, C. and Miller, P. (eds) *The Foucault Effect: Studies in Governmentality*, Chicago: University of Chicago Press.

Fouracre, P. and Maunder, D. 1987. *Travel Demand in Three Medium Sized Indian Cities*, Crowthorne: TRRL RR 121.

Freund, P. and Martin, G. 1993. *The Ecology of the Automobile*, Montreal: Black Rose Books.

Friedman, M. and Savage, L. 1948. The utility of choices involving risks. *Journal of Political Economy*, 56, 279–304.

Friend, J. and Jessop, N. 1969. *Local Government and Strategic Choice: An Operational Research Approach to the Processes of Public Planning*, Oxford: Pergamon.

Frommelt, O. 2008. Strategy, scenarios and strategic conversation: an exploratory study in the European truck industry. Doctor of Business Adminstration thesis, University of Nottingham.

Geels, F. 2002. Technological transitions as evolutionary reconfiguration processes: a multi-level perspective and a case-study. *Research Policy*, 31, 1257–1274.

—— 2011a. The multi-level perspective as a new perspective for studying socio-technical transitions. In Geels, F., Kemp, R., Dudley, G. and Lyons, G. (eds) *Automobility in Transition? A Socio-Technical Analysis of Sustainable Transport*, London: Routledge.

—— 2011b. The multi-level perspective on sustainability transitions: responses to seven criticisms. *Environmental Innovation and Societal Transitions*, 1, 24–40.

Geels, F. and Schot, J. 2007. Typology of sociotechnical transition pathways. *Research Policy*, 36, 399–417.

Geels, F., Kemp, R., Dudley, G. and Lyons, G. (eds) 2011. *Automobility in Transition?: A Socio-Technical Analysis of Sustainable Transport*, London: Routledge.

Geurs, K. and Van Wee, B. 2000. *Environmentally Sustainable Transport: Implementation and Impacts of Transport Scenarios for the Netherlands for 2030*, Bilthoven, The Netherlands: National Institute for Public Health and the Environment.

—— 2004. Backcasting as a tool for sustainable transport policy making: the environmentally sustainable transport study in the Netherlands. *European Journal of Transport Infrastructure Research*, 4, 47–69.

Giddens, A. 1984. *The Constitution of Society: Outline of the Theory of Structuration*, Cambridge: Polity Press.

—— 1991. *Modernity and Self Identity*, Cambridge: Polity Press.

—— 2009. *The Politics of Climate Change*, Cambridge: Polity.

Giddens, A. and Dallmayr, F. 1982. *Profiles and Critiques in Social Theory*, London: Macmillan.

Gilbert, R. and Perl, A. 2010. *Transport Revolutions: Moving People and Freight Without Oil*, Philadelphia: New Society.

GIZ Deutsche Gesellschaft Für Technischer Zusammenarbeit. 2008. *Fuel Prices, International Comparative Data*. Eschborn, Germany: GIZ and World Bank.

Gladwell, M. 2000. *The Tipping Point: How Little Things Can Make a Big Difference*, London: Little, Brown.

Glaeser, E. 2011. *Triumph of the City*, London: Macmillan.

Goffman, E. 1959. *The Presentation of Self in Everyday Life*, London: Penguin, 1990 (originally published by Anchor Books).

Goodwin, P. 1995. Car dependence. *Transport Policy*, 2, 151–152.

Gordon, P. and Richardson, H. 1989. Gasoline consumption and cities: a reply. *Journal of American Planning Association*, 55, 342–345.

—— 1995. Sustainable congestion. In Brotchie, J., Batty, M., Blakely, E., Hall, P. and Newton, P. (eds) *Cities in Competition: Productive and Sustainable Cities for the 21st Century*, Melbourne: Longman.

Government of India 2007. White Paper on Pollution in India. Delhi: Ministry of Environment and Forests.

Government of National Capital Territory of Delhi. 2010. *Statistics of Delhi At a Glance* (Online). Delhi. (Accessed April 2011).

Government Office for the South East 2009. *South East Plan*. Guildford: GOSE.

Graham, D. and Glaister, S. 2002. *Review of Income and Price Elasticities of Demand for Road Traffic*, London: Imperial College London.

Greater London Authority 2003. *Population and Household Forecasts*, SDS Technical Report 23, London: GLA.

—— 2004. *London Plan: Spatial Development Strategy for London*, London: GLA.

—— 2007. *Climate Change Action Plan*, London: GLA.

—— 2009. *London Plan (Draft Revised): Spatial Development Strategy for London*, London: GLA.

—— 2011. *London Plan. Spatial Development Strategy for London*, London: GLA.

Grübler, A. 1990. *The Rise and Fall of Infrastructures: Dynamics of Evolution and Technological Change in Transport*, Heidelberg, Germany: Physica.

—— 2004. *Technology and Global Change*, Cambridge: Cambridge University Press.

Guiliano, G. 1985. A multicriteria method for transportation investment planning. *Transportation Research A*, 19A, 29–41.

Gwilliam, K. 2002. *Cities on the Move. A World Bank Urban Transport Strategy Review*, Washington, DC: World Bank.

Habermas, J. 1981. *The Theory of Communicative Action: Reason and the Rationalization of Society*, Cambridge: Polity Press (1984).

Hajer, M. A. 1995. *The Politics of Environmental Discourse: Ecological Modernization and the Policy Process*, Oxford: Clarendon Press.

Hall, P. 1963. *London 2000*, London: Faber and Faber.

—— 1980. *Great Planning Disasters*, London: Weidenfeld and Nicolson.

—— 1988. *Cities of Tomorrow: An Intellectual History of Urban Planning and Design in the Twentieth Century*, Oxford: Basil Blackwell.

—— 1989. *London 2001*, London: Unwin Hyman.

Hall, P. and Falk, N. 2013. *Good Cities, Better Lives*, Abingdon: Routledge.

Hall, P. and Pain, K. 2006. *The Polycentric Metropolis: Learning from Mega-City Regions in Europe*, London: Earthscan.

Hall, P., Hamiduddin, I., Hickman, R., Jones, P. and Osborne, C. 2013. *S-MAP 2030. An Action Plan for Seamless Mobility in North West Europe*, London: UCL.

Handy, S. L., Boarnet, M. G., Ewing, R. and Killingsworth, R. E. 2002. How the built environment affects physical activity: views from urban planning. *American Journal of Preventive Medicine*, 23, 64–73.

Harvey, D. 2005. *A Brief History of Neo-Liberalism*, Oxford: Oxford University Press.

Haub, C. and Sharma, O. 2006. Population bulletin, Washington, DC: Population Reference Bureau.

He, K. 2010. *Study of the Transport System in a Low Carbon Society: The Chinese Regional Study*, Tsinghua University, ITPS Cooperation Research Project.

Headicar, P. (ed.) 2009. *Transport Policy and Planning in Great Britain*, London: Routledge.

Headicar, P. 2010. PPG13: evidence of the strategic deficit. *Town and Country Planning*, February.

Headicar, P. and Curtis, C. 1998. The location of new residential developments: its influence on car-based travel. In Banister, D. (ed.) *Transport Policy and the Environment*, London: Spon.

Hebbert, M. 1998. *London: More by Fortune than Design*, Chichester: John Wiley and Sons.

Heinberg, R. 2003. *The Party's Over: Oil War and the Fate of Industrial Society*, British Columbia: New Society Publishers.

Heller, J. 1961. *Catch-22*, London: Random House (1994).

Hickman, R. and Banister, D. 2005. Reducing travel by design: what happens over time? In Williams, K. and Burton, E. (eds) *Spatial Planning, Urban Form and Sustainable Transport*, Aldershot: Ashgate.

—— 2007a. Looking over the horizon: transport and reduced CO_2 emissions in the UK by 2030. *Transport Policy*, 14, 377–387.

—— 2007b. Transport and reduced energy consumption: What role can urban planning play? Working paper (ref. 1026). University of Oxford TSU.

—— 2012. Transport and energy: planning beyond incrementalism? EPSRC Retrofit 2050. Expert Review Paper.

Hickman, R., Saxena, S. and Banister, D. 2008. *Breaking the Trend. Visioning and Backcasting for Transport in India and Delhi. Scoping Report*, London: Halcrow Group for the Asian Development Bank.

Hickman, R., Ashiru, O. and Banister, D. 2009a. *20% Transport. Visioning and Backcasting for Transport in London. Executive Summary*, London: Halcrow Group.

—— 2009b. Achieving carbon efficient transport: backcasting from London. *Transportation Research Record*, 2139, 172–182.

Hickman, R., Seaborn, C., Headicar, P. and Banister, D. 2009c. *Planning for Sustainable Travel: Summary Guide*, London: Halcrow and Commission for Integrated Transport.

Hickman, R., Ashiru, O. and Banister, D. 2010a. Transport and climate change: simulating the options for carbon reduction in London. *Transport Policy*, 17, 110–125.

Hickman, R., Ashiru, O., Seaborn, C. and Walters, G. 2010b. *INTRA-SIM Oxfordshire, Final Report*, London: Halcrow.

Hickman, R., Seaborn, C., Headicar, P. and Banister, D. 2010c. Planning for sustainable travel: integrating spatial planning and transport. In Givoni, M., and Banister, D. (eds) *Integrated Transport: From Policy to Practice*, London: Routledge.

Hickman, R., Ashiru, O. and Banister, D. 2011. Transitions to low carbon transport futures: strategic conversations from London and Delhi. *Journal of Transport Geography*, 19(6), 1553–1562.

Hickman, R., Fremer, P., Breithaupt, M. and Saxena, S. 2011. *Changing Course in Sustainable Urban Transport: An Illustrated Guide*, Manila: Asian Development Bank.

Hickman, R., Ashiru, O., Seaborn, C. and Austin, P. 2012a. *INTRA-SIM Auckland, Final Report*, London: Halcrow.

Hickman, R., Saxena, S., Banister, D. and Ashiru, O. 2012b. Examining transport futures with scenario analysis and MCA. *Transportation Research Part A*, 46, 560–575.

Hickman, R., Hall, P. and Banister, D. 2013. Planning more for sustainable mobility. *Journal of Transport Geography*, in press, online August 2013.

Hidalgo, D. 2009. *Bus Rapid Transit in Asia*, Washington, DC: Transportation Research Board.

Hidalgo, D. and Pai, M. 2009. *Delhi Bus Corridor: An Evaluation*, Washington, DC: EMBARQ, World Resources Institute.

Hillman, M. and Fawcett, T. 2004. *How We Can Save The Planet*, London: Penguin.

HM Treasury 2006. *The Eddington Transport Study* (Rod Eddington), London: The Stationery Office.

—— 2007. *The King Review of Low Carbon Cars* (Julia King), London: The Stationery Office.

Holden, E. and Linnerud, K. 2011. Sustainable transport: the troublesome leisure travel. *Urban Studies*, 48, 3087–3106.

Hook, W. and Replogle, M. 1996. Motorization and non-motorized transport in Asia: transport system evolution in China, Japan and Indonesia. *Land Use Policy*, 13, 69–84.

Illich, I. 1974. *Energy and Equity*, London: Calder and Boyars.

Intergovermental Panel on Climate Change 1990. *First Assessment Report. Working Group I Scientific Assessment of Climate Change*, Geneva: IPCC.

—— 1995. *Second Assessment Report*, Geneva: IPCC.

—— 2001. *Third Assessment Report. Synthesis Report*, Geneva: IPCC.

—— 2007. *Fourth Assessment Report on Climate Change. Synthesis Report*, Geneva: IPCC.

International Energy Agency 2004. *Energy Technologies for a Sustainable Future*, Paris: IEA.

—— 2009. *Transport Energy and CO2*, Paris: IEA.

—— 2010a. *CO2 Emissions from Fuel Combustion: Highlights*, Paris: IEA.

—— 2010b. *Key World Energy Statistics*, Paris: IEA.

—— 2012. *World Energy Outlook*, Paris: IEA.

Ionesco, E. 1967. *Exit the King*, New York: Grove Press (first performed 1962, Paris).

Jackson, T. 2009. *Prosperity Without Growth: Economics for a Finite Planet*, London: Earthscan.

Jacobs, J. 1961. *The Death and Life of Great American Cities*, New York: Random House.

Jinan Municipal Government 2011. *12th Five Year Plan (2011–2015) for Economic and Social Development*, Jinan, China: Jinan Municipal Government.

Jinan Statistics Bureau 2009. *Jinan Statistics Yearbook*, Beijing: China Statistics Press.

Joffé, H. 1999. *Risk and 'The Other'*, Cambridge: Cambridge University Press.

Johansson, T. B. and Steen, P. 1978. *Solar Sweden. An Outline of a Renewable Energy System*, Stockholm: Secretariat for Energy Studies.

Johansson, T., Steen, P., Fredriksson, R. and Bogren, E. 1983. Sweden beyond oil: the efficient use of energy. *Science*, 219, 335–361.

Jungmar, M. 1995. *Progress Report: A Low Waste/Ecocyclic Society and its Boundaries*, Stockholm University.

Kafka, F. 1925. *The Trial*, London: Random House (1999).

Kahn, H. 1960. *On Thermonuclear War*, Princeton, NJ: Princeton University Press (1967).

—— 1962. *Thinking About the Unthinkable*, New York: Horizon Press, p. 254.

—— 1965. *On Escalation, Metaphor and Scenarios*, New York: Praeger.

—— 1984. *Thinking About the Unthinkable in the 1980s*, New York: Simon and Schuster.

Kahn, H. and Wiener, A. 1967. *The Year 2000: A Framework for Speculation on the Next Thirty Three Years*, New York: Macmillan.

Karnani, A. and Wernerfelt, B. 1987. Competitive strategy under uncertainty. *Strategic Management Journal*, 8, 42–46.

Kaufmann, V. 2002. *Re-thinking Mobility: Contemporary Sociology*, Aldershot: Ashgate.

Kemp, R. 1994. Technology and the transition to environmental sustainability: the problem of technological regime shifts. *Futures*, 26(10), 1023–1046.

Kemp, R., Geels, F. and Dudley, G. 2012. Sustainability transitions in the automobility regime and the need for a new perspective. In Geels, F., Kemp, R., Dudley, G. and Lyons, G. (eds) *Automobility in Transition? A Socio-Technical Analysis of Sustainable Transport*, Abingdon: Routledge.

Kennedy, C., Steinberger, J., Gasson, B., Hansen, Y., Hillman, T., Havranek, M., Pataki, D., Phdungsilp, A., Ramaswami, A. and Villalba Mendez, G. 2009. Greenhouse gas emissions from global cities. *Environmental Science and Technology*, 43, 7297–7302.

Kenworthy, J. 2011. An international comparative perspective on fast rising motorization and automobile dependence. In Dimitriou, H. and Gakenheimer, R. (eds) *Urban Transport in the Developing World: Perspectives from the First Decade of the New Millennium*, Cheltenham: Edward Elgar.

Khare, M. and Sharma, P. 2003. Fuel options. In Hensher, D. and Button, K. (eds) *Handbook of Transport and the Environment*, Oxford: Elsevier.

King, J. 2007. *The King Review of Low Carbon Cars, Part I: The Potential for CO2 Reduction*, HM Treasury. Norwich: The Stationery Office.

—— 2008. *The King Review of Low Carbon Cars, Part 2: Recommendations for Action*, HM Treasury. Norwich: The Stationery Office.

Kondratieff, N. D. 1935. The long waves in economic life. *Review of Economic Statistics*, 17, 105–15.

Kuhn, T. 1962. *The Structure of Scientific Revolutions*, Chicago: University of Chicago Press.

Kurosaki, T., Yasuyuki, S., Banerji, A. and Mishra, S. 2007. Rural urban migration and urban poverty: socio-economic profiles of rickshaw pullers and owener contractors in north-east Delhi. CIRJE Discussion Paper. Tokyo: University of Tokyo.

Kurzweil, R. 2005. *The Singularity is Near: When Humans Transcend Biology*, New York: Viking.

Landcare Research 2007. *Four Future Scenarios for New Zealand*, Auckland: Landcare Research.

Latour, B. 1992. Where are the missing masses? The sociology of a few mundane artifacts. In Bijker, W., Hughes, T. and Pinch, T. (eds) *The Social Construction of Technical Systems*, Cambridge, MA: MIT Press.

Levine, D. 1997. Knowing and acting: on uncertainty in economics. *Review of Political Economy*, 9, 5–17.

Levinson, D. 2010. Equity effects of road pricing: a review. *Transport Reviews*, 30, 33–57.

Lindblom, C. 1959. The science of muddling through. *Public Administration Review*, 19, 79–88.

—— 1979. Still muddling, not yet through. *Public Administration Review*, 39, 517–526.

Litman, T. 2010. *Transportation Demand Management (TDM) Encyclopedia* (Online). Victoria Transport Policy Institute. (Accessed March 2010).

Liverman, D. 2008. Conventions of climate change: constructions of danger and dispossession of the atmosphere. *Journal of Historical Geography*, 35, 279–296.

Lloyd Wright, F. 1935. Broadacre City: a new community plan from architectural record. In LeGates, R. and Stout, F. (eds) *The City Reader*, Abingdon: Routledge, 1996, pp. 344–349.

Lönnroth, M., Johansson, T. and Steen, P. 1983. Sweden beyond oil: The efficient use of energy. *Science*, 219, 355–361.

Lovins, A. 1977. *Soft Energy Paths: Toward a Durable Peace*, Cambridge, MA: Ballinger Publishing.

Lucas, K. and Jones, P. 2009. *The Car in British Society*, London: RAC Foundation.

Lucas, K., Blumenberg, E. and Weinberger, R. 2011. *Auto Motives: Understanding Car Use Behaviours*, Bingley: Emerald.

Lupton, D. 1999. *Risk*, London: Routledge.

Ma, L. 2009. Chinese urbanism, in Kitchin, R. and Thrift, N. (eds) *Encyclopaedia of Human Geography*, Oxford: Elsevier.

Macharis, C., De Witte, A. and Turcksin, L. 2010. The multi-actor multi-criteria analysis (MAMCA) application in the Flemish long-term decision making process on mobility and logistics. *Transport Policy*, 17, 303–311.

Mahoney, J. 2000. Path dependence in historical sociology. *Theory and Society*, 29, 507–548.

Malthus, T. 1798. *An Essay on the Principle of Population*, Cambridge: Cambridge University Press (1989).

Mannheim, K. 1936. *Ideology and Utopia: An Introduction to the Sociology of Knowledge*, London: Harvest/Harcourt Brace Jovanovich.

March, J. and Herbert, S. 1958. *Organisations in Action*, New York: Wiley.

Marcuse, H. 1964. *One-Dimensional Man: Studies in the Ideology of Advanced Industrial Society*, London: Routledge and Kegan Paul.

Markovits, C. 2004. *A History of Modern India, 1480–1950*, Anthem South Asian Studies. Delhi: Anthem Press.

Marshall, S. 2001. The challenge of sustainable transport. In Layard, A., Davoudi, S. and Batty, S. (eds) *Planning for a Sustainable Future*, London: Spon.

Maunsell 2008. *ARC Carbon Futures Stage 1: Baseline Data Review*, Auckland: Maunsell.

—— 2009. *ARC Carbon Futures Stage 2: Development of Mitigation Options*, Auckland: Maunsell.

May, G. 1982. The argument for more future-oriented planning. *Futures*, 14, 313–318.

McKinnon, A. 2007. *CO2 Emissions from Freight Transport in the UK. Background Report*, London: Commission for Integrated Transport.

McLuhan, M. 1964. *Understanding Media: The Extensions of Man*, London: Routledge and Kegan Paul.

Meadows, D., Meadows, D., Randers, J. and Behrens, W. 1972 *The Limits to Growth*, New York: Universe Books.

Mees, P. 2010. *Transport for Suburbia: Beyond the Automobile Age*, London: Earthscan.

Metz, D. 2008. The myth of travel time saving. *Transport Reviews*, 28, 321–336.

Meyer, A. 2000. *Contraction and Convergence: The Global Solution to Climate Change*, Totnes: Global Commons Institute, Green Books.

—— 2013. Contraction and convergence graphic (Online). London. Available: www.gci.org.uk/index.html (Accessed January 2013).

Millard-Ball, A. and Schipper, L. 2010. Are we reaching peak travel? Trends in passenger transport in eight industrialized countries. *Transport Reviews*, 31, 357–378.

Miller, A. 1949. *Death of a Salesman*, London: Penguin Books (Penguin Classics, 2000).

Ministry for the Environment 2009. *Net Position Report: New Zealand's Projected Balance of Kyoto Protocol Units During the First Commitment Period*, Wellington: MoE.

Ministry of Transport 2005. *Getting There – On Foot, by Cycle: A Strategy to Advance Walking and Cycling in New Zealand Transport*, Wellington: Ministry of Transport.

—— 2012. Mode share of trip legs people aged 5 and over by region 2007–11, Auckland region. Wellington: Ministry of Transport. www.transport.govt.nz/ourwork/TMIF/Pages/TP002.aspx (Accessed October 2012).

Ministry of Transport and Buchanan, C. 1963. *Traffic in Towns: A Study of the Long Term Problems of Traffic in Urban Areas. Reports of the Steering Group and Working Group appointed by the Minister of Transport* (Chairman of Working Group, Sir Colin Buchanan), London: HMSO.

Mitchell, A. 1972. *The Half Gallon Quarter Acre Pavlova Paradise*, Christchurch: Whitcombe and Tombs.

Mitric, S. 2008. *Urban Transport for Development: Towards an Operationally-Orientated Strategy*, Washington, DC: World Bank.

Mohan, D. 2002. Road safety in less motorised environments: future concerns. *International Journal of Epidemiology*, 31, 527–532.

—— 2006. Squandering public funds for a handful of people. *Business Standard*, New Delhi, 7 October. www.business-standard.com/article/opinion/dinesh-mohan-squandering-public-funds-for-a-handful-of-people-106100701026_1.html (Accessed 22 July 2013).

Mohan, D. and Tiwari, G. 1999. Sustainable transport systems: linages between environmental issues, public transport, non-motorised transport and safety. *Economic and Political Weekly*, 34, 1580–1596.

Mokhtarian, P. 1988. An empirical evaluation of the travel impacts of teleconferencing. *Transportation Research Part A: General*, 22, 283–289.

Mokhtarian, P. and Salomon, I. 2001. How derived is the demand for travel? Some conceptual and measurement considerations. *Transportation Research Part A: Policy and Practice*, 35, 695–719.

More, T. 1516. *Utopia*, Toronto: Broadview Press (2010).

Motortrend Forum. 2010. Top 50 best selling cars (Online). Available: http://forums.motortrend.com (Accessed February 2011).

Mumford, L. 1968. *The Urban Prospect*, New York: Harcourt, Brace and World.

Murphy, J. and Cohen, M. 2001. Sustainable consumption: environmental policy and the social sciences, in Murphy, J. and Cohen, M. (eds) *Exploring Sustainable Consumption: Environmental Policy and the Social Sciences*, Amsterdam: Elsevier.

Murty, M., Dhavala, K., Ghosh, M. and Singh, R. 2006. *Social Cost-Benefit Analysis of Delhi Metro*, New Delhi: Institute of Economic Growth.

Naess, P. 2009. Residential self selection and appropriate control variables in land use: travel studies. *Transport Reviews*, 29, 293–324.

Naisbitt, J. 1996. *Megatrends Asia: The Eight Asian Megatrends That Are Changing the World*, London: Nicholas Brealey.

Newman, P. and Kenworthy, J. 1989. *Cities and Automobile Dependence: An International Sourcebook*, Aldershot: Gower.

—— 1999. *Sustainability and Cities: Overcoming Automobile Dependence*, Washington, DC: Island Press.

Ng, W-S. and Schipper, L. 2005. China motorisation trends: policy options in a world of transport challenges. In Bradley, R. and Baumert, K. (eds) *Growing in the Greenhouse: Protecting the Climate by Putting Development First*, Washington, DC: World Resources Institute.

Ni, J. 2008. *Motorization, Vehicle Purchase and Use Behavior in China: A Shanghai Survey*, Research Report UCD-ITS-RR-08-27. ITS, University of California–Davis.

Nijkamp, P., Ubbels, B. and Verhoef, E. 2003. Transport investment appraisal and the environment. In Hensher, D. and Button, K. (eds) *Handbook of Transport and the Environment*, London: Elsevier.

Nordhaus, W. 2008. *A Question of Balance: Weighing the Options on Global Warming*, New Haven, CT: Yale University Press.

Office for National Statistics 2012. 2011 *Census*. (Online) www.ons.gov.uk/ons/publications/re-reference-tables.html?edition=tcm%3A77-257414 (Accessed October 2012).

Oram, R. 2009. *Auckland 2060*, Auckland: Royal Commission on Auckland Governance.

Organisation for Economic Cooperation and Development 1995. *Motor Vehicle Pollution: Reduction Strategies Beyond 2010*, Paris: OECD.

—— 2000. *EST! Environmentally Sustainable Transport. Futures, Strategies and Best Practice. Synthesis Report*, Paris: OECD.

Orwell, G. 1937. *The Road to Wigan Pier*, London: Victor Gollancz (republished by Penguin Classics, 2001).

Oxford City Council 2008. *Oxford Local Development Framework, Core Strategy*, Oxford: OCC.

—— 2011. Population estimate (Online). Oxford: OCC. Available: www.oxford.gov.uk/PageRender/decC/ Population_statistics_occw.htm (Accessed December 2012).

Oxfordshire County Council 2000. *Road Traffic Reduction Report*, Oxford: OCC.

—— 2006. *Local Transport Plan 2*, Oxford: OCC.

—— 2007. *Population Estimate*, Oxford: OCC.

—— 2011. *Local Transport Plan3*, Oxford: OCC.

Pacala, S. and Socolow, R. 2004. Stabilization wedges: solving the climate problem for the next 50 years with current technologies. *Science*, 305, 968–972.

Peñalosa, E. 2011. 'Challenges and Opportunities of Developing Country Cities', Seminar, Oxford: Smith School of Enterprise and the Environment.

Peters, M., Lieb, R. and Randall, H. 1998. The use of third party logistics by European industry. *Transport Logistics*, 1(3), 167–179.

Peters, G., Andrew, R., Boden, T., Canadell, J., Ciais, P., Le Quéré, C., Marland, G., Raupach, M. and Wilson, C. 2013. The challenge to keep global warming below 2°C. *Nature Climate Change*, 3, 4–6.

Peterson, G., Cumming, G. and Carpenter, S. 2003. Scenario planning: a tool for conservation in an uncertain world. *Conservation Biology*, 17, 358–366.

Pharoah, T. 1992. *Less Traffic, Better Towns*, London: Friends of the Earth.

Pharoah, T. and Apel, D. 1995. *Traffic Concepts in European Cities*, Aldershot: Avebury Publishing.

Pinter, H. 1960. *The Birthday Party*, London: Methuen and Co. (republished by Faber and Faber, 1991).

Plato, 2007. *The Republic*, ed. Lee, H. and Lane, M., London: Penguin (written c.380 BC).

Popper, K. 1957. *The Poverty of Historicism*, London: Routledge and Kegan Paul.

Porter, M. 1980. *Competitive Strategy: Techniques for Analyzing Industries and Competitors*, New York: Free Press.

—— 1985. *Competitive Advantage: Creating and Sustaining Superior Performance*, New York: Free Press.

—— 1990. *The Competitive Advantage of Nations*, London: Macmillan.

Potter, S., Enoch, M. and Fergusson, M. 2001. *Fuel Taxes and Beyond: UK Transport and Climate Change*. Godalming: World Wildlife Fund.

Pred, A. 1985. Interpenetrating processes: human agency and the becoming of regional spatial and social structures. *Papers of the Regional Science Association*, 57, 7–17.

Preval, N., Chapman, R. and Howden-Chapman, P. 2010. For whom the city? Housing and locational preferences in New Zealand. In Howden-Chapman, P., Stuart, K. and Chapman, R. (eds) *Sizing up the City: Urban Form and Transport in New Zealand*, Wellington, NZ: Steele Roberts Publishers.

Priemus, H., Flyvbjerg, B. and Van Wee, B. 2008. *Decision-Making on Mega-Projects: Cost-Benefit Analysis, Planning and Innovation*, Cheltenham: Edward Elgar.

Prins, G. and Rayner, S. 2008. *The Wrong Trousers: Radically Rethinking Climate Policy*, Oxford: James Martin Institute for Science and Civilization.

Pucher, J. and Buehler, R. 2008. Making cycling irresistible: lessons from the Netherlands, Denmark and Germany. *Transport Reviews*, 28, 495–528.

Pucher, J., Peng, Z.-R., Mittal, N., Zhu, Y. and Korattyswaroopam, N. 2007. Urban transport trends and policies in China and India: impacts of rapid economic growth. *Transport Reviews*, 27, 379–410.

Quinet, E. 2000. Evaluation methodologies of transportation projects in France. *Transport Policy*, 7, 27–34.

Quist, J., Thissen, W. and Vergragt, P. 2011. The impact and spin off of participatory backcasting: from vision to niche. *Technological Forecasting and Social Change*, 78, 883–897.

Reddy, K. 2003. *Indian History*, New Delhi: McGraw-Hill.

Ringland, G. 1998. *Scenario Planning: Managing for the Future*, Chichester: John Wiley.

RITES. 2008. *BRT Proposal for Delhi* (Online). Delhi: RITES. Available: www.reinventingtransport.org/ 2008/04/will-delhis-brt-be-given-chance-to.html (Accessed December 2012).

Rittel, H. and Webber, M. 1973. Dilemmas in a general theory of planning. *Policy Sciences*, 4, 155–169.

Robinson, J. 1982. Energy backcasting: a proposed method of policy analysis. *Energy Policy*, 10, 337–344.

—— 1990. Futures under glass: a recipe for people who hate to predict. *Futures*, 22, 820–842.

Robinson, J., Burch, S., Talwar, S., O'Shea, M. and Walsh, M. 2011. Envisioning sustainability: recent progress in the use of participatory backcasting approaches for sustainability research. *Technological Forecasting and Social Change*, 78, 756–768.

Roychowdhury, A., Chattopadhyaya, V., Shah, C. and Chandola, P. 2006. *The Leapfrog Factor: Clearing the Air in Asian Cities*, New Delhi: Centre for Science and Environment.

Santos, G. 2005. Urban congestion charging: a comparison between London and Singapore. *Transport Reviews*, 25, 511–534.

Sassen, S. 2000. *Cities in a World Economy*, London: Pine Forge Press.

Saxena, S. 2012. Low carbon transport pathways in Delhi. D.Phil. (unpublished), University of Oxford.

Sayers, T. M., Jessop, A. T. and Hills, P. J. 2003. Multi-criteria evaluation of transport options: flexible, transparent and user-friendly? *Transport Policy*, 10, 95–105.

Schäfer, A. and Victor, D. 2000. The future mobility of the world population. *Transportation Research Part A: Policy and Practice*, 34, 171–205.

Schäfer, A., Heywood, J., Jacoby, H. and Waitz, I. 2009. *Transportation in a Climate-constrained World*, Cambridge, MA: MIT Press.

Schipper, L., Marie-Lilliu, C. and Gorham, R. 2000. *Flexing the Link Between Transport and Greenhouse Gas Emissions: A Path for the World Bank*, Paris: IEA.

Schoemaker, P. 1998. Twenty common pitfalls in scenario planning. In Fahey, L. and Randall, R. (eds) *Learning from the Future: Competitive Foresight Scenarios*, New York: Wiley.

Schoemaker, P. and Gunther, R. 2002. *Profiting from Uncertainty: Strategies for Succeeding No Matter What the Future Brings*, New York: Free Press.

Schumpeter, J. 1939. *Business Cycles*, New York: McGraw-Hill (reprinted 1982, Philadelphia: Porcupine Press).

Schwanen, T. and Mokhtarian, P. 2005. What if you live in the wrong neighborhood? The impact of residential neighborhood type dissonance on distance traveled. *Transportation Research Part D*, 10, 127–151.

Schwanen, T., Banister, D. and Anable, J. 2011. Scientific research about climate change mitigation in transport: a critical review. *Transportation Research Part A*, 45(10), 993–1006.

—— 2012. Rethinking habits and their role in behaviour change: the case of low-carbon mobility. *Journal of Transport Geography*, 24, 522–532.

Schwartz, P. 1996. *The Art of the Long View: Paths to Strategic Insight for Yourself and Your Company*, New York and London, Currency Doubleday.

Schwartz, P. and Ogilvy, J. 1998. Plotting your scenarios. In Fahey, L. and Randall, R. (eds) *Learning from the Future: Competitive Foresight Scenarios*, New York: John Wiley and Sons.

Self, P. 1970. Nonsense on stilts: cost benefit analysis and the Roskill Commission. *The Political Quarterly*, 41, 249–260.

Self, W. 1999. *Tough, Tough Toys for Tough, Tough Boys*, Harmondsworth: Penguin.

Sen, A. 2009. *The Idea of Justice*, London: Allen Lane.

Shell International 2011. *Shell Energy Scenarios to 2050*, The Hague: Shell International.

Sheller, M. 2004. Automotive emotions: feeling the car. *Theory, Culture and Society*, 21, 221–242.

Sheller, M. and Urry, J. 2004. The city and the car. *International Journal of Urban and Regional Research*, 24, 737–757.

—— 2006. The new mobilities paradigm. *Environment and Planning A*, 38, 207–226.

Shove, E. 2010. Beyond the ABC: climate change policy and theories of social change. *Environment and Planning A*, 42, 1273–1285.

Simmel, G. 1978. *The Philosophy of Money*, London: Routledge and Kegan Paul.

Simon, H. 1991. Bounded Rationality and Organizational Learning. *Organization Science*, 2, 125–134.

Simons, D. J. and Chabris, C. 1999. Gorillas in the midst: sustained international blindness for dynamic events. *Perception*, 28, 1059–1074.

Sivam, A. 2003. Housing supply in Delhi. *Cities*, 20, 135–141.

Sloman, L., Cairns, S., Newson, C., Anable, J., Pridmore, A. and Goodwin, P. 2010. *The Effects of Smarter Choice Programmes in the Sustainable Travel Towns: Summary Report*, London: Department for Transport.

Solnit, R. 2000. *Wanderlust: A History of Walking*, London: Viking.

Sperling, D. and Gordon, D. 2009. *Two Billion Cars: Driving Toward Sustainability*, New York: Oxford University Press.

Statistics New Zealand 2011. Subnational population estimates. www.stats.govt.nz/browse_for_stats/population/estimates_and_projections/subnational-pop-estimates-tables.aspx. Wellington: Statistics New Zealand (Accessed October 2012).

Stauffer, D. 2002. Five reasons why you still need scenario planning. *Harvard Management Update*, 7, 3–5.

Stead, D. 2001. Relationships between land use, socioeconomic factors and travel patterns in Britain. *Environment and Planning B: Planning and Design*, 28, 499–528.

Steen, P. 1997. Transport in a sustainable society: Sweden 2040. World Conference on Transport Research, Antwerp.

Steg, L. 2005. Car use: lust and must. Instrumental, symbolic and affective motives for car use. *Transportation Research Part A: Policy and Practice*, 39, 147–162.

Stern, N. 2007. *The Economics of Climate Change: The Stern Review*, Cambridge: Cambridge University Press.

—— 2009. *A Blueprint for a Safer Planet: How to Manage Climate Change and Create a New Era of Progress and Prosperity*, London: Bodley Head.

Stopher, P. 2004. Reducing road congestion: a reality check. *Transport Policy*, 11, 117–131.

Strahan, D. 2007. *The Last Oil Shock: A Survival Guide to the Imminent Extinction of Petroleum Man*, London: John Murray.

Swift, J. 1726. *Gulliver's Travels*, London: Penguin (1994).

Taleb, N. 2007. *The Black Swan: The Impact of the Highly Improbable*, London: Penguin.

Taylor, B. 2004. The politics of congestion mitigation. *Transport Policy*, 11, 299–302.

The Economist 2012. The driverless road ahead. 20 October.

The Guardian. 2012. *How many gigatons of carbon dioxide?* (The Guardian Datablog, with Information IsBeautiful.net) (Online). London. (Accessed 7 December 2012).

Thetransportpolitic. 2009. HSR rail map (Online). Available: www.thetransportpolitic.com/2009/01/12/high-speed-rail-in-china (Accessed December 2012).

Thomson, J. 1977. *Great Cities and Their Traffic*, London: Gollancz.

—— 1983. Towards better urban transport in developing countries. Working Paper 600, Washington, DC: World Bank.

Thrift, N. 2004. Driving in the city. *Theory, Culture and Society*, 21, 41–59.

Thynell, M., Mohan, D. and Tiwari, G. 2010. Sustainable transport and the modernisation of urban transport in Delhi and Stockholm. *Cities*, 27, 421–429.

Tin Tin, S., Woodward, A., Thornley, S. and Ameratunga, S. 2009. Cycling and walking to work in New Zealand, 1991–2006: regional and individual differences, and pointers to effective interventions. *International Journal of Behavioural Nutrition and Physical Activity*, 6, 64.

Tiwari, G. and Jain, D. 2010. Bus rapid transit projects in Indian cities: a status report. *Built Environment*, 36, 353–362.

Toffler, A. 1972. *Future Shock*, London: Pan Books.

Transport for London 2006. *Transport 2025: Transport Vision for a Growing City*, London: TfL/GLA.

—— 2007. *Travel in London*, London: Transport for London.

—— 2009. *Transport Strategy for London (Draft Revision)*, London: TfL, GLA.

—— 2010. *Transport Strategy for London*, London: TfL, GLA.

—— 2011. *Travel in London, Report 4*, London: Transport for London.

Tuchman, B. 1984. *The March of Folly: From Troy to Vietnam*, London: Abacus.

UNDP 2010. *China Human Development Report 2009–2010. China and a Sustainable Future Towards a Low Carbon Economy and Society*. Beijing: Renmin University of China for UNDP China.

UN Habitat 2011. *Cities and Climate Change: UN Human Settlements Programme*, London: Earthscan.

United Nations Framework Convention on Climate Change 2011. *Report of the In-depth Review of the Fifth National Communication of New Zealand*, Bonn: UNFCCC (Accessed September 2011).

Unruh, G. 2000. Understanding carbon lock-in. *Energy Policy*, 28, 817–830.

URBED, TCPA. 2002. *A City of Villages. Promoting a Sustainable Future for London's Suburbs*, London: URBED and TCPA for Greater London Authority.

Urry, J. 2000. *Sociology Beyond Societies: Mobilities for the Twenty-first Century*, London: Routledge.

—— 2007. *Mobilities*, Cambridge: Polity.

—— 2011. *Climate Change and Society*, Cambridge: Polity.

US Energy Information Administration. 2009. World proved reserves of oil and natural gas, most recent estimates (Online). Available: www.eia.gov/international/reserves.html (Accessed October 2011).

Utley, T., Austin, T., Howell, M. and Fergusson, E. 2011. *VIBAT Auckland: Background to Policy Packages*, Auckland: University of Auckland.

Van den Belt, A. 1988. *Constructive Technology Assessment: Towards a Theory*, University of Amsterdam Press.

Van der Heijden, K. 1996. *Scenarios: The Art of Strategic Conversation*, Chichester: John Wiley.

Van Notten, P., Rotmans, J., Van Asselt, M. and Rothman, D. 2003. An updated scenario typology. *Futures*, 35, 423–443.

Vasconcellos, E. 2001. *Urban Transport, Environment and Equity: The Case for Developing Countries*, London: Earthscan.

Veblen, T. 1899. *The Theory of the Leisure Class: An Economic Study in the Evolution of Institutions*, New York: Macmillan.

Voltaire (François-Marie Arouet) 2005. *Candide*, New York: Pocket Books (originally published 1759).

Von Neumann, J. and Morgenstern, O. 1944. *Theory of Games and Economic Behavior*, Princeton, NJ: Princeton University Press

Vonnegut, K. 1963. *Cat's Cradle*, London: Victor Gollancz (Penguin Classics, 2008).

Wack, P. 1985a. Scenarios: shooting the rapids. *Harvard Business Review*, November, 139–150.

—— 1985b. Scenarios: unchartered waters ahead. *Harvard Business Review*, September, 73–89.

Weber, M. 2004. Expectations, foresight and policy portfolios: shaping of or adapting to the future? Paper presented at the Expectations in Science and Technology Research Workshop, Risoe National Laboratory, Denmark.

Wegener, M. and Fürst, F. 1999. *Land-use Transport Integration: State of the Art (Deliverable 2a, TRANSLAND)*, Dortmund: University of Dortmund, European Commission FP4.

Weinert, J., Ogden, J., Sperling, D. and Burke, A. 2008. The future of electric two wheelers and electric vehicles in China. *Energy Policy*, 36, 2544–2555.

Wells, P., Niewenhaus, P. and Orsato, R. 2012. The nature and causes of inertia in the automotive industry. In Geels, F., Kemp, R., Dudley, G. and Lyons, G. (eds) *Automobility in Transition? A Socio-Technical Analysis of Sustainable Transport*, Abingdon: Routledge.

West, S. 2003. Croesus' second reprieve and other tales of the Persian court. *Classical Quarterly*, 53, 416–437.

Wheeler, S. 2012. *Climate Change and Social Ecology: A New Perspective on the Climate Challenge*, London: Routledge.

Wilbur Smith Associates 2008. *Traffic and Transportation Policies and Strategies in Urban Areas in India*, Delhi: Ministry of Urban Development.

Williams, H. 1991. *Autogeddon*, New York: Arcade Publishing.

Wolf, E. (ed.) 2007. *Ilf and Petrov's American Road Trip*, New York: Princeton Architectural Press (original travelogue from Ilya Ilf and Evgeny Petrov in 1935).

Woodcock, J., Banister, D., Edwards, P., Prentice, A. and Roberts, I. 2007. Energy and transport. *The Lancet*, 370, 1078–1088.

Woodcock, J., Edwards, P., Tonne, C., Armstrong, B., Ashiru, O., Banister, D., Beevers, S., Chalabi, Z., Chowdhury, Z., Cohen, A., Franco, O., Haines, A., Hickman, R., Lindsay, G., Mittal, I., Mohan, D.,

Tiwari, G., Woodward, A. and Roberts, I. 2009. Public health benefits of strategies to reduce greenhouse-gas emissions: urban land transport. *The Lancet*, 374, 1930–1943.

World Bank 2010a. *World Development Indicators Database*, Washington, DC: World Bank.

—— 2010b. *World Development Indicators. Country Data*, Washington, DC: World Bank.

—— 2010c. *World Development Report 2010: Development and Climate Change*, Washington, DC: World Bank.

World Commission on Environment and Development 1987. *Our Common Future*, New York: Oxford University Press.

World Health Organization 2009. *Global Status Report on Road Safety*, Washington, DC: WHO.

Wright, L. 2010. Bus rapid transit: a public transport renaissance. *Built Environment*, 36, 269–273.

Wright, L. and Fulton, L. 2005. Climate change mitigation and transport in developing nations. *Transport Reviews*, 25, 691–717.

Wu, F. 2012. China's eco-cities. *Geoforum*, 43, 169–171.

Wyndham, J. 1953. *The Kraken Wakes*, Harmondsworth: Penguin, 1979 (originally published 1953 by Chivers).

Xiaohong, C. and Zhang, H. 2012. Evaluation of the effects of car ownership policies in Chinese megacities: a contrastive study of Beijing and Shanghai. Paper no.12–3257, presented at the Transportation Research Board, 91st Annual Conference, Washington, DC.

Zhao, J. 2011. Can the environment survive China's craze for automobiles? Working paper, Ann Arbor: University of Michigan Press.

Zhou, H. and Sperling, D. 2001. *Transportation Scenarios for Shanghai, China*. Transportation in developing countries series, Arlington, VA: Pew Centre.

Index

Note: Page references in *italics* refer to Figures and Plates; those in **bold** refer to Tables